D. T. Suzuki on the Unconscious in Zen Art, Meditation & Enlightenment

SUNY series, Perspectives in Contemplative Studies

Harold D. Roth and Judith Simmer-Brown, editors

D. T. Suzuki on the Unconscious in Zen Art, Meditation & Enlightenment

Steve Odin

SUNY PRESS

Cover Credit: Miyamoto Musashi (1584–1645). *Shrike on a Dead Branch* (枯木鳴鵙図).
Ink painting.
Published by State University of New York Press, Albany
© 2025 State University of New York
All rights reserved
Printed in the United States of America

No part of this book may be used or reproduced in any manner whatsoever without written permission. No part of this book may be stored in a retrieval system or transmitted in any form or by any means including electronic, electrostatic, magnetic tape, mechanical, photocopying, recording, or otherwise without the prior permission in writing of the publisher.

Links to third-party websites are provided as a convenience and for informational purposes only. They do not constitute an endorsement or an approval of any of the products, services, or opinions of the organization, companies, or individuals. SUNY Press bears no responsibility for the accuracy, legality, or content of a URL, the external website, or for that of subsequent websites.

EU GPSR Authorised Representative:
Logos Europe, 9 rue Nicolas Poussin, 17000, La Rochelle, France
contact@logoseurope.eu

For information, contact State University of New York Press, Albany, NY
www.sunypress.edu

Library of Congress Cataloging-in-Publication Data
Names: Odin, Steve, author
Title: D. T. Suzuki on the unconscious in Zen art, meditation, and enlightenment / Steve Odin, author.
Description: Albany : State University of New York press, [2025] | Series: SUNY series in Perspectives in Contemplative Studies | Includes bibliographical references and index.
Identifiers: ISBN 9798855803044 (hardcover : alk. paper) | ISBN 9798855803020 (e-book)
Further information is available at the Library of Congress.

Contents

List of Illustrations	*ix*
Acknowledgments	*xi*
Cover Art	*xiii*
Introduction	1

PART ONE. THE UNCONSCIOUS IN ZEN THEORY AND PRACTICE

Chapter 1. Suzuki's Zen Doctrine of the Cosmic Unconscious	13
No-Mind as the Unconscious	13
The Unconscious as Emptiness	27
The Unconscious as Indra's Net	36
The Unconscious as the Storehouse Consciousness	44
The Unconscious as Ordinary Mind	54
Suzuki's Zen Map of the Unconscious	61
The Mu Koan and Other Zen Meditation Techniques for Accessing the Unconscious	66
Chapter 2. The Unconscious in Suzuki's Zen Aestheticism	87
Zen Aestheticism in Japanese Culture	87
Suzuki and Nishida on Beauty as *Muga* or Ecstasy	92
Chapter 3. The Unconscious in Zen and *Bushidō*: The Religio-Aesthetic Way of the Martial Arts	95
The Art of Swordsmanship	95
The Art of Archery	100
Suzuki's "Samurai Zen" in Critical Perspective	105
Chapter 4. The Unconscious in Zen and *Geidō*: The Religio-Aesthetic Way of the Fine Arts	117

Sumie Ink Painting 117
Tea Ceremony 126
Haiku Poetry 128
The Impact of Suzuki's Zen Aetheticism on the
   Avant-Garde Artworld 133

PART TWO: ZEN AND WESTERN MODELS OF THE UNCONSCIOUS

Chapter 5. The Unconscious in Zen and American Thought 145

   Zen and William James 146
   Zen and A. N. Whitehead 159

Chapter 6. The Unconscious in Zen and German Philosophy 165

   The Abyss in Jacob Boehme's Philosophical Mysticism 166
   The Monadology of G. W. F. Leibniz 167
   Obscure Representations in the Transcendental
      Idealism of Immanuel Kant 171
   The Unconscious in the Aesthetic Idealism of F. W. J. Schelling 173
   The Grand Synthesis in Eduard von Hartmann's *Philosophy
      of the Unconscious* 178

Chapter 7. The Unconscious in Zen and German Psychology 183

   Zen and Freudian Psycholanalysis 184
   Erich Fromm on Zen and Psychoanalysis 193
   Zen and Jungian Psychology 195
   Zen, the Jungian Psychology of Kawai Hayao,
      and the Fiction of Murakami Haruki 206

Chapter 8. The Unconscious in Zen and French Thought 213

   Rancière and Suzuki on the Aesthetic Unsconscious 213
   Zen, Derrida, and Lacan on the Unconscious as a Möbius Band 215
   Zen and Sartre on the Transparency of Consciousness 222
   Zen and the Rhizomatic Unconscious of Deleuze-Guattari 226

Chapter 9. The Unconscious in Zen and Transpersonal Psychology 237

   Satori, Peak Experience, and the Unconscious in Zen

and Abraham Maslow 238
The Unconscious in Zen and Ken Wilber's
   Spectrum of Consciousness 242
D. T. Suzuki, G. I. Gurdjieff, and the Zen Unconscious of
   Hubert Benoit 244
Superconsciousness in Zen and Roberto Assagioli's
   Psychosynthesis 249
Psychedelic Experience and Suzuki's Zen Critique
   of Drug-Induced Satori 254

Epilogue: D. T. Suzuki and Jean Gebser on Zen Satori as a Shift to the Integral Structure of Consciousness as Openness, Radiance, and Transparency *261*
Abbreviations for the Works of D. T. Suzuki and Related Texts *265*
Notes *267*
Bibliography *277*
Indices *301*

List of Illustrations

Figure I.1. D. T. Suzuki (ca. 1953)	2
Figure 1.1. The relation between self-nature, the unconscious, and empirical mind	19
Figure 1.2. Levels of mind from the cosmic unconscious to consciousness	63
Figure 4.1 Splashed-Ink Landscape by Sesshū Tōyō	119
Figure 4.2. The Ten Oxherding Pictures by Shūbun	125
Figure 5.1 The Focus/Fringe Structure of Trans-Marginal Consciousness	158
Figure 8.1. Hakuin's Möbius Strip	219
Figure 9.1. Relation between satori, sleep, and waking	247
Figure 9.2. Assagioli's Oval Diagram of the Mind	250
Figure 9.3. Suzuki's Oval Diagram of the Unconscious	252

Acknowledgments

First, I would like to offer my gratitude to the Center for Japanese Studies at the University of Hawaii, which financially supported this project with a Japanese Studies Endowment award during my 2019 sabbatical in Japan, followed by additional summer research grants. At the international East-West Philosophers' Conference at the University of Hawaii held from May 24-31, 2024, I organized a plenary panel on the Zen Buddhism of D. T. Suzuki, celebrating Suzuki not only as the one who introduced Zen to the West but also for his enormous contributions to our East-West Philosophers' Conference in 1939, 1949, 1959, and 1964. I would therefore like to sincerely thank the outstanding scholars who participated in this auspicious event, including Moriya Tomoe and Steven Heine, along with Benjamin Hoffman, the moderator of our panel. I am further grateful to Benjamin Hoffman for skillfully editing this book manuscript for final publication. I want to thank Mareka Little for using her expertise in computer graphic art to create one of the diagrams in this work illustrating Suzuki's Zen map of the Unconscious. Moreover, I am especially grateful to my colleague Tamara Albertini, who introduced me to the remarkable German-Swiss philosopher Jean Gebser, resulting in the epilogue to this volume, wherein Suzuki's account of Zen satori is interpreted in terms of Gebser's phenomenology of mutations in the structures of consciousness, including the leap to a new integral structure of openness, radiance, and transparency. This work is dedicated to my amazing wife Megumi and to my wonderful talented daughter Riko.

Cover Art

The cover art is a Japanese ink painting titled *A Shrike on a Dead Branch* by the famous samurai warrior Miyamoto Musashi (1584–1645). In the Zen aestheticism of Suzuki, Miyamoto Musashi was a paradigm of one who realized Zen *mushin* or "no-mind" as the cosmic Unconscious of absolute nothingness. Because of his awakening to Zen no-mind, Miyamoto Musashi could express spontaneous creative impulses from the cosmic Unconscious through the fine art of ink painting and the martial art of swordsmanship, while at the same time articulating the Zen philosophy of emptiness in his classic treatise *The Book of Five Rings*. This exquisite Japanese ink painting of natural beauty is admired for its profound expression of Zen no-mind, emptiness, and silence. However, amidst the peace, tranquility, and harmony of nature shown in this painting, it also portrays a hunter and its prey along with impending violence and death thus revealing the fierce samurai aspect of Miyamoto Musashi. In this painting, the shrike, notorious as a predatory songbird that tortures its victims, looks down at a caterpillar slowly climbing toward the top of the branch, at which time the shrike will impale the creature, watch it suffer in agony, and then consume it with pleasure.

Introduction

The present volume critically examines D. T. Suzuki's views on Zen art, meditation, and enlightenment based on what I refer to as his philosophical psychology of the Unconscious. It is my claim that Suzuki applies his Zen doctrine of the subliminal mind to interpret all aspects of Zen and Mahayana Buddhism while also postulating a new concept of the unconscious as a multileveled spectrum, which at its deepest level he terms "the cosmic Unconscious." Furthermore, I demonstrate that for Suzuki, Zen satori or "enlightenment" is to become fully conscious of the cosmic Unconscious in what he calls superconsciousness. Although Suzuki was profoundly influenced by various Western theories of the unconscious, it is shown that he ultimately defines his Zen concept of the cosmic Unconscious in Mahayana Buddhist terms, including Zen *mushin* or "no-mind"; Prajnaparamita sunyata or "emptiness"; the Huayan/Kegon (Avatamsaka) dharma world of nonobstructed harmonious interpenetration between one and many as visualized by the holographic image of Indra's net; the Yogacara storehouse consciousness emptied of all karmic defilements; and the Zen doctrine of no-mind as the ordinary mind of everyday life. For Suzuki, Mahayana Buddhist concepts denoting ultimate reality, including Dharmakaya, Buddha nature, Buddha mind, Original Enlightenment, Tathagatagarbha, Prajna, Sunyata, the Unborn, and the Storehouse Consciousness, as well as the Dao of Chinese Daoism, are to be comprehended in modern psychological terms as functions of the cosmic Unconscious.

Suzuki further maintains that the Zen Buddhism of traditional Japanese culture blossomed into a "Zen aestheticism." According to Suzuki, beyond the personal unconscious of repressed instincts in Freudian psychoanalysis, and the collective unconscious of archetypes in Jungian analytical psychology, Zen aestheticism posits a deeper level of the cosmic Unconscious, which as spacelike dharmakaya emptiness or absolute nothingness, is the reservoir of infinite creative potentialities and the fountainhead of all Zen artworks. Hence, for Suzuki, Zen meditation is a process of rapid descent into the depths of our unconscious mind, and Zen satori or enlightenment is a sudden breakthrough to the bottomless abyss of the cosmic Unconscious, while Zen-inspired artworks are spontaneous creative products of the cosmic Unconscious as the transparent openness of absolute nothingness, wherein emptiness is fullness and fullness is emptiness, so that all things are disclosed just as they are in the aesthetic immediacy of their concrete particular suchness.

Zen Buddhism was introduced to the West by Suzuki Daisetsu Teitarō (鈴木大拙貞太郎), better known as D. T. Suzuki, or Daisetz Teitarō Suzuki. To give just a brief synopsis of his remarkable life, Suzuki Teitarō (1870–1966) was born in Kanazawa in Ishikawa Prefecture, Japan, the son of a medical doctor. His father, who died when Suzuki was only five years old, had family ties to Rinzai Zen, while his mother was a member of a Shin Pure Land Buddhist

Figure I.1. D. T. Suzuki (ca. 1953). *Source*: Wikimedia Commons. Public domain.

movement with secret teachings. He attended the Fourth High School in the area where he met Nishida Kitarō, who was to become founder of the Kyoto School of modern Japanese philosophy. At the suggestion of Nishida, Suzuki began studying philosophy at Tokyo Imperial University. In Tokyo, Suzuki worked as an English teacher at a primary school, taking courses at Tokyo University in a nondegree program. Both Suzuki and Nishida started Zen training under Setsumon, a priest of Kokutaiji. While living in Tokyo, Suzuki then began practicing *zazen* or "seated meditation" with the great Zen master Imakita Kōsen (1816–1892) in 1891 at Engakuji, a Rinzai Zen temple in Kamakura, Japan. As documented by Janine Sawada (2004, 132), Imakita was a pioneering Zen modernizer who broke with convention and initiated a new program for "lay Zen" at Engakuji, and it was through this outreach program that Suzuki underwent his own Zen training. In 1923 the *Kojirin* or "laypeople's grove" was formally established at Engakuji as a center where everyone could now practice Zen meditation. When Imakita passed away, Suzuki continued his Zen practice with Shaku Sōen (1859–1919), Imakita's successor at Engakuji, who further developed this progressive modernization program for lay practitioners. It was Shaku Sōen who bestowed Suzuki with the Buddhist name "Daisetsu" (大拙) meaning "absolute simplicity." The first koan given to Suzuki by Imakita was Hakuin's "Sound of One Hand." Shaku Sōen, however, changed Suzuki's koan from Hakuin's "Sound of One Hand" to Jōshū's "Mu!" At Engakuji, Suzuki immersed himself in the zazen koan practice of concentration upon the keyword Mu, finally being certified as having achieved an initial breakthrough to satori by Shaku Sōen. Having met with Suzuki on many occasions, and carefully studying his writings, Fukushima Keido Roshi (d. 2011), an acclaimed Rinzai Zen master who became head abbot of Tofukuji in Kyoto, testifies that he regards Suzuki as a great scholar and teacher who through intensive practice attained satori as a lay practitioner of Zen (2017, 88).

In 1911 Suzuki married an American woman interested in Buddhism and Theosophy named Beatrice Lane Suzuki (1878–1939). As documented in *Tokyo Boogie-woogie and D. T. Suzuki* by Yamada Shōji (2022), Beatrice and Suzuki adopted a half-Caucasian and half-Japanese boy who they named Alan Masaru Suzuki. But due to Alan's excessive drinking, womanizing, and other scandalous activities, Suzuki cut off all relations with him. Nonetheless, Alan had his own moment of fame when he co-wrote the hit song *Tokyo Boogie-woogie* (1947), which became a sensation in post-war Japan. From 1911 until 1919 Beatrice and Suzuki lived in a cottage on the Zen temple grounds at Engakuji in Kamakura, afterward moving to Kyoto, where Suzuki began a professorship at Ōtani University in 1921 at the age of fifty-one. That same year Suzuki and his wife founded *The Eastern Buddhist*, a journal devoted to Mahayana Buddhism and the Kyoto School of modern Japanese philosophy. After a lifetime spreading Zen throughout the United States and other Western countries, Suzuki passed away at 95 years of age. In 2011 the D. T. Suzuki Museum (Suzuki Daisetsu Kan) was opened near the home of his birth in Kanazawa. As part of his enduring legacy, Suzuki left behind more than thirty major works in English and a forty-volume *Collected Works* in Japanese.

It was the lectures, classes, and writings of Suzuki that ignited the "Zen boom" that exploded like a bomb in postwar America during the 1950s, the seismic aftershocks of which are still resounding today. Suzuki disseminated Zen throughout American culture, pop culture, and counterculture while also profoundly influencing Western academic fields such as philosophy, psychoanalysis, comparative religions, and aesthetics. Moreover, Suzuki's Zen aestheticism had an enormous impact on the avant-garde artworld of modernist painters, poets, novelists, architects, musicians, sculptors, and other experimental artists. But to adapt Zen Buddhism to his Western audience, Suzuki gave Zen a modern psychological interpretation based on his Zen doctrine of the Unconscious. According to Suzuki, the *summum bonum* or ultimate goal of Zen is the immediate experience of *satori* (悟り), awakening, illumination, or enlightenment. Psychologically speaking, however, Suzuki interprets Zen satori as a sudden breakthrough to the Unconscious or what he otherwise refers to as the cosmic Unconscious, the recognition of which he terms superconsciousness. Another name for satori in Suzuki's Zen writings is *kenshō* (見性), "seeing into one's [Buddha] nature." Again, in psychological terms, Suzuki explains Buddha nature, Original Enlightenment, or Tathagatagarbha (the womb or generative matrix of Buddhahood), as our own deeper subliminal mind, such that kensho is direct insight into the Unconscious. Buddha nature as prajna wisdom of emptiness is a very subtle awareness that is always present, but ordinarily goes unrecognized or unnoticed, and is therefore referred to by Suzuki in psychological terms as *subconscious*, *unconscious*, and *subliminal*. Zen satori is the noetic act of recognizing or noticing this very subtle awareness, hence, to awaken from the sleep of unconsciousness. In his Zen mysticism, Suzuki regards zazen meditation as a discipline whereby consciousness gradually plunges ever deeper into its source in the bottomless well of the Unconscious, while satori is a radical breakthrough to the Unconscious, thereby to illuminate it from within in an explosive burst of sudden enlightenment. Suzuki's psychologization of Zen thus views satori-kensho as an act of recovering the entire Unconscious as spacelike dharmakaya emptiness and thereupon making it fully conscious in what he calls superconsciousness or supraconsciousness. According to the Rinzai Zen of Suzuki, it is concentration of the whole bodymind upon the keyword of a koan such as *Mu* that opens up a shortcut path to satori, whereby there is an abrupt realization of the cosmic Unconscious. Through Zen koan practice, awareness penetrates into the depths of the cosmic Unconscious as the luminous void of emptiness or nothingness, normally associated with sleep or death, while at the same time remaining fully lucid, alert, and awake, thereby to attain satori as what Suzuki otherwise paradoxically calls unconscious consciousness or conscious unconsciousness. In Suzuki's Zen aestheticism, Zen satori and its spontaneous expressions in Zen-inspired art have their origin in the cosmic Unconscious, which as the radiant transparent openness of absolute nothingness is the ontological source of creativity. As will be further demonstrated, in Suzuki's Zen aestheticism, satori is the aesthetically immediate experience of interdependently arisen phenomena in the natural beauty of their emptiness-suchness. Moreover, using the "two truths" doctrine of Mahayana Buddhism, Suzuki argues that prior to enlightenment a large part of our mind remains unknown, unnoticed, or unrecognized at the level of dualistic ego-consciousness and is therefore *provisionally* designated in conventional terms as "the Unconscious." But at the *ultimate* level of discourse, the nondual Zen experience of satori makes the Unconscious conscious in superconsciousness, whereupon the total spectrum of our mind becomes fully "transparent" to itself in the diaphanous clarity of absolute nothingness, all out in the open with nothing hidden. It can thus be said that the cosmic Unconscious is the key notion operative in Suzuki's modern psychological interpretation of Zen art, meditation, and enlightenment.

A recurrent theme in Suzuki's writings is the *trikāya* or "three bodies" doctrine of Mahayana Buddhism. To further elucidate Suzuki's Zen concept of the cosmic Unconscious, I use C. G. Jung's application of the "three bodies" doctrine of Mahayana Buddhism as a hermeneutical framework for analyzing the infrastructure of the unconscious psyche as a full spectrum with multiple levels. Jung wrote the foreword to Suzuki's *An Introduction to Zen Buddhism,* wherein the former interprets Zen satori as an inflow of the contents of the collective unconscious into consciousness thereby activating the individuation process as a quest for wholeness in the hero's journey toward Self-realization. In in his psychological commentaries on Mahayana and Vajrayana Buddhism, Jung employs the *trikāya* doctrine to classify the three levels of the unconscious, arguing that Freudian psychoanalysis is restricted to *nirmāṇakāya* or the physically embodied personal unconscious of repressed libidinal instincts. Moreover, Jung claimed that his own method of analytical psychology focuses on *sambhogakāya* or the enjoyment body as the dreamlike *mundus imaginalis* or imaginal realm of the collective unconscious and its archetypal images. But here I demonstrate that in contrast to Freud's "personal unconscious" corresponding to *nirmāṇakāya*, and Jung's "collective unconscious" corresponding to *sambhogakāya*, Suzuki's Zen concept of the "cosmic Unconscious" is explicitly identified with *dharmakāya* as the spacelike transparent openness of sunyata or emptiness, also referred to as the plenary void of absolute nothingness.

I will further clarify that Suzuki formulates a modern hybrid Zen theory of the Unconscious derived from an integral synthesis of Mahayana Buddhism and Daoism with American and continental schools of philosophical psychology. Moreover, it will be shown how Suzuki's Zen doctrine of the Unconscious itself influenced subsequent theories of the unconscious psyche, both in Japan and the West. In this work the Unconscious is thus developed as an intercultural theme for East-West comparative philosophy, psychology, religion, and aesthetics. On the Western side, Suzuki was familiar with the aesthetic spirituality of the psychologized American tradition, including William James's subconscious or transmarginal consciousness, A. N. Whitehead's process metaphysics based on *prehension* or unconscious feeling, and the extremely popular New Thought metaphysics based on the notion that the human mind has a threefold intrapsychic division between the conscious, the subconscious, and the superconscious. In addition, Suzuki was knowledgeable about European, and especially the

German, theories of the unconscious mind, running through such luminaries as Boehme, Leibniz, Kant, Schelling, and Schopenhauer, including their grand synthesis in Eduard von Hartmann's *Philosophy of the Unconscious* (1869). Here I make reference to historical overviews of the unconscious in Western thought, including John Bargh (2017), Henri Ellenberger (1970), Jon Mills (2014), Leonard Mlodinow (2013), Frank Tallis (2012), Joel Weinberger and Valentina Stovicheva (2021), and others. But these studies do not incorporate Eastern perspectives on the unconscious psyche. Also, these histories generally neglect modern/postmodern French theories of the unconscious developed by Henri Bergson, Jacques Lacan, Jean-Paul Sartre, Jacques Derrida, Jacques Rancière, Gilles Deleuze, Félix Guattari, and others. Moreover, they fail to include new concepts of a deeper, wider, and higher unconscious developed in transpersonal psychology, including such representative figures as Abraham Maslow, Ken Wilber, Hubert Benoit, G. I. Gurdjieff, Roberto Assagioli, and Stanislov Grof. The present volume can therefore serve as an updated East-West global survey about theories of the subliminal mind in American, European, and Asian traditions, as viewed through the lens of Suzuki's Zen doctrine of the cosmic Unconscious.

In this work, I have not attempted to provide a comprehensive intellectual biography of Suzuki's entire life and teachings, or to give an exhaustive account of his writings, but only to elucidate his Zen concept of the Unconscious, especially as found in his works aimed at introducing Zen to the West.[1] At the same time, it will be discussed how Suzuki also provides detailed presentations on the Unconscious in his untranslated Japanese works, such as *Mushin to iu koto* (*On No-mind/On the Unconscious*, 2012). Although various commentators sometimes make passing reference to Suzuki's Zen doctrine of the Unconscious, none have identified it as a central and recurrent motif pervading his work. Hence, in the present volume I have endeavored to demonstrate through abundant textual citations, both from English and Japanese texts, that the cosmic Unconscious is *the* master concept operative in Suzuki's modern psychological interpretation of Zen and Mahayana Buddhism, from beginning to end.

It is my position that there is enormous value in revisiting the works of Suzuki today. In the twentieth century, the Unconscious became a major concept, especially owing to the depth psychology of Freud and Jung, not only in academia but also in popular culture, including the aesthetic world of painting, sculpture, literature, film, theater, and other creative arts. In this volume I want to demonstrate that beyond his pioneering role as a translator and expositor of Zen and Mahayana Buddhist texts, the genius of Suzuki and his most significant contribution as an original thinker was to have developed a modern philosophical psychology that reinterprets every aspect of Zen art, meditation, and enlightenment as a spontaneous function of the Unconscious while also positing a new Zen concept of the cosmic Unconscious, which as spacelike transparent dharmakaya emptiness or absolute nothingness is the inexhaustible wellspring of unlimited creative potentialities and the source of all Zen-inspired arts. I thus contend that Suzuki's Zen Buddhist philosophical psychology of the cosmic Unconscious makes a valuable and enduring contribution to our knowledge of the full spectrum of the human mind in its totality.

Critiques of Suzuki's Zen

Although Suzuki has received much acclaim as the one who introduced Zen to the West, his writings have also been strongly criticized.[2] Suzuki's Zen has been questioned for its alleged support of militarism, ethnocentrism, colonialism, imperialism, apologism, and ultranationalism, along with the triumphalism of his *nihonjinron* views propagating the myth of Japanese uniqueness and superiority. Furthermore, some buddhologists have objected that Suzuki's Zen is not authentic or traditional Zen/Chan Buddhism but rather a Westernized, modernized, decontextualized, psychologized, and hybridized Zen. Others have criticized Suzuki's ahistorical view of Zen satori as an immediate or pure experience that transcends all historical, cultural, and social conditions. In the present volume, I develop my own critique of Suzuki's Zen aestheticism, focusing on his apologetic discourse on the "samurai Zen" of Bushido as the art of swordsmanship, insofar as it has come to be viewed by some as misusing Zen *mushin* or no-mind as the cosmic Unconscious to illicitly support dangerous ideologies, such as ultranationalism, imperialism, colonialism, militarism, and totalitarian emperor-system fascism during World War II in Japan.

A paradigmatic example of critical scholarship leveled against Suzuki's Zen is to be found in a famous debate between the Chinese philosopher Hu Shih and Suzuki, which took place at an East-West Philosophers' Conference at the University of Hawaii. On this occasion, Hu Shih argued that Suzuki neglects the historical and cultural aspects of Zen to which Suzuki countered that Hu Shih only knows the outside of Zen, but that from its inside, the awakening of Zen satori is a pure experience that transcends history and culture. The most important effort to mediate disputes between Suzuki's Zen and his various critics is to be found in Steven Heine's *Zen Skin, Zen Marrow* (2008). In this truly exceptional work, Heine posits two competing approaches to Zen: traditional Zen narrative (TZN) versus historical and cultural criticism (HCC). According to Heine, Suzuki and his followers are among those to be classified as TZN, which can be regarded as a romanticized, idealized, and dehistorized approach to Zen, while Hu Shih and other antagonists are classified as HCC. Scholars of HCC generally attempt to discredit Suzuki's version of Zen/Chan Buddhism, some of his detractors having adopted an extremist attitude that becomes dogmatically one-sided, excessively hypercritical, and arrogantly dismissive. In Heine's more inclusive, judicious, and edifying approach, however, the goal is to balance TZN and HCC, with a Buddhist middle way standpoint that incorporates insights from both positions. What Heine calls TZN as represented by scholars like Suzuki is based on three principles: (1) ineffability as a process of "special transmission outside the scriptures" (*kyōge betsuden*) undertaken "without relying on words and letters" (*furyū monji*); (2) nonduality, or the espousing of a philosophy based on direct, immediate, or pure experience; and (3) societal harmony (*wa*), as embracing equality of all beings by virtue of their possessing the common endowment of original enlightenment (*hongaku*) or innate Buddha nature (*busshō*) (2008, 6–7). By contrast, HCC asserts that Zen is based on three opposing principles: (1) speech, or the use of language, writing, and conversation; (2) mediation, or the widespread use of rituals and supernaturalism in the spread of Zen throughout East Asia, especially ceremonies for practical this-worldly benefits (*genze riyaku*); and (3) discrimination, or the unfortunate contributions of Zen to problems of gender and class conflict, militarism, and nationalism (2008, 8–9). According to Heine, this approach "provides a methodological framework for the constructive juxtaposition that enables a creative interaction and dialogue instead of opposition and polarization between the TZN and HCC positions" (2008, 29). Heine's comprehensive, balanced, and insightful approach thereby opens up a way to develop Suzuki's Zen Buddhist philosophical psychology of the Unconscious along with those criticisms questioning his views in light of HCC.

A special issue of *The Eastern Buddhist* (Vol. 47, No. 2, 2016) reported on an event at Ōtani University in Kyoto commemorating the fiftieth anniversary of the passing of Suzuki Daisetsu. Sueki Fumihiko clarifies how starting with the initial period of acclaim, followed by a period of critical reaction, there has begun a new period of reevaluating Suzuki's work from a more informed perspective that takes into account these criticisms (2016, 1–3). He discusses the great renewal of interest in Suzuki along with the new directions in research on his writings: "With the year 2016 marking the fiftieth anniversary of his death, scholars have been turning a fresh eye to D. T. Suzuki (1870–1966)" (2016, 1).[3] As explained by Sueki, in the first period of Japanese scholarship on Suzuki, research was carried out by scholars who were taught or influenced by him, such as Furuta Shōkin, Kirita Kiyohide, Ueda Shizuteru, and Akizuki Ryōmin, and were therefore aimed at honoring the importance of the man and his work. Starting around the 1980s, however, a second period of critical studies began to appear in response to existing research with its slant toward praising Suzuki. This development, which began overseas, included Brian Victoria's *Zen at War* (2006), along with the work of Robert Sharf and Bernard Faure. These scholars focused on Suzuki's war cooperation and nationalism. Sueki then goes on to discuss the third period of scholarship on Suzuki's works: "In recent years, Suzuki's thought has begun to be reexamined in a new way, which takes into account such criticisms. This is the third, and still ongoing period in the history of research on D. T. Suzuki" (2016, 2).[4]

In the final chapter of *Global Origins of the Modern Self, from Montaigne to Suzuki* (2019), Avram Alpert persuasively argues that Suzuki, like many other non-Western and non-European thinkers, has been marginalized and thus excluded from the established canon of world philosophy. Alpert thus provides an alternative non-Eurocentric reading of Suzuki's Zen notion of global selfhood, thereby to now include Suzuki within an expanded canon of world philosophy that is creolized, deracialized, and decolonized. Hence, against the many recent Western scholars who have attempted to undermine or arrogantly dismiss Suzuki's enormous contributions to East-West dialogue, Alpert's postcolonial reading of Suzuki recognizes his landmark contributions to Zen and comparative philosophy.

This renewal of interest in and reevaluation of Suzuki's writings is especially indebted to a four-volume series, *The Selected Works of D. T. Suzuki* (2015, 2015, 2016, 2021) edited by Richard M. Jaffe, the foremost American scholar of Suzuki.[5] In accordance with this third wave of recent scholarship, the present volume highlights the remarkable contributions made by Suzuki, focusing on what I regard to be his signature concept of the cosmic Unconscious to interpret all aspects of Zen art, religion, and philosophy. Yet at the same time I address some of the important objections raised against Suzuki Zen while also developing my own critique of Suzuki's militarized apologistic discourse on samurai Zen aestheticism, insofar as it is based on his modern philosophical psychology of satori as sudden awakening to *mushin* or no-mind as the cosmic Unconscious.

Part 1 examines how Suzuki (re)interprets every aspect of Zen and Mahayana Buddhism in terms of his modern philosophical psychology of the cosmic Unconscious, focusing especially on his psychologized understanding of Zen art, meditation, and enlightenment. Part 2 develops Suzuki's modern Zen concept of the cosmic Unconscious in relation to Western theories formulated in the American, German, and French traditions as well as the field of transpersonal psychology. Finally, the epilogue reexamines Suzuki's notion of Zen satori in light of Jean Gebser's phenomenology of unfolding "structures of consciousness" in European history, especially the leap or mutation beyond the egocentric mental-rational structure to the ego-free integral structure of openness, clarity, diaphaneity, and transparency. It is in such a manner that the present volume endeavors to critically analyze and reevaluate Suzuki's interpretation of Zen art, meditation, and enlightenment based on his modern philosophical psychology of the cosmic Unconscious.

Part One

The Unconscious in Zen Theory and Practice

Part one focuses on Suzuki's Zen concept of the cosmic Unconscious as formulated in Mahayana Buddhist terms, including Zen *mushin* or "no-mind," Prajnaparamita teachings of sunyata or emptiness as absolute nothingness, Kegon/Huayan philosophy of interpenetration between many and one visualized as Indra's net, the Yogacara psychology of the storehouse consciousness functioning as our deeper subliminal mind, and the Zen/Chan teaching that no-mind is the ordinary mind of everyday life. Also, there is an analysis of Suzuki's Zen aestheticism, which views Zen art and Zen aesthetics in psychological terms as a spontaneous expression of the cosmic Unconscious as the wellspring of creativity. Moreover, there is an exposition of Suzuki's view of Zen meditation and other spiritual exercises that awaken us to the cosmic Unconscious in superconsciousness, especially Rinzai Zen koan practice, foremost of which is concentration of the whole bodymind on the keyword MU!

Chapter 1

Suzuki's Zen Doctrine of the Cosmic Unconscious

No-Mind as the Unconscious

The Sino-Japanese Zen/Chan Buddhist term *mushin* (C. *wuxin/wu-hsin*, 無心) is commonly translated as "no-mind." D. T. Suzuki also frequently translates *mushin* as "no-mind," or sometimes as "empty-mind." But he argues that psychologically speaking, *mushin* is best rendered as "the Unconscious." Furthermore, Suzuki demonstrates how the Zen notion of *mushin* or no-mind is equivalent to *munen* (C. *wunian/wu-nien*, 無念) or "no-thought," which is therefore likewise translated in psychological terms as "the Unconscious." He further identifies *mushin* or no-mind and *munen* or no-thought with *muga* (Skt: *anātman*), "no-self or nonego," also interpreted as the Unconscious. Just as Suzuki psychologically interprets Zen no-mind as the Unconscious, he explains Zen *satori* (悟り) or enlightenment as awakening to the Unconscious: "*Satori* is the *raison d'*être of Zen without which Zen is not Zen" (AIZB, 95). Moreover, he describes satori in psychological terms: "satori is to realize the Unconscious" (EZB II, 21). He adds: "As far as the psychology of satori is considered, a sense of the Beyond is all we can say about it. . . . I have called it elsewhere the Unconscious, though this has a psychological taint" (EZB II, 19). An alternate Zen Buddhist term for satori or enlightenment is *kenshō* (見性), "seeing into one's [Buddha] nature." In Suzuki's own words: "Another name for satori is *ken-sho* (*chien-hsing* in Chinese) meaning 'to see essence or nature'" (ZKMA, 25). From the standpoint of his philosophical psychology, Suzuki's "satori Zen" thus interprets satori-kensho as a sudden flash of insight into the Unconscious or what he otherwise terms the cosmic Unconscious.

Suzuki historically traces back the Zen doctrine of *mushin* or no-mind as the Unconscious to Bodhidharma (fifth century CE), the legendary first patriarch of the Chan/Zen school. According to Buddhist legend, it was Bodhidharma (C. Putidamo; J. Daruma) who transmitted the Chan/Zen (Skt. *dhyāna*, "meditation") teachings from India to China. Using his own translations from classical Chinese, Suzuki cites the words of Bodhidharma on the Zen doctrine of no-mind as the Unconscious.[1] A disciple asks Bodhidharma: "O Master, if it is the Unconscious that prevails everywhere. . . . Why do all beings transmigrate in the six paths of existence and constantly go on through birth and death?" (EZB III, 10). Bodhidharma answers:

> Where there is the Unconscious, they erroneously imagine the reality of a conscious mind. Thus various sorts of deeds are performed, and there is really transmigration in the six paths of existence. Such beings are advised to see a good friend, great [in his spiritual insight], and to practice meditation which will lead them to the realisation of the Unconscious. . . . As the sunlight once penetrating into the darkness dispels all that is dark, all their sins are destroyed when they realize the Unconscious. (EZB III, 10; brackets in original)

Through the arising of subject-object bifurcation there emerges dualistic ego-consciousness, the karmic cause for transmigration in the material world of samsara with all its suffering, just as by awakening to the Unconscious through meditation practice under the guidance of a Chan/Zen master, one attains enlightenment. Bodhidharma is further cited: "Therefore, let it be known that all things rise when a conscious mind is asserted, and that all things cease to exist when the Unconscious is realized" (EZB III, 11). As translated/interpreted by Suzuki, Bodhidharma declares: "The Unconscious is the true Mind, the true Mind is the Unconscious. . . . Only let us be awakened to the Unconscious in all things, in all our doings – this is the way of discipline, there is no other way. Thus we know that when the Unconscious is realized, all things cease to trouble us" (EZB III, 12). For Bodhidharma, one must therefore follow the way of discipline through Chan/Zen meditation in everyday life as the method for awakening to our true Mind as the Unconscious.

Suzuki cites from his own translation of a Dunhuang cave text attributed to Bodhidharma, titled *Mushinron* (C. Wuxinlun, 無心論) or "Treatise on Mushin," a text that is considered representative of the Southern School of Chan/Zen Buddhism (EZB III, 8–12). He first explains in a footnote the origin of this discussion in Keiki Yabuki's *Echoes of the Desert* (folio 77) containing collotype reproductions of some Dunhuang Buddhist manuscripts (EZB III, 8, fn. 3). This text was among those approximately three hundred Chan/Zen manuscripts discovered in the Dunhuang caves near the Gobi Desert, and Suzuki was the first to translate parts of this manuscript from Chinese into English. The Dunhuang Zen/Chan manuscript *Mushinron* (無心論) can be translated by convention as "Treatise on No-Mind," but in accordance with Suzuki's modern psychological approach, it can be alternately translated as "Treatise on the Unconscious." Discussing Bodhidharma's Zen notion of *wuxin/mushin* or no-mind, Suzuki writes: "Let us start with Bodhidharma, the father of Chinese Zen, who writes on *Wu-hsin* (literally, 'no-mind')" (EZB III, 8). But as Suzuki goes on to say, "In the present case, *Wu-hsin* is 'unconsciousness'" (EXB III, 8–9, fn. 3).

Next, Suzuki goes on to consider the Zen doctrine of "no-mind" (C. *wuxin*; J. *mushin,* 無心) or "no-thought" (C. *wunian*; J. *munen,* 無念), as "the Unconscious" propounded by Huineng (J. Enō 慧能, 638–713), the legendary Sixth Patriarch of Chan/Zen Buddhism: "According to Hui-neng, the concept of the unconscious is the foundation of Zen Buddhism" (ZDNM, 58). He elsewhere states: "*Wu-nien,* the Unconscious, according to Hui-neng, is the name not only for ultimate reality but for the state of consciousness in which the ultimate presents itself. . . . Consciousness must be made somehow to relate to the Unconscious . . . and this realization is known to be the *Wu-nien,* literally a state of 'thoughtlessness'" (EZB III, 17). Suzuki maintains that the central aim of Huineng's teaching is "sudden enlightenment" (C. *tunwu*; J. *tongo,* 頓悟), comprehended as instantaneous awakening to the Unconscious: "The doctrine of the Unconscious (*wu-nien*) together with that of immediate understanding (*tun-wu*) was the chief topic of interest in the days of Hui-neng and his followers" (EZB III, 18). He points out that while Bodhidharma uses the term *wuxin* or "no-mind," Huineng generally prefers the term *wunian* or "no-thought" to designate the Unconscious. Moreover, he explains that Huineng criticized "gradual enlightenment" and instead emphasized "sudden enlightenment," described as an abrupt or immediate experience of the Unconscious: "The consciousness of Zen specifically as the 'immediate experience of the understanding' of the Unconscious dawned in the mind of Hui-neng. If Bodhidharma used the term, *wu-hsin,* for the Unconscious, Hui-neng replaced *hsin* by *nien.* . . . The use of *wu-nien* . . . in the sense of 'unconsciousness,' and pregnant with a deep spiritual significance, as far as I can gather, begins with Hui-neng" (EZB III, 14–15). He continues: "Let us now see what Hui-neng has to say about the Unconscious (*wu-nien*)" (EZB III, 15). Suzuki translates Huineng's discourse on sudden awakening to the Unconscious as proclaiming: "Good friends, to have an insight for once is to know what Buddhahood means. . . . To recognize the inmost mind is emancipation. When emancipation is attained, Prajñā-Samādhi obtains. To realize Prajñā-Samādhi means to have the Unconscious" (EZB III, 18). Huineng's discourse proceeds:

> What is the Unconscious? It is to see all things as they are and not to become attached to anything; it is to be present in all places and yet not to become attached anywhere. . . . This is to realize Prajñā-Samādhi, to be master of oneself, to become emancipated, and is known as living the Unconscious. . . . He who understands the teaching of the Unconscious has a most thorough going knowledge of all things. He who understands the teaching of the Unconscious sees into the spiritual realm of all Buddhahood. He who understands the "abrupt" teaching of the Unconscious reaches the stage of Buddhahood. (EZB III, 18)

According to Suzuki, then, Huineng imparted the Zen teaching of kensho as a sudden act of directly seeing into Buddhahood or Buddha nature as the Unconscious, our innate prajna wisdom of emptiness-compassion.

It should be remembered that during his employment with Paul Carus at Open Court Press, Suzuki translated Laozi's *Daodejing* (1898) and other Daoist texts from classical Chinese into English. Suzuki thus further explains how Huineng's Chan/Zen doctrine of *wunian* (no-thought) or *wuxin* (no-mind) as the Unconscious corresponds to Laozi's Daoist notion of *wuwei* (J. *mui*, 無為) or "non-action": "In one sense the Laotsuan teaching of Non-action (*wu-wei*) may be said to be living in the Unconscious of Hui-neng" (EZB III, 18). Daoist *wuwei* or non-action is a functional equivalent to Chan/Zen *wuxin/mushin* or no-mind, and *wunian/munen* or no-thought, as the Unconscious, in that it signifies a noncoercive attitude of letting things be what they are without clinging, grasping, or attachment. Just as Chan/Zen *wuxin/mushin* or no-mind as the Unconscious is compared by Suzuki to Laozi's *wuwei* or nonaction, so he further relates it to Zhuangzi's Daoist practice of "mind-fasting" (*xin zhai*), an emptiness where the life force of *qi*-energy is open, receptive, and freely responding to all that is present (ZJC, 149). Chan/Zen *wuxin/mushin* or no-mind, like Daoist *wuwei*, is a spontaneous action performed with "effortless naturalness." Reminiscent of Daoist *wuwei*, Suzuki describes *wuxin* or no-mind and *wunian* or no-thought, psychologically interpreted as the Unconscious, as designating actions performed without "conscious striving" (ZDNM, 72, fn. 3). He argues that in *wuxin* or no-mind the Buddha functions naturally, instinctively, effortlessly, and unconsciously: "Hence it is declared that *fo wu hsin*, 'Buddha is unconscious', or 'By Buddhahood is meant the unconscious'. Philosophically speaking, therefore, no special conscious strivings are necessary" (ZDNM, 73, fn. 4). He adds: "That is, the Buddha with all his worldly activities among us lies on the plane of unconsciousness, in a world of effortlessness" (ZDNM, 73, fn. 3). According to Suzuki, "no-mind" of Sino-Japanese Chan/Zen Buddhism as the Unconscious is parallel to "the Laozian doctrine of the action of nonaction" (SWS I, 180). Elsewhere, he again describes Laozi's Daoist principle of *wuwei* in relation to Zen *mushin* as follows: "This is the practical application of the Lao-tzuan doctrine of 'doing by not doing.' . . . The Heavenly Way is above the self, which is *mushin*, 'no-mind,' or *munen*, 'no-thought'" (ZJC, 133). Both the *wuxin/mushin* or no-mind of Chan/Zen Buddhism, and the *wuwei* or nonaction of Daoism, are a creative function of the Unconscious that operates automatically, effortlessly, and unconsciously in the spontaneous flow of nature and everyday life. Indeed, here I would like to point out the striking parallels between the philosophical psychology of Chan/Zen *wuxin* (J. *mushin*) or no-mind and Daoist *wuwei* (J. *mui*) or nonaction as the Unconscious in Suzuki's Zen aestheticism and the views of Li Zehou, widely regarded as the greatest contemporary Chinese philosopher. In a section titled "The Unconscious" from his work *The Chinese Aesthetic Tradition*, Li thus claims that "the unconscious" (*wuyishi*) has been a central theme running throughout the history of

Chinese aesthetics, especially in the traditions of Daoism and Chan Buddhism: "This idea of the unconscious has exercised a tremendous influence on Chinese aesthetics. Whether in poetry, prose, painting, or calligraphy, the question of an unconscious creative principle has been a matter of almost constant discussion" (Zehou 2010, 110).

The Zen Doctrine of No Mind (1949) is Suzuki's partial translation of, and commentary on, the *Platform Sutra* (*Lu-tso T'an-ching*; J. *Rokuso dangyo*) attributed to Huineng. In this work Suzuki argues that "sudden enlightenment" as realization of "no-mind," "no-thought," or "nonego," comprehended in psychological terms as "the Unconscious," is the central notion operating in the *Platform Sutra* of Huineng. In this work, Suzuki explains his psychological interpretation of Zen no-mind or no-thought as the Unconscious: "As Zen is more concerned with experience and hence with psychology, let us go further into the idea of the Unconscious. The original Chinese is *Wu-nien* (*mu-nen*) or *Wu-hsin* (*mu-shin*), and literally means 'no-thought', or 'no-mind' . . . *wu-nien* and *wu-hsin* point to the same state of consciousness" (ZDNM, 57). Explaining his translation of the Chinese terms *wunian* (J. *munen*) or no-thought and its equivalent *wuxin* (J. *mushin*) or no-mind as "the Unconscious," Suzuki writes: "*Wu-nien* is 'no-consciousness', thus the unconscious . . . *Wu-nien* thus also means 'the unconscious'" (ZDNM, 57). In this and other works, Suzuki often translates *mushin* as "no-mind," and *munen* as "no-thought." But when he endeavors to clarify the modern psychological aspects of no-mind or no-thought, he renders them as "the Unconscious." Further clarifying Huineng's Zen doctrine of sudden enlightenment as an abrupt realization of no-mind as the Unconscious, Suzuki asserts: "That the process of enlightenment is abrupt means that there is a leap, logical and psychological, in the Buddhist experience . . . the psychological leap is that the borders of consciousness are overstepped and one is plunged into the Unconscious, which is not, after all, unconscious . . . this is 'Seeing into one's Self-nature'" (ZDNM, 54). It should be noted how Suzuki tells us that while the term unconsciousness is used, our Buddha nature or true Mind is not actually unconscious but what he elsewhere describes as cosmic consciousness, superconsciousness, and supraconsciousness. Zen *mushin* or no-mind hence designates a very subtle awareness that is always present but normally goes unrecognized, and the task of Zen practice is to recognize this very subtle awareness by awakening to our Buddha nature in superconsciousness.

According to Suzuki, Huineng's Chan/Zen doctrine of seeing into self-nature as true Mind or the Unconscious is to be understood as "no-mind" (C. *wuxin*; J. *mushin*, 無心), which he elucidates in terms of "no-thought" (C. *wunian*; J. *munen*, 無念), "no-form" (C. *wuxiang*; J. *musō*, 無想), and "no-abiding" (C. *wuzhu*; J. *mujū*, 無住), all of which in psychological terms refer to "the Unconscious." Citing the words of Huineng: "I establish no-thought-ness (*wu-nien*) the Unconscious as the Principle [of my teaching], formlessness as the Body, and abodelessness as the Source" (ZDNM, 102). He continues: "This declaration is the foundation of Zen teaching . . . *Wu-nien* (no-thought) is psychological, *wu-hsiang* (no-form) ontological, and *wu-chu* (no-abode) is moral. . . . They all practically and ultimately mean the same thing, but Zen is most interested in psychology, in realizing the Unconscious" (ZDNM, 102). Suzuki then explains Mazu's concept of Buddha mind in terms of the Unconscious: "The most famous saying of Ma-tsu is, 'This mind is the Buddha himself,' which has been in fact one of the main thoughts advocated by all the Zen masters preceding him; but to this Ma-tsu added: 'One's everyday thought (or mind) is the Tao.' . . . This may correspond to what I have called the Unconscious (*wu-hsin* or *wu-nien*)" (ZDNM, 106). He continues: "When Ma-tsu and other Zen leaders declare that 'this mind is the Buddha himself', it does not mean that there is a kind of soul lying hidden in the depths of consciousness, but that a state of unconsciousness, psychologically stated, which accompanies every conscious and unconscious act of mind is what constitutes Buddhahood" (ZDNM, 106). It is here again clarified how Mazu's famous declaration that "mind is Buddha" is to be understood as making reference to the Unconscious, or the deep subliminal mind that underlies all conscious and unconscious processes. Hence, "the Unconscious" is Suzuki's epithet for Buddha, Buddha nature, Buddha mind, Dharmakaya, Tathagatagarbha, the Unborn, and other Mahayana Buddhist terms denoting ultimate reality, as well as the nondual primordial awareness cognizing that reality.

The Zen Doctrine of No Mind further develops Suzuki's psychological interpretation of Huineng's prajna-intuition as the act of directly seeing into one's self-nature as the Unconscious: "Another point I have to make clearer in their connection is that Prajñā is the name given to Self-nature according to Huineng, or the Unconscious, as we call it, when it becomes conscious of itself . . . Prajñā therefore points in two directions to the Unconscious and to a world of consciousness which is now unfolded" (ZDNM, 21). He then sums up his psychologized view of Zen *mushin* or no-mind and *munen* or no-thought as unconsciousness: "What is *mushin* (*wu-hsin* in Chinese)? What is meant by 'no-mind-ness' or 'no-thought-ness'? It is difficult to find an English equivalent except the Unconscious" (ZDNM, 120). Furthermore, he explains: "In order to explain how one comes to realize the state of *mushin* (*wu-hsin*) or *munen* (*wu-nien*), I have given a diagrammatic analysis of Self-nature" (ZDNM, 142). At this point, Suzuki represents his view of Huineng's Chan/Zen notion of self-nature as *mushin* or no-mind and *munen* or no-thought, defined in psychological terms as the Unconscious, using a schematic diagram (Fig. 1.1) (ZDNM, 125; ZB, 253).

Explaining his diagrammatic scheme of the Unconscious and its various levels, Suzuki continues: "In this [diagram] the Unconscious *A*, *B*, and *C* belong to the transcendental order, and are essentially of one and the same nature, whereas the unconscious D is of the empirical mind which is the subject of psychology" (ZDNM, 125). According to Suzuki's diagram of the unconscious mind, then, levels A, B, and C together represent the Zen concept of no-mind

Figure 1.1. The relation between self-nature, the unconscious, and empirical mind. *Source*: Created by the author.

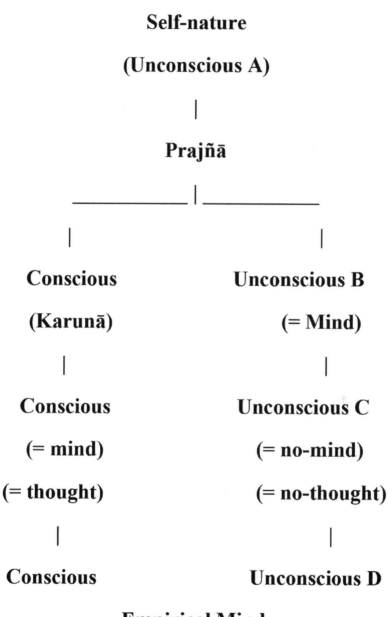

or no-thought as the cosmic Unconscious realized through prajna wisdom of emptiness, whereas D is the empirical unconscious of Western psychology.

Suzuki cites from the words of Shenhui (686–760), a disciple of Huineng: "To see into the Unconscious is to understand self-nature" (ZDNM, 63). Explaining the Zen doctrine of no-mind or the Unconscious in Shenhui and Huineng, he adds, "'to see' self-nature . . . means to wake up in the Unconscious" (ZDNM, 64). Again: "The Chinese *wu-hsin*, 'without mind', and *wu-nien*, 'without thought', mean both the Unconscious and being unconscious" (ZDNM, 71). He goes on to clarify that for Huineng, the Unconscious is not to be reified into a material substance with permanent or separate existence: "The conception of the Unconscious leads to many wrong interpretations when it is taken as pointing to the existence of an entity to be designated 'the Unconscious'" (ZDNM, 71). According to Huineng and Shenhui, the Unconscious is neither to be conceived in substantialistic terms as a material entity nor in nihilistic terms as mere nothingness. To see into self-nature as the Unconscious is to realize the middle way between existence and nonexistence or being and nothingness: "The Unconscious is not describable as either existent nor non-existent" (EZB III, 19). Moreover, "To go beyond the dualism of being and non-being, and to love the track of the Middle Way — this is the Unconscious" (ZDNM, 63–64). Discussing self-nature as *wu-nien* or no-thought as the Unconscious, Shenhui declares: "Hence Wu-nien is neither real or unreal" (ZDNM, 29). The Unconscious is therefore not a substantial entity nor is it a nihilistic void but the unreified and unreifiable emptiness-suchness, thereby to designate the middle way between eternalism and nihilism. Elsewhere, Shenhui is again translated as saying: "Those who see into the Unconscious have their senses cleansed of defilements. Those who see into the Unconscious are moving towards Buddha-wisdom. Those who see into the Unconscious are known to be with Reality. Those who see into the Unconscious are in the Middle Path, in the ultimate truth itself. . . . Those who see into the Unconscious embrace all things within themselves" (EZB III, 21).

Suzuki then discusses how this Zen doctrine of the Unconscious espoused by Bodhidharma, Huineng, Shenhui, and Mazu is further developed by Ta-chu Hui-hai: "This view of the Unconscious is thoroughly confirmed by Ta-chu Hui-hai, a chief disciple of Ma-tsu, in his *Essential Teaching of the Abrupt Awakening*." Ta-chu Hui-hai propounds: "The Unconscious means to have no-mind in all circumstances. . . . The Unconscious is thus known as to be truly conscious of itself. . . . 'To see the Unconscious' is to be conscious and yet to be unconscious of self-nature. . . . The Unconscious is thus the ultimate reality, the true form, the most exquisite body of Tathāgatahood" (ZDNM, 62–63). A further linguistic clarification can be made about Suzuki's translation/interpretation of Zen *mushin* (無心) or no-mind in psychological terms as "the Unconscious." In Suzuki's *Zen Buddhism and its Influence on Japanese Culture* (1938), translated from English into Japanese by Kitagawa Momo'o as *Zen to bunka* (禅と文化, 1964), "the Unconscious" is translated by the standard Japanese term *muishiki* (無意識). To provide just a few examples, when the original English text reads "for the mastery of [Zen] art, there are certain intuitions directly reaching what I call Cosmic Unconscious" (ZNB, 228), the Japanese translation for "Cosmic Unconscious" is *uchūteki muishiki* (宇宙的無意識) (ZNB, 229). Suzuki holds that Zen arts of *mushin* or no-mind such as tea, ink painting, calligraphy, haiku poetry, flower arrangement, noh drama, swordsmanship and archery, are all alike, rooted in the cosmic Unconscious as the fountain of creativity and that the cosmic Unconscious is to be understood as an egoless state of being consciously unconscious, or unconsciously conscious. Where the English text reads "to be unconsciously conscious" (ZNB, 112), the Japanese translation is *muishiki ni ishiki suru koto* (無意識に意識すること) (ZNB, 113).

Suzuki's Zen doctrine of *mushin* or no-mind was instrumental in the reinterpretation of Theravada Buddhism by Buddhadāsa Bikkhu (1906–1993), modern Thailand's most highly original and profoundly influential Buddhist philosopher. Among the distinctive contributions of Buddhadāsa to Theravada Buddhist philosophy was to have exhaustively searched the Pali canon to find the Buddha's own teachings on *suñña* or "void" and *suññatā* or "voidness," thereby to argue that the fundamental doctrine of Theravada Buddhism, like Mahayana Buddhism, is the doctrine of voidness or emptiness as interdependent coorigination. As demonstrated by Peter Jackson's work *Buddhadāsa: Theravada Buddhism and Modernist Reform in Thailand,* the cornerstone of Buddhadāsa's reinterpretation of Theravada Buddhist philosophy is the Zen-inspired notion of *chit wang* or "void mind," the liberated mind emptied of all attachment to a substantial ego-self: "In placing *chit wang* [void mind] at the centre of his presentation of Theravada doctrine, Buddhadāsa has in fact drawn heavily on Mahayana and Zen Buddhist teaching" (2003, 69).[2] Moreover, he underscores the impact of Suzuki on Buddhadāsa's reconstruction of Theravada Buddhism: "Buddhadāsa finds a soulmate in such Zen authors as Suzuki" (2003, 193). Jackson goes on to document how Buddhadāsa's core notion of *cit wang* or "void mind" was especially influenced by Suzuki's writings on the Zen doctrine of *mushin* or "no-mind" emptied of egoism (2003, 182, 193). Hence, it must be said that Suzuki's Zen doctrine of *mushin* or no-mind as the Unconscious not only influenced the dissemination of Zen Buddhism in the West but also profoundly impacted Buddhadāsa's radical reconstruction of Theravada Buddhism in Thailand.

Problematizing *Mushin* as "the Unconscious"

In English scholarship it was Suzuki who first claimed that *mushin* (C. *wuxin*) was the central notion of Zen/Chan Buddhism, and often he just translates it in the conventional way as "no-mind." Fukushima Keido Roshi, the esteemed Rinzai Zen master who served as the head abbot of Tofukuji in Kyoto, discusses

Suzuki's translation of *mushin*: "Mushin is sometimes translated as 'no mind.' D. T. Suzuki usually translated mushin in this way. . . . But as with Mu, I think it's better not to translate mushin at all, because it has so many meanings. . . . So mushin includes empty mind, free mind, fresh mind, creative mind and pure mind" (2017, 14–15). In the view of Fukushima Keido Roshi, it is best not to translate the Zen concept of *mushin* at all, because it is a polyvalent term with a plurality of meanings and therefore cannot be reduced to any one single meaning in the English language. As said by Fukushima Keido Roshi, *mushin* can signify no mind, empty mind, void mind, openness mind, clear mind, free mind, creative mind, and so forth. From the perspective of modern depth psychology, however, Suzuki argues that *mushin/wuxin* is the Unconscious and that *satori* or enlightenment is noetic insight into the Unconscious. Suzuki holds that from the psychological standpoint, the terms *mushin/wuxin* or no-mind and *munen/wunian* or no-thought can be rendered as the Unconscious in its literal translation as "no-consciousness." To repeat Suzuki's words: "'*Wu-nien*' is 'no-consciousness', thus the unconscious" (ZDNM, 57). Moreover, even though Suzuki often just directly translates *mushin* as the Unconscious, elsewhere he more carefully says, "*mushin*, which may be regarded in a way as corresponding to the concept of the unconscious" (ZJC, 94; ZNB, 112–113).

Buddhologists such as Bernard Faure (1993, 63–64) and David McMahan (2008, 271, fn. 7) have expressed reservations about Suzuki's translation of *mushin* as "the Unconscious," noting that it is problematic and potentially misleading. Moreover, at the outset of his essay "Treatise on No-Mind: A Chan Text from Dunhuang," the Zen/Chan scholar Urs App states: "This paper presents the first complete English translation of a short Chan text that is regarded as representative of the teachings of the Southern school of Chan: the *Wuxinlun* 無心論 (Jap. *Mushinron*), or Treatise on No-Mind" (1995, 70). App explains that the *Treatise on No-Mind* was discovered by Suzuki in Yabuki Keiki's photographed collection of the Dunhuang manuscripts, whereupon Suzuki included its partial translation in the Third Series of his *Essays in Zen Buddhism* (1995, 72). App, however, then goes on to express his reservation about Suzuki's translation of *wuxin* as "unconsciousness": "[I]n 1949, Suzuki published an English book entitled *The Zen Doctrine of No-Mind,* a study of the teaching of the *Platform sutra*. In this work, Suzuki confirmed his view of *wuxin* as the central doctrine of Zen. He was evidently still struggling to explain the meaning of *wuxin* to Westerners; and various inconsistencies, contradictions, the choice of the word "unconscious" for *wuxin* were less helpful in this endeavor" (1995, 75). But as noted by App (1995, 73), Suzuki himself fully acknowledges the problem translating the Sino-Japanese term *wuxin/wu-hsin* (J. *mushin,* 無心) into English. In Suzuki's own words: "*Wu-hsin* [*wuxin*] is one of those difficult Chinese words which are untranslatable. *Wu* is a negative term and *hsin* comprises various meanings. It is 'mind,' 'heart' . . . 'consciousness' . . . etc. In the present case, *Wu-hsin* is 'unconsciousness' in its ordinary, empirical sense, and at the same time it means the Unconscious as underlying all our activities mental and bodily, conscious and unconscious" (EZB III, 8–9, fn. 3).

Suzuki often comments that there is no satisfactory word by means of which to render *mushin*, thus it can only be expressed as "X" or unconsciousness: "Because of its being outside the ordinary field of consciousness we have no word for it except to give it a negative name, X, or the unconscious. The unknown, or X, is too vague . . . it may be not inappropriately designated as the unconscious" (ZP, 22). Elsewhere, Suzuki further points out that the Chan/Zen terms *wuxin/mushin* or no-mind and *wunian/munen* or no-thought are difficult to translate with precision and that even his own choice of the Unconscious could be misleading: "Chinese or Sanskrit terms when translated literally are frequently subject to gross misunderstandings. *Wu-nien* is one of them, for 'thoughtlessness' will surely be a most undesirable state of mind as the goal of Zen discipline, in fact as the goal of any spiritual exercise. Even 'the Unconscious' may not be a very appropriate term" (EZB III, 17). For Suzuki, then, there is no perfect way to translate certain Chan/Zen terms, so that even his own rendering of *wuxin/mushin* as "the Unconscious" may not be satisfactory. Yet as he further argues, the standard translation of *wuxin/mushin* by "no-mind" or "mindlessness" and *wunian/munen* by "no-thought" or "thoughtlessness" can be even less satisfactory, insofar as they give rise to nihilistic interpretations of Zen (EZB III, 17).

Thomas Kasulis argues that Suzuki's rendering of *mushin* or no-mind is misleading insofar as it implies a state of drowsiness: "No-thought or no-mind is not an unconscious state at all; it is an active, responsive awareness of the contents of experience as directly experienced" (1981, 47–48). For similar reasons, Alan Watts expresses reservations about translating *mushin* as the unconscious, saying that it is "a highly aware *unself*consciousness" (1972, 319). In his autobiography, Watts recalls his meeting with C. G. Jung, at which time the latter asked if there was a Sanskrit word for "the unconscious." Watts suggested that the nearest to it was the Yogacara Buddhist term ālaya-vijñāna, the "storehouse consciousness," which was somewhat like Jung's collective unconscious as the supraindividual origin of those archetypes, which we use to organize experience (1972, 319). He continues: "I pointed out that Suzuki had sometimes used the phrase 'the unconscious' in a very different way, to translate the Japanese *mushin* ('no-mind') which, so far from being unconscious, was a highly aware un*self*consciousness" (1972, 319). Elsewhere, Watts makes a similar point when describing the Zen experience of satori as awakening to *mushin/wuxin* as no-mind or unconsciousness: "Their 'unconsciousness' is not coma, but what the exponents of Zen later signified by *wu-hsin*, literally 'no-mind,' which is to say un-self-consciousness. It is a state of wholeness in which the mind functions freely and easily" (1989, 23). Moreover, Eric Fromm questions Suzuki's translation of *mushin* as the unconscious, instead preferring to call it the "Cosmic Consciousness" (ZP, 134).

Although he does not mention Suzuki by name, in an essay titled "Oriental Nothingness" the Kyoto School philosopher Hisamatsu Shin'ichi articulates his concerns about understanding Zen no-mind or nothingness as unconsciousness. Hisamatsu argues that what he terms "oriental nothingness" is not to be understood as the negation of being, an abstract concept, an imagined nothingness, or as unconsciousness (2011, 221–222). He continues: "Oriental nothingness is not, again, nothingness in the . . . sense of *unconsciousness*. . . . Oriental nothingness . . . is 'perfectly lucid and clear'" (2011, 223). His objections to characterizing Zen no-mind or oriental nothingness as "unconsciousness" is then further explained as follows: "Whether we speak of oriental nothingness as 'no-mind,' 'no-consciousness,' the 'great death itself,' or 'nirvana,' it is not the unconsciousness of sleep, fainting, or ordinary death. . . . There in no condition in which one is so clearly aware as in 'no-mind' or 'no-consciousness' . . . this is not a blank loss of consciousness. On the contrary. This is rather supreme awareness in which there is not the slightest unawareness or unclarity" (2011, 223–224).[3]

Satori as Awakening to the Cosmic Unconscious in Superconsciousness

It has now been seen how several leading scholars in Japan and the West have raised questions about Suzuki's translation of *mushin* or no-mind as "the unconscious" or "unconsciousness" insofar as it might imply a dull, unresponsive, and nonreactive state of mental torpor. To avoid this kind of misunderstanding, the term *mushin* is therefore alternately described by Kasulis as an "active, responsive awareness" (1981, 47–48), by Watts as a highly aware "un*self*consciousness" (1989, 23), by Bret Davis as a "nondualistic-consciousness" (2022, 228), and by Fromm as "Cosmic Consciousness" (ZP, 134). The modern Japanese philosopher Nishitani Keiji criticizes the view that religion can be explained in terms of consciousness or self-consciousness but also argues that it is not based on a regression to the preconscious or subconscious, instead maintaining that it requires a radical breakthrough to the more encompassing Zen Buddhist standpoint of emptiness (1982, 13). Hisamatsu objects to conceiving the absolute nothingness of *mushin* or no-mind as unconsciousness, instead characterizing it as a supreme awareness that is "perfectly lucid and clear" (2011, 223).

For Suzuki, however, the satori of Zen is *not* an infantile regression to the preconscious, subconscious, or unconscious of Western psychoanalysis but instead signifies a realization of the "cosmic Unconscious" in *superconsciousness*: "Psychologically speaking, *satori* is super-consciousness, or consciousness of the Unconscious. The Unconscious is, however, not to be identified with the one psychologically postulated. The Unconscious of satori is . . . the cosmic Unconscious" (AZL, 62; LZ, 88). Suzuki's notion of "superconsciousness" can itself be traced back to William James's chapter on Mysticism in *The Varieties of Religious Experience* (1982), where the latter makes reference to the renowned Hindu yogi-philosopher Swami Vivekananda (1863–1902), the leading apostle of India's famous saint, Sri Ramakrishna (1836–1886). It should be remembered that at the 1893 World's Parliament of Religions in Chicago, Illinois, Suzuki's Zen teacher Shaku Sōen introduced Japanese Mahayana Buddhism, while Anagarika Dharmapala from Sri Lanka introduced Theravada Buddhism, and Swami Vivekananda from India introduced the nondual Hindu mystical traditions of Yoga, and Vedanta. According to Vivekananda, the human mind has three intrapsychic levels: consciousness, unconsciousness, and superconsciousness. In *Raja Yoga* (1986), Vivekananda proclaims: "the mind itself has a higher state of existence, beyond reason, a superconscious state." Vivekananda continues: "All the different steps in yoga are intended to bring us scientifically to the superconscious state of samâdhi. . . . Just as unconscious work is beneath consciousness, so there is another work which is above consciousness, and which, also, is not accompanied with the feeling of egoism" (cited by James 1982, 400). Similarly, Suzuki argues that Zen satori involves a yogic contemplative process of becoming fully conscious of the cosmic Unconscious in superconsciousness. Indeed, for the modern Zen of Suzuki in Japan, as for the twentieth-century yoga philosophy of Vivekananda, the *summum bonum* or supreme goal of human existence is to overcome dualistic ego-consciousness by realizing the ultimate nondual state of enlightenment in the rapture of superconsciousness.

In *Living Zen*, Suzuki further explicates his key notion of satori as awakening to the cosmic Unconscious in superconsciousness: "Zen is never satisfied with such intellectual chimeras; Zen wants to take hold of the one who breathes through every fibre of your tissue and vibrates with every beat of your pulse. This is what might be called superconsciousness or unconscious consciousness. In regular Buddhist terminology, it is undiscriminated discrimination, the mind of mindlessness, or unthought thought" (LZ, 135). Thus, according to Suzuki, the great awakening of satori as *mushin* or no-mind is not a coma-like trance state of unconsciousness as erroneously said by his critics but is a "superconsciousness," expressed in terms of his paradoxical *soku hi* logic as "unconscious consciousness," or what in more traditional Buddhist vocabulary is "undiscriminated discrimination" (*mufunbetsu no funbetsu*, 無分別の分別). In *The Awakening of Zen*, Suzuki tells us: "There must be along with the physiological or psychological consciousness, another form of consciousness, which is a sort of unconsciousness but not in the ordinary sense of the term. For this unconscious consciousness we have no suitable logical or metaphysical term" (AZ, 36). Here it is admitted that there is no adequate word to convey this paradoxical Zen notion of an unconscious consciousness or conscious unconsciousness. It is in this context that Suzuki describes nondual Zen satori in *mushin* or no-mind, *munen* or no-thought, and *muga* or nonego, as becoming fully conscious of the cosmic Unconscious in superconsciousness: "Can there be something more here where our minds are attuned to the Divine Mind, a kind of superconsciousness transcending our ordinary sensuous limited consciousness which functions on the plane of human psychology? Is this not a superconsciousness, which is frequently designed by Buddhists as 'mindlessness' or 'thoughtlessness' or 'unconscious consciousness'! And is it not this that constitutes the divine-human mind?" (AZ, 39–40).

In his book *Toward a Philosophy of Zen Buddhism,* Izutsu Toshihiko (1914–1993) describes the *mushin* or no-mind of Zen satori as a paradoxical state that is both conscious and unconscious in *supra*consciousness: "This is what we would call supra-consciousness. And this is no other than the 'no-mind'" (1977, 17). Moreover, "what Zen considers to be the original experience of the Buddha is primarily an awakening to a dimension of supra-consciousness" (1977, 149). For Izutsu, Zen satori is "supraconsciousness" as realization of the Field (place, locus, topos) of absolute nothingness encompassing subject and object, discrimination and nondiscrimination, consciousness and unconsciousness, and all other dualities. *Toward a Philosophy of Zen Buddhism* makes no reference to Suzuki. However, the Japanese philosopher Nishihira Tadashi demonstrates that Izutsu's "supraconsciousness" is an attempt to further illuminate Suzuki's Zen doctrine of *mushin* or no-mind (2015; 2024).[4] To begin with, Nishihira points out that there is no standard definition of *mushin/wuxin* in Sino-Japanese literature, so that its meaning varies widely according to context (2015, 2). In *The Philosophy of No-Mind* and various essays, Nishihira expounds on Izutsu's view that "no-mind is not unconsciousness" (2024, 74–77). He first discusses Izutsu's view of Zen *mushin* or no-mind as a refined psychological flow state of mental clarity along with its spontaneous expression through artistic creativity (2015, 3). Nishihira then cites Izutsu's example of a virtuoso musician absorbed in his music to illustrate the Zen notion of *mushin* or no-mind-ness as a paradoxical state of enlightenment where the musician is fully conscious, yet at the same time no longer conscious of his playing (2015, 3; Izutsu 1977, 16). He continues: "What, then, shall we term this state of consciousness which is neither the consciousness governed by ordinary self nor unconsciousness? Izutsu came up with the term 'supra-consciousness' . . . *supra* is the Latin prefix meaning 'above, over'. It can be contrasted, therefore, with pre (semi) consciousness and subconscious" (Nishihira, 2015, 3; 2024, 77). Nishihira sums up Izutsu's understanding of Zen *mushin* or no-mind-ness as a "new consciousness which is neither the ordinary, everyday ego-based consciousness nor unconsciousness. It is a special conscious state which Izutsu called 'supra-consciousness'" (2015, 4; 2024, 77).

Although Nishihira provides a very insightful analysis of Izutsu's interpretation of Zen *mushin* or no-mind-ness, it must be emphasized here that it was *not* Izutsu who first coined the term "supraconsciousness" to clarify Zen *mushin* or no-mind. Suzuki himself uses the term "supraconsciousness" in such works as *An Introduction to Zen Buddhism* (AIZB, 108). Moreover, as demonstrated so far, the characterization of Zen *mushin* as "supraconsciousness" to denote a paradoxical state of unconscious consciousness is also termed "superconsciousness" throughout Suzuki's writings. When Izutsu employs the word "supraconsciousness" to describe *mushin* or no-mind, he is therefore only elucidating Suzuki's own concept of Zen satori as awakening to the cosmic Unconscious in superconsciousness, or what he also terms "supraconsciousness."

The Unconscious as Emptiness

Suzuki defines his notion of the cosmic Unconscious in Mahayana Buddhist terms, including the *mushin* or "no-mind" of Zen/Chan Buddhism, the ālaya-vijñāna or "storehouse consciousness" of Yogacara Buddhist depth psychology, the dharma realm of *rijimuge* or "unobstructed interpenetration between multiplicity and unity" as visualized by Indra's net in Kegon/Huayan Buddhism, the sunyata or "emptiness" as taught in the *Prajñāpāramitā* wisdom literature, and their integration in the Zen doctrine that *mushin* or no-mind is itself *heijōshin* or the "ordinary mind" of everyday life. Although he defines his Zen notion of the Unconscious in terms of various Mahayana Buddhist categories, the *Prajñāpāramitā* wisdom literature teachings of sunyata or emptiness is always at their core. Indeed, Suzuki tells us: "The Unconscious is no other than Prajñāpāramitā itself" (ZDNM, 61). For Suzuki the nondual Zen concept of *śūnyatā* (J. *kū*, 空) is a multivalent term, which in various contexts designates emptiness, suchness, voidness, nonsubstantiality, absence of self, lack of inherent existence, dependent origination, interconnectedness, zero, vacuity, spaciousness, creative potentiality, openness, and transparency. Moreover, for Suzuki, emptiness is synonymous with "nothingness" (J. *mu*, 無), but like Nishida and the Kyoto School of modern Japanese philosophy, he distinguishes its negative meaning as "relative nothingness" or nihilism from its positive meaning as the enveloping space of "absolute nothingness," comprehended as the infinite openness where emptiness is fullness and fullness is openness, whereupon all things are viewed "just as they are" (*sono mama*) in their concrete particular suchness.

The Cosmic Unconscious as Dharmakaya Emptiness

The Unconscious as *mushin* or "no-mind" is also translated by Suzuki as "empty-minded-ness" (ZJC, 114). His identification of Zen *mushin* as the Unconscious with sunyata or emptiness is frequently made explicit by juxtaposing the two words, such as when he speaks of "Emptiness or no-mind-ness" (ZJC, 113). The cosmic Unconscious as no-mind, void-mind, or empty-mind is itself prajna-intuition of sunyata or emptiness. He thus declares: "'Emptiness' (*śūnyatā*) is the gospel of the *Prajñāpāramitā-sūtra* and also the fountainhead of all the Mahayana philosophies and practical disciplines" (SWS IV, 147).

Suzuki renders Zen no-mind in psychological terms as the cosmic Unconscious, which he in turn equates with primordial awareness of sunyata or emptiness and *mu* or nothingness. He also describes the cosmic Unconscious as "the Void" (WZ, 95). Discussing Zen *kokoro* (心, mind, heart, spirit) in its relationship to no-mind as the Unconscious, Suzuki writes: "So with the 'no-mind,' it means . . . *kokoro*, or its nothingness or emptiness (*śūnyatā*)" (WZ, 33). As Richard M. Jaffe explains: "Suzuki would use such terms as 'will,' 'Unconscious,' 'Self,' and the Japanese *kokoro* to represent the 'abyss of absolute nothingness' for the source from which "all things are produced" and to which they all return. According to Suzuki when properly understood the encounter dialogues of the Zen teachers were all 'expressions directly bursting out of an abyss of absolute nothingness,' that is, *kokoro*" (SWS I, xlvii). Likewise, Abe Masao speaks of "Emptiness, Void, or Cosmic Unconsciousness" as equivalent terms in Suzuki's Rinzai Zen concept of the true self or authentic Person as absolute nothingness (1985, 75).

Suzuki discusses the Zen doctrine of no-mind or empty-minded-ness as the Unconscious attributed to Bodhidharma in relation to the teachings on "emptiness" credited to Daoxin/Tao-hsin (580–651), who is traditionally regarded as the fourth patriarch of Chan Buddhism in China. In this context, he cites the words of Daoxin, who advocates "meditating on Emptiness: whereby the [conscious] mind is emptied. . . . The mind in its absolute purity is the Void itself" (EZB III, 12). This is followed by Suzuki's commentary: "It can readily be seen that Bodhidharma and Tao–shin are speaking of the subject from different angles of understanding. Bodhidharma's *Wu-hsin*, 'the Unconscious,' is 'the Empty,' 'the Serene,' 'the Abysmal,' of Tao-hsin. The one uses psychological terms while the other is inclined to Prajñā philosophy" (EZB III, 14). The conclusion of Suzuki's analysis is that Bodhidharma's *wuxin* or no-mind as "the Unconscious," and Daoxin's "the Empty," are synonymous terms. But while Daoxin's notion of "the Empty" or "the Void" is based on Prajnaparamita wisdom teachings of emptiness, Bodhidharma's Zen doctrine of "the Unconscious" is articulated from a different perspective in psychological terms.

Suzuki traces back his Zen concept of *mushin* (C. *wuxin*) or no-mind as the Unconscious to the legendary Huineng: "The doctrine of the Unconscious (*wu-nien*) . . . was the chief topic of interest in the days of Hui-nêng and his followers . . . 'the Unconscious' is the Chinese way of describing the realisation of Emptiness (*śūnyatā*)" (EZB III, 18). As asserted by Suzuki in a previously quoted passage (ZDNM, 62–63), Huineng's Zen concept of the Unconscious designates the illuminated mind that cognizes sunyata or emptiness. Moreover, he goes on to say that Huineng's concepts of *mushin* or no-mind, and *munen* or no-thought, are based on the early Buddhist notion of *anātman* (J. *muga*), no-self or nonego: "*Mushin*, or *munen*, is primarily derived from *muga*, *wu-wo*, *anātman*, 'non-ego', 'selflessness' which is the principal conception of Buddhism" (ZDNM, 120). Suzuki continues: "When the intellectualization went further and deeper the doctrine of *anātman* assumed a more metaphysical aspect, and the doctrine of Śūnyatā developed" (ZDNM, 120). He further clarifies that a basic concept of Huineng's Zen philosophy is "self-nature" and that sudden enlightenment is referred to as *kenshō* (C. *chien-hsing*, 見性) or "seeing into one's self-nature." Huineng's Zen concept of self-nature or Buddha nature is then equated with no-mind as the Unconscious, and the Unconscious is identified with nondual prajna wisdom of sunyata or emptiness: "In Hui-neng's *T'an-ching* the Buddha-nature and self-nature are subjects of constant reference. They mean the same thing, and they are primarily by nature pure, empty, Śūnyā, non-dichotomic, and unconscious. This pure, unknown Unconscious moves, and Prajñā is awakened" (ZDNM, 121). Suzuki further explains: "In this Self-nature there is a movement, an awakening, and the Unconscious becomes conscious of itself" (ZDNM, 194). Seeing into self-nature as prajna wisdom of sunyata or emptiness is the original act of illumination whereby consciousness awakens to its source in the Unconscious. He adds: "In the traditional terminology of Buddhism, self-nature is Buddha-nature . . . it is absolute Emptiness, *Śūnyatā*, it is absolute Suchness, *Tathatā* . . . I will for convenience' sake call it Mind, with the capital initial letter, and also the Unconscious . . . Mind and the Unconscious, are here used as synonymous with Self-nature" (ZDNM, 123). According to Suzuki, then, Huineng's Zen philosophy is based on seeing into one's self-nature, and self-nature is the true Mind or Buddha nature, which in psychological terms is "the Unconscious." Moreover, Buddha nature as the cosmic Unconscious is identified with prajna wisdom of emptiness or nothingness: "The first declaration made by Hui-neng regarding his Zen experience was that 'From the first not a thing is', and then he went on the 'Seeing into one's self-nature', which self-nature, being 'not a thing', is nothingness. Therefore, 'seeing into one's self-nature' is 'seeing into nothingness'" (ZDNM, 31). In this passage Suzuki clarifies the Zen doctrine of no-mind as the Unconscious in terms of Huineng's key teaching: "From the first not a thing is" (J. *honrai mu ichi motsu*, 本来無一物) (ZDNM, 22). Moreover, he explains that self-nature is "nothingness," whereas kensho or seeing into self-nature is "seeing into nothingness." He continues: "When Hui-neng declared, 'From the first not a thing is', the keynote of his Zen thought was struck. . . . Hui-neng's concept of nothingness (*wu-i-wu*) may push one down into a bottomless abyss. . . . The philosophy of Prajñāpāramitā, which is also that of Hui-neng, generally has this effect. To understand it a man requires deep religious intellectual insight into the truth of Śūnyatā" (ZDNM, 24).

From the standpoint of this Zen doctrine of no-mind as the Unconscious, in its meaning as prajna wisdom of emptiness or seeing into nothingness, Suzuki analyzes the contrasting views of the two Chan masters, Huineng (638–713) and his rival Shenxiu (Junshu, ca. 606–706). As declared by Huineng above: "He who understands the 'abrupt' teaching of the Unconscious reaches the stage of Buddhahood" (EZB III, 18). Based on his substantialized notion of mind, Shenxiu teaches gradual enlightenment, whereas based on his nonsubstantial concept of mind as no-mind or empty-mind, Huineng teaches sudden enlightenment in the Unconscious. According to Shenxiu, the mind is originally like a bright mirror but becomes covered by the "dust" of habitual thoughts, and therefore it should be constantly wiped clean by the gradual practice of Chan/Zen meditation. As expressed by the poetic verse of Shenxiu: "The body is the Bodhi tree, The mind is a like a mirror bright; Take heed to keep it always clean, And let no dust collect on it" (ZDNM, 17). Shenxiu's reified picture of mind as a mirror, and of Chan/Zen meditation as a process of mirror-wiping, serves as the basis for his view of "gradual enlightenment." By contrast, Huineng proclaimed: "From the very first not a thing is." According to Huineng's doctrine of nothingness, the mind is originally void, or empty of substance. Since for Huineng, the true mind as *wuxin* is "no-mind" or "empty-minded-ness," there is nowhere for defilements to accumulate and therefore no need to continuously polish the mirror through the practice of meditation (ZDNM, 22). Suzuki translates Huineng's famous verse as follows: "There is no Bodhi-tree, Nor stand of mirror bright. Since all is void, Where can the dust alight?" (ZDNM, 22). Although historical research has shown that this contest between Shenxiu and Huineng is no doubt fictional, it is a legend that has been used in popular Rinzai Zen teachings to clarify the distinction between gradual versus sudden enlightenment. For Suzuki, the verse attributed to Huineng illustrates how the possibility of sudden enlightenment is itself based on the Zen concept of no-mind or the Unconscious as nondual prajna wisdom of emptiness.[5]

Suzuki's Zen concept of the Unconscious in its meaning as nondual prajna-intuition of emptiness is summed up as follows: "This Unconscious is a metaphysical concept, and it is through *satori* that we become conscious of the Unconscious. . . . To *satoru* means to become conscious of the Unconscious, and this Unconscious is all the time along with consciousness. *Satori* makes the Unconscious articulate. The cosmic Unconscious in terms of space is 'Emptiness' (*śūnyatā*)" (AZL, 62; LZ, 88). Here as elsewhere, Suzuki gives a modern psychological interpretation of Zen satori as becoming conscious of the cosmic Unconscious, although he admits that his view has "a psychological taint" (EZB II, 19). Nonetheless, Suzuki does not fall into the error of "psychologism," whereby events are reduced to psychological categories, insofar as his Zen doctrine of the Unconscious is itself ultimately comprehended in terms of the Prajnaparamita philosophy based on prajna wisdom of sunyata or emptiness as interdependent origination. As Suzuki explicitly declares in the above passage: "The cosmic Unconscious in terms of space is 'Emptiness' (*śūnyatā*)" (AZL, 62). And elsewhere he tells us: "Zen masters, ultimately deriving their philosophy from the Buddhist doctrine of *śūnyatā* and *prajñā* describe the Unconscious" (ZJC, 192–193).

Suzuki's Zen doctrine of the cosmic Unconscious can be further analyzed in terms of the *tri-kāya* or "three bodies" of Buddha theory prevalent in both the exoteric Mahayana and esoteric Tantrayana (or Vajrayana) Buddhist traditions. In his exposition of the *tri-kāya* doctrine, Suzuki explains that *nirmāṇakāya* is Buddha's coarse physical body, *sambhogakāya* is Buddha's subtle enjoyment body, and dharmakaya is Buddha's very subtle truth body of emptiness. Suzuki identifies his Zen concept of the cosmic Unconscious with the *dharmakāya* (J. *hosshin,* 法身) as the Void of emptiness or absolute nothingness. The cosmic Unconscious is explicitly identified with dharmakaya emptiness, for instance, when he speaks of "the Dharmakāya [which is the Unconscious]" (EZB III, 16; brackets in original text). Elsewhere, he tells us: "Suchness is also termed 'Mind' (*citta*) from the psychological point of view. . . . When, however, even 'Mind' is regarded too intellectual the Buddhists call it Dharmakāya . . . The doctrine of the Triple Body (*trikāya*) has thus evolved from the notion of Dharmakāya. . . . It is Emptiness or Void (*śūnyatā*)" (SWS II, 82). Throughout his works Suzuki equates his Zen doctrine of the cosmic Unconscious with dharmakaya and identifies the dharmakaya with sunyata or emptiness. He thus contends that psychologically speaking, Zen satori is to attain full consciousness of the cosmic Unconscious as absolute nothingness in superconsciousness, which in terms of Prajnaparamita teachings is ultimately conceived as the infinite spacelike transparent openness of dharmakaya emptiness.

Emptiness and Overcoming Nihilism

Explaining the Zen Buddhist philosophy of the Middle Way, Suzuki asserts: "The ultimate truth is not to be found in eternalism, or nihilism" (EZB I, 93). In accordance with the Mahayana Buddhist philosophy of the Middle Way, Suzuki argues that his Zen doctrine of the cosmic Unconscious neither falls into "eternalism," whereby it is reified into a substantial entity, nor into "nihilism" so as to be conceived as a meaningless void, insofar as it is based on the Prajnaparamita wisdom teachings of sunyata or emptiness. He admits that various notions related to his Zen doctrine of the Unconscious such as *mushin* or no-mind, *munen* or no-thought, *muga* or no-self, *kū* (*śūnyatā*) or emptiness, *mu* or nothingness, and *nirvāṇa* or extinction appear to have negative connotations that might suggest extreme nihilism thereby leading to a pessimistic attitude of resignation from life and total renunciation of the world. In Suzuki's Zen philosophy, however, all negative expressions result in a higher dialectical affirmation. Thus, while Suzuki defines his Zen concept of no-mind or the Unconscious as spacelike dharmakaya emptiness, it is not the negative emptiness of nihilism but a positive emptiness as the plenary vacuum where nothingness and fullness are the same.

Suzuki attempted to correct the initial Western understanding of Buddhism as an extreme nihilism propagated by Arthur Schopenhauer. Throughout his works Suzuki accords an ontological primacy to the cosmic force of "the Will" over against the Western rationalist tradition, which prioritizes reason, and to this extent agrees with the voluntarism of Schopenhauer. Based on German translations of early Indian Buddhist texts, Schopenhauer argued that unconscious blind will as desire for existence is the origin of suffering, and negation of the will through detached resignation of the mystics is to realize nirvana as total annihilation of self in nothingness, thus to achieve the end of suffering. Nietzsche, however, criticizes the worldviews of both Schopenhauer and early Buddhism as life-denying nihilism. Suzuki, like the voluntarism of Schopenhauer, declares that "Will" is the ultimate metaphysical principle and then explicitly identifies the will with his notion of the "cosmic Unconscious" while also identifying both will and the cosmic Unconscious with the abyss of nothingness. In Suzuki's words: "The one great will from which all these wills, infinitely varied, flow is what I call the Cosmic (or ontological) Unconscious, which is the zero-reservoir of infinite possibilities" (ZP, 51). Although to some extent Suzuki's primacy of unconscious will over conscious reason approximates Schopenhauer, at the same time he clearly differentiates the positive teachings of Zen and Mahayana Buddhism from Schopenhauer's nihilism, negativism, and pessimism (SWS IV, 107; EZB I, 157). Suzuki then further distinguishes the life-affirming teachings of Buddha from the life-denying nihilism of Schopenhauer: "His [the Buddha's] teaching is based upon affirmative propositions. . . . The Buddha pointed the way to escape this [suffering] by Enlightenment and not by annihilation. . . . The Buddha thus wants an illumined will and not the negation of it. . . . His aversion to asceticism and nihilism as well as to hedonism becomes intelligible in this light" (EZB I, 158–159; SWS IV, 108–109).

In *Shūkyō to wa nani ka* (1961), later translated into English as *Religion and Nothingness* (1982), Nishitani Keiji argues that the basic problem for philosophy and religion today is that of overcoming nihilism (1982, 47; 1961, 54). The major sources of inspiration for overcoming nihilism in the modern Zen philosophy of Nishitani are Buddhism in the East along with the existentialism of Nietzsche and Heidegger in the West. Following his teacher Nishida Kitarō (1870–1945), founder of the Kyoto School of modern Japanese philosophy, Nishitani establishes an East-West philosophy and Buddhist-Christian interfaith dialogue based on a Zen concept of *mu* or nothingness. Nishitani posits three ontological standpoints, including (1) "being" (*yū*, 有); (2) "relative nothingness" (*sōtaiteki mu*, 相対的無), or "nihilility" (*kyomu*, 虚無); and (3) "absolute nothingness" (*zettai mu*, 絶対無) or "emptiness" (*kū*, 空). Emptiness or absolute nothingness is therefore the standpoint of the "middle way" (*chūdō*, 中道) between the extreme views of "substantialism" and "nihilism." In the Zen enlightenment process, these function as three stages whereby all things reified into permanent material substance on the field of being are dissolved into a nihilistic void on the field of relative nothingness but are then affirmed just as they are on the field of emptiness or absolute nothingness. In Nishitani's words: "To speak in Nietzschean terms, this field is the field of the Great Affirmation, where we can say Yes to all things" (1982, 123–124; 1961, 140). As stated by Nishitani, in contrast to "nihilism" (*kyomu*, 虚無) as the "field of nullification" (*muka no ba*, 無化の場), "emptiness" (*kū*, 空) is the "field of affirmation" (*kōtei no ba*, 肯定の場) where one can say "Yes!" (*shikari*, 然り) to all things in their concrete, particular, and individual "suchness" (*kono mama*, 此儘) (1961, 140). Using the language of Heidegger's existential phenomenology, Nishitani defines absolute nothingness as the "infinite openness" (*mugen na hirake,* 無限な開け) where emptiness is fullness and fullness is emptiness, so that all things are affirmed just as they are in their concrete particular suchness or isness (1961, 250; 1982, 228).

Although the theme of overcoming nihilism by awakening to Zen emptiness or absolute nothingness has been made well-known by the modern Japanese philosopher Nishitani Keiji, it has in fact been a major theme running throughout the writings of Suzuki. As early as 1906, Suzuki published an essay "Is Buddhism Nihilistic?" in the journal *Light of Dharma* 6 (3–7; IBN), where he endeavored to dispel initial Western responses to Buddhist philosophy as nihilism. In a chapter titled "Is Zen Nihilistic?" from his 1934 work *Introduction to Zen Buddhism* (AIZB), first published in 1914 as an essay in *The New East*, Suzuki admits that the language of Zen is often expressed in negative terms and thus appears to be a kind of nihilism. After citing various primary texts of Zen Buddhism, he comments: "These are passages taken at random from the vast store of Zen literature, and they seem to be permeated with the ideas of emptiness (*sunyata*), nothingness (*nasti*), quietude (*santi*), no-thought (*acinta*), and other similar notions, all of which we may regard as nihilistic or as advocating negative quietism" (AIZB, 50). Suzuki acknowledges that characteristic Zen terms such as emptiness, nothingness, and voidness, as well as no-thought, no-mind, no-self, non-ego, and non-attachment, altogether might seem to suggest life-denying nihilism. The Zen doctrine of no-mind or no-thought as prajna-intuition of emptiness has thus often been misconstrued as being nihilistic, pessimistic, and quietistic.

Throughout his writings, Suzuki argues that such Zen concepts of no-mind, no-thought, no-self, and emptiness do not signify "nihilism" (AIZB, 39, 50, 68; ZJC, 36), or what he also refers to as "pessimism" (WZ, 85) and "sheer negativism" (HRN, v). In response to the question as to whether Zen Buddhism is nihilistic, Suzuki answers that Zen does not lead to nihilism, pessimism, or negativism but is itself the standpoint of a higher affirmation (AIZB, 66–73). He thus proclaims: "Nihilism is not Zen" (AIZB, 68). Moreover, Suzuki asserts: "Do not imagine, however, that Zen is nihilism. All nihilism is self-destructive, it ends nowhere. Negativism is sound as method, but the highest truth is an affirmation. When it is said that Zen has no philosophy ... we must not forget that Zen is holding up in this very act of negation something quite positive and eternally affirmative" (AIZB, 39). Suzuki repeatedly asserts that Zen no-mind as the cosmic Unconscious is coextensive with sunyata or emptiness as the clear skylike openness of empty space, such as when he declares: "The cosmic Unconscious in terms of space is 'Emptiness'" (AZL, 62; LZ, 88). Moreover, he also emphasizes that sunyata or emptiness is not nihilistic, negativistic or pessimistic: "Śūnyatā theory is not nihilism" (EZB I, 58). As he elsewhere clarifies: "Zen emptiness is not the emptiness of [nihilistic] nothingness, but the emptiness of fullness" (SWS III, 222). Hence, throughout his many works, both in English and Japanese, Suzuki aims to demonstrate how Zen overcomes the negative emptiness of nihilism through a higher dialectical affirmation in a positive emptiness as the infinite transparent openness where emptiness and fullness are paradoxically different and yet the same.

Like Nishida Kitarō, Nishitani Keiji, and others in the Kyoto School of modern Japanese philosophy, Suzuki makes a fundamental distinction between the negative standpoint of "relative nothingness" or "relative emptiness" as the locus of nihilism and the positive standpoint of "absolute nothingness" or "absolute emptiness." Although Suzuki describes sunyata as absolute emptiness, he further clarifies: "*Śūnyatā* is not the Absolute as it is usually understood, when the Absolute is regarded as something standing by itself. Such an Absolute is really non-existent, for there is nothing in this world which is absolutely separable from the rest of it" (AZ, 81). In contrast to relative nothingness wherein all things are negated in a meaningless void, absolute nothingness is the spatial locus of sunyata or emptiness that affirms all things as they are in their isness, suchness, openness, and fullness.[6] In Suzuki's words: "This Sunyata is what was referred to before as the Absolute, but the Absolute and Sunyata, the Void, are synonymous, as pertaining to non-distinction. This Void, or emptiness, however, as I have said repeatedly, is not to be taken as mere [nihilistic] nothingness. Sunyata is absolute, not relative nothingness" (WZ, 95). Hence, in contrast to the relative nothingness of nihilism, it is the positive conception of absolute emptiness or absolute nothingness that Suzuki identifies with his Zen notion of the cosmic Unconscious (ZDNM, 123; EZB, III, 18; AZL, 62; LZ, 88). Nishida Kitarō, Nishitani Keiji, and others in the Kyoto School of modern Japanese philosophy, confer an ontological primacy to "space," understood as emptiness, voidness or openness, which in technical terms Nishida calls *mu no basho* (無の場所), the "field (place, locus, topos) of nothingness." But in the Zen Buddhism of Suzuki, the spacelike field of dharmakaya emptiness or absolute nothingness is now restated in psychological terms as the "cosmic Unconscious."

In his discussion of a koan by Unmon Bun'en (Yunmen Wenyan, 864–949) recorded in *Blue Cliff Records,* Suzuki refers to the poetic commentary by Setchō Jūken (Xuedoe Chongxian, 980–1052), whereupon he distinguishes the negative void of relative emptiness or nihilism as mere absence, from sunyata or emptiness in its positive meaning as absolute nothingness:

> Setchō now naturally proceeds to make reference to the teaching of sunyata (void or emptiness) in the Prajñāpāramitā sutras. This doctrine is very much misunderstood even among Buddhist scholars, for they take it for sheer emptiness from the relativistic point of view. Emptiness in their [view] means the absence of a reality . . . and not absolute nothingness or emptiness as advocated in the philosophy of Prajñāpāramitā. Such a relative conception of sunyata has nothing creative or operative

in it . . . Buddhism and Zen have nothing to do with it. No birds fly in it, no grasses grow from it, no clouds, no vapors rise out of it, no waves surge over its surface. (SWS I, 102)

As stated here, sunyata or emptiness is not the mere absence of relative nothingness but the boundless creativity of absolute emptiness. Again: "Buddhist *śūnyatā* does not mean absence. . . . Buddhist *śūnyatā* does not mean extinction. . . . Buddhist *śūnyatā* does not mean vacancy. . . . Buddhists' Emptiness is not on the plane of relativity. It is Absolute Emptiness transcending all forms of mutual relationship, of subject and object, birth and death, God and the world, something and nothing, yes and no, affirmation and negation" (MCB, 23). In a further point of clarification, Suzuki adds: "Emptiness is not a vacancy, it holds in it infinite rays of light" (MCB, 25). For Suzuki, the sunyata or emptiness of Zen Buddhism is not a relative emptiness signifying mere absence, lack, or vacancy but is the nondual spacelike field of absolute emptiness filled with the positive content of effulgent infinite light whereby events radiate into appearance. Suzuki thus argues that sunyata or emptiness is not nihilism but, in its positive designation, is the spacelike openness, luminosity, and transparency where all things are revealed just as they are in suchness.

Suzuki's Zen/Chan concept of the cosmic Unconscious is ultimately formulated in terms of the Prajnaparamita doctrine of sunyata or emptiness, as summed up when he propounds: "'The Unconscious' is the Chinese way of describing the realisation of Emptiness (*śūnyatā*)" (EZB III, 18). Again, when speaking of Huineng's notion of self-nature as Buddha nature: "It is absolute Emptiness . . . the Unconscious" (ZDNM, 123). The Prajnaparamita doctrine of sunyata or emptiness in its meaning as spaciousness or skylike transparent openness is further revealed as the ultimate philosophical basis for Suzuki's Zen concept of the cosmic Unconscious when he proclaims: "The cosmic Unconscious in terms of space is 'Emptiness' (*śūnyatā*)" (AZL, 62; LZ, 88). However, when Suzuki refers to his Zen concept of the cosmic Unconscious as sunyata or emptiness, it is not the negative or life-denying relative emptiness of nihilism but the positive and life-affirming standpoint of absolute emptiness as the luminous transparent openness of the void where nothingness is fullness and fullness is emptiness so that all things are affirmed just as they are in their concrete particular suchness. He thus declares: "Emptiness is suchness in which there is nothing empty. Emptiness unites in itself both fullness and nothingness" (SWS II, 82).

The Unconscious as Indra's Net

At the metaphysical level of discourse, Suzuki's Zen concept of the cosmic Unconscious as the psychological locus of sunyata as emptiness or absolute nothingness is further identified as what in Kegon (C. Huayan; Skt. Avatamsaka) Buddhism is called the *dharmadhātu* (J. *hokkai*, 法界), the transparent spacelike "dharma world" of unhindered harmonious interpenetration between unity and multiplicity or subjectivity and objectivity. Moreover, the Zen-Kegon concept of nonobstructed harmonious interpenetration between one and many is itself ultimately based on the Prajnaparamita doctrine of sunyata or emptiness as interdependent origination. Hence, as claimed by Suzuki in *The Training of the Zen Buddhist Monk*: "The philosophy of Zen is, of course, that of Buddhism, especially that of the *Prajñāpāramitā*, highly coloured with the mysticism of the Avatamsaka" (TZBM, xxiii).

In Kegon Buddhism, this dharma world of interpenetration between one and many is itself imaginatively visualized through the holographic metaphor of "Indra's net" (*Indara no ami*, インダラの網). The Kegon school argues that since every dharma event in the all-encompassing matrix of Indra's net is sunya or empty, they are devoid of substance, whereupon there is said to be harmonious nonobstructed interpenetration between parts and the whole, objects and space, or solid and void. In phenomenological terms, Kegon Buddhism describes this simultaneous mutual penetration of parts and the whole as interfusion between objects discriminated in the foreground focus of attention and the nondiscriminated encompassing background field of emptiness or absolute nothingness. Furthermore, sunyata or emptiness as dependent co-arising explains how the transparent dharma realm of Indra's net is a nondual spacelike continuum wherein all things are interrelated, interdependent, interconnected, and interpenetrating. In the philosophical psychology of Suzuki, Zen satori is awakening to the cosmic Unconscious of dharmakaya emptiness or absolute nothingness in superconsciousness, envisioned as the Kegon dharmadhatu of unimpeded interpenetration between the many and the one, whereupon the illuminated buddhamind now perceives all events as shining jewels in Indra's net that reflect the entire universe from their own perspective, both containing and pervading the continuum of nature as a microcosmos of the macrocosmos.[7]

According to Suzuki, Sino-Japanese Mahayana Buddhist thought reached its apex in the Huayan/Kegon philosophy of unobstructed harmonic interpenetration between many and one. Moreover, the Huayan/Kegon teachings were assimilated into the Chan/Zen contemplative tradition, which emphasized how interfusion of parts and the whole is directly experienced through meditation on nature, art, and everyday life. Indeed, the Kegon/Huayan philosophy of interpenetration between unity and multiplicity came to permeate the entire Japanese Buddhist tradition, including not only Zen Buddhism but also the teachings of Shingon and Pure Land Buddhism, along with Nishida Kitarō and the Kyoto School of modern Japanese philosophy.[8]

Summing up the Kegon/Huayan teachings and their relation to Zen/Chan Buddhism, Suzuki writes: "Kegon is the climax of Chinese speculative thought as influenced by Indian metaphysics which developed within the system of Mahayana Buddhism, whereas Zen marks another critical point in the history of Chinese Buddhism wherein the earthiness of the Chinese mentality kept itself close to this world minding all the mysteries of life in our daily surroundings. Yet Zen managed to leave enough room for the high-flying Kegon imagination to enter into the fabric of Zen thought" (HRN, v). For Suzuki the subconscious mind at its deepest level is the "cosmic Unconscious," precisely because it signifies homologization of psyche and cosmos. But this correspondence between inner psyche and outer cosmos remains unnoticed, unrecognized, or unconscious, until its recognition in the awakening of satori. In the philosophical psychology of Suzuki, the cosmic Unconscious as the locus of emptiness is itself identified with the Kegon/Huayan (Skt. Avatamsaka) Buddhist "dharma realm" (Skt. *dharmadhātu*) of unobstructed harmonious interpenetration between the many and the one, part and whole, or microcosm and macrocosm. The teachings of Kegon/Huayan Buddhism are based on *The Avataṃsaka Sūtra* (J. Kegon-kyō; C. Huayan-jing, 華厳経), or "Flower Garland Scripture." Early in his career, Suzuki edited the Sanskrit text of *The Avataṃsaka Sūtra* and endeavored to translate it into English. Although he never published a complete translation of this massive work, it remained basic to his understanding of Zen and Mahayana Buddhism. Suzuki frequently explains the Zen Buddhist philosophy of emptiness from the standpoint of the Japanese Kegon School, which he otherwise refers to as the Chinese Huayan (Hua-yen) sect, tracing it back to the ancient Indian Sanskrit work *Avataṃsaka Sūtra* often calling it by the name of its last chapter, "The Gaṇḍavyūha Sutra." Suzuki describes the "amalgamation of Zen and Hua-yen (Kegon) philosophy," as especially seen in thinkers such as Zongmi/Tsung-mi (J. Shūmitsu, 780–841), who was a lineage patriarch of both the Chan/Zen and Huayan/Kegon schools in Chinese Buddhism (ZJC, 50–51; SWS III, 97). In his writings Suzuki refers to this consolidation of Zen and Kegon teachings as "the Zen-Kegon interpretation of Mahayana Buddhist thought" (ZJC, 308; SWS III, 130). This is how Suzuki clarifies the worldview of Zen-Kegon philosophy: "To Zen students, the One is the All and the All is the One" (ZJC, 32). In Kegon philosophy, the interpenetration of One and All and All in All is visualized by the holographic metaphor of "Indra's net" credited to Dushun (557–640), who established the Huayan sect of Chinese Buddhism based on teachings of *The Avataṃsaka Sūtra*.

Much of Suzuki's *Essays in Zen Buddhism* (third series) focuses on the relationship between Zen/Chan Buddhism and the Kegon/Huayan scripture, known in Sanskrit as *The Avataṃsaka Sūtra*, the culminating section being called "The Gaṇḍavyūha Sūtra," which describes Sudhana's experience of ocean mirror samadhi in the Tower of Maitreya, exquisitely adorned with jewels that mirror each other ad infinitum, just as each ornamented tower contains all the other towers, in an expansive metaphysical vision of the cosmos as a spectacle of unity-in-plurality and plurality-in-unity. In Suzuki's words: "Sudhana the young pilgrim sees himself in all the towers as well as in each single tower, where all is contained in one and each contains all" (EZB III, 133). Suzuki follows the classical Chinese commentaries on this sutra by Fazang (643–712), the third patriarch of Chinese Huayan Buddhism. The first section of Suzuki's *Essays on Zen Buddhism* (third series), titled "From Zen to the *Gaṇḍavyūha*" (EZB III, 1–53), states that the key teaching of *The Gaṇḍavyūha Sūtra* and Zen Buddhism is "the Unconscious" and that the Unconscious as a psycho-cosmic homologization reveals the Kegon/Huayan or Avatamsaka teachings of Indra's net as an infinite network of relationships between parts and the whole. After discussing the Unconscious in the Chan/Zen tradition of Bodhidharma, Huineng, Shenhui, and Tai-chu Hui-hai, Suzuki relates the Zen tradition to the Kegon/Huayan (Avatamsaka) Buddhist teachings: "Aided by this monograph of Fa-tsang, we shall be able to grasp the ultimate teaching of *The Gaṇḍavyūha Sūtra* and also its relation to Zen Buddhism. When all is said, Zen discipline consists in realizing the Unconscious which is at the basis of all things, and this Unconscious is no other than Mind-only in the *Ganda* as well as the *Lanka*" (EZB III, 52). For Suzuki, then, Zen/Chan and Kegon/Huayan Buddhism culminate in an astonishing panoramic vision of the dharmadhatu of unobstructed harmonious interpenetration between all events as depicted through the metaphor of Indra's net, which he in turn identifies with the prajna wisdom of the cosmic Unconscious.

In *The Awakening of Zen*, Suzuki explains Zen satori as insight into the cosmic Unconscious in terms of the Kegon Buddhist vision of total unobstructed harmonious interpenetration between multiplicity and unity: "[I]t was in the Far East that a system of thought developed in the seventh-century which is known as the Kegon school of philosophy. The Kegon is based on the ideas of interfusion, or interpenetration, or interrelatedness, or mutual unobstructedness" (AZ, 67). For Suzuki, Kegon Buddhism is based on the "philosophy of the interrelatedness of things" (AZ, 67). According to Suzuki: "In Zen, each individual is an absolute entity, and as such he is related to all other individuals: this nexus of infinite interrelationships is made possible in the realm of Emptiness" (ZJC, 349). Moreover, he explains that the image/concept for the Zen-Kegon philosophy of interrelatedness, interdependence, or interpenetration between one and many is that of Indra's net, wherein ultimate reality is described as an interconnected network of causal relationships: "This perfect network of mutual relations has received the technical name of interpenetration in the hands of Mahayana philosophers" (SWS IV, 155). The Kegon Buddhist dharmadhatu as the nonobstructed realm of interpenetration between all events constitutes a "network of mutual dependence" (AZ, 67). Again, the Kegon dharmadhatu is "an infinitely complicated network of interrelationships" (AZ, 67). And elsewhere, "the net of the universe spreads out both in time and space from the center known as 'myself'" (SWS IV, 125). The dharmadhatu is a "causal net"

(OIMB, 58), insofar as it is a dynamic network of causal relationships wherein each event produced by interdependent co-origination is a "cause" that *influences* everything else while also being an "effect" that is *influenced* by everything else in the pluralistic multiverse. Ultimate reality is described by Kegon Buddhism as "a network of pearls" wherein each iridescent pearl is like a mirror reflecting all the others in realm of Indra's net (SWS IV, 89). Describing the Kegon metaphor of the golden lion, wherein each hair of the lion contains an infinity of golden lions, he writes that in the dharmadhatu, "the complete network of interrelationships of all things rests on the point of a single hair" (SWS IV, 90). According to this Kegon Buddhist philosophy of interpenetration between one and many, "the existence of each individual, whether or not he is conscious of the fact, owes something to an infinitely expanding and all-enwrapping net of loving relationship" (AZ, 66–67; SWS III, 195). As indicated here, although each moment of our existence is a reflection of the whole cosmos from a unique perspective within the interconnected matrix of Indra's net, it often goes unnoticed or unrecognized, such that it occurs at a subliminal level of awareness in what Suzuki terms the cosmic Unconscious.

Kegon Buddhism describes the dharmadhatu as the Jewel Net of Indra, or what Suzuki also refers to in the plural as "jewel nets" (OIMB, 188) and "nets of mani-jewels" (OIMB, 190). The empty, luminous, and transparent dharmadhatu is to be envisioned as a "net of light" where every shining jewel in the cosmic web of Indra's net radiates without obstruction the clear light of Buddha nature from its own perspective (SWS IV, 157). Similarly, Indra's net is characterized as a "net of illumination" (OMB, 158). Suzuki, hence, tells us that the "Light of Dharmakaya is like a full moon. . . . Its reflection is seen in every drop or body of clear water" (OMB, 135). The notion of the transparent dharmadhatu as a "network of mutual dependence," a "network of interrelationships," a "causal net," an "all-enwrapping net of relationships," a "network of pearls," a "net of light, or "net of illumination" is thus poetically depicted in Kegon (Huayan/Avatamsaka) Buddhist literature as "Indra's net," a holographic vision of nature as an infinite network, mesh, web, lattice, or matrix of interconnected events. Suzuki therefore refers to "nets of Indra" (OIMB, 189) where there is total nonimpeded interfusion of each part with all the other parts and with the whole. Moreover, he speaks of the dharmadhatu of Indra's net as the abode "where such an exquisitely beautiful and altogether inconceivable spectacle takes place" (OIMB, 198). Each event in the dharmadhatu of unobstructed harmonious interpenetration between many and one permeates the whole space-time continuum, both containing the universe as contracted and pervading the universe as expanded, thus to reflect totality from its own standpoint in nature as a brilliant gem on Indra's net as an individual microcosmos of the all-inclusive macrocosmos.

In *What is Zen?* Suzuki again emphasizes how Zen enlightenment is insight into the cosmic Unconscious, comprehended in terms of the Kegon/Huayan (Avatamsaka) dharmadhatu of *riji muge* (理事無碍) or "unhindered interpenetration of particulars and the whole" and *jiji muge* (事事無碍) or "unhindered interpenetration between particulars and particulars," as poetically depicted by the metaphor of Indra's net, wherein each dharma event arising through emptiness as interdependent co-origination is a shining jewel reflecting every other jewel in the cosmic web of relationships from its own unique perspective as a mirror of totality: "The climax of Buddhist philosophy is reached in the Kegon conception of Jiji-mu-ge (literally, each thing no hindrance). As I see it, this is the summit of oriental thought as developed by the finest Buddhist minds, and represents Japan's contribution to world philosophy" (WZ, 93). The Zen-Kegon pluralistic multiverse of Indra's net, characterized by *jiji muge* or unhindered interpenetration of parts and *riji* muge or unhindered interpenetration of parts and the whole, is further explained by Suzuki with the metaphor of the Hall of Mirrors:

> To explain this conception, Kegon uses the analogy of ten mirrors, placed in the zenith, the nadir and the eight points of the compass. Each mirror reflects the other nine, individually and together. . . . In this concept of interpenetration or reflection, it will by noted that there is no reference to the Absolute, or to any transcending reality. The world of everyday is taken in its entirety, and the world of multiplicity is affirmed. This may be called a form of radical empiricism. (WZ, 96–97)

This analogy of the Hall of Mirrors illustrates how in the dharmadhatu of Indra's net, all perspectival events are reflected from the standpoint of every other event, such that each nonlocal dharma event both pervades and contains the universe from its own point of view as multiplicity-in-unity and unity-in-multiplicity. Elsewhere, Suzuki tells us how the great Chinese teacher Fazang disclosed the Kegon dharma world of interpenetration to the empress, showing how each moment is like a mirror reflecting the effulgent light of Buddha nature from its own perspective: "He had first a candle lighted, and then encircling it had mirrors on all sides. The central light reflected itself in every one of the mirrors, and every one of these reflected lights was reflected again in every mirror, so that there was a perfect interplay of lights, that is, of concrete universals" (SWS IV, 158).[9]

Throughout his various writings, Suzuki explicitly relates the Kegon philosophy of *riji muge* or unhindered interpenetration of concrete particulars and the universal-whole as visualized by the image of Indra's net to his Zen concept of the cosmic Unconscious: "*Ri* (*li*) and *Ji* (*shih*) are terms used very much in Kegon philosophy. *Ji* is a particular object or event, and *ri* is a universal principle. As long as these two are kept separate, life loses its freedom and spontaneity, and one fails to be master of oneself. Psychologically speaking, this is the unconscious breaking into the field of consciousness when consciousness loses itself, abandoning itself to the dictates of the unconscious" (ZJC, 101–102, fn. 9). For Suzuki, then, Zen satori as a flash of insight into the cosmic

Unconscious is realization of the Kegon Buddhist dharma realm of *riji muge* or nonobstructed harmonious interpenetration of the parts and the whole, as seen in the kaleidoscopic, panoramic, and holographic vision of Indra's net, wherein each shining jewel in the cosmic web of relationships mirrors the universe from its own standpoint as one-in-many and many-in-one.

According to Suzuki, the Zen-Kegon philosophy of impermanence is based on interpenetration of the moment with eternity in the cosmic Unconscious, or what he also calls unconscious consciousness: "For this reason our consciousness of change and impermanence is deeply interfused with an unconscious consciousness of eternity, unchangeability or timelessness. This interfusion of consciousness and unconsciousness or, in Buddhist terminology, of the Many and the One, of Form (*rūpam*) and Emptiness (*śūnyatā*), the Distinction (or Discrimination) and Non-distinction (or non-discrimination) is, we can say, the philosophy of Zen" (AZ, 36). Suzuki thus clarifies how the Zen-Kegon philosophy of harmonious interpenetration between the many and the one, the moment and eternity, form and emptiness, or discrimination and nondiscrimination is to be comprehended in psychological terms as the unobstructed interfusion of consciousness (multiplicity) and unconsciousness (unity). Elsewhere he explains that in Zen satori there is a sudden awakening to the cosmic Unconscious, whereupon there is an experience of eternity in the moment, a vision of the entire cosmos in each minute particle of dust, or what Kegon Buddhism expresses as unimpeded interfusion between the whole and its parts. To illustrate this Zen experience of satori as awakening to the cosmic Unconscious, Suzuki cites a verse from the mystical poetry of William Blake: "To see a world in a grain of sand/And a heaven in a wild flower/Hold infinity in the palm of your hand/And eternity in an hour" (ZB, 141).

At the level of moral discourse, Suzuki elucidates the Zen-Kegon philosophy of interrelatedness, interconnectedness, and interpenetration as the basis for a Buddhist ethics of *karuṇā* (J. *jihi*, 慈悲) or compassion: "When this [Zen-Kegon] philosophy of the interrelatedness of things is, rightly understood, love begins to be realized, because love is to recognize others and to take them into consideration in every way of life. To do to others what you would like them to do to you is the keynote of love, and this this is what naturally grows out of the realization of mutual relatedness" (AZ, 67; SWS III). Elsewhere, Suzuki further explains this link between the Zen-Kegon philosophy of interrelatedness and the nondual Mahayana Buddhist ethics of compassion when he declares: "As long as we remain in the realm of dualistic logic this world of Jiji-mu-ge, controlled by the great Compassion, will be unintelligible, and as a result we shall encounter all manner of suffering in our daily life" (WZ, 100). He adds: "The Kegon doctrine of interpenetration must be intuitively understood.... For interpenetration is not an intellectual experience, but comes directly from the spirit, manifesting itself as a great Compassionate Heart" (WZ, 99). Thus, in Zen-Kegon philosophy it is direct perception of sunyata or emptiness as the interrelatedness of all things in the all-embracing matrix of Indra's net that functions as the basis for an altruistic morality of compassion, and perception of interrelatedness is not acquired by discursive reason but directly grasped by prajna-intuition of the cosmic Unconscious as the holographic vision of Indra's net.

Suzuki further clarifies how the Kegon/Huayan (Skt. Avatamsaka) Buddhist philosophy of interpenetration between unity and multiplicity as envisioned by Indra's net along with other poetic metaphors such as the Hall of Mirrors, the Tower of Maitreya, Moonlight in a Dewdrop, and the Ocean and its Waves is the basis for the Zen aesthetic, artistic, and poetic appreciation of beauty in nature: "Here we must remember that the experience of mere oneness, is not enough for the real appreciation of Nature. . . . The balancing of unity and multiplicity or, better, the merging of self with others as in the philosophy of the Avatamsaka (Kegon) is absolutely necessary to the [Zen] aesthetic understanding of Nature" (ZJC, 354). Moreover, it is this Kegon Buddhist metaphor of Indra's net as harmonious interpenetration of unity and multiplicity or subjectivity and objectivity that serves as the basis for a Zen Buddhist environmental ethics grounded in an ecological view of the undivided aesthetic continuum of nature as Indra's net where everything is connected to everything else, thereby requiring compassion for all sentient beings, along with conservation of nature through an aesthetic *wabi*-lifestyle of voluntary simplicity, frugality, and spiritual poverty: "Zen proposes to respect Nature, to love Nature, to live its own life; Zen recognizes that our Nature is one with objective Nature . . . in the sense that Nature lives in us and we in Nature. For this reason, Zen asceticism advocates simplicity, frugality . . . making no attempt to utilize Nature for selfish purposes" (ZJC, 351–352). According to the Zen-Kegon moral directive guiding this artistic *wabi*-lifestyle of voluntary simplicity, one takes from the aesthetic continuum of nature only what one needs and gives back everything one takes, such that the sparing use of natural resources is not too much or too little, but "just enough" (ZJC, 295).[10] This Zen moral-aesthetic principle of "just enough" thus functions as a Buddhist middle way, or as it were, an Aristotelian "golden mean" establishing a via media between extremes of excess and deficit.

Based on his Zen-Kegon metaphysics of unhindered harmonious interpenetration between multiplicity and unity as propounded in *The Avataṃsaka Sūtra*, Suzuki argues for a primacy of "synaesthesia" or the synaesthetic experience of intersensory fusion in Zen satori as awakening to the cosmic Unconscious. David L. McMahan examines descriptions of synaesthesia in "The Gaṇḍavyūha Sūtra," the final chapter of *The Avataṃsaka Sūtra* (J. Kegon-kyō), which expounds the nonobstructed interpenetration of many and one as visualized by the Buddhist metaphor of Indra's net: "Another way the text relates vision to sound and speech is through synaesthesia, the phenomenon of sensory cross-over; such that one seems to 'hear visions' or 'see sounds.' Passages that cross sensory boundaries are fairly frequent in the *Gaṇḍavyūha*" (2002, 126). Likewise, Suzuki applies his Zen-Kegon philosophy of harmonious interpenetration between multiplicity and unity to the aesthetic-mystical experience of synaesthesia as the harmonious interfusion of diverse sense modes. As Suzuki explains in *Manual of Zen Buddhism*:

> When this source [the Unconscious] is penetrated by means of Prajna, the entrance is effected to the inner sanctuary, where all the senses are merged in one. Let the Prajna penetration enter through the auditory sense as was the case with Kwannon Bosatsu, and the distinction of the six senses will thereby be effaced; that is to say, there will then take place an experience called "perfect interfusion." The ear not only hears but sees, smells, and feels. All the barriers between the sensory functions are removed, and there is a perfect interfusion running between them; each Vijnana then functions for the others. (MZB, 69)[11]

In the cosmic Unconscious of sunyata or emptiness as interdependent co-origination, there is an unobstructed synaesthetic interpenetration between diverse sense qualities whereby one "sees music" and "hears colors," as exemplified by Kannon (観音), the bodhisattva of compassion whose name literally means to "see the sounds" of the world. According to Suzuki's Zen-Kegon metaphysics of harmonious interfusion between many and one in the all-embracing interconnected matrix of Indra's net, and the Yogacara Buddhist depth psychology of the *ālaya-vijñāna* as the subliminal mind, while the five sense-consciousnesses (*vijñānas*) of sight, sound, taste, scent, and touch appear as discrete atomic sensations at the surface level of ego-consciousness with its discriminative intellect and correlate subject-object dualism, the senses are merged into synaesthetic multiplicity-in-unity when grasped as an interrelated aesthetic whole by the nondual prajna-intuition of sunyata or emptiness in Zen satori as consciousness of the cosmic Unconscious in superconsciousness.[12]

Just as Suzuki explains his Zen concept of the cosmic Unconscious in terms of Prajnaparamita literature as sunyata or emptiness, and Yogacara Buddhist depth psychology as the alaya-vijnana or storehouse consciousness, he further elucidates its content, structure, and dynamics with the Kegon metaphysics of *riji muge* or interpenetration between many and one. From the standpoint of his own philosophical psychology of the cosmic Unconscious, Suzuki interprets Kegon Buddhist harmonious unobstructed interpenetration between multiplicity and unity as the interfusion of consciousness and unconsciousness or discrimination and nondiscrimination. In immediate experience there is a foreground/background pattern whereby one is normally conscious of particular sense-objects clearly articulated in the foreground focus of attention, while the rest of the universe recedes into unconsciousness in the nonarticulated background field of emptiness as interdependent co-origination. When consciousness awakens to the cosmic Unconscious, there is psycho-cosmic homologization whereby all objects discriminated in the foreground now disclose the entire universe in the undiscriminated background of emptiness, such that the whole is disclosed in each part, just as each part reveals the whole. According to Suzuki's Zen-Kegon metaphysics of unobstructed harmonious interpenetration between the parts and the whole, then, nondual Zen satori is a sudden awakening of consciousness to the cosmic Unconscious in supraconsciousness, whereupon each minute particle in the undivided aesthetic continuum of nature is likened to a sparkling jewel on Indra's net that reflects totality from its own unique perspective as an individual microcosmos of the all-embracing macrocosmos thereby to multiply the beauty, splendor, and majesty of the universe ad infinitum.

The Unconscious as the Storehouse Consciousness

The philosophical psychology of Suzuki relates his Zen concept of "the Unconscious" to the *ālaya-vijñāna* or "storehouse consciousness," a central notion in *The Laṅkāvatāra Sūtra* and *The Awakening of Faith in Mahayana* (C. Dàshéng Qǐxìn Lùn; J. Daijōkishinron, 大乗起信論), as well as in Yogacara Buddhism. Thus, while Suzuki's modern Zen concept of the Unconscious was profoundly influenced by Western psychology and philosophy, it is nonetheless also deeply rooted in the alaya-vijnana of Mahayana Buddhism. It should be noted that the alaya-vijnana or "storehouse consciousness" is itself designated as a mode of "consciousness" (*vijñāna*) but a *very subtle* consciousness that normally functions outside the normal margins of awareness, and so is still unrecognized or unnoticed, at which time it is referred to by Suzuki in psychological terms as "the Unconscious." Although this very subtle consciousness of the alaya-vijnana usually operates at the subliminal levels, it is not inaccessible but can become fully aware of itself through a shift of attention by yoga meditation practices. In this chapter, I will first briefly discuss the notion of the alaya-vijnana as the unconscious mind in the Indian (Waldron, 2003), Chinese (Tao Jiang, 2006), and Japanese (Tagawa Shun'ei, 2009) traditions of Yogacara Buddhism. Following this preliminary discussion, it will be then demonstrated how, from his earliest writings, Suzuki explains the alaya-vijnana in psychological terms as the subconscious, unconscious, nonconscious, or subliminal mind. As will be seen, Suzuki relates the alaya-vijnana to various Western concepts of the subliminal mind, including "the Unconscious" of Eduard von Hartmann, the "trans-marginal consciousness" of William James, and the "collective unconscious" of C. G. Jung. Nonetheless, he argues that the alaya-vijnana is ultimately comprehended in terms of his Zen concept of the "cosmic Unconscious."

The Alaya-Vijnana in Indian, Chinese, and Japanese Buddhism

In *The Buddhist Unconscious: The ālaya-vijñāna in the context of Indian Buddhist thought*, William S. Waldron argues that the earliest notion of the unconscious was formulated by the Indian school of Yogacara Buddhism. According to Waldron, it was "the Indian Yogācāra Buddhists who first systematically conceptualized this awareness of unawareness. . . . They not only explicitly differentiated a dimension of the unconscious mental processes — called ālaya vijñāna, the 'basal, store, or home' consciousness — from the processes of conscious cognitive awareness — called *pravritti-vijñāna*. They also articulated a variety of experiential, logical and exegetical arguments in support of this concept of unconscious mind" (2003, xi). For Waldron the Yogacara Buddhist notion of alaya-vijnana thus constitutes what he terms the "Buddhist unconscious" (2003, xi). Moreover, as Waldron emphasizes above, Yogacara Buddhism was not only the first to explicitly and systematically formulate the concept of an unconscious mind, but also to rigorously argue for this concept through the testimony of experience, logic, and scripture.

Waldron further clarifies how even in the early canonical Pali sources of Theravada Buddhism, *bhavanga-citta* (life-constituent mind) was used as a synonym for the ālaya-vijñāna (2003, 131) in its function as the unconscious. Similar to the alaya-vijnana, the notion of *bhavanga-citta* was used in Theravada Buddhism as the subliminal mind that explained the continuity of human experience, even though it is constituted as a ceaseless flux of discontinuous momentary events with no eternal soul or permanent self to function as an underlying substratum. Moreover, like alaya-vijnana, the Theravada Buddhist notion of *bhavanga-citta* operates as the unconscious mind that establishes continuity throughout the mental states of waking, dream, and deep sleep, as well as from life to life in the rebirth process of transmigration. Similar to the alaya-vijnana of Yogacara Buddhist psychology, the early Theravada Buddhist notion of *bhavanga-citta* is the unconscious mind that contains *anusaya* as "latent dispositions" karmically inherited from the past that condition each moment of experience. This Theravada Buddhist concept of *anusaya*, hence, refers to those dormant predispositions, inclinations, and habitual tendencies that lie sleeping beneath consciousness at the subliminal levels of awareness.

Tao Jiang provides an historical analysis of the alaya-vijnana as the subliminal layer of mental functioning in the Chinese tradition of Yogacara Buddhism. In *Contexts and Dialogue: Yogācāra Buddhism and Modern Psychology on the Subliminal Mind*, Jiang states: "Ālayavijñāna, usually translated as the storehouse consciousness, is a key concept in the Yogācāra system. It is a subliminal reservoir of memories, habits, tendencies, and future possibilities. The subliminal nature of the ālayavijñāna renders it susceptible to being interpreted as the Buddhist version of the unconscious. On the other hand, the notion of the unconscious looms large in modern psychology as well as in popular parlance"

(2006, 8). He then argues that while various scholars have interpreted the alaya-vijnana using the psychology of Freud or Jung, one must first establish the historical "context" of the subliminal mind in Indian and Chinese Yogacara Buddhism, prior to establishing "dialogue" with modern Western concepts of the unconscious (2006, 15).

Although Jiang considers differences between the models of the unconscious developed in Western psychology by Freud and Jung in contrast to the Chinese Yogacara Buddhism of Xuan Zang (602–664), of special interest is his analysis of differences in *access* to the unconscious in the three models. In Freud's view, the "royal road" to the unconscious is interpretation of dreams, so the personal unconscious can be accessed only in an *indirect* way by decoding camouflaged dream symbolism (Jiang 2006, 132). Similarly, in Jung's analytical psychology, the archetypes of the collective unconscious cannot be directly known in themselves but can only be *indirectly* viewed through their historical and cultural expressions by what he calls symbols or primordial images (Jiang 2006, 137). Xuan Zang, however, argues that in Chinese Yogacara Buddhism, the buddhas and bodhisattvas who are adept in yoga meditation can *directly* access the unconscious depths of the storehouse consciousness upon achieving enlightenment (Jiang 2006, 139).

In *Living Yogacara: An Introduction to Consciousness-Only Buddhism*, Tagawa Shun'ei describes the conscious/subconscious infrastructure of the mind in the Japanese "Consciousness-only" (*yuishiki,* 唯識) school of Yogacara Buddhism. This conscious/subconscious infrastructure of the total psyche is constituted by the "shallow mind" comprised of the five sense-consciousnesses plus thinking consciousness, and their underlying "deep consciousness," including *manas* or the mind of self-attachment, and beneath that the ālaya-vijñāna or the storehouse consciousness (2009, 18). Whereas the shallow mind signifies ordinary consciousness, the deep mind refers to the subconscious. Tagawa explains: "The Yogācārins deliberating on the composition of our mind and its functions of conscious awareness, came to be convinced that there had to be an additional, deeper layer of mind. . . . Thus, they posited a subconscious region of the mind, comprised of the two deep layers of consciousness of *manas* and ālaya-vijñāna" (2009, 12).

The Alaya-vijnana in the Zen Buddhism of Suzuki

Throughout his vast corpus of writings, Suzuki explicitly and systematically relates the alaya-vijnana with the unconscious, subconscious, or subliminal mind. In later essays such as "Awakening of a New Consciousness in Zen," Suzuki explains the alaya-vijnana of Yogacara Buddhist psychology as a function of unconscious processes: "The *Alaya* may be considered as corresponding to 'the Unconscious'" (SWS I, 139). Likewise, in his early 1907 text *Outlines of Mahayana Buddhism*, Suzuki explains: "The All-Conserving Mind (Alaya) in a certain sense resembles the Unconscious" (OMB, 84). Elsewhere in the same work, Suzuki describes "how potential karma stored from time out of mind is saturated in every fibre of our subliminal consciousness or in the Alaya-vijnana, as Buddhists might say" (OMB, 84). What Suzuki refers to above as "the Unconscious" or "subliminal consciousness" of the alaya-vijnana is further referred to in this text as "the dark recesses of unconsciousness" (OMB, 84), "a state of absolute unconsciousness" (OMB, 72), the "non-conscious," "unconscious or subconscious intelligence" (OMB, 187), and "an unconscious intellect" (OMB, 191, fn. 2). He further explains the alaya-vijnana in its workings as the subconscious mind by what in the radically empirical psychology of William James is described as "trans-marginal consciousness" (OMB, 72). Again, referring to *Philosophy of the Unconscious* (*Philosophie des Unbewussten*, 1869) by Eduard von Hartmann, Suzuki discusses the alaya-vijnana as "Hartmann's *Unbewusste Geist* (unconscious spirit)" (OMB, 84). And indeed, Suzuki makes reference to von Hartmann's concept of *das Unbewusste* or "the Unconscious" in one of his first published essays treatises dated 1894 (PPOH, 135). It can therefore be seen how throughout his long and prolific career, even from his earliest writings, Suzuki interpreted the alaya-vijnana in terms of his philosophical psychology of the Unconscious.

In the introduction to his groundbreaking 1927 *Essays in Zen Buddhism* (first series), Suzuki explains his Zen concept of the cosmic Unconscious as follows:

> Some think that there is still an unknown region in our consciousness which has not yet been thoroughly and systematically explored. It is sometimes called the Unconscious or the Subconscious.... Just as our ordinary field of consciousness is filled with all possible kinds of images ... so is the Subconscious a storehouse of every form of occultism or mysticism, understanding by the term all that is known as latent or abnormal or psychic or spiritualistic. The power to see into the nature of one's own being may lie also hidden there, and what Zen awakens in our consciousness may be that. At any rate, the masters speak figuratively of the opening of a third eye. "Satori" is the popular name given to this opening or awakening. (EZB I, 19)

In this passage Suzuki refers to his central notion of "the Unconscious," which he alternately refers to as "the Subconscious." He then describes the Unconscious as a "storehouse" of latent contents hidden beneath normal waking consciousness. This description of the Unconscious as a storehouse makes reference to the alaya-vijnana or storehouse consciousness in the Lankavatara and Yogacara Buddhist traditions. Moreover, he explains Zen satori as opening to this deeper unconscious mind: "Satori is to realize the Unconscious" (EZB II, 21). For Suzuki, "the Unconscious" of Zen, like the alaya-vijnana or storehouse consciousness, is not just the underside of consciousness, but is the all-inclusive Mind, insofar as it designates "the Unconscious as underlying all our activities mental and bodily, conscious and unconscious" (EZB III, 8–9, fn. 3).

Suzuki translated two important Mahayana Buddhist source texts for the Yogacara Buddhist concept of the storehouse consciousness as a subconscious, unconscious, or subliminal mind operating beneath the surface of ego-consciousness. In 1900 Suzuki published a translation from Chinese into English of *Aśvaghosha's Discourse on the Awakening of Faith in Mahayana* (AFM). In 1930 he published a work titled *Studies in the Lankavatara Sutra*. Soon afterward *The Laṅkāvatāra Sūtra* was translated by Suzuki from Sanskrit into English and published in 1932. Suzuki further emphasizes the special importance of *The Laṅkāvatāra Sūtra* in the tradition of Zen/Chan Buddhism, since it was said by a legend to be the only text brought by Bodhidharma to China (SLS, 89). Together, these three works about the storehouse consciousness became foundational for Suzuki's Zen concept of the Unconscious and his view of Zen satori as awakening to the cosmic Unconscious.

In his translation of Aśvaghosha's *Discourse on the Awakening of Faith in Mahayana,* the alaya-vijnana or storehouse consciousness is rendered as the "all-conserving mind."[13] Referring to unconscious operations of the all-conserving mind, the text states that through "perfuming" or contamination by subliminal karmic dispositions forming in the alaya-vijnana, ego-consciousness and its subject-object dualism arise, resulting in awareness of temporal succession of past, present, and future, whereby the mind "unconsciously recollects things gone by, and in imagination anticipates things to come" (AFM, 77). Again, the all-conserving mind is described as "an unconscious activity . . . originating in the mind as it achieves a most hidden activity" (AFM, 125). Moreover, the *manas* or dualistic ego-consciousness that forms by habitual tendencies within the all-conserving mind is defined as "the subjective mind which believes consciously or unconsciously in the existence of the ego-soul" (AFM, 151).

In *Studies in the Lankavatara Sutra*, Suzuki holds that while *citta* or mind in its general sense designates the whole system of mental operations, in other cases it specifies the ālaya-vijñāna or storehouse consciousness (SLS, 179). Moreover, in its functioning as the alaya-vijnana, *citta* is identified as the subconscious mind: "Psychologically, the Citta may thus be regarded as corresponding to the Subconscious" (SLS, 249). As he clarifies elsewhere in the same text: "The Ālaya is the reservoir of things good and bad, but it is perfectly neutral and not conscious of itself, as there is as yet no differentiation in it" (SLS, 197). When the alaya is still in its original undiscriminated state, it is unconscious, or "not conscious of itself," while upon becoming discriminated into subject and object, it becomes conscious. It is further explained that supreme enlightenment occurs when there is a sudden revolution or turning around (*parāvritti*) of consciousness, which is the psychological process of conversion whereby the alaya is cleansed of all karmic dispositions. Once again, in psychological terms, Suzuki describes this process of conversion in terms of his philosophical psychology of the Unconscious: "The unconscious process that preceded it may have been gradual, but as far as his conscious mind is concerned, the revulsion has taken place instantaneously" (SLS, 207, fn. 1). Suzuki's translator's introduction to *The Laṅkāvatāra Sūtra* describes the text as including a system of Buddhist depth psychology: "What may be termed Buddhist psychology in the *Lanka* consists in the analysis of mind, that is, in the classification of the Vijñānas. To understand thus the psychology of Buddhism properly the knowledge of these terms is necessary: *citta, manas, vijñāna, manovijñāna*, and ālaya-vijñāna" (LS, xxi). In his *Studies of the Lankavatara Sutra*, Suzuki outlines the structure of the human mind as divided into eight consciousnesses: "There are eight Vijñānas: (1) The Tathāgata-garbha, known under the name of the Ālayavijñāna, (2) Manas, (3) Manovijñāna, and the five sense-vijñānas grouped together as is pointed out by the philosophers" (SLS, 198). Hence, the mind is a psychical continuum with eight levels, including the five *vijñānas* or sense-consciousness, *mano-viñāna* or the intellectual center, *manas* or the principle of individuation responsible for egocentrism or self-grasping, and the *ālaya-vijñāna* or storehouse consciousness, the all-conserving mind functioning as a repository for accumulated *vāsanās* or habitual tendencies inherited from the past, referred to by Suzuki in psychological terms as "the Unconscious."

This is Suzuki explaining that all Mahayana Buddhist scriptures have their ultimate source in Buddha mind as the innermost depths of the cosmic Unconscious: "The sutras, especially Mahayana sutras, are direct expressions of spiritual experiences; they contain intuitions gained by digging down deeply into the abyss of the Unconscious" (EZB III, 7). Suzuki translated *The Laṅkāvatāra Sūtra* from Sanskrit into English and edited for publication the Sanskrit version of *The Gaṇḍavyūha Sūtra* (the final chapter of *The Avataṃsaka Sūtra*). These texts strongly influenced Suzuki's interpretation of Zen Buddhism. *The Laṅkāvatāra Sūtra* is a source text for Yogacara Buddhism that formulates an Eastern psychology of the unconscious mind as the alaya-vijnana. *The Gaṇḍavyūha Sūtra* is a source text for the Huayan/Kegon (Avatamsaka) doctrine of interpenetration between all events in the cosmic web of Indra's net. Moreover, *The Gaṇḍavyūha Sūtra* incorporates the Mind-only (Skt. *cittamātra*) doctrine of Yogacara Buddhism, teaching that because in the transparent dharmadhatu of Indra's net, all discriminated objects imputed by thought are Mind-only, they are void of substance, such that there is unimpeded harmonious interfusion between the many and the one in sunyata or emptiness as interdependent origination. Suzuki here describes Zen as a process of realizing the Unconscious while further identifying the Unconscious with the "Mind" or "Mind-only" doctrine of the *Ganda* and *Lanka* traditions of Mahayana Buddhism: "Aided by this monograph of Fa-tsang, we shall be able to grasp the ultimate teaching of the *Gaṇḍavyūha* and also its relation to Zen Buddhism. When all is said, Zen discipline consists in realizing the Unconscious which is at the basis of all things, and this Unconscious is no other than Mind-only in the *Ganda* as well as in the *Lanka*" (EZB III, 52).

In the philosophical psychology of Suzuki, the experience of Zen satori as awakening to the cosmic Unconscious is the realization of the *araya-shiki* (阿頼耶識, アラヤ識) or storehouse consciousness after it has been transformed into *mumotsushiki* (無没識) as "consciousness sunk into nothingness." In a discussion on the unconscious in Suzuki and Western psychoanalysis, Heinrich Dumoulin takes up the Yogacara Buddhist notion of storehouse consciousness: "In the Buddhist doctrine of consciousness (*vijñānavāda*) the eighth consciousness is the 'storehouse consciousness' (*ālayavijñāna*; Japanese: *arayashiki*), also called *mumotsushiki* in Japanese (literally consciousness sunk into nothingness); this can be interpreted as the unconscious or as a cosmic unconscious. It is frequently invoked by Japanese Zen masters in clarifying the process of enlightenment" (1992, 92). In Suzuki's philosophical psychology, the alaya-vijnana as *mumotsushiki* or "consciousness sunk into nothingness" corresponds to Zen satori as awakening to the cosmic Unconscious, in its meaning as the space-like transparent openness of dharmakaya emptiness or absolute nothingness.

In various places throughout his work Suzuki identifies his Zen notion of the cosmic Unconscious with the Yogacara Buddhist *ādarśana jñāna* or "great mirror wisdom," which appears when the alaya-vijnana or storehouse consciousness has been cleansed, purified, and transformed into the boundless light of dharmakaya emptiness through the "turning around" (*parāvritti*) of satori or kensho. The alaya-consciousness has two phases, the first phase of the impure alaya-vijnana contaminated or perfumed by karmic habitual tendencies and the second phase of the purified alaya-vijnana after it has been cleansed of all dormant habitual tendencies by the *parāvritti* or "revolution of consciousness" in Zen satori awakening (LS, xvii). It is this second phase of the Unconscious as alaya-vijnana, after all residual defilements have been eliminated through yogic practice, that Suzuki identifies as the *ādarśana jñāna* or "great mirror wisdom" of dharmakaya emptiness.

Following the Rinzai Zen koan tradition of Hakuin, Suzuki incorporates the Yogacara Buddhist concept of the alaya-vijnana based on the four ways of knowing, the three bodies, and the eight consciousnesses.[14] Suzuki explicitly identifies the Yogacara Buddhist doctrine of "great mirror wisdom" as dharmakaya emptiness at the level of the purified storehouse consciousness with the no-mind state of Zen satori, which in psychological terms he refers to as the "cosmic Unconscious." Suzuki thus describes "the Buddhist epistemology of the 'great mirror wisdom' . . . which is the state of no-mindedness" (ZJC, 121). Further clarifying kensho as the great mirror knowing of dharmakaya emptiness, Suzuki writes: "*Ādarśana jñānam*, in Sanskrit which is one of the four knowledges (*jñānam*) given by the Yogācāra or Vijñāptimātra School of Buddhism. It is the fundamental poetic quality of consciousness in general, which is here compared to the illuminating quality of the mirror" (ZJC, 121, fn. 22). Elsewhere in the same text, while referring to the spontaneous workings of *ki*-energy in Zen no-mind-ness or the cosmic Unconscious in swordsmanship and other arts, Suzuki again discusses the "great mirror wisdom" of dharmakaya emptiness at the level of the storehouse consciousness: "Emptiness is one mind-ness, one mind-ness is no-mind-ness, and it is no-mind-ness that achieves wonders" (ZJC, 165). He adds: "This [emptiness or no-mind-ness] corresponds to the modern conception of the 'cosmic unconscious,' which may be taken as reflecting something of the *ālaya-vijñāna* (*arayashiki* in Japanese) after it has been transformed into *ādarśana jñāna*, 'mirror wisdom' (*daienkyōchi* in Japanese)" (ZJC, 165, fn. 18). As clearly stated here, the cosmic Unconscious is equated by Suzuki with the alaya-vijnana or storehouse consciousness but only *after* it has been purified, cleansed, and transformed by Zen meditation into *ādarśana jñāna*, the "great mirror wisdom." Suzuki thus maintains that after the alaya-vijnana is cleansed of all karmic dispositions it transcends the collective unconscious of Jung thereby to become the *ādarśana jñāna* or great mirror knowing as spacelike transparent dharmakaya emptiness: "When all these limits are transcended — which means going even beyond the so-called collective unconscious — one comes upon that which is known in Buddhism as *ādarśana jñāna*, 'mirror knowledge.' The darkness of the unconscious is broken through and one sees all things as one sees one's face in the brightly shining mirror" (ZP, 56). Elsewhere he describes the process of breaking through the alaya-vijnana as the Jungian collective unconscious to the deeper level of the Zen Buddhist cosmic Unconscious, here identified with *kokoro* or the natural unfabricated heartmind as the abyss of absolute nothingness:

> The *kokoro* is not to be confused with the ālayavijñāna of the Yogācāra. . . . The *kokoro* reveals itself only when the ālaya is broken through. The ālaya is more than mere Unconscious as distinguished from the Conscious for it comprises both. The *kokoro*, however, is not the ālaya, in which, I would say, there is still something savoring of intellect. The *kokoro* is thoroughly purged of all sorts of intellection, it is an abyss of absolute nothingness. (SWS I, 139)

In Suzuki's philosophical psychology, when the alaya-vijnana is still karmically perfumed by *vāsanās* or latent habit-energies, it functions similar to the Jungian "collective unconscious" of psychically inherited archetypal patterns that condition human experience. Yet, he further explains that when the alaya-vijnana or storehouse consciousness is cleansed of all latent karmic dispositions, it is transmuted into *ādarśana jñāna* or "great mirror wisdom" as the boundless clear light of dharmakaya emptiness that is realized in the "turning around" (*parāvritti*) of satori-kensho; and it is this all-illuminating great mirror wisdom of spacelike transparent dharmakaya emptiness that Suzuki identifies with his Zen concept of the cosmic Unconscious as the abyss of absolute nothingness.

The Alaya-Vijnana as the Unconscious in Suzuki's *Mushin to iu koto*

Suzuki delivered a series of Japanese lectures in Tokyo on the theme of *mushin* in 1938, and subsequently published them as a book in 1939 with the Japanese title *Mushin to iu koto* (無心と言うこと, "On No-Mind," or "On the Unconscious").

At the start of Suzuki's 1939 Japanese publication titled *Mushin to iu koto* or "On the Unconscious," he asserts:

> I think that *mushin* (no-mind/the Unconscious) forms the core of Buddhist thought and is the pivot of the Oriental spiritual civilization.... One may recognize that what distinguishes the West from the East is that in the West, there is no *mushin,* and that in the East there is. Or rather: I propose that among the items that distinguishes the eastern spirit and thought from their western equivalents, *mushin* has a definite place. This is why I would like to explain it to westerners. (M, i)

In this work Suzuki interprets Zen *mushin* or no-mind in psychological terms as *muishiki* (無意識), the standard Japanese word for "the unconscious" (M, 196–197). Again, in this same work Suzuki explains *mushin* by means of another Japanese term, *mujikaku* (無自覚), or the unconscious, and *mujikakusei* (無自覚性), unconsciousness or unawareness (M, 191–197). According to Suzuki, what distinguishes Japanese spirituality from the West is that it based on satori as sudden awakening to *mushin* or no-mind as the Unconscious. Suzuki thus regarded *mushin* as the core teaching of Zen Buddhism and undertook as his lifelong mission the task of spreading this Zen doctrine of *mushin* or no-mind as the cosmic Unconscious to the West.

Suzuki's treatise interprets *mushin* or no-mind from three perspectives: the psychological, the ethical, and the religious. The psychological explains *mushin* in terms of the Buddhist notion of *muga* (無我) or nonego, comprehended as unconsciousness. The second type of *mushin* explains the altruistic moral aspect, whereby the Buddhist theory of no-mind or no-self means to remove all selfishness and egoism. The third type of Zen *mushin* is the religious aspect of acting spontaneously without conscious effort, conscious awareness, and conscious intention, which in Pure Land Buddhist terms means to abandon self-power for the Other-power grace of Amida Buddha and in Christian terms is to abandon self-will so as to act in accordance with God's will (M, 39). Zen, Pure Land Buddhism, Christianity, and other religions all involve "receptivity" (*judōsei*, 受動性) or openness to the unconscious Other-power grace for salvation/enlightenment. Although in this work Suzuki does not extensively analyze *mushin* or the Unconscious from an aesthetic point of view, at the outset he cites a poem about the beauty of nature by Tao Yuanming (365–427), a Chinese poet influenced by Confucianism, Daoism, and Buddhism. A verse from Tao

Yuanming's poem "Returning Home" reads as follows: "An aimless cloud rises from the peaks. A bird, wary of flying, knows it is time to return home" (M, 5). In his discussion of this poem, Suzuki focuses on the meaning of "aimless cloud," or "cloud of no intention" (J. *unmushin*, 雲無心). A cloud aimlessly floating in the sky is characterized by *mushin* (C. *wuxin*) or no-mind, moving without any conscious intention or rational deliberation, thereby to wander freely, naturally, spontaneously, and unconsciously.

In chapter 6 ("The Experience of *Mushin*," M, 199–214), Suzuki explains *mushin* or no-mind as "the Unconscious" (*muishiki*, 無意識) through a detailed analysis of Yogacara Buddhism, with its depth psychology of the mind organized into eight successive layers, the deepest layer of which is the ālaya-vijñāna (J. *araya-shiki*) or "storehouse consciousness" (*zōshiki*, 蔵識), here explicitly formulated as the subliminal awareness underlying all operations of the body and mind. Moreover, Suzuki alternately explains *mushin* using the Japanese term *mujikaku* (無自覚) or "unconscious," as well as *mujikakusei* (無自覚性) and *mujikakumen* (無自覚面) signifying "unconsciousness" or "unawareness" (M, 191–197). Alongside the kanji characters for *muishiki*, he sometimes writes "unconscious" in katakana script (無意識, アンコンシャス) (M, 192) just as alongside the terms *mujikakusei* and *mujikakumen*, he also sometimes writes "unconsciousness" in katakana (無自覚面, アンコンシャスネス) (M, 193). To briefly summarize part of this discussion, he tells us that the first layer of the upper phase of the mind is called the "five consciousnesses" (五識), which perceives the five senses of sight, sound, smell, taste, and touch. According to the Consciousness-only school (*Yuishiki-ha*, 唯識派) of Yogacara Buddhism, *mano-vijñāna* is the intellectual center that supervises the five sense consciousnesses. There is another layer of consciousness beneath the *mano-vijñāna*, termed *manas* (末那識), which posits the fictional "self" (自分, 我). Beneath *manas* is the deeper unconscious level of mind called the *araya-shiki*. The level of *manas* establishing attachment to our false ego-self is pivotal insofar as it has two sides, one side directed toward consciousness and the other directed toward unconsciousness: "The 'self' 我 overlaps both the conscious (*yuishiki*, 有意識) and the unconscious (*muishiki*, 無意識)" (M, 192). He explains: "*Manas* 末那識 is endowed with both consciousness and unconsciousness. Accordingly, one aspect is connected to the five senses; and the other is sunk into the world of nothingness of *araya-shiki*" (一面は、阿頼耶識の無の世界に没入している) (M, 194). Suzuki here refers to the Yogacara Buddhist notion of the *araya-shiki* as "consciousness sunk into nothingness" (*mumotsushiki*, 無没識). He further emphasizes that realization of *araya-shiki* or the Unconscious in its spacelike void aspect as emptiness or nothingness is based on the Perfection of Wisdom (J. *Hannya no chie*, 般若の智慧) teachings expounded by Prajnaparamita literature (M, 197–202). Suzuki tells us: "By using the perfection of wisdom, it starts to enable us to shift from consciousness to unconsciousness" (M, 195). Like Nishida's concept of *basho* (topos) as the spatial locus, field or place of absolute nothingness, Suzuki describes the Unconscious as a vast and boundless "space" (*kūkan*, 空間) encompassing ordinary consciousness: "If I illustrate the human mind as space, this area of the unconscious would be wider or deeper than the area of consciousness" (M, 193). Finally, at its widest and deepest level, *araya-shiki* is recognized as the storehouse of "light" (*kōmyō*, 光明) (M, 197–199). In Yogacara Buddhism, then, liberation is attained when the darkness of *araya-shiki* at the bottom of the unconscious is purified of all karmic dispositions, whereupon it reveals the storehouse of infinite clear light as *ādarśana jñāna* or "great mirror knowing" (J. *daienkyochi*, 大円鏡智), the illuminated wisdom of spacelike transparent dharmakaya emptiness that like a great round mirror functions to clearly reflect all things just as they are in their emptiness-suchness.

The Unconscious as Ordinary Mind

Above it has been shown how for Suzuki the apex of Zen is satori or enlightenment, and that in psychological terms, satori makes the Unconscious conscious in superconsciousness. Moreover, drawing from his extensive translations of various Mahayana Buddhist texts, he interprets the Unconscious in terms of Zen no-mind, Prajnaparamita emptiness, Kegon interpenetration of part and whole visualized as Indra's net, and the Yogacara storehouse consciousness as our subliminal mind emptied of all karmic dispositions. He goes on to integrate these doctrines in the central Zen teaching that "ordinary mind is the Way," whereupon no-mind as the cosmic Unconscious is identified with the ordinary mind of everyday life. Hence, while the Zen satori experience of awakening to the cosmic Unconscious is characterized in negative terms as "no-mindedness" (SZIP, 183), or "empty-mindedness" (ZJC, 181), if articulated in positive terms, "Zen is our 'ordinary mindedness'" (ZB, 154).

According to Suzuki, Indian Buddhism was "other-worldly" or directed toward transcendence, whereas Chinese Buddhism, due to its transformation by Confucianism and Daoism, was *this*-worldly in its orientation, thus to be directed toward immanence. The Chinese traditions of Confucianism, Daoism, and Buddhism therefore all emphasized the unity of Dao and everyday life: "While the Chinese mind was profoundly stimulated by the Indian way of thinking . . . it never neglected the practical side of our daily life" (ZJC, 3). Suzuki makes reference to the Zen/Chan saying, "the Tao is no more than one's everyday life experience" (ZJC, 11). In this context he cites the Confucian teachings of Mencius (J. Mōshi, 372–289 BC): "The Tao is near and people seek it far away. . . . This means that the Tao is our everyday life itself" (ZJC, 11). He then dispels the erroneous view that this reduces Dao to mundane existence devoid of spiritual and moral aspects (ZJC, 11). According to the philosophical psychology of Suzuki, then, Zen/Chan Buddhism, Daoism, and Confucianism all proclaim the inseparability of Dao with ordinary events, and Dao is the cosmic Unconscious as it spontaneously functions in nature and everyday life.

In contrast to the monastic life of Indian Buddhist monks, in the Chan Buddhist temples of China, "all members were equally to engage in manual labor" (ZJC, 4). As a result of this cultural attitude of "practical-mindedness" (ZJC, 5), the exercise of focusing attention during everyday manual labor was cultivated throughout the Chan/Zen monasteries of China and Japan. Zen mindfulness exercises such as concentrated attention on koans were practiced not only while sitting in the meditation hall but during ordinary tasks of daily life such as cooking, eating, washing, and sweeping. In this context Suzuki cites the words of "Hō Koji" (P'ang Chü-shih), a Zen lay practitioner of the eighth century, who declares: "How wondrous this, how mysterious! I carry fuel, I draw water" (ZJC, 16). Suzuki comments that Zen practice during manual labor is calm abiding in the ordinary mind that chops wood and carries water yet remains nonattached, empty, and awake at each moment of daily life.

For Suzuki the *summum bonum* of Zen is satori awakening to no-mind or the cosmic Unconscious as prajna-intuition of emptiness disclosed by ordinary events. In terms of its language, the Zen concepts of no-mind, no-thought, no-self, unconsciousness, and emptiness suggest a doctrine of nihilism. But at the same time Suzuki refutes the view that Zen is nihilistic: "Nihilism is not Zen" (AIZB, 68). The antinihilistic character of Zen is seen by the fact that Zen *mushin* (無心) or "no mind" is a negative term for what in its positive aspect is expressed as *heijōshin* (平常心), "ordinary mind" or "everyday mind." Zen *mushin* as no-mind or the Unconscious is not a life-denying nihilism but is wholly life-affirming in its natural operation as *heijōshin* or "ordinary mind." In Suzuki's words: "'To be of no-mind' (*mushin*) means the 'everyday mind' (*heijō-shin*)" (ZJC, 147). According to Suzuki's philosophical psychology, Zen no-mind or the Unconscious in its aspect as ordinary mind is the deeper subliminal awareness working beyond the edge of consciousness that sustains all bodily functions during all of the common activities of daily experience. Moreover, to perform these daily activities in no-mind or the Unconscious in its aspect as the ordinary mind is to function naturally, automatically, and spontaneously, without conscious effort.

While discussing Zen no-mind or the Unconscious in its positive aspect as everyday mind, Suzuki cites the words of Pen-hsien (941–1008), who counters the nihilistic tendencies of quietism by teaching that Zen enlightenment is "'your everyday thought,' of 'sleeping when tired and eating when hungry,' of 'sipping tea which is offered to you, of responding 'yes' when called to; that is to say, of following the dictates of the Unconscious" (ZDNM, 111). Further explaining how these common Zen sayings express no-mind or the cosmic Unconscious as everyday mind: "'When I feel sleepy, I sleep; when I want to sit, I sit.' Or: 'When hungry I eat, when tired, I sleep. . . .' Are these not our everyday acts, acts done naturally, instinctively, effortlessly, and unconsciously?" (ZDNM, 106–107). Again: "Do we not also here have tidings of 'your everyday thought which is the Tao'? Do we not trace here the working of the Unconscious which responds almost 'instinctively' to the requirements of the occasion?" (ZDNM,

110). In this context, the cosmic Unconscious as "ordinary mind" corresponds to what in modern neuroscience is termed the autonomic nervous system that normally operates beneath the threshold of awareness to regulate all bodily functions such as respiration, blood pressure, digestion, heartbeat, and body temperature but which, through Zen meditation, can become fully conscious in satori as superconsciousness.

Explaining the *locus classicus* for the Zen doctrine of "ordinary mind," Suzuki often makes reference to the encounter dialogue between Nanquan/Nan-ch'uan (J. Nansen) and Zhaozhou/Chao-chou (J. Jōshū) as recorded in case 19 from the *Gateless Barrier* (J. *Mumonkan*, 無門関): "When Chao-chou came to study Zen under Nan-ch'uan, he asked, 'What is the Tao (or the Way)' Nan-ch'uan replied, 'your everyday mind, that is the Tao'" (ZB, 160). For Suzuki this koan proclaims the fundamental doctrine characterizing Zen/Chan Buddhism: "Ordinary mind is the Way," or "everyday mind is Dao" (J. *heijōshin kore dō/byōjōshin kore dō*, 平常心是道).

Just as Suzuki expounds the Zen teaching that "everyday mind is Dao," so he explicitly identifies *Dao* (道) with "the Unconscious."

> Consciousness was awakened from the unconscious sometimes in the course of evolution. . . . Consciousness is a leap, but the leap cannot mean a disconnection in its physical sense. For consciousness is in constant, uninterrupted communion with the unconscious. Indeed, without the latter the former could not function; it would lose its basis of operation. This is the reason that the Tao is "one's everyday mind." By Tao, Zen of course means the unconscious, which works all the time in our consciousness. (ZP, 18)

For Suzuki, the Dao as the spontaneous creative flow of Nature is expressed through the Daoist *wuwei* or nonaction of Laozi, and *wuwei* is to be identified with Zen *mushin* or no-mind as the cosmic Unconscious: "In one sense the Laotsuan teaching of Non-action (*wu-wei*) may be said to be living in the Unconscious of Hui-neng" (EZB III, 18). Suzuki affirms this connection between *wuxin* or "no-mind" and *wuwei* or "nonaction" in their Chan/Zen-Daoist meaning as "effortless naturalness," but in psychological terms, he interprets these notions as "the Unconscious." Thus, in the modern psychologized Zen of Suzuki, our everyday mind is Dao, and Dao is the cosmic Unconscious. Furthermore, Zen *mushin* or no-mind and Daoist *wuwei* or nonaction are identified with ordinary actions springing from the cosmic Unconscious thereby to be performed naturally, instinctively, effortlessly, and unconsciously.

For Suzuki, the koan practice of Rinzai Zen culminates in an illumination of the quotidian: "The object of Zen training consists in making us realize that Zen is our daily experience" (ZJC, 13). In the Rinzai Zen of Suzuki, the aim of Zen is to experience satori, and satori is an awakening of consciousness to no-mind or the Unconscious, which is itself the ordinary mind of our everyday life. He cites a famous public case record from Rinzai Zen koan teachings: "Jōshū Jūshin (778–897) was once asked by a monk, 'What is my Self?' Jōshū said, 'Have you finished the morning gruel?' 'Yes, I have finished.' Jōshū then told him, 'If so, wash your bowl'" (ZP, 29). Suzuki further clarifies how the recurrent pattern of koans is that students ask a question, such as "what is Dao?" Although they expect to receive an abstract, metaphysical, or speculative answer, instead the Zen master points to some concrete, particular event in the qualitative immediacy of its emptiness-suchness, thereby to show how no-mind or the Unconscious functions as ordinary mind in daily experience: "Both in Te-Shan and Huang-Po, Zen is taught to be something in direct contact with our daily life, there are no speculations soaring heavenward, no abstractions. . . . Facts of daily experience are taken as they come to us, and from them a state of no-mind-ness is extracted. . . . The Unconscious, the recognition of which makes up *mushin*, lines every experience which we have through the senses and thoughts" (ZDNM, 132). He adds:

> These passages are enough to show the Zen masters' attitude toward the so-called metaphysical or theological questions. . . . They never resort to discussions of a highly abstract nature, but respect their daily experiences which are ordinarily grounded under the "seen, heard, thought, and known." Their idea is that in our "everyday thought" (*ping-chang-hsin*) the Unconscious is to be comprehended, if at all, for there is no intermediary between it and what we term "the seen heard, thought, and known." Every act of the latter is lined with the Unconscious. (ZDNM, 137; ZB, 266–267)

In the quotation above, Suzuki hence sums up what he regards to be the quintessential teaching of the foremost Rinzai Zen masters in the lineage of Huineng: "Their idea is that in our 'everyday thought' (*ping-chang-hsin*) the Unconscious is to be comprehended" (ZDNM, 137).

Suzuki analyzes an encounter dialogue about Zen master Unmon (Yunmen, 864–949) from the *Blue Cliff Records* (Hekiganroku, case 6) that cultivates satori experience of no-mind or the Unconscious as the ordinary mind of everyday life. In this koan, Unmon gave a sermon: "As to what precedes the fifteenth, I have nothing to ask you about; but when the fifteen is over, let me have from you one statement [expressing the ultimate truth of Buddhism]" (SWS I, 95; brackets in original). The first fifteen days of the month are prior to satori, and Unmon asks for "one statement" (*ikku*, 一句) to express the realization of Zen after satori awakening. No monk came forward to venture an answer. Thereupon the master gave his own statement: "Everyday is a fine day" (SWS I, 95). Unmon's proclamation, "Everyday is a fine day" (*nichi nichi kore kō jitsu*, 日日是好日), is one of the most universally acclaimed sayings not only by Zen monks but also by tea masters, artists, craftsmen, and others who devote themselves to being fully present, open, and awake at each moment of everyday life through tranquil abiding in no-mind as the cosmic Unconscious.

An illuminating example of Zen no-mind or the Unconscious as the ordinary mind of everyday life is given by Suzuki in his account of Chao-pien, a government official of the Sung dynasty, who was also a lay disciple of a Chan/Zen master. Chao-pien records his experience of sudden enlightenment while performing routine work at the office (ZB, 124). Suzuki remarks: "Satori is experienced in connection with any ordinary occurrence in one's daily life" (ZB, 125). Adding his psychological view of Zen enlightenment: "Satori is to realize the Unconscious" (ZB, 126). Moreover, he clarifies that while the Avatamsaka (Kegon/Huayan) texts of Indian Buddhism record astonishing visions of multitudinous interpenetrating phenomena radiating infinite light that shines with resplendent brilliance throughout the cosmos, Zen describes satori as triggered by the plain, ordinary, and everyday moments of commonplace existence: "But the Zen feeling of exaltation is rather a quiet feeling of self-contentment, it is not at all demonstrative when the first glow of it passes away. The Unconscious does not proclaim itself so boisterously in the Zen consciousness" (ZB, 126).

In *The Awakening of Zen* Suzuki employs Kegon metaphysics of interpenetration between many and one to analyze Zen satori as awakening to the cosmic Unconscious in superconsciousness or unconscious consciousness as realized in daily existence: "For this reason our consciousness of change and impermanence is deeply interfused with an unconscious consciousness of eternity, unchangeability or timelessness. This interfusion of consciousness and unconsciousness or, in Buddhist terminology, of the Many and the One, or Form (*rūpam*) and Emptiness (*śūnyatā*), the Distinction (or Discrimination) and Non-distinction (or Non-discrimination) is, we can say, the philosophy of Zen" (AZ, 36). Suzuki here explains the notion of Zen satori as superconsciousness in terms of the "interfusion of consciousness and unconsciousness," which he then identifies with Kegon/Huayan (Avatamsaka) Buddhist "interpenetration of Many and One." Furthermore, this unobstructed interfusion of consciousness and unconsciousness, many and one, or discrimination and nondiscrimination, is realized in Zen satori as awakening to superconsciousness in the midst of ordinary, everyday life: "It [superconsciousness] is indeed so interfused with our psychological consciousness that we are utterly unconscious of its presence. It requires certain spiritual training to be awakened to it, and it is Zen that has for the first time in the world history of mental evolution pointed out this fact. In a word, it is Zen that has become aware of the truth of superconsciousness in connection with the most commonplace doings in our daily life" (AZ, 40). In ordinary experience our Buddha nature as prajna wisdom of sunyata or emptiness is always unconsciously functioning in the nonarticulated metaphysical background surrounding all objects articulated in the foreground, and it is through Zen training that one becomes aware of this encompassing background field of emptiness or absolute nothingness in satori as superconsciousness. He continues: "People generally conceive of things spiritual as going beyond our prosaic everyday experience. But the plainest truth is that everything we experience is saturated, interfused, interpenetrated with spiritual signification, and for this reason my handling the lute, my standing in the snow, my feeling hungry or thirsty after a hard day's work, is surcharged with superconsciousness, with unconscious consciousness" (AZ, 40). He adds: "The superconsciousness which is possessed by every human being as long as he is created in God's image cannot be separable from the relative sensuous consciousness which performs most useful functions in this world of particulars. The superconsciousness must be thoroughly and in the most perfect manner interfused with the one in daily use: otherwise the superconsciousness cannot be of any significance to us" (AZ, 40).

In Suzuki's philosophical psychology, the Zen concept of no-mind or the cosmic Unconscious as the ordinary mind of everyday life is also derived from the Chan/Zen teachings of Mazu Daoyi (709–788) and his lineage of successors, including Baizhang Huaihai (720–814), Nanquan Puyuan (ca. 749–835), Zhaozhou Congshen (778–897), Huangbo Xiyun (d. 850), and Linji Yixuan (d. 866). This line of great Chan masters running through Mazu to Linji taught that "ordinary mind is the Way" (C. *pingchangxin shi dao*), according to which "ordinary mind" is understood as the natural, uncontrived, and spontaneous mind that functions unconsciously with effortless naturalness in daily life, whether sitting, standing, walking and reclining, or while responding to every situation as needed. In his essay "D. T. Suzuki's Notion of 'Person,'" Sueki Fumihiko explains Suzuki's idea of "the Person" as the "supra-individual Person" that is also "one individual person." Sueki further clarifies how Suzuki's idea of the true self or Person is especially influenced by the Chan/Zen teachings of Linji (J. Rinzai) as expounded in the *Record of Linji* (C. Linjilu; J. Rinzairoku): "Suzuki identified the 'Person' or true self as comprising the fundamental thought of the *Linjilu*" (2016, 16). Linji describes the Person by such terms as "doing nothing" (C. *wushi*; J. *buji*, 無事), or in the words of Mazu (J. Baso, 709–788), "ordinary mind is the path" (C. *pingchangxin shi dao*; J. *byōjōshin kore dō*, 平常心是道) (2016, 19). In the Chan/Zen Buddhist lineage of Mazu and Linji, the Person is further characterized by the phrase "ordinary doing nothing" (C. *pingchang wushi*; J. *byōjō buji*, 平常無事). For Mazu and Linji, the true self or authentic Person is one who makes no conscious effort but is just ordinary and everyday. Moreover, this Person of the ordinary and everyday is what Linji calls "the true person of no rank" (C. *yi wuwei zhenren*; J. *ichi mui shinnin*, 一無位真人). Summing up Linji's Chan/Zen teachings as assimilated into Suzuki's thought, Sueki writes: "Linji belonged to Mazu's lineage. In fact, Linji frequently spoke of 'doing nothing' and 'ordinariness.' For example, he said, 'As to the Buddhadharma, no effort is necessary. You have only to be ordinary, with nothing to do — defecating, urinating, wearing clothes, eating food, and lying down when tired,' asserting that there is no Buddhadharma outside of everyday life" (2016, 23).

In Sueki's analysis, Suzuki's Zen concept of the supra-individual Person as ordinary and everyday also contains elements of Shin Buddhism as expounded in the Pure Land teachings of Shinran: "We could say that in the case of Shinran, the 'supra-individual Person' is expressed in the context of the individual who is an ordinary being (or *bonbu* 凡夫), and in the case of Linji that the 'genuine individual' is expressed in living in the 'supra-individual,' having gone beyond the self" (2016, 12). For Suzuki, the selfless state of the *bonbu* or "ordinary being" is what Shinran refers to as one who abides in *jinen hōni* (自然法爾) or "naturalness," which is itself a spontaneous function of the "Other-power" (*tariki*, 他力) of Amida, the compassionate Buddha of infinite light. Moreover, for Suzuki the paradigm of a *bonbu* or "ordinary being" who without conscious effort lives in accordance with the naturalness of Amida Buddha's Other-power grace is the *myōkōnin*, (妙好人), the "wonderful good person" of Shin Pure Land Buddhist tradition that lives a simple and ordinary life of faith while continuously abiding in an ecstatic blissful state of *nembutsu-samādhi*.

Suzuki maintains that Linji's ordinary and everyday self of no rank is an authentically existing Person who is both individual and supra-individual and therefore an integration of consciousness and cosmic Unconsciousness. His understanding of Linji's individual/supra-individual Person as a unity of consciousness and cosmic Unconsciousness is explained by the Kyoto School philosopher Abe Masao: "Suzuki characterizes this 'Person' as absolute Subjectivity, '*reiseiteki jikaku*' [spiritual self-awareness]', 'the Cosmic Unconsciousness or *prajñā*-intuition'" (1985, 73). Again, "Suzuki emphasizes that Lin-chi's 'Person' is supra-individual as well as individual. 'Person' is supra-individual because Lin-chi's 'Person is identical with 'Emptiness', 'Seeing', or to use Suzuki's terminology, 'Cosmic Unconsciousness'" (1985, 75). Abe continues:

> "Person" has two aspects — one exists as a finite individual, and at the same time, one is a "bottomless abyss". The bottomless abyss is, needless to say, "Emptiness", "Void" or "Cosmic Unconsciousness" which is supra-individual. One often mistakes Emptiness, Void or Cosmic Unconsciousness as something separated from an individual existence. . . . The supra-individual Emptiness or Cosmic Unconsciousness cannot manifest itself directly unless it materializes in an individual existence. On the other hand, an individual existence is really individual only insofar as the supra-individual Emptiness or Cosmic Unconsciousness manifests itself in and through it. Lin-chi's "Person" is nothing but a living individual who is always (therefore, right here and right now) Emptiness, Cosmic Unconsciousness or Seeing. In other words, the living non-duality of the individual and the supra-individual is "Person". (1985, 75)

In Suzuki's psychological account of Linji's Chan/Zen Buddhism, the authentic Person is not just individual consciousness but also supra-individual emptiness of the cosmic Unconscious. According to Suzuki, then, Linji's true self of no rank that makes no conscious effort but is just ordinary and everyday is the single individual that is also a supra-individual Person, thus to be a paradoxical identity of consciousness and unconsciousness in the cosmic Unconscious as superconsciousness.

It has now been seen how for Suzuki, the fundamental Chan/Zen koan teaching in the encounter dialogue between Nanquan (J. Nansen) and Zhaozhou (J. Jōshū) as recorded by case 19 of the *Gateless Barrier*, as well as the noble Chan/Zen line from Mazu to Linji, is that "ordinary mind is the Dao," or "everyday mind is the Way." However, while Zen enlightenment in its final stages is characterized by a return to the ordinary and everyday, it is not the ordinary as trivial, insignificant, or meaningless, but the ordinary as transfigured into something extraordinary, wondrous, and profound. Another saying of Zen is "the ordinary is extraordinary" (*heibon wa hibon de aru*, 平凡は非凡である). In Suzuki's words: "'Extraordinary' does not mean supernatural or miraculous. When true understanding is attained, the ordinaries transform themselves into extraordinaries" (AZ, 64, fn. 4). For Suzuki, then, Zen satori is a sudden awakening to *mushin* or no-mind as the cosmic Unconscious of absolute nothingness in its natural function as *heijōshin* or the ordinary mind of everyday life, whereupon Zen becomes a joyous celebration of the wonder of the ordinary as extraordinary.

Suzuki's view of Zen no-mind or the cosmic Unconscious as the ordinary mind of everyday life is conveyed by Alan Watts in *The Way of Zen*, where he reports how on one occasion Suzuki described his own experience of Zen satori: "Professor D. T. Suzuki was once asked how it feels to have attained satori, the Zen experience of 'awakening,' he answered, 'Just like ordinary everyday experience, except about two inches off the ground!'" (1989, 22).

Suzuki's Zen Map of the Unconscious

Having examined Suzuki's Zen concept of the Unconscious in its multivariate aspects, we can now outline his Zen "map" of the Unconscious. Suzuki's cartography of the human psyche is here referred to as his Zen map of "the Unconscious," because of his view that *wuxin/wu-hsin* (J. *mushin*) as the cosmic Unconscious is the basis for *all* psychosomatic operations of human bodymind experience: "*Wu-hsin* is 'unconsciousness' in its ordinary, empirical sense, and at the same time it means the Unconscious as underlying all our activities mental and bodily, conscious and unconscious" (EZB III, 8–9, fn. 3).

Suzuki's Zen map of the human mind is a multi-layered spectrum, including (1) consciousness; (2) semiconsciousness; (3) the unconscious; (4) the collective unconscious; and (5) the cosmic Unconscious. Although the following is a single passage from Suzuki's *Zen and Japanese Culture*, for the sake of clarification I have provided numbers and headings from this section of his work, followed by a depiction of Suzuki's topographical map of the Unconscious with a schematic diagram:

I. Consciousness:

The human mind can be considered to be made up, as it were, of several layers of consciousness, from a dualistically constructed consciousness down to the Unconscious. The first layer is where we generally move; everything here is dualistically set up, polarization is the principle of this stratum. (ZJC, 242)

II. Semi-consciousness:

The next layer below is the semiconscious plane; things deposited here can be brought up to full consciousness any time they are wanted; it is the stratum of memory. (ZJC, 242)

III. The Unconscious:

The third layer is the Unconscious, as it is ordinarily termed by the psychologist; memories lost since time immemorial are stored up here. (ZJC, 242)

IV. The Collective Unconscious:

This unconscious layer of the mind is not the last layer; there is still another which is really the bedrock of our personality, and may be called "collective unconscious," corresponding somewhat to the Buddhist idea of ālayavijñāna, that is, "the all-conserving consciousness." The existence of this *vijñāna* or unconscious may not be experimentally demonstrated, but the assumption of it is necessary to explain the general fact of consciousness. (ZJC, 242)

V. The Cosmic Unconscious:

Psychologically speaking, this ālayavijñāna or "collective unconscious" may be regarded as the basis of our mental life; but when we wish to open up the secrets of the artistic or religious life we must have what may be designated "Cosmic Unconscious." The Cosmic Unconscious is the principle of creativity. . . . All creative works of art, the lives and aspirations of religious people, the spirit of inquiry moving the philosophers – all those come from the fountainhead of the

Cosmic Unconscious, which is really the store-house (ālaya) of possibilities. (ZJC, 242–243)

Suzuki's cartography of the human mind can be illustrated with a triangle-shaped diagram based on the familiar "iceberg model" of Western psychology, where ego-consciousness is depicted as the tip of an iceberg above the surface of the ocean, while beneath the surface are multiple levels of unconsciousness. In Suzuki's Zen map of the human psyche, however, there is an additional layer revealing a wider, larger, and deeper layer of the subliminal mind: namely, the cosmic Unconscious. Beyond the "personal unconscious" of Freudian psychoanalysis, and the "collective unconsciousness" of Jungian analytical psychology, Suzuki posits the "cosmic Unconscious" of Zen Buddhism. Finally, in Zen satori one becomes fully conscious of all layers of the unconscious psyche, down to the bottomless abyss of the cosmic Unconscious, in what Suzuki terms *super*consciousness: "Psychologically speaking, *satori* is super-consciousness, or consciousness of the Unconscious" (AZL, 62; LZ, 88).

As shown in the schematic diagram in Fig. 1.2, the first layer in Suzuki's map is (1) "Consciousness," designating the state of waking consciousness as characterized by ego-centeredness, mental discrimination, and subject-object dichotomy. According to Suzuki, it is this bifurcation of Mind into subject

Figure 1.2. Levels of mind from the cosmic unconscious to consciousness. *Source*: Created by the author.

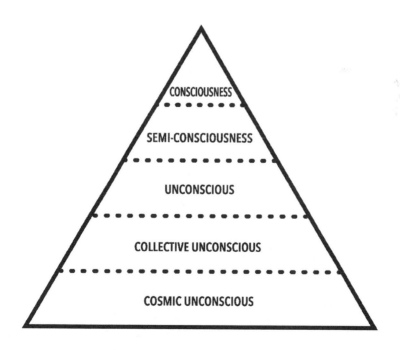

and object or seer and seen that establishes dualistic "consciousness," while the more subtle levels of awareness fall into the sleep of unconsciousness; (2) "Semi-consciousness" is similar to Freud's preconscious, where information stored beneath the threshold of awareness can be retrieved by an act of will; (3) the "Unconscious" corresponds to Freud's personal unconscious as the level of repressed instincts, forbidden desires, and traumatic memories that are prevented from surfacing into consciousness through the censorship of defense mechanisms; (4) the "Collective unconscious" directly refers to Jung's collective unconscious as the *mundus imaginalis* or imaginal realm, the reservoir of archetype images inherited from the past that organize experience into numinous patterns; and (5) the "Cosmic Unconscious" of Zen Buddhism, which Suzuki identifies as prajna-intuition of emptiness or absolute nothingness. The cosmic Unconscious as articulated by Suzuki is not merely subjective or psychical but now becomes an integrated psycho-cosmic homologization wherein the internal self merges with external nature and the universe as a microcosm of the macrocosm. Hence, in Suzuki's Zen map of the human psyche, there is a gradual expansion from the individual to the collective to the cosmic dimensions of the unconscious mind. Suzuki tells us: "The Cosmic Unconscious is the principle of creativity," adding that as absolute nothingness, it is the ultimate source of inexhaustible creative potentiality functioning as the basis for all Zen art, religion, and philosophy. Moreover, in Suzuki's philosophical psychology the Jungian collective unconscious is identified with the Yogacara Buddhist notion of *ālaya-vijñāna* in its impure aspect as the "storehouse" perfumed by karmic defilements, while the cosmic Unconscious corresponds with the Yogacara Buddhist storehouse after it has been purified of all karmically inherited predispositions and transformed into *ādarśana jñāna* or the all-illuminating "great mirror wisdom" of dharmakaya emptiness (ZJC, 165, fn. 18). Again, the cosmic Unconscious is the deepest level of mind beyond the *ālaya-vijñāna* when it is cleansed of all habitual karmic tendencies whereupon it becomes *mumotsushiki*, "consciousness sunk into nothingness." In the map, the various levels of the psyche are only divided with broken lines, thereby indicating how each level is porous, open, and permeable, thus to interpenetrate with all the other layers within the total undivided bodymind continuum. As said by Suzuki himself while describing another diagram representing his map of the human psyche: "Throughout the whole figure there runs a line of demarcation setting the Conscious against the Unconscious, but in Self-nature itself there is no such distinction" (ZDNM, 143). It should further be emphasized that in Suzuki's Zen map of the psyche, semiconsciousness, the personal unconscious, the collective unconscious, and the cosmic Unconscious, are said to be "unconscious" only because they have not yet been integrated with consciousness. When at the moment of satori awakening, the contents of the Unconscious are fully assimilated into consciousness, the "conscious/unconscious" distinction is eradicated, whereupon the mind becomes "transparent" to itself in supraconsciousness, all out in the open with nothing hidden.

Elsewhere, Suzuki again describes his transpersonal Zen map of the human psyche as a multilevel spectrum, which descends even below Jung's collective unconscious, finally reaching down to the *mushin* or no-mind as the cosmic Unconscious: "To reach the bedrock of one's being means to have one's Unconscious entirely cleansed of egoism, for the ego penetrates even the Unconscious so-called. Not the 'Collective Unconscious' but the 'Cosmic Unconscious' must be made to reveal itself unreservedly. This is why Zen so emphasizes the significance of 'no-mind' (*mushin*) or 'no-thought' (*munen*), where we find infinite treasures well preserved" (ZJC, 226). Using his geological metaphor of the "bedrock" of the cosmic Unconscious as prajna-intuition of emptiness, Suzuki proclaims: "The highest act of our consciousness is indeed to penetrate all the conceptual deposits and reach the bedrock of Prajñā the Unconscious" (ZDNM 154). Suzuki again briefly adumbrates his map of the Unconscious while further summing up his Zen Buddhist depth psychology: "The function of human consciousness, as I see it, is to dive deeper and deeper into its source, the unconscious. And the unconscious has its strata of variable depths: biological, psychological, and metaphysical. One thread runs through them, and Zen discipline consists in taking hold of it in its entirety, whereas other arts, such as swordsmanship or tea, lead us to the comprehension of respectively particularized aspects of the string" (ZJC, 143, fn. 3). According to Suzuki, "consciousness rises from an unconscious source" (OIMB, 171). In his psychological interpretation of Zen Buddhism, Suzuki maintains that the aim of human consciousness is to descend ever deeper into its ground, source, and origin in the cosmic Unconscious. For Suzuki the cosmic Unconscious is primordial awareness of dharmakaya emptiness or the spacelike transparent openness of absolute nothingness. Within this continuum of the cosmic Unconscious, however, Suzuki distinguishes "particularized aspects" of the Unconscious (ZJC, 143, fn. 3). The Zen art of swordsmanship based on *mushin* or no-mind reaches down to the "instinctual Unconscious" (ZJC, 199) as a particularized aspect of the cosmic Unconscious to explicate the spontaneous, lightening-fast reaction of the samurai warrior to his life-and-death situation at any moment (ZJC, 199). When the samurai warrior enters *mushin* or no-mind in its particularized aspect as the *instinctual unconscious*, he "acts instinctually in response to what is presented to him. . . . His unconscious automatically takes care of the whole situation" (ZJC, 146). At another level, he distinguishes the particularized aspect of an *aesthetic unconscious*, or what he otherwise terms "the artistic aspect of the Unconscious" (ZJC, 226), comprehended as the fountainhead of unlimited creative possibilities and the source of all Zen-inspired arts. While no-mind as the instinctive unconscious of a samurai functions in battle, and no-mind as the aesthetic unconscious operates in the appreciation or creation of profound beauty in art, the awakened no-mind of the Zen unconscious pervades every aspect of daily life. Beyond the instinctual unconscious of the samurai, and the aesthetic unconscious of the artist, it is the fully enlightened Zen master alone who realizes satori and penetrates down to the bedrock layer of the cosmic

Unconscious as the bottomless abyss of absolute nothingness where emptiness and fullness are the same (ZJC, 226). Thus, for Suzuki the path of Zen attains to its *summum bonum* with the immediate experience of satori as awakening to our own deeper unconscious mind: "Satori is to realize the Unconscious" (EZB II, 21). In the philosophical psychology of Suzuki, then, while it is the reified Ego and its subject-object dualism that makes the Unconscious unconscious, it is the function of Zen practice to make the Unconscious conscious in satori as superconsciousness.

The Mu Koan and other Zen Meditation Techniques for Accessing the Unconscious

Suzuki not only develops a philosophical psychology of the Unconscious as primordial awareness of spacelike dharmakaya emptiness but also discusses Zen meditation techniques for directly accessing the Unconscious, especially Rinzai Zen koan practice. Suzuki's presentation of Zen to his Western audience was sectarian insofar as he promoted Rinzai Zen to the neglect of the Sōtō Zen tradition of Dōgen (1200–1253). Yet he does provide an analysis of Dōgen's teachings in his important essay "Dōgen, Hakuin, Bankei: Three Types of Thought in Japanese Zen" (SWS I, 68–93). In this essay, Suzuki's bias against Sōtō Zen is seen in his criticism of Dōgen's "silent illumination" (*mokushō*, 默照) method of "sitting-only" (*shikantaza*, 只管打坐) as a form of inactivity, quietism, and gradualism, revealing his clear sectarian preference for Hakuin's dynamic koan practice as the method of sudden enlightenment. For Suzuki the passive-receptive method of Dōgen's silent illumination technique of zazen meditation leads to mental dullness, whereas the active-concentrative method of Hakuin's koan practice results in satori as a sudden flash of noetic insight into the Unconscious.[15] In this context he discusses Hakuin's own experience of abrupt awakening through the koan method of one-pointed concentration on Mu (SWS I, 89). Elsewhere, however, Suzuki gives a more balanced presentation of the Rinzai and Sōtō Zen schools as complementary traditions (FZ, 95). Nonetheless, it will be seen that Suzuki is an advocate of Rinzai Zen koan practice, especially the *watō* technique of focusing on the keyword of a koan. Above all else, Suzuki promotes concentration of the whole bodymind upon the keyword "Mu!" in the lower abdomen as the shortcut method for realizing satori as a sudden breakthrough to the cosmic Unconscious in superconsciousness.

Mu and Zen Koan Practice

Although Suzuki's "satori Zen" puts the emphasis on satori or sudden enlightenment, the experience of satori and Zen koan practice are inseparable. As said by Victor Sōgen Hori: "Satori and koan are not two independent topics in Suzuki's account" (2016, 59). It is true that Suzuki emphasizes *prajñā* (wisdom) over *dhyāna* (meditation) in the sense that *prajñā* is itself the cosmic Unconscious in its natural function as seeing into nothingness, while *dhyāna* is an expedient means by which to realize the Unconscious. Nevertheless, it is clear that Suzuki follows Huineng in emphasizing the identity of dhyana meditation and prajna wisdom of emptiness and, thus, the simultaneity of practice and enlightenment. Moreover, in the tradition of Huineng's doctrine of sudden enlightenment, Suzuki's Rinzai Zen maintains that both dhyana meditation and prajna wisdom of emptiness are indistinguishable in the cosmic Unconscious. In Suzuki's own words: "Those who emphasize Prajñā, like Hui-neng, and his school, tend to identify Dhyāna with Prajñā, and insist on an abrupt, instantaneous awakening in the Unconscious. . . . According to Hui-neng's Prajñā school, Prajñā and Dhyāna become identical in the Unconscious" (ZDNM, 64–65). Suzuki rejects any dualism between koan practice as a "means" and satori or enlightenment as an "end." Following the nondual teachings of sudden enlightenment transmitted by Huineng and the Linji/Rinzai tradition of Chan/Zen Buddhism, Suzuki emphasizes that dhyana and prajna, or meditation and wisdom, are inseparable. Referring to the "essence-function" or "body-use" (C. *ti-yong*; J. *tai-yō*, 体用) doctrine to explain this nondual relationship between dhyana and prajna, Huineng is cited by Suzuki as proclaiming: "And, friends, do not be deceived and led to thinking that Dhyāna and Prajñā are separable. They are one, and not two. Dhyāna is the Body of Prajñā, and Prajñā is the Use of Dhyāna" (ZDNM, 46). Citing Huineng, Suzuki explains how based on the nondual "body-use" doctrine, meditation and enlightenment are as inseparable as a lamp and its light (ZDNM, 47).

According to Suzuki, the method of Rinzai Zen koan meditation is a practice whereby the emptiness-suchness of all things is not intellectually explained through the discursive reason of ego-consciousness but something directly shown or demonstrated through dynamic actions and performative utterances coming from out of the cosmic Unconscious.

> No one had ever thought that beating, kicking, and other rough methods of treatment would be accorded to the students. "Mere seeing" is gone, and acting has taken its place. . . . What has undergone change is the method used. The spirit is that of Huineng, who declares: "I establish no-thought-ness (*wu-nien*, the Unconscious) as the Principle. . . . This declaration is the foundation of Zen teaching. . . . Zen is most interested in psychology, in realizing the Unconscious. (ZDNM, 102)

According to Suzuki, then, Huineng declares that no-thought or no-mind as the Unconscious is the basic principle of Zen Buddhism. Moreover, at the level of practice, acts such as beating, kicking, and shouting function to awaken the student to the cosmic Unconscious.

Suzuki claims that Zen koans such as "Mu" have their origins in the cosmic Unconscious, so that it is by concentration upon koans that unconscious contents surface to consciousness in satori: "The koan is within ourselves, and what the Zen master does is no more than to point it out for us so that we can see it more plainly than before. When the koan is brought out of the unconscious to the field of consciousness, it is said to have been understood by us" (ZP, 44). Even though Suzuki often discusses the need to study koans with an authorized Zen master, at the same time, he warns against dependence on the teacher, such that concentration is directed toward the koan itself, the paradigm case of which is focusing on Mu: "In Zen this kind of relationship between master and pupil is rejected as not conducive to the enlightenment experience on the part of the pupil. For it is the koan '*Mu!*,' symbolizing the ultimate reality itself, and not the master, that will rise out of the pupil's unconscious" (ZP, 58). For Suzuki, then, latent koans such as Mu surface from the Unconscious during Zen practice, and it is by focusing on Mu that one achieves satori as opening to the Unconscious.

In *The Zen Koan as a Means of Attaining Enlightenment*, Suzuki describes the Zen practice of concentration on Mu and other koans in a psychological process involving three stages: the first stage is the effort to overcome subject-object dualism where *one is still conscious of the koan* as an external object; the second is an intermediate stage of samadhi concentration wherein *one is no longer conscious of being separate from the koan*; and third is the stage of Zen satori or enlightenment as *awakening to the Unconscious in everyday life*. We are told that when undertaking the practice of koan meditation,

> the time will come to you without your specifically seeking it when the mind attains a state of perfect concentration. That is to say, when you are sitting, you are not conscious of the fact; so with your walking or lying or standing, you are not at all conscious of what you are doing; nor are you aware of your whereabouts . . . the day is like the night and *vice versa*. But this is still midway to satori, and surely not satori itself. (ZKMA, 117)

Becoming one with the Mu koan at the second stage of samadhi is here described as a state of perfect concentration that is "midway to satori," in which the Zen practitioner is not conscious of the body, of sitting in meditation, or of the koan as an external object. After entering the unconscious trance state of samadhi concentration, however, one must break through to satori or enlightenment, thereby to become fully conscious of the cosmic Unconscious in super-consciousness.

At the conclusion of *The Training of the Zen Buddhist Monk*, Suzuki again interprets the practice of Mu and other koans in terms of his philosophical psychology of the Unconscious. The teachings of various Zen masters are here cited to further describe the role of unconsciousness in samadhi as a transitional state toward satori in the threefold process of Rinzai Zen koan meditation:

"When your mind is steadily and intensely and without interruptions on the koan, you will begin to be unconscious of your bodily existence, while the koan occupies the centre of your consciousness. At this stage, however, you have to be careful not to give up yourself to unconsciousness. . . . The time will come when together with the koan everything vanishes out of your mind including the mind itself" (TZBM, 108). Moreover, we are told, "keep this up until a state of satori breaks upon your consciousness" (TZBM, 109). To this is added the instructions for koan practice by another Zen master: "Keep this koan in your mind and never allow yourself to think that quietude or a state of unconsciousness is the *sine qua non* in your koan exercise" (TZBM, 109). The text continues:

> "The spirit of inquiry" so intensely working out its own way, there is no conscious effort on your part to continue the koan exercise. After a while even this is swept away, and you attain a state of unconsciousness in which there is neither the koan nor the one who holds it. This is what is known as the stage of objectlessness. Is it a final one? No, by no means. Says an ancient master: "Don't think the state of unconsciousness is the truth itself, for there is still another frontier-gate which is now to be broken through." (TZBM, 110)

The above instructions for Zen koan meditation conclude by saying that while in the trance state of unconsciousness, described as being without any conscious effort, and devoid of consciousness of oneself as a subject or of the koan as a separate object, there occurs an unexpected sound or sight that elicits a sudden breakthrough to satori, whereupon one bursts out into laughter (TZBM, 110).

Suzuki was a Zen Buddhist layman who trained according to the Rinzai koan method under two great Zen masters at Engakuji in Kamakura — Imakita Kōsen (1816–1892) and Shaku Sōen (1859–1919) — finally attaining his own breakthrough to satori with the Mu koan (SWS I, 209). In *The Gateless Gate*, "Jōshū's *Mu*" is the first koan or public case record that opens up the gateway of Zen and is widely regarded as the most important koan in Rinzai Zen. Suzuki tells about the origin of Jōshū's Mu koan, while also giving simple instructions on how to practice Mu:

> Jōshū Jūshin (778–897, Zhaozhou Congshen in Chinese) was one of the great Zen masters of the T'ang dynasty. He was asked once by a monk, "Has a dog the Buddha-nature?" Answered the master, "Mu!" "Mu!" (*wu*) literally means "no." But when used as a koan the meaning does not matter, it is simply "Mu." . . . The disciple is told to concentrate his mind on the meaningless sound "Mu!" regardless of whether it means "yes" or "no" . . . Just "Mu!" "Mu!" "Mu!" (SWS I, 167; ZP, 46)

In his autobiographical essay "Early Memories" Suzuki describes his own initial experience of satori during a *sesshin* or intensive meditation retreat at

Engakuji, while doing Rinzai Zen koan meditation focusing on the single word Mu (SWS I, 209–210):

> Up till then I had always been conscious that *Mu* was in my mind. But so long as *I* was conscious of *Mu* it meant that I was somehow separate from *Mu*, and that is not a true samadhi. But toward the end of that *sesshin*, about the fifth day, I ceased to be conscious of *Mu*. I was one with *Mu*, identified with *Mu*, so that there was no longer the separateness implied by being conscious of *Mu*. This is the real state of *samadhi*. (SWS I, 209; FZ, 10)

Suzuki goes on to say:

> I have no idea how long I was in that state of samadhi, but I was awakened from it by the sound of the bell. I went to *sanzen* with the Rōshi, and he asked me some of the *sassho* or test questions about *Mu*. I answered all of them except one, which I hesitated over, and at once he sent me out. But the next morning early I went to *sanzen* again, and this time I could answer it. (SWS I, 209; FZ, 10–11)

Based on his own experience of Zen satori, Suzuki explains that when practicing the Mu koan, as long as one is still conscious of oneself concentrating on Mu there is ego and subject-object dualism so that one reflects on Mu as if it is an external object of meditation that stands apart from the internal subject. Next, upon becoming unconscious of the koan as a separate object through one-pointed concentration on Mu during the practice of dhyana or meditation, the practitioner becomes one with Mu and thereby enters the ecstatic trance state of samadhi. The unconsciousness of samadhi concentration, however, is only a transitional phase to the ultimate breakthrough experience of full awakening in satori or kensho as pranja-intuition of emptiness:

> But this samadhi alone is not enough. You must come out of that state, be awakened from it, and that awakening is Prajna. That moment of coming out of the samadhi and seeing it for what it is — that is satori. When I came out of that state of samadhi during that *sesshin* I said, "I see. This is it." . . . After that I did not find passing koans at all difficult. Of course other koans are needed to clarify *kenshō*, the first experience. (SWS I, 209–210; FZ, 10–11)

Suzuki then recalls how the following evening he experienced a moment of satori-kensho or awakening to the cosmic Unconscious as he descended the stairs to the gate at Engakuji temple: "I remember that night as I walked back from the monastery to my quarters in the Kigen'in temple, seeing the trees in the moonlight. They looked transparent and I was transparent too" (SWS I, 209–210; FZ, 11).

It should be noticed that Suzuki's remembrance of his initial satori-kensho experience by focusing on the Mu koan is parallel to his description of three stages marking the Buddha's awakening to Bodhi or supreme enlightenment. Suzuki raises the question: "If dhyāna had no positive object except in pacifying passions and enjoying absorption in the unconscious, why did the Buddha leave his seat under the Bodhi-tree and come out into the world?" (EZB I, 85–86). He answers that having become unconscious of both self and nature in samadhi concentration, the Buddha then realized full awakening in satori, thereby returning to the world of everyday life out of compassion for the benefit of all sentient beings. In *The Field of Zen* Suzuki gives an account of the Buddha's enlightenment during the final week under the Bodhi tree, as explained in terms of his modern Zen psychology of the Unconscious:

> During that week the Buddha must have suffered a terrible trial. . . . When the trouble reaches its climax the consciousness of subject and object dies, as it were, and sinks into unconsciousness. . . . This is what is called samadhi, being absorbed in meditation. . . . There is psychologically a complete state of unconsciousness. But when this state is reached, even this is not final. There must be awakening, and this awakening usually takes place through sense-stimulation. When Buddha was in this state, he happened to look at the morning star. The rays of the star passed through his eye and touched the nerve and passed to the brain, as we might say today, and he was awakened from unconsciousness and passed to the state of consciousness. . . . But what Buddhists call enlightenment is when the unconscious begins to move into the state of consciousness, or awareness of subject and object. The instant when we begin to be aware is the moment of enlightenment. (FZ, 17)

Suzuki regards the Buddha's enlightenment as paradigmatic for the threefold psychological process undergone by all Buddhist practitioners as they move from discrimination of subject and object in consciousness to the nondiscrimination of subject and object in the unconsciousness of samadhi concentration to Bodhi as awakening to nonduality, whereupon one becomes fully conscious of the Unconscious. Prior to his experience of supreme enlightenment beneath the Bodhi tree, the Buddha entered into an ecstatic samadhi trance as a state of unconsciousness. Similarly, when Suzuki ceased being conscious of the koan as an object separate from himself as a subject, he entered into the unconsciousness of samadhi concentration through the meditative practice of dhyana. Just as the Buddha is shocked into awakening by the sense-stimulation of brilliant rays from the morning star, Suzuki is jolted out of samadhi trance into satori-kensho by the resonant sound of the temple bell. Finally, whereas after supreme enlightenment the Buddha saw everything as empty or void of substance, after satori-kensho Suzuki viewed himself and all objects as "transparent," manifesting just as they are in their emptiness-suchness, all out in the open with nothing hidden. Suzuki thus underscores the movement from dualistic consciousness to unconsciousness in dhyana or meditation to prajna wisdom of emptiness in the awakening of satori, whereupon one becomes fully conscious of the cosmic Unconscious in the paradoxical state of conscious unconsciousness, or what he otherwise terms superconsciousness. Or as Suzuki elsewhere asserts: "When this paradox is understood we are in possession of *nirvāna* . . . To be consciously unconscious, or to be unconsciously conscious, is the secret of *nirvāna*" (ZJC, 140).

Although Suzuki discusses many koans, he especially advocates the Rinzai Zen koan practice of intense concentration with one's whole bodymind upon the keyword "Mu" at the *hara* center in the lower abdomen as the most effective way to realize satori as noetic insight into the Unconscious. As said by Suzuki, the Mu koan "originates from Jōshū (778–897) of the T'ang Dynasty" (LZ, 147). However, Suzuki traces the earliest use of Mu as a koan to Chan/Zen master Goso Hōyen: "The 'Mu' as koan was probably first used by Goso Hoyen (d. 1104), of the Sung Dynasty. No doubt it was one of the koan, or *watō*, which he adopted as the means of opening the eyes of his disciples to the truth of Zen, but later it came to be almost exclusively used as the first eye-opening koan" (LZ, 147). Here Suzuki makes reference to the koan practice of *watō* (C. *hua tou*; K. *hwadu,* 話頭) as the "keyword" or "key phrase" shortcut technique for achieving sudden enlightenment that was first made widespread in the Linji/Rinzai lineage by Chan master Dahui Zonggao (1089–1163). By this method, even if one studies in detail the entire case record of an encounter dialogue between master and disciple, with all of its scholarly commentaries, capping phrases, literary interpretations, puns, word games, and poetic verses, while actually practicing the koan, one focuses only on the abbreviated key phrase or keyword.

The paradigm case of a *watō* or "keyword" used for Rinzai Zen koan practice is Jōshū's Mu (case 1) as recorded in the collection of 48 koans titled *The Gateless Gate* (J. Mumonkan; C. Wumenguan, 無門関), compiled by Zen master Mumon Ekai (C. Wumen Huikai, 1183–1260). When Jōshū (C. Zhaozhou) is asked if a dog has Buddha nature, he answers with the single word "Mu!" During Zen practice of the Mu koan, one breathes in Mu and breathes out Mu and then becomes Mu. According to Suzuki this one-pointed, single-minded, and whole-hearted concentration of the entire bodymind on Mu is practiced while sitting, walking, standing, or reclining, both day and night, throughout the periods of waking, dreaming and sleeping, until there is an explosive breakthrough to satori as awakening to the cosmic Unconscious (SWS I, 167). In his book on the history and philosophy of the Mu koan, Steven Heine cites scholars and practitioners of Zen/Chan Buddhism that acclaim Mu as the "the koan of koans," such that all the rest of the hundreds or thousands of cases are simply a process of refining what is originally seen in Mu (2014a, 1). Heine discusses how among the thousands of cases, Mu emerged as foremost among the keywords for koan meditation throughout East Asia. Explaining the widespread practice of *watō* as the key phrase or keyword technique focusing on the Mu koan, Heine remarks on "the notion of the key-phrase in the philosophy endorsed by Dahui, Jinul, Hakuin, D.T. Suzuki, and Sheng Yen" (2014a, 112). Heine points out that starting from the early 1930s the Zen writings of Suzuki "portray the development of the Keyword Meditation [*Watō*] as a high point not only in the history of Chan, but in the development of East Asian Buddhism overall" (2014a, 82; brackets in original). Moreover, commenting on Suzuki's role in disseminating the Mu koan throughout the English-speaking world, Heine explains: "The Mu Kōan was also championed as the essential component of Zen training by two leading Japanese scholars who have greatly influenced modern scholarship: Yanagida Seizan, who revolutionized historiographical studies of Zen, and D. T. Suzuki (Daisetsu), whose impact based on years of publishing and teaching in English was remarkably wide-ranging" (2014a, 10). It can thus be said that in the West, the Rinzai Zen koan practice of focusing on the keyword Mu was first made widely known by Suzuki.

Suzuki maintains that the aim of *zazen* (座禅) or "seated meditation" in Rinzai Zen koan practice is to directly experience satori as awakening to the Unconscious: "The sitting crossed-legged is the form of Zen, while inwardly the Zen consciousness is to be nursed to maturity. When it is fully matured, it is sure to break out as satori, which is an insight into the Unconscious" (ZK, 56–57; EZB II, 46). According to Suzuki's philosophical psychology, in the tradition of Rinzai Zen the koan practice of focusing on the keyword Mu is the shortcut path to satori as sudden awakening to the cosmic Unconscious in superconsciousness. Throughout his work Suzuki discusses experiences of samadhi concentration followed by satori-kensho awakening elicited with the Mu koan practice as reported by the great masters in the history of Zen Buddhism. In his essay "The Koan and the Five Steps," he explains how through repetition of Mu, the subject-object dualism is overcome such that the practitioner is no longer conscious of being separate from Mu: "We now can say that the 'Mu!' and the 'I' and the Cosmic Unconscious — the three are one and the one is three. When this state of uniformity or identity prevails, the conscious is in a unique situation, which I call 'consciously unconscious' or 'unconsciously conscious'" (SWS I, 167; ZP, 46). For Suzuki it is through ceaseless repetition of Mu that leads to an experience of total nondual interpenetration between "the 'Mu!' and the 'I' and the Cosmic Unconscious" (SWS I, 167; ZP, 46–47). Suzuki, however, identifies this pure experience of one-pointed concentration on Mu with samadhi or tranquility, which is only *midway* toward the deeper realization of satori as consciousness of the cosmic Unconscious.

> But this is not yet a satori experience. We may regard it as corresponding to what is known as samadhi meaning "equilibrium," "uniformity," or "equanimity," or "a state of tranquility." For Zen this is not enough; there must be a certain awakening which breaks up the equilibrium, and brings one back to relative consciousness, when a satori takes place . . . it is the borderland

between the conscious level and the unconscious. Once this level is touched, one's ordinary consciousness becomes infused with the tidings of the unconscious. (SWS I, 167; ZP, 46–47)

Having become unconscious of Mu as a separate object in samadhi concentration, with additional practice one breaks through to satori by returning from the absolute to the relative plane thereby awakening to no-mind as the cosmic Unconscious, which at its deepest level is the ordinary mind of everyday life.

In his essay "The Koan and the Five Steps" Suzuki further describes "Jōshū's "Mu!," Hakuin's "sound of one hand," and other koans as aporias or paradoxical utterances beyond the logical categories of reason: "These paradoxical propositions will no doubt tax one's intellect to the highest degree of tension" (SWS I, 169). Intellect alone is not able solve the aporia, contradiction, or paradox of a koan needed to reach satori as breakthrough to the cosmic Unconscious, also referred to in the following quote as the "ontological unconscious": "Whatever we may say about the intellect, it is after all superficial, it is something floating on the surface of consciousness. The surface must be broken through in order to reach the unconscious. But as long as this unconscious belongs to the domain of [Western] psychology, there cannot be any satori in the Zen sense. The psychology must be transcended and what may be termed the 'ontological unconscious' must be tapped" (SWS I, 169).

The koan method of focusing attention on Mu is a spirit of inquiry, skeptical doubt, and radical questioning that brings the mind to a concentrated state of maximum intensity, whereupon it finally achieves satori as an explosive breakthrough to the Unconscious:

> Why is it necessary to keep up the spirit of inquiry through the koan exercise? . . . What is the Mind . . . or the Unconscious that is always posited behind the multitudinousness of things, and that is felt to be within ourselves? They [the Zen masters] desired to grasp it directly, intuitively, as the Buddhas of the past had all done. Impelled by this desire to know, which is the spirit of inquiry, they reflected within themselves so intensely, so constantly, that the gate was finally opened to them, and they understood. (EZB II, 106–107)

For Suzuki, the great Rinzai Zen masters achieved satori as direct realization of the Unconscious through constant inquiry into the expansive nature of their own mind as spacelike transparent dharmakaya emptiness by using koans, foremost of which is Jōshū's Mu. He discusses how in the teachings of Zen master Hakuin, the koan practice of focusing on keywords such as "Mu," or key phrases such as "Sound of One Hand" is a method of inquiry that arouses the intense concentration of "great doubt" (*daigi*, 大疑), what he alternatively translates here as "great fixation." Suzuki cites the words of Hakuin: "Therefore, you are instructed to inquire into the koan of '*Mu*' (*wu*) and see what sense there is in it. If your inquiring spirit is never relaxed, always intent on '*Mu*' (*wu*) and free from all ideas and emotions and imaginations, you will most decidedly attain the stage of great fixation" (ZK, 125). Suzuki then gives a psychological interpretation of this state of great doubt or great fixation aroused by sustained inquiry into the Mu koan: "This Zen state of consciousness ... is also known as a state of *daigi* [great doubt] or 'fixation.' This is the point where the empirical consciousness with all its contents both conscious and unconscious is about to tip over its border-line, and get noetically related to the Unknown, the Beyond, the Unconscious" (ZK, 96; EZB II, 84). Hence, for Suzuki it is the focused mental state of great doubt or great fixation in samadhi aroused by one-pointed concentration on Mu and other paradoxical koans that trigger satori-kensho as breakthrough to the Unconscious.

Suzuki's psychological analysis of the keyword Mu emphasizes that Zen koan practice is a function of "Will" and that the locus of the will center is the *hara* (腹) or lower abdomen below the navel as the "ocean of energy" (*kikai*, 気海). Moreover, in Suzuki's psychosomatic bodymind schema, while the head is the center of consciousness, the abdomen is the center of the Unconscious (ZP, 55–56). It should be recalled that in a book coauthored with his Rinzai Zen teacher Shaku Sōen Roshi, Suzuki writes: "According to the zazen method at hand, one strives to always keep the lower abdomen full of power, the breathing always uniform, the heart beat tranquil, the muscles of the whole body always resilient" (SWS I, 6–7). Counting breaths is an important aspect of Zen meditation practice. Although breathing is normally an unconscious involuntary process, it can also be done consciously or voluntarily through Zen mindfulness. The breath is therefore a vital link between conscious and unconscious processes. The autonomic nervous system controls the somatic operations that normally occur at subliminal levels beneath the threshold of conscious awareness, such as blood pressure, digestion, heartbeat, body temperature, breathing, and other life-sustaining functions. In the Rinzai Zen tradition of Hakuin, focusing on Mu and other koans is accompanied by deep, full, rhythmic breathing into the lower abdomen. It is through attention to breathing in Zen mindfulness practice that one becomes aware of these subliminal operations of the autonomic nervous system, thereby to make the Unconscious conscious. Hakuin proclaimed that the supreme Zen koan practice for attaining satori is concentration on the keyword Mu in the lower abdomen, which leads to great doubt, great death, and great enlightenment (Yampolsky 1971, 144–145).[16] According to Hakuin: "In general, for the hero who would seek enlightenment ... nothing surpasses the Mu koan" (1971, 144). He further enjoins his disciples that when practicing the koan, to "always set in the area below the navel Chao-chou's Mu" (1971, 145).

One of the most remarkable aspects of Hakuin's training is that he claims to have learned secret Daoist alchemical yoga methods of embryonic abdominal breathing for health and longevity from a Daoist master named Hakuyushi living in the mountains of Shirakawa. In his autobiographical essay *Oretagama* and other works, Hakuin describes this secret Daoist yoga as generating inner heat by focusing on the *tanden* or elixir field at the warm furnace below the navel, finally visualizing an ambrosial liquid atop the head flowing down and spreading throughout the body like soft melted butter, producing an exquisite sensation of great bliss (1999, 92–107; also, see Yampolsky 1971, 30–32).[17] In his essay "The Way Zazen Works" Suzuki himself gives instructions for doing Zen meditation and abdominal breathing exercises while also discussing Hakuin's method of Daoist yoga, suggesting that Hakuin "is transmitting the classic Daoist theory of embryonic breathing" (WZW). Suzuki thereby came to advocate Hakuin's Rinzai Zen Buddhist method of focusing attention on the keyword Mu at the umbilical region of the navel center in the lower abdomen, which he then interpreted with his modern philosophical psychology as the way to achieve bodymind unity through integration of consciousness and unconsciousness in the cosmic Unconscious.

Hakuin proclaimed that in Zen practice "nothing surpasses the Mu koan" (Yampolsky 1971, 144). Yet, later in his career Hakuin devised his own famous koan, "sound of one hand" (*sekishu no onjō*, 隻手の音声). Suzuki explains: "Hakuin, a great Zen master of modern Japan, used to raise one of his hands before his followers, demanding: 'Let me hear the sound of one hand clapping'" (SWS I, 169). In some of his Zen ink paintings Hakuin also depicts himself showing the sound of one hand clapping. But as Suzuki emphasizes: "At all events the koan is not to be solved with the head; that is to say, intellectually or philosophically. . . . the koan is destined to be finally settled with the abdominal parts" (SWS I, 173). Meditation on the keyword "Mu" or the key phrase "sound of one hand" in Zen koan training brings about a radical shift from the head as the center of rational ego-consciousness down to the "second brain" in the lower abdomen as the center of the cosmic Unconscious. When the Zen koan practitioner focuses on a keyword such as "Mu" at the *hara* as the center of the Unconscious, he or she mindfully sits upright in the cross-legged lotus posture while breathing deeply and rhythmically into the lower abdomen. By shifting the focus on this keyword "Mu" from rational ego-consciousness in the head center down to the lower abdomen at the energetic navel center, the koan practice of Rinzai Zen thereby recovers the whole person as a nondual bodymind unity through integration of consciousness and unconsciousness or reason and will in the cosmic Unconscious as superconsciousness.

Suzuki also calls the cosmic Unconscious the ontological unconscious insofar as it is identified with "the Will" as the ultimate source of reality itself. Throughout his writings Suzuki underscores the ontological primacy of the will over intellect in Zen Buddhism: "The truth is that what involves the totality of human existence is not a matter of intellection but of the will in its most primary sense of the word" (SWS I, 169; ZP, 48). This ontological priority accorded to will over reason in Suzuki's Zen Buddhism is in some ways reminiscent of Schopenhauer's voluntaristic metaphysics in the West, itself influenced by Indian Buddhist and Hindu philosophy. For Schopenhauer, the body and all phenomena of nature are objectifications of desire as a blind or unconscious will. In an important passage, Suzuki clarifies the ontological primacy of the will in its function as the Unconscious, while further clarifying how Zen meditation on the keyword "Mu" takes one down to the source of will in the lower abdomen as the somatic locus of the cosmic Unconscious: "The one great will from which all these wills, is infinitely varied, flow is what I call the 'Cosmic (or ontological) Unconscious,' which is the zero-reservoir of infinite possibilities. The 'Mu!' thus is linked to the unconscious by working on the conative plane of consciousness. The koan that looks intellectual or dialectical, too, finally leads one psychologically to the conative center of consciousness and then to the Source itself" (SWS I, 171; ZP, 51). Hence as said above, the primary will is "the Cosmic (or ontological) Unconscious," and the center of will power in the human bodymind is the *hara* in the lower abdomen: "The master is likely to continue, 'You must not think with the head but with the abdomen, with the belly'" (SWS I, 171; ZP, 52). Suzuki explains that when Zen masters do koan practice, they bring the keyword Mu from the intellect in the head as the center of consciousness, down into the lower abdomen beneath the navel as the locus of will and the center of the cosmic Unconscious: "The head is conscious while the abdomen is unconscious. When the master tells his disciples to think with the lower part of the body, he means that the koan is to be taken down to the unconscious and not to the conscious field of consciousness. The koan is to 'sink' into the whole being and not stop at the periphery" (ZP, 55; SWS I, 174). As Suzuki explicitly asserts here: "The head is conscious while the abdomen is unconscious." He further clarifies that when the Zen master instructs the student to concentrate on a koan such as Mu in the lower part of the body, "he means that the koan is to be taken down to the unconscious." Through concentration on Mu in the lower abdomen one thus achieves bodymind oneness by psychosomatic integration of conscious and the unconscious processes in the cosmic Unconscious as superconsciousness.

In his psychological explanation of Zen koan practice Suzuki describes how a koan such as Mu is brought down from consciousness in the head center to the unconscious in the navel center, so that the koan descends into deeper and deeper levels of unconsciousness, finally breaking through to the cosmic Unconscious, also termed the "ontological unconscious": "Whatever we may say about the intellect, it is after all superficial, it is something floating on the surface of consciousness. The surface must be broken through in order to reach the unconscious. But as long as this unconscious belongs in the domain of psychology, there cannot be any *satori* in the Zen sense. The psychology must be transcended and what may be termed the 'ontological unconscious' must be tapped" (SWS I, 169; ZP, 49). As Zen practice continues, the Mu koan "sinks" even below the *ālaya-vijñāna*: "But when we realize that the bottom of the unconscious where the koan 'sinks' is where even the *ālaya-vijñāna*, the all-conserving consciousness, cannot hold it, we see that the koan is no more in the field of intellection, it is thoroughly identified with one's Self" (ZP, 55–56; SWS I, 174). In his description of how the Mu koan "sinks" beneath consciousness to deeper levels of the unconscious mind, Suzuki refers to the Yogacara Buddhist doctrine adopted by Rinzai Zen master Hakuin, whereby there are two aspects of the *ālaya-vijñāna*: (1) the storehouse consciousness perfumed with latent karmic tendencies, which Suzuki identifies with Jung's collective unconscious and its archetypes that condition human experience, and (2) the storehouse consciousness *after* it has been cleansed of all latent karmic tendencies, whereupon it becomes transformed into *ādarśana jñāna* or "great mirror wisdom" of dharmakaya emptiness, which he identifies with his own Zen concept of the cosmic Unconscious as the abyss of nothingness. "When all these limits are transcended — which means going even beyond the so-called collective unconscious — one comes upon that which is known in Buddhism as *ādarśanajnāna*, 'mirror knowledge.' The darkness of the unconscious is broken through and one sees all things as one sees one's face in the brightly shining mirror" (ZP, 56; SWS I, 174). Here as elsewhere, Suzuki makes reference to Jung's hallmark notion of the "collective unconscious." But for Suzuki, even the Jungian collective unconscious, here identified with the ālaya-vijnāna in its impure aspect as the universal reservoir of karmically inherited habitual tendencies, must be inwardly transcended as one "sinks" even further into the depths of the embodied mind, finally realizing the luminous "mirror knowledge" of *ādarśana jnāna*, the storehouse consciousness, now purified of all karmic conditioning, whereupon there occurs a breakthrough to the cosmic Unconscious: "The *ādarśanajnāna* which reveals itself when the bottom of the unconscious, that is, of the *ālaya-vijñāna*, is broken through, is not other than *prajñā*-intuition. The primary will out of which all beings come is not blind and unconscious; it seems so because of our ignorance (*avidyā*) which obscures the mirror, making us oblivious even of the fact of its existence" (ZP, 58; SWS I, 175). Thus it is finally with prajna wisdom of emptiness acquired through intense Zen koan meditation upon the single keyword Mu at the *hara* in the lower abdomen as the center of will that the Mu koan "sinks" below rational ego-consciousness into the unconscious, then descending even further below the Jungian collective unconscious or the *ālaya-vijñāna* as the storehouse of latent habitual tendencies, down to the level where the storehouse is cleansed of all karmic dispositions and transformed into *ādarśana jnāna* or all-illuminating mirror wisdom of spacelike dharmakya emptiness, thereby to realize the deepest bedrock layer of the fully awake cosmic Unconscious as the bottomless abyss of absolute nothingness.

Bankei's Unborn

One of Suzuki's contributions to Zen scholarship was his bringing to light the significance of Japanese Rinzai Zen master Bankei Yōtaku (1623–1693). Bankei proclaimed that Zen enlightenment is to abide without conscious striving in the uncontrived, unfabricated, and unborn emptiness of everyday life and nature.

Although Suzuki was himself devoted to the koan system of Rinzai Zen developed by Hakuin and others, he learned from Bankei not to be trapped or limited by any rigid system of koans. Suzuki clarifies how Bankei rejected Dōgen's quietistic Sōtō Zen sitting-only method of silent illumination. However, Bankei also rejected the Rinzai Buddhist koan system as too artificial, too difficult, and too complex. Bankei further rejects any kind of artificial, contrived, or unnatural doubt aroused by koans. In opposition to the Sōtō Zen silent illumination and Rinzai Zen koan methods, Bankei instructed his followers to just live their daily life in a joyful state of naturalness that he called "the Unborn" (*fushō*, 不生). Suzuki interprets Bankei's notion of the Unborn in terms of his philosophical psychology of the cosmic Unconscious, when he says: "Bankei's teaching centered on the Unborn.... It is the Unconscious" (LZ, 176). Bankei abandons the "silent illumination" method of Sōtō Zen as well as the koan method of Rinzai Zen, instead teaching his disciples to just awaken to the Unborn operating naturally, effortlessly, automatically, and unconsciously in everyday life: "Bankei, one of the great modern Japanese Zen masters, used to teach the doctrine of the Unborn. To demonstrate his idea, he pointed to facts of our daily experience such as hearing a bird chirp, seeing a flower in bloom etc., and that that these are all due to the presence of the Unborn" (ZP, 18–19). He concludes that for Bankei, the Unborn is no-mind or the cosmic Unconscious as the source of creativity, which is itself the "ordinary mind" of everyday life: "For Bankei's Unborn is the root of all things.... Our 'everyday mind,' or our daily experience ... as far as they are considered in themselves, have no special value and significance. They acquire these only when they are referred to the Unborn or what I have called the 'Cosmic Unconscious.' For the Unborn is the fountainhead of all creative possibilities" (ZP, 19).

Zen and Pure Land Buddhism

Although Suzuki is especially known as the one who introduced Zen to the West, in later years he also dedicated himself to the propagation of Pure Land Buddhism, especially the Jōdo Shinshū (浄土真宗) or True Pure Land Buddhism of Shinran (親鸞, 1173–1263), what he also termed "Shin Buddhism." Indeed, one of Suzuki's accomplishments as a scholar of Mahayana Buddhism was to have translated Shinran's masterwork *Kyōgyōshinshō*.

In *Japanese Spirituality* (*Nihonteki reisei,* 日本的霊性), Suzuki argues that Zen Buddhism and Shin or Pure Land Buddhism are the two major expressions of the Japanese spirit and that both are rooted in the selflessness of *mushin* or no-mind, which in psychological terms he calls the Unconscious. He also establishes the difference between these two schools whereby Zen Buddhism is based on *jiriki* (自力) or "self-power," and Pure Land Buddhism is based on *tariki* (他力) or "Other-power." Zen meditation is a path of prajna wisdom, direct seeing into nothingness as a function of self-power rooted in the "will" at the *hara* center of the lower abdomen beneath the navel. Shin Buddhism, however, is *bhakti* yoga (ZB, 132), a devotional path based on "faith" (*shinjin*, 信心) in the Other-power grace of Amida Buddha's compassion rooted in the heart center. Generally speaking, Suzuki regards Zen Buddhism as emphasizing *prajñā* wisdom of emptiness and Shin Pure Land Buddhism as prioritizing *karuṇā* or compassion. Suzuki, however, regards the self-power of Zen and the Other-power of Pure Land Buddhism as complementary. Moreover, for Suzuki both schools are abrupt or sudden teachings, so that like Rinzai Zen "sudden enlightenment" (J. *tongo*, 頓悟; *totsuzen no satori*, 突然の悟り), salvation by faith in the compassionate Other-power grace of Amida Buddha in Shin Buddhism culminates in an instantaneous "crosswise *leap*" (*ōchō*, 横超). Ultimately, Suzuki holds that sudden enlightenment through the *jiriki* or self-power of Zen Buddhism and salvation through a leap of faith in the *tariki* or Other-power grace of Shin Pure Land Buddhism are the subliminal activity of *mushin* or no-mind as the cosmic Unconscious.

According to Suzuki's psychology of religion, Zen and Shin or Pure Land Buddhism result in sudden enlightenment/salvation as awakening to the cosmic Unconscious, achieved by a psychological effect induced through sustained focused attention and constant repetition. In Rinzai Zen practice this repetition is achieved by single-minded, one-pointed, and whole-hearted concentration on the keyword of a koan such as "Mu." In Pure Land Buddhism, repetition is achieved by focusing attention on the *nembutsu* (念佛) of "Namu Amida Butsu" (南無阿弥陀佛), meaning "I take refuge in Amida Buddha," or "Adoration to the Buddha of infinite light." In Suzuki's philosophical psychology, the sudden enlightenment of Zen Buddhism realized through koan practice and salvation by a leap of faith in Pure Land Buddhism achieved with the nembutsu as an invocation of the name of Amida Buddha are to be explained as a function of our own unconscious mind. Suzuki explains rebirth into the Pure Land of peace, light, and bliss through repetition of the nembutsu as the Pure Land Buddhist method for invoking the compassionate Other-power grace pouring out from its source in the cosmic Unconscious: "This is saying the Nenbutsu, that is, invoking the name of Amida; Namu Amida Butsu. . . . The conscious object of course is to be embraced in the grace of Amida by repeatedly pronouncing his name, but psychologically it is to prepare the mind in such a way as to suspend all the surface activities of consciousness and to wake from its unconscious sources a power greater than the empirical ego" (SWS IV, 139–140). Moreover, Pure Land Buddhism holds that opposed to samsaric existence bound to karma as the law of cause and effect, the Unconscious is the inexhaustible source of Amida's Other-power grace that leads to salvation by a leap of faith:

> [W]hile our limited consciousness urges us to conform ourselves to the working of karma, the Unconscious attracts us away to the Unknown beyond karma. The Unconscious and the Unknown are not terms to be found in the dictionary of our

ordinary life, but they exercise a mysteriously irresistible power over us to which our logic and psychology are inapplicable. This most fundamental contradiction which appears in every section of human life refuses to be reconciled in no other way than by the "other-power" teaching of Mahayana Buddhism. (SWS II, 81).

In his introduction to an essay titled "The Shin Sect of Buddhism" from *Japanese Spirituality* by Suzuki, James Dobbins explains the function of the Unconscious in Suzuki's modern psychological interpretation of Shin or Pure Land Buddhism as a religion of faith in Other-power grace as follows: "Throughout Suzuki's essay he presupposes that religious experience is at the heart of Shin Buddhism. Sometimes he expresses this in psychological terms — as a yearning of the "Unconscious." . . . In explaining Shin Buddhism in this way, Suzuki helps redefine it as a modern religious worldview with a rich and fulfilling inner life instead of as an antiquated belief system centered on a mythic other-worldly paradise" (SWS II, 76–77). According to Suzuki, awakening to the Unconscious in Shin or Pure Land Buddhism is due to the psychological effect of ceaseless repetition of the nembutsu: "In my view, the reason is to be sought not in the magical effect of the name itself, but in the psychological effect of its repetition" (SWS II, 62). He further maintains that the psychological effects from continuous repetition of nembutsu in Shin Pure Land Buddhism has its parallel in the koan practice of Rinzai Zen Buddhism: "Do we not see here something of Zen psychology in which '"Wu," "Wu." all day today, and "Wu," "Wu," over again all day tomorrow,' is practiced? Hence the exhortation to say the Nembutsu all day, or every day regularly, or so many times a day — ten thousand times, fifty thousand, and even up to a hundred thousand times a day" (SWS II, 63).

The vocal nembutsu (*shōmyō*, 唱名) whereby one chants *Namu-amida-butsu* achieves the psychological effect of single-minded concentration in nembutsu-samadhi through repetition of the potent name of Amida Buddha, just as through the koan practice of Zen one attains samadhi trance followed by satori as prajna-intuition of emptiness through one-pointed focus on the keyword of a koan, uttering Mu! Mu! Mu! in Japanese, or Wu! Wu! Wu! in Chinese, thereby to enter satori as a flash of insight into the Unconscious. Suzuki thus asserts: "When the Nembutsu is turned into pronouncing a Dharani without any conscious reference to its meaning literary and devotional, its psychological effect will be to create a state of unconsciousness in which ideas and feelings superficially floating are wiped off" (SWS II, 64). Suzuki goes on to describe how repetition of a koan such as Mu in Zen Buddhism, or repetition of nembutsu in Pure Land Buddhism, is similar to the practice of *dhikr* or repetition of the holy name of "Allah" in Sufi mysticism, thereby leading to *fana* or "dissolution of self." In Suzuki's words: "The perpetual reiteration of *Namu-amida-butsu* has its parallel in Sufism whose followers repeat the name 'Allah'" (SMW II, 64).

Using the method of repetition, the koan of Rinzai Zen, the nembutsu of Pure Land Buddhism, and the *dhikr* of Sufism, all use one-pointed, single-minded, and whole-hearted concentration in samadhi to achieve a breakthrough to the Unconscious. Suzuki therefore asserts: "Whatever aspects of the Unconscious there may be, they can never be tapped unless one experiences *samādhi* or *sammai*, which is the state of one-pointedness (*ekāgratā*), that is, of concentration" (ZJC, 226).

In his account of the one-pointed concentrative state of nembutsu-samadhi induced by repetition of Namu-Amida-Butsu, Suzuki emphasizes the importance of an attitude of "sincerity," "devotion," and "faith" while uttering the name of Amida. He explains that although one endeavors to sincerely pronounce the name of Amida, if it is a conscious attitude, it is not real sincerity: "To utter the name once with trustfulness and sincerity is enough, but generally we do not pronounce it sincerely" (BIL, 32). Moreover: "We may think that we are sincere and in possession of faith or belief in Amida, but real sincerity, real trust, is altogether devoid of such consciousness" (BIL, 32). "When we say Amida's name while such consciousness remains we cannot be born in the Pure Land. Therefore, to pronounce NAMU-AMIDA-BUTSU is to forget altogether, not to be conscious at all, of saying NAMU-AMIDA-BUTSU.... Even when I feel that it is the Name itself pronouncing itself, it is not sincere if consciousness still remains" (BIL, 33). As said here, to be sincere in the state of nembutsu-samadhi is "not to be conscious at all, of saying NAMU-AMIDA-BUTSU," such that one is reciting the name of Amida Buddha naturally, effortlessly, automatically, and unconsciously. Suzuki concludes with a psychological account of how the nembutsu of Namu-Amida-Buddha must be recited with sincerity in an effortless state of unconsciousness: "'Sincerity' is perfect forgetting of oneself. ... Religious or spiritual forgetfulness is something that one must experience for oneself. That is, one has to experience it personally to know what kind of forgetfulness or unconsciousness we are talking about" (BIL, 33).

In *Japanese Spirituality*, Suzuki endeavors to clarify the meaning of "Japanese spirituality" (*Nihonteki reisei*, 日本的霊性), the exemplars for which are Zen and Pure Land Buddhism. Moreover, he defines "Japanese spirituality" by means of his signature concept of no-thought or no-mind, interpreted psychologically as the Unconscious: "When the 'bright and pure heart' of the Japanese ceases to work on the surface of consciousness and begins to move submerged in its deepest parts, when it is moving *unconsciously*, with non-discrimination, without thought, then Japanese spirituality can be understood. The singularity of Japanese spirituality is manifested in this feature of 'no-thought'" (JS, 22; italics added). Or as he elsewhere defines Japanese spirituality: "To be conscious yet not conscious of anything at all is the true spiritual consciousness" (WZ, 90–91; SWS IV, 209).

One of Suzuki's important contributions to modern Japanese Buddhist scholarship was to introduce the *myōkōnin*, (妙好人), the "wonderful good men" of Pure Land Buddhism. Suzuki describes how Myokonin Asahara Saichi

(1850–1932) perpetually lived in a joyful, carefree state of nembutsu-samadhi that he describes as "the believing heart's unconscious consciousness" (SWS II, 168). He further tells us: "All expressions should enable us to see Saichi living immersed in a 'Namu-Amida-Butsu' samadhi. He had from the first no interest in reason or logic. . . . *But spirituality is not something that always appears on the surface of consciousness, it operates constantly hidden in the unconscious area of the heart*" (JS 201; italics added). Suzuki here again states that the character of Japanese spirituality is that it operates naturally, spontaneously, effortlessly, and unconsciously beneath the surface of dualistic ego-consciousness. Furthermore, he explains that Japanese spirituality as an egoless state of unconsciousness is what Shinran calls *jinen honi*, (自然法爾), naturalness, effortlessness, and spontaneity (BIL, 60–67). Although the actions and sayings of the Myokonin often run counter to common sense, Saichi and other liberated Myokonin do not act from the logic of rational ego-consciousness but from the spontaneous inner workings of the Unconscious.

According to the teachings of Pure Land Buddhism, Dharmākara (J. Hōzō, 法蔵), whose name means "storehouse of dharma," through lifetimes of striving became the universal savior Amida Buddha. Elsewhere I have discussed how the modern Pure Land Buddhist scholar Soga Ryōjin (1875–1971) reinterpreted Amida Buddha/Dharmākara in psychological terms as a personification of the Yogacara Buddhist alaya-vijnana or storehouse consciousness in its meaning as the unconscious mind (Odin 2005). As said by Mark L. Blum: "Soga's aim was to identify Amida Buddha as the religious dimension of the Yogācāra notion of the unconscious (ālaya-vijñāna) and to identify Dharmākara Bodhisattva, the monk who through diligent practice became Amida Buddha, as the true savior of mankind" (Heisig et al. 2011, 273). According to Soga, Amida/Dharmākara as the alaya-vijnana is the "deep consciousness" (*shinsō ishiki*, 深層意識). Furthermore, Soga tells us that Amida/Dharmākara in its soteriological function as the storehouse consciousness is supraconsciousness: "Many years ago I called the ālaya-vijñāna, this supraconsciousness in which all dharmas are stored, this 'storehouse-consciousness,' 'Dharmākara consciousness'" (1982, 228).

It should be noted that although the native Japanese religious tradition of Shinto (神道) as the "way of the gods" is claimed by some to be the heart and soul of Japanese spirituality, for Suzuki it differs from Zen spirituality in that it fails to recognize "the Unconscious" operating beneath the surface levels of normal ego-consciousness: "Because of this Shinto, which is considered the essence of Japaneseness, came under the influence of Zen. This 'Zen-ization' reveals all the more, because it was unconscious, the Zen character of Japanese spirituality. Shintoists would consciously deny this 'unconscious' process beneath the surface" (JS, 19; italics added). Suzuki's view of Japanese spirituality can be summed up by his assertion: "spirituality is not something that always appears on the surface of consciousness, it operates constantly hidden in the unconscious area of the heart" (JS, 201). He therefore claims, "when it is moving unconsciously, with non-discrimination, without thought, then Japanese spirituality can be understood" (JS, 22). According to Suzuki's philosophical psychology, then, the Unconscious is the inner source of Japanese spirituality, the paradigms for which are both Zen and Pure Land Buddhism. It can therefore be said that Suzuki's modernization, detraditionalization, and demythologization of Japanese Buddhism involves a process of *psychologization*, whereby both Zen satori and Shin Buddhist rebirth in the Pure Land are hermeneutically reinterpreted as sudden awakening to the cosmic Unconscious in supraconsciousness.

Christian-Buddhist Mysticism

In his essay "What is Religion?" Suzuki contends that mystical experience is at the inner core of all religions, further arguing that every religion articulates this experience by means of an ultimate principle: "In all religions there is something ultimate which we may call God, the Buddha-nature, Élan vital, Substance, Thought, the Unconscious, the Absolute Spirit, the Atman, or anything else you like" (SWS III, 103). For Suzuki the religious ultimate of Zen Buddhism is designated by such terms as Emptiness, Buddha-nature, or Dharmakaya, but which in psychological terms he refers to as "the Unconscious." Although Suzuki especially focuses on the operation of "the Unconscious" in Zen and Mahayana Buddhism, he also applies it in his writings on Christian-Buddhist dialogue and comparative religions. Here it should be pointed out that in *Mystics and Zen Masters*, Thomas Merton interprets Suzuki's Zen concept of no-mind as the Unconscious based on the latter's translation of texts attributed to Huineng and Bodhidharma, explaining the Unconscious in Christian biblical terms of John 1:1 as the Logos or Word, the divine Light that illuminates us from within (1967, 24–28).

Suzuki maintains that repetition of a koan such as Mu in Zen Buddhism and recitation of nembutsu in Shin or Pure Land Buddhism are similar to the practice of *dhikr* or repetition of "Allah" and other divine names in Sufi mysticism (SMW II, 64). In Suzuki's essay "Shin and Zen — A Comparison," he goes on to argue that repetition of nembutsu in Shin Buddhism and koans such as Mu in Zen are similar to recitation of the Jesus Prayer of Eastern Orthodox Christian mysticism ("Lord Jesus Christ, Son of God, have mercy upon me"), while explaining all three spiritual practices in terms of his philosophical psychology of the Unconscious:

> In repeating the Nembutsu, as with the Jesus prayer, the repetition is done with the same rhythm, sound and movement so many times. . . . If consciousness is occupied with just one thought, that consciousness is equivalent to the unconscious. When consciousness contains two things, we become conscious of consciousness. This bifurcation, subject and object,

is needed to make us aware of consciousness. When consciousness is only preoccupied with one thought it loses itself, i.e., we become unconscious of consciousness. (FZ, 74)[18]

In the apophatic tradition of *via negativa* Christian mysticism, salvation is achieved through detachment from the world and kenotic self-emptying into the Godhead of nothingness. It is this via negativa tradition of mystical Christianity that Suzuki finds to have the closest proximity with Zen mysticism based on the experience of no-mind or the Unconscious as spacelike dharmakaya emptiness. In *Mysticism: Christian and Buddhist*, Suzuki focuses especially on parallels between Zen and the kenotic via negativa Christian mysticism of the Dominican theologian Meister Eckhart (1260–1327). At the outset of this work, he announces: "I attempt to call the reader's attention to the closeness of Meister Eckhart's way of thinking to that of Mahāyāna Buddhism, especially of Zen Buddhism" (MCB, 1). In this work Suzuki makes comparisons between Zen sunyata or emptiness and Eckhart's apophatic negative theology based on such notions as breakthrough to the Godhead of nothingness, detachment from the world, emptying oneself into nothingness, salvation by dwelling in nothingness of Godhead through voluntary poverty, and overcoming nihilism by realizing the Godhead of nothingness as the is-ness of things: "It is now necessary to examine Eckhart's close kinship with Mahāyāna Buddhism and especially with Zen Buddhism in regard to the doctrine of Emptiness" (MCB, 10). Suzuki regards both Zen Buddhism and the apophatic Christian mysticism of Eckhart as via negative paths to salvation/enlightenment having their apex in the beatific experience of nothingness, emptiness, and silence. For Suzuki, Zen and via negativa Christian mysticism teach the virtue of letting go, whereby Zen "nonattachment" (*mushūjaku*, 無執着) and Eckhart's "absolute detachment" (*abegescheidenheit*) culminate in a kenotic act of self-emptying to nothingness. Speaking of Eckhart, Suzuki therefore asserts: "What then is the content of absolute detachment? . . . It is pure nothing (*bloss nicht*)" (MCB, 11). Further demonstrating the close proximity between Zen mysticism and the Christian mysticism of Eckhart, Suzuki says "we really enter into the realm of emptiness where the Godhead keeps our discriminatory mind altogether 'emptied out to nothingness'" (MCB, 14). Summing up the basic point of correspondence between Zen and the Christian mysticism of Eckhart, Suzuki asserts: "Eckhart is in perfect accord with the Buddhist doctrine of *sūnyatā*, when he advances the notion of Godhead as 'pure nothingness'" (MCB, 13). However, Suzuki goes on to emphasize how like Zen satori, the via negativa Christian mysticism of Eckhart culminates in a kenotic or self-emptying realization of the Godhead of infinite nothingness, but then returns to everyday life to affirm ordinary things in their "is-ness" (MCB, 67–70).

Suzuki explains in psychological terms how Zen and Eckhart refer to the experience of nothingness as *unconsciousness*, or what Eckhart also terms the state of "unknowing" (MCB, 23), when the self loses conscious awareness of itself and all things in the Godhead of nothingness. Suzuki cites Eckhart's own description of the state of blessedness wherein the soul becomes absorbed into the pure nothingness of Godhead without knowing it at all thereby to become completely "unconscious" of any distinction between subject and object or knower and known: "For the foundation of spiritual blessing is this: that the soul look at God without anything between; here it receives its being and life and draws its essence from the core [*grund*] of God, unconscious of the knowledge process, or love or anything else. Then it is quite still in the essence of God, not knowing at all where it is, knowing nothing but God" (MCB, 73; brackets in original). Suzuki thus regards Zen and Eckhart's via negativa Christian mysticism as attaining their consummation in a breakthrough to the Unconscious as the abyss of nothingness.

In his development of a Christian-Buddhist interfaith dialogue, Suzuki finds another significant parallel whereby the inwardness of faith in Jesus Christ's sacrifice on the cross as a ransom for the sins of all humankind leads to salvation in Christianity through "vicarious atonement," just as sincere faith in Amida Buddha's "transference of merit" (*pariṇāmanā*) leads to salvation by Otherpower blessings in the Pure Land teachings of Shin Buddhism, both of which are psychologically interpreted as a sudden inflow of grace from the Unconscious into consciousness to give it enlightenment: "Whatever theological or ethical interpretation may be given to this, the truth or fact, psychologically speaking, remains the same with Christians and Buddhists: it is the experience of a leap from the relative plane of consciousness to the Unconscious" (SWS II, 98). Elsewhere, while pointing out similarities and differences between Zen and the Christian mysticism of Saint Ignatius Loyola, Saint Francis of Assisi, and other Catholic writers, Suzuki concludes: "But so far as its psychological experience is concerned, both the Zen masters and the Catholic leaders aim at bringing about the same state of mind, which is no other than realizing the Unconscious in our individual consciousnesses" (ZDNM, 69).

Chapter 2

The Unconscious in Suzuki's Zen Aestheticism

In works such as *Zen and Japanese Culture*, Suzuki formulates a "Zen aestheticism," the cornerstone of which is his Zen concept of the "cosmic Unconscious." Suzuki's Zen aestheticism claims that Zen has exerted a pervasive influence on traditional Japanese arts while further maintaining that Zen-inspired arts spring from *mushin* or no-mind as the cosmic Unconscious, which as the abyss of absolute nothingness, is the inexhaustible source of unlimited creative possibilities.

Zen Aestheticism in Japanese Culture

Suzuki argues that the Zen-inspired arts have their origin in *mushin* or no-mind as the cosmic Unconscious and therefore manifest the emptiness-suchness of things in absolute nothingness. According to Suzuki's Zen aestheticism, the Unconscious is the source of unlimited creative possibilities that underlies *geidō* (芸道) or the religio-aesthetic way of the arts, such as sumie ink painting, calligraphy, haiku poetry, noh theater, and tea ceremony, and *bushidō* (武士道) or the religio-aesthetic way of the martial arts such as archery and swordsmanship. It has been seen how in the philosophical psychology of Suzuki, Zen no-mind or the Unconscious in its aspect as ordinary mind is the deeper subliminal awareness of our autonomic nervous system underlying the common activities of everyday life, such as eating when hungry, drinking when thirsty, and sleeping when tired. Likewise, in Suzuki's Zen aestheticism it is no-mind or the cosmic Unconscious acting as the ordinary mind that guides the lightning-fast sword of the samurai, the graceful brushstrokes of the sumie painter, the effortless gestures of the noh actor, and the elegant movements of the tea master. For this reason, *mushin* or no-mind as the cosmic Unconscious is the key notion operative in Suzuki's modern psychological interpretation of Zen, Zen art, and Zen aesthetics.

Two characteristics of Suzuki's Zen aestheticism based on his philosophical psychology of the Unconscious is that it includes an "everyday aesthetics" and a "somaesthetics." According to the Zen aestheticism of Suzuki, it is *mushin* or no-mind as the cosmic Unconscious in its function as *heijōshin* or ordinary mind that inspires the creation and enjoyment of *wabi-sabi* art exhibiting the plain and natural beauty of ordinary things in everyday life. Suzuki's *wabi-sabi* Zen aestheticism is therefore a Japanese paradigm of "everyday aesthetics."[1] In Suzuki's Zen aestheticism, *mushin* or no-mind as the Unconscious is an egoless state beyond the subject-object distinction in which the artist is so immersed in his or her art that the bodymind spontaneously acts without conscious effort. Hence, in Suzuki's Zen aestheticism there is a *psychosomatic* aspect to all the Zen-inspired arts rooted in *mushin* or no-mind, insofar they involve cultivation of the whole bodymind. Suzuki's Zen aestheticism can therefore be further elucidated in terms of what American pragmatist Richard Shusterman calls a "somaesthetics." According to Shusterman, *somaesthetics* is a study of the experience and use of one's physical body as the locus of sensory-aesthetic appreciation and creative self-cultivation. Shusterman furthermore cites *zazen* seated meditation practice with its emphasis on correct bodily posture, deep rhythmic breathing, and mindfulness of bodily sensations as a Japanese form of somaesthetics (2008, 173–174). In the present volume I further extend somaesthetics to the specific traditional Japanese artforms developed under the influence of Zen as analyzed by Suzuki, such as noh theater, sumie ink painting, tea ceremony, and swordsmanship, insofar as they require cultivation of unified bodymind awareness through integration of conscious and unconscious processes.

Suzuki maintains that the development of Zen Buddhism in Japan culminated in "Zen aestheticism" (*Zen no "bi" ron,* 禅の「美」論: ZNB, 38–39; ZJC, 27). According to Suzuki's philosophical psychology, Zen aestheticism is itself rooted in *mushin* or no-mind as the cosmic Unconscious, which functions as the principle of creativity and the inexhaustible source of all Zen-inspired arts: "The Cosmic Unconscious is the principle of creativity. . . . All creative works of art . . . come from the fountainhead of the Cosmic Unconscious" (ZJC, 242–243). He asserts that *mushin* or no-mind as the cosmic Unconscious "is where all arts merge into Zen" (ZJC, 94). Moreover, in Zen satori as awakening to *mushin* or the cosmic Unconscious, there is a fusion of aesthetic and religious experience: "Aestheticism now merges into religion" (ZJC, 355). This merging of aesthetic and spiritual experience, of art and religion, of the beautiful and the mystical, is what is referred to as *geidō* or the religio-aesthetic way of the artist.

Suzuki's view of spontaneous playful activity in aesthetically immediate experience based on a philosophical psychology of the Unconscious is already present in his early 1907 work *Outlines of Mahayana Buddhism*, where he expounds on the attainment of "unconscious or subconscious intelligence" in the higher stages of a compassionate bodhisattva:

> This knowledge is also called non-conscious or non-deliberate knowledge. . . . It is a sort of unconscious or subconscious intelligence, or immediate knowledge. . . . The conscious striving that distinguished all his former course has now given way to a state of spontaneous activity . . . of divine playfulness. . . . He is nature herself. . . . This state of perfect ideal freedom may

be called esthetical, which characterizes the work of a genius. There is no trace of consciously following some prescribed laws, no pains of elaborately confirming to the formula. (OMB, 187–188)

Throughout this same work, Suzuki cites Mahayana Buddhist texts to support his view of the bodhisattva who realizes this kind of nonconscious, unconscious, or subconscious knowing in dharmakaya emptiness, which like the Daoist *wuwei* or effortless naturalness of Laozi, abandons all conscious strivings, thereby to act out of spontaneity, immediacy, playfulness, and freedom characteristic of an aesthetic mode of existence.

In his discussion of Zen aestheticism, Suzuki declares: "Every one of us, however ordinary he may be, has something in him, in his Unconscious, that is hidden away from the superficial level of consciousness" (ZJC, 226). For Suzuki, Zen satori as insight into the deeper unconscious mind is best realized by koan practices focusing on keywords such as "Mu" or key phrases such as Hakuin's "sound of one hand." Moreover, Zen satori as awakening to the Unconscious is also realized through the creation and enjoyment of art: "This supreme moment in the life of an artist, when expressed in Zen terms, is the experience of satori. To experience satori is to become conscious of the Unconscious (*mushin,* no-mind), psychologically speaking. Art has always something of the Unconscious about it" (ZJC, 220). In the Zen aestheticism of Suzuki, all the Zen-inspired arts surge upward from the cosmic Unconscious as prajna wisdom of sunyata or emptiness, understood in the context of art as the source of infinite creative possibilities:

> Underneath all the practical technique or the methodological details necessary for the mastery of an art there are certain intuitions directly reaching what I call the Cosmic Unconscious. . . . It is indeed firmly believed by Japanese generally that the various specific intuitions acquired by the swordsman, the tea master, and masters of other branches of art and culture are no more than particularized applications of one great experience . . . but the fundamental experience is acknowledged to be an insight into the Unconscious itself as the source of all creative possibilities, all artistic impulses. (ZJC, 193).

He adds: "Zen masters, ultimately deriving their philosophy from the Buddhist doctrine of *śūnyatā* and *prajñā* describe the Unconscious. . . . For the Unconscious then permits its privileged disciples, masters of the arts, to have glimpses of its infinite possibilities" (ZJC, 192–193). The Zen-influenced arts require years of training to master various techniques. But Suzuki distinguishes between the technical skill of an artist involving conscious effort and the effortless naturalness of Zen art that comes from the cosmic Unconscious. Zen artforms in the style of *myō* or mystery require an artist to ultimately forget all contrived techniques so as to spontaneously act from unconscious creative impulses: "What is known as *myō* or *myōyū* in Japanese arts comes out when the rationality of things ceases to be valued. In fact, all works of original creativity are the products of the unconscious that go beyond rationalistic schematizations" (ZJC, 140). Suzuki establishes a fundamental axiom in his psychology of Zen art: "All works of original creativity are the products of the unconscious." According to Suzuki's Zen aestheticism, however, this means that all creative works of art produced by the Zen-trained artists have their origin in what he terms the cosmic Unconscious as spacelike transparent dharmakaya emptiness, which is revealed in the artwork through an encompassing metaphysical background of absolute nothingness.

In his explanation of the Zen aesthetic principle of *myō* (妙) or "mystery," also called *myōyū* (妙用), Suzuki further clarifies that the Japanese sense of beauty as *myō* springs from what Zen master Bankei called "the Unborn" and which in psychological terms, he refers to as "the Unconscious": "[I]t is only when we are out of an intellectual grip of any kind that . . . we can work freely in the mysterious realm of the Unborn, where the artists can display *myō* in all its varieties. A 'view' or 'thought' is the outcome of intellection, and wherever this is found this creativity of the Unborn or the Unconscious meets all sorts of obstacles" (ZJC, 141). Anything in art, nature, and everyday life that spontaneously expresses the indistinct atmospheric beauty of *myō* or mystery, or the aesthetic quality of *yūgen* as profound mystery and depth, has its origin in the cosmic Unconscious: "*Myōyū* (*miao-yung* in Chinese) . . . or simply *myō* . . . is a certain artistic quality perceivable not only in works of art but in anything in Nature or life . . . *myō* is something original and creative growing out of one's own unconscious" (ZJC, 142, fn. 3). Suzuki elsewhere comments: "When an art, therefore, presents those mysteries in a most profound and creative manner, it moves us to the depths of our being: art then becomes a divine work" (ZJC, 219).

Suzuki's Zen aestheticism based on the cosmic Unconscious as the source of creativity is part of his sustained effort to overcome nihilism. It has been seen that throughout his works, Suzuki identifies his Zen notion of the cosmic Unconscious with dharmakaya emptiness (EZB, III, 16, 18; AZL, 62; LZ, 88). Yet he further clarifies that sunyata or emptiness is not a nihilistic void but an emptiness-fullness that discloses the qualitative immediacy of aesthetic events just as they are in the beauty of their suchness, thisness, or isness. Suzuki defines the Zen concept of beauty as follows: "When beauty is expressed in terms of Buddhism it is a form of self-enjoyment of the suchness of things" (SWS I, 108). And elsewhere: "In a way we can say that in the Zen conception of *tathatā* there is something reminding us of an aesthetic appreciation of works of art or of beauties of nature" (ZB, 325). The Zen aestheticism of Suzuki thus counters nihilism by showing how *śūnyatā* or "emptiness" designates the beauty of *tathatā* or "suchness": "*śūnyatā* ('emptiness') is *tathatā* ('suchness'), and *tathatā* is *śūnyatā*: *śūnyatā* is the world of the Absolute, and *tathatā* is the world of particulars. One of the commonest sayings in Zen is 'Willows are green and flowers red' or 'bamboos are straight and pine trees gnarled.' Facts of experience are accepted as they are; Zen is not nihilistic" (ZJC, 36). Hence, when Suzuki formulates his concept of the cosmic Unconscious as prajna-intuition of emptiness, it is not the life-negating view of nihilism but a life-affirming perspective that celebrates the directly felt aesthetic qualities of events in their emptiness-suchness, which in Zen is poetically expressed by the aphorism: "Willows are green and flowers red."

Suzuki establishes a contrast between the abstractions of scientific analysis based on the intellectualizations of consciousness versus Zen aesthetic intuition of mysterious subtle beauty rooted in the Unconscious. For Suzuki the Unconscious is the creative matrix of all aesthetic productivity in Zen art and literature: "The sciences deal with abstractions . . . Zen plunges itself into the source of creativity and drinks from it all the life there is in it. This source is Zen's Unconscious" (ZP, 12). He continues: "While the scientist murders, the [Zen] artist attempts to recreate. . . . He therefore uses canvas and brush and paint and tries to create out of his unconscious. When this unconscious sincerely and genuinely identifies itself with the Cosmic Unconscious, the artist's creations are genuine. . . . He paints a flower which, if it is blooming from his unconscious is a new flower and not an imitation of nature" (ZP, 12–13). Suzuki here returns to a theme pervasive throughout his work, stating that the aesthetic creativity of Zen-inspired art has its source in the Unconscious, further clarifying that this is not the unconscious of Western psychology but what he calls the cosmic Unconscious. Zen art that emerges from the cosmic Unconscious is not an "imitation" but an original recreation of nature that infuses life with the aesthetic value of beauty. Psychologically speaking, Zen-influenced artforms such as noh drama, sumie ink painting, haiku poetry, and the tea ceremony, as well as martial arts such as archery and swordsmanship, have their genesis in the cosmic Unconscious as prajna-intuition of emptiness. The directly felt aesthetic qualities characteristic of Zen art such as *wabi* (simplicity), *sabi* (loneliness), *shibumi* (understatement), *myō* (mystery), *yūgen* (depth), *ma* (negative space), and *furyū* (windblown elegance) likewise spring from their ontological source of creativity in the cosmic Unconscious as the abyss of absolute nothingness and, therefore, function to depict things as they are in the ephemeral beauty of their emptiness-suchness.

In *Zen Buddhism and Psychoanalysis*, Suzuki again returns to his theme that the cosmic Unconscious is the ontological source of creativity and the ultimate origin of traditional Zen-inspired arts:

> I do not know if it is correct to call this kind of unconscious the Cosmic Unconscious. The reason I like to call it so is that what we generally call the relative field of consciousness vanishes away somewhere into the unknown, and this unknown, once recognized, enters into ordinary consciousness and puts into good order all the complexities there which have been tormenting us to greater or lesser degree. . . . May we not call this

unknown the Cosmic Unconscious, or the source of infinite creativity whereby not only arts of every description nourish their inspirations, but even we ordinary beings are enabled . . . to turn his life into something of genuine art? (ZP, 17)

He goes on to describe the Zen artist as one whose everyday life has its deepest source in no-mind as the cosmic Unconscious, or what he also terms here "the creative unconscious" (ZP, 31): "To such a person his life reflects every image he creates out of his inexhaustive source of the unconscious. To such, his every deed expresses originality, creativity . . . His Self has touched the unconscious, the source of infinite possibilities. His is 'no-mind'" (ZP, 16). It can now be seen how Suzuki's Zen aestheticism is used to counter nihilism. According to Suzuki, Zen aestheticism overcomes life-denying nihilism insofar as it is an affirmation of beauty as the intrinsic value of all things in nature, art, and everyday life arising through the spontaneous creativity of the cosmic Unconscious. According to Suzuki's Zen aestheticism, it is by tapping the cosmic Unconscious as the dharmakaya of absolute nothingness that a Zen-trained artist manifests the uncontrived beauty of ordinary things in nature and life just as they are in the haecceity of their emptiness-suchness. Suzuki's Zen aestheticism based on his philosophical psychology of the cosmic Unconscious proclaims that Zen achieves its zenith when the canvas of our own life becomes a work of art as if to be a sumie ink painting, a haiku poem, or a noh play: "We cannot all be expected to be scientists, but we are so constituted by nature that we can all be artists — not, indeed, artists of special kinds, such as painters, sculptors, musicians, poets, etc., but artists of life" (ZP, 15). The Zen aestheticism of Suzuki is thus a celebration of the mystery and wonder of the ordinary as extraordinary that results in a creative transformation of everyday life into art.

Suzuki and Nishida on Beauty as *Muga* or Ecstasy

The central role of Suzuki and Nishida Kitarō in establishing the vocabulary for modernist discussions of Zen art and Zen aesthetics is highlighted by Gregory Levine: "In the case of Nishida Kitarō (1870–1945) and Suzuki, Zen works of art, as well as their proper understanding and explanation, were seen to derive from 'pure experience' (*junsui keiken*), 'absolute nothingness' (*zettai mu*), and the corollary states of *muga* (no self/ego), *mushin*, and *mu'nen*. Although these last three terms are not modern neologisms, they came to steer much of the discourse on Zen art as it spread internationally in the early twentieth century" (Levine, 80). In what follows, it is explained how Suzuki and Nishida describe Zen art as emerging from *muga* or no-self, otherwise called *mushin* or no-mind and *munen* or no-thought, while further clarifying its significance in aesthetic and mystical discourse as an egoless state of "ecstasy." Suzuki and Nishida develop an aesthetics of beauty as "ecstasy" (ancient Greek: *ek-stasis*), meaning to be transported beyond oneself in an intoxicated state of rapture. Moreover, I demonstrate that how Suzuki differs from Nishida is that he analyzes the Zen concepts of *muga*, *mushin*, and *munen* in terms of his modern philosophical psychology of the cosmic Unconscious as the all-encompassing spatial locus of nonego, emptiness, and absolute nothingness.

According to Suzuki's Zen aestheticism, the traditional Japanese arts developed under the aegis of Zen Buddhism, such as sumie inkwash landscape painting, haiku poetry, noh drama, swordsmanship, archery, and the tea ceremony, are rooted in the egoless state of *mushin* or no-mind as cosmic unconsciousness. Throughout his writings on Zen aestheticism, Suzuki regularly equates *mushin* (無心) or no-mind and *munen* (無念) or no-thought with the Buddhist notion of *muga* (無我) as no-self or nonego (ZJC, 127). Moreover, Suzuki argues that all Zen-influenced artforms emerge from out of nonego (*muga*) or the Unconscious as the wellspring of creativity:

> [I]t may be better to regard the Buddhist teaching of Non-ego [*muga*] as the practical method of expounding the philosophy of the Unconscious . . . Buddhism now teaches to abandon the thought of an ego-soul, to be free from this clinging . . . for it is thus that the Unconscious regains its original creativity. . . . Great things so called seem to be achieved always by our direct appeal to the unconscious. Not only great spiritual events but great moral, social and practical affairs are the results of the immediate working of the Unconscious. Egolessness is meant to direct our attention to this fact. (EZB III, 317)

In this passage Suzuki maintains that the Zen Buddhist teaching of *muga* (Skt. *anātman*) or nonego is best comprehended in terms of what he calls "the philosophy of the Unconscious." Suzuki not only identifies Zen *muga* or nonego with the Unconscious but argues that the Unconscious is the source of all aesthetic creation, as well as all spiritual, moral, and practical activity. He further explains how lesser artworks are tinged with self-grasping, egoism, and pride, while Zen-inspired works of art are spontaneously produced in the ecstatic state of *muga* or *mushin* as the Unconscious:

> The feeling of "self" is a great hindrance to the execution of a work [of art]. . . . We instinctively turn away from it [the artwork] not directly coming from the Unconscious. Anything from the latter . . . has a peculiar charm of its own as being a first work of the Unconscious. That we can feel this charm bears testimony to the Unconscious. The aim of all the artistic discipline in Japan gathers around the self-appreciation of it [the Unconscious]. . . . "Muga" or "Mushin" or effortlessness is thus the consummation of art. (EZB III, 318)

In a key statement, Suzuki goes on to say: "To the Japanese mind, 'Muga' and 'Mushin' signify the same thing. When one attains the state of 'Muga,' the state of 'Mushin,' the Unconscious, is realized. Muga is something identified with a state of ecstasy in which there is no sense of 'I am doing it'" (EZB III, 318). In his explanation of Zen aestheticism in traditional Japanese art culture, then, Suzuki equates *muga* or "nonego" with *mushin* or "no-mind" while further identifying both with "the Unconscious." Moreover, it is said that beauty produced without conscious effort from *muga* or *mushin* is "the consummation of art." Finally, he asserts that *muga* is a state of "ecstasy" (EZB III, 318).

Suzuki's connection between *mushin* or no-mind, *munen* or no-thought, and *muga* or no-self as the basis of Zen art, understood as a state of "ecstasy," can be further clarified through the aesthetics of Nishida. His essay "An Explanation of Beauty" (*Bi no setsumei,* 1900), which I have elsewhere translated in full, is an original treatise on the Japanese sense of beauty that synthesizes elements from Eastern and Western aesthetics (Odin, 1987b). He begins the essay with an effort to formulate an adequate definition of "beauty" (*bi*, 美) and concludes that it is *muga* or "ecstasy." Nishida reformulates the Kantian sense of beauty as disinterested pleasure, or artistic detachment from egoistic desires, in terms of the Zen notion of *muga* 無我 (Skt: *anātman*), "no-self," "nonego," "self-effacement," or "ecstasy" (1987b, 216). In Nishida's words: "Only this *muga* is the essential element of beauty" (Odin, 1987b, 216). As emphasized by Valdo H. Viglielmo (1971, 555), in Nishida's early writings on aesthetics, his use of the term *muga* to define aesthetic experience of beauty is best translated in its dictionary meaning as "ecstasy".[2] It can therefore be said that Nishida, like Suzuki, argues that aesthetic experience has its basis in Zen *muga* as no-self, selflessness, or nonego. Also, Suzuki and Nishida hold that in Japanese aesthetics, *muga* denotes the egoless state of "ecstasy," an ecstatic feeling of *losing oneself* in the beauty of art, nature, and everyday life. Moreover, Suzuki and Nishida elsewhere describe the *muga* or ecstasy of aesthetic and religious modes of nondual experience in terms of "pure experience" and "absolute nothingness." But what distinguishes the views of these two Japanese thinkers is that for Suzuki the aesthetic experience of beauty rooted in Zen *mushin* or no-mind and *muga* or nonego, understood as a mystical state of ecstasy, is further interpreted in psychological terms as the cosmic Unconscious. In his analysis of the Zen sense of beauty in art and aesthetic experience, Suzuki thus asserts: "When one attains the state of 'Muga', the state of 'Mushin,' the Unconscious, is realized. Muga is something identified with a state of ecstasy" (EZB III, 317–318).

Chapter 3

The Unconscious in Zen and *Bushidō*

The Religio-Aesthetic Way of the Martial Arts

In *Zen and Japanese Culture* and other writings, Suzuki describes what he regards to be the connection between Zen and the Japanese martial arts, holding that both are grounded in *mushin* or no-mind in its natural function as *heijōshin* or the ordinary mind of everyday life, while further explaining *mushin* in psychological terms as the cosmic Unconscious. Suzuki's psychologized Zen interpretation of *bushidō* (武士道) as the religio-aesthetic path of the samurai (侍) based on no-mind is no doubt fascinating, but as will be discussed, it is also one of the most contested, controversial, and criticized aspects of Suzuki's Zen, or what is also referred to as Suzuki's "samurai Zen."

The Art of Swordsmanship

In his presentation of traditional Japanese artforms that he claims to have been influenced by Zen aestheticism, Suzuki includes the martial arts of *kendō* (剣道) or the art swordmanship and *kyudō* (弓道) or the art of archery, both of which became highly developed in Bushido as the *dao* or religio-aesthetic way of the samurai warrior. Suzuki argues that mastery in the art of swordsmanship, like sumie painting, haiku poetry, noh drama, the tea ceremony, and other Zen-influenced Japanese arts, involves emptying the self into nothingness and attaining *mushin* or no-mind as the Unconscious. The Zen-trained swordsman transcends rational ego-consciousness and acts from unconscious intuition, which at the deeper subliminal level is attuned to its total surroundings and can therefore instantly react to the demands of its situation. Suzuki argues that when the samurai "empties himself of all thoughts . . . both man and sword turn into instruments in the hands, as it were, of the unconscious" (ZJC, 146). He continues: "Furthermore, the body and the mind are not separated, as they are in the case of intellectualization. The mind and the body move in perfect unison" (ZJC, 146). Hence, for Suzuki the Zen art of swordsmanship is a somaesthetic practice for realizing satori by cultivating nondual experience of bodymind oneness through integration of conscious and unconscious processes.

Summing up the connection between Zen and the samurai, Suzuki asserts: "Zen and the Sword's Way are one in this, that both ultimately aim at transcending the duality of life and death" (ZJC, 127). Both Zen and the art of swordsmanship arrive at the insight that in the state of *mushin* or no-mind, life and death are the same, and it is this paradoxical insight that liberates the samurai warrior from any fear of death (ZJC, 71). The ethics of Bushido consists in the cultivating of the Confucian virtues of loyalty, filial piety, and benevolence. He adds, "But to fulfill these duties successfully two things are needed: to train oneself in moral asceticism . . . and to be always ready to face death" (ZJC, 70). Suzuki relates the samurai's contemplation of impending death and nothingness to the moral code of Bushido, which is right action based on performance of "duty" (*giri*, 義理) versus "human feelings" (*ninjō*, 人情). He cites *Primer of Bushido* by the seventeenth-century warrior Daidōji Yūsan: "The idea most vital and essential to the samurai is that of death, which he ought to have before his mind day and night, night and day . . . you will come to consider every day of your life your last and dedicate it to the fulfillment of your obligations" (ZJC, 72). The samurai overcomes existential fear of mortality, death, and nothingness in the egoless state of *mushin* or "no-mind" as the cosmic Unconscious and is always prepared to die, such that he discharges his obligations without delay. Suzuki cites the teachings of Zen-trained master swordsman Yamaoka Tesshū (1836–1888), according to which the samurai's realization of no-mind or the Unconscious as the abyss of absolute nothingness is itself the satori experience of pre-mortem death, or the death of ego-consciousness, otherwise known in Zen as "the Great Death": "Tesshū knew from his long experience in Zen that a man has to die, for once, to his ordinary consciousness in order to awaken the Unconscious. . . . 'The great death' Zen-men talk so much about thus comes also to be experienced by him" (ZJC, 197).

Suzuki argues that "no-mind" (*mushin*, 無心) as the cosmic Unconscious is itself the "ordinary mind" (*heijōshin*, 平常心) of everyday life that functions as the source for creativity in the Zen aestheticism of traditional Japanese art culture, including the martial arts of Bushido: "The swordsman calls this unconscious 'the mind that is no-mind' (*mushin no shin*), or 'the mind that knows no stopping' (*tomaranu kokoro*) . . . or 'the everyday mind' (*heijō-shin*) . . . the mind that is no-mind is the last stage in the art of swordplay. 'To be of no-mind' (*mushin*) means the 'everyday mind' (*heijō-shin*)" (ZJC, 146–147). In Japanese swordplay, *mushin* or no-mind is a negative expression for what is in positive terms the "everyday mind": "When things are performed in a state of 'no-mind' (*mushin*) or 'no-thought' (*mu-nen*), which means the absence of all modes of self or ego-consciousness, the actor is perfectly free from inhibitions and feels nothing thwarting his line of behavior. . . . This is one's 'everyday mind' (*heijō-shin*)" (ZJC, 147). To master the Zen art of swordsmanship, the samurai must enter no-mind or the cosmic Unconscious as the field of emptiness devoid of subject-object bifurcation, whereupon the swordsman becomes one with his opponent: "The moment of intense concentration is the moment when perfect identification takes place between subject and object. . . . When this is not reached, it means that the field of consciousness has not yet been completely cleared up: that there still remains a 'subtle trace of thought' (*misai no ichinen*) which interferes with an act directly and straightforwardly issuing from the person — that is, psychologically speaking, from the Unconscious" (ZJC, 183). In his discussions of Zen and Bushido, Suzuki explains how the samurai is taught to access the boundless source of *ki* (気) or bioenergetic life-force pouring out from their cosmic Unconscious (ZJC, 193). He describes the inexhaustible power surging from its source in the lower abdomen of *hara* (腹) as the ocean of *ki*-energy cultivated by the discipline of swordsmanship, explaining that the reservoir of this inexhaustible energy supply is the Unconscious (ZJC, 193). Thus, similar to his discussions of Zen koan practice, Suzuki emphasizes that swordsmanship and other somaesthetic martial arts spring from the *hara* in the lower abdomen as the vital center of the cosmic Unconscious.

According to Suzuki, what Zen Buddhism terms prajna-intuition is a function of subliminal processes, so that to act intuitively is to depend on spontaneous impulses from the cosmic Unconscious as the principle of artistic creativity and the aesthetic experience of ecstasy. To attain mastery in the Zen art of swordsmanship, all technique must be forgotten so that the samurai warrior's unified bodymind acts intuitively, automatically, and unconsciously: "However well a man may be trained in the art, the swordsman can never be the master of his technical knowledge unless his psychic hindrances are removed, and he can keep the mind in the state of emptiness. . . . The entire body . . . will move as if automatically, with no conscious efforts on the part of the swordsman himself. . . . All the training is there, but the mind is entirely unconscious of it" (ZJC, 152–153). He adds: "When life is not intellectually and therefore consciously conditioned but left to the inner working of the Unconscious, it takes care of itself in an almost reflex automatic fashion, as in the case of the physiological functioning of an organic body" (ZJC, 197).

The "samurai Zen" of Suzuki uses the writings of the famous Rinzai Zen priest Takuan Sōho (1573–1645) to establish the historical relationship between Zen and swordsmanship. Moreover, in *Zen and Japanese Culture* Suzuki translates "Takuan's Letter to Yagyū Tajima no Kami Munenori" as a basis for his psychological interpretation of this Zen art of swordsmanship as an automatic function of the Unconscious (ZJC, 95–113). Suzuki describes Takuan's view of swordsmanship as recounted by Yagyū Tajima: "It is his Unconscious, not his analytical intelligence, that controls his behavior. Because of this the swordsman feels that the sword is controlled by some agent unknown to him and yet not unrelated to him. All the technique he has consciously and with a great deal of pains learned now operates as if directly from the fountainhead of the Unconscious" (ZJC, 438). As pointed out by Suzuki, Takuan was renowned not only as a master swordsman but also as a great connoisseur of the Japanese *wabi*-style of tea ceremony (ZJC, 276–278). Moreover, he was an expert in the Zen art of calligraphy. For Takuan, the elegant movements of a tea master, the graceful brushstrokes of calligraphy or ink painting, and the lightning-fast strikes of the samurai in the art of swordsmanship are done without conscious effort when they spontaneously originate from *mushin* or no-mind as the Unconscious. When acting from no-mind as the cosmic Unconscious of dharmakaya emptiness, the attention of the samurai warrior does not stop, cling, or attach to anything but continually flows without hindrance like the Dao, just as he does not focus on any localized object but expands his awareness to spread throughout the total situation. Although for Takuan it is good to concentrate on the *hara* as the center of *ki*-energy to accumulate its power, the samurai's awareness should not be exclusively localized in the lower abdomen but must be allowed to pervade everywhere so as to spontaneously, automatically, and unconsciously react to his circumstances as needed. Explaining the original mind of Zen as no-mind or the cosmic Unconscious, Suzuki writes: "The original mind is a mind unconscious of itself. . . . The conscious mind is *ushin no shin* contrasting with *mushin no shin*, mind unconscious of itself. *Mushin* literally means 'no-mind,' it is a mind negating itself, letting go itself from itself" (ZJC, 110). Here the words of Takuan's "The Mind of No-Mind" (*Mushin no shin*) are cited from Suzuki's own translation as follows:

> A mind unconscious of itself . . . is always flowing, it never halts, nor does it turn into a solid . . . it fills the whole body, pervading every part of the body, and nowhere standing still. If it should find a resting place anywhere, it is not a mind of no-mind. A no-mind keeps nothing in it. It is called *munen*, "no-thought." *Mushin* and *munen* are synonymous. When *mushin* or *munen* is attained, the mind moves from one object to another, flowing like a stream of water, filling every possible corner. For this reason the mind fulfills every function required of it. (ZJC, 111)

Suzuki further emphasizes that for Takuan, the psychology of no-mind-ness as the cosmic Unconscious is itself correlated with a Zen metaphysics of sunyata (*kū*, 空), emptiness: "Takuan is never tired of dilating on the doctrine of emptiness (*śūnyatā*), which is the metaphysics of *mushin no shin* ('mind of no-mind')" (ZJC, 113). He continues: "The [swordsman] must turn himself into a puppet in the hands of the unconscious. The unconscious must supersede the conscious. Metaphysically speaking, this is the philosophy of *śūnyatā* ('emptiness'). The technique of swordsmanship is based on its psychology, and the psychology is a localized application of the metaphysics" (ZJC, 117). Hence, according to Suzuki's interpretation of Takuan's writings, swordsmanship and other somaesthetic artforms of traditional Japanese culture are to be conceived in terms of a Zen psychology of no-mind as the cosmic Unconscious and its underlying metaphysics of sunyata or emptiness.

Further applying his philosophical psychology of the cosmic Unconscious to the Zen art of swordsmanship, Suzuki asserts: "Takuan, being a Zen master, sees into the very source of reality, which we may call the metaphysical or cosmic Unconscious" (ZJC, 199). He adds: "Psychologically stated, the sword now symbolizes the Unconscious in the person of the swordsman. He then moves as a kind of automaton. He is no more himself. He has given himself up to an influence outside his everyday consciousness, which is no other than his own deeply buried Unconscious, whose presence he was never hitherto aware of" (ZJC, 209). Thus for Suzuki, the master swordsman is one who realizes satori as insight into the egoless Zen state of *mushin* or no-mind, such that all actions of the samurai are automatic, instinctive, lightning-fast reactions to the immediate situation as directed by spontaneous impulses from the cosmic Unconscious.

While explaining the role of the Unconscious in Yagyū's "Sword of Mystery," Suzuki writes: "The Unconscious dormant at the root of existence is awakened, it now directs instinctually all the movements not only of the conscious mind but of the physical body" (ZJC, 163). He adds: "It is the Unconscious which works behind the field of consciousness. Ordinarily it is the consciousness that creates all sorts of inhibitions and obstructs the free movements of the man. . . . The Unconscious, therefore, must be brought out and made to occupy the entire field of mentation. . . . This is the wielding of Yagyū's Sword of Mystery" (ZJC, 162–163). Suzuki then goes on to say: "By thus applying the modern psychology of the Unconscious to the art of swordplay we may be able to interpret not only Yagyū's methodology but also that of other schools" (ZJC, 163). But as he further clarifies: "Perhaps the secret sword belongs in the spiritual or metaphysical domain which must be postulated as lying beyond the psychological unconscious" (ZJC, 163). For Suzuki this means that although the swordsman must learn to tap the creative power of his unconscious mind, it is not the empirical unconscious posited by Western psychology but the deeper, higher, and wider unconscious level of our mind realized in Zen satori that he refers to as the cosmic Unconscious.

Elsewhere, Suzuki further elaborates on Takuan's instructions about prajna wisdom of emptiness in no-mind as the Unconscious to his swordsman disciple Yagyu Tajima-no-kami: "*Prajña,* which Takuan calls 'immovable *prajñā*' . . . is the immovable mover which unconsciously operates in the field of consciousness" (ZP, 20–21). He continues: "When the swordsman stands against his opponent . . . He just stands there with his sword which, forgetful of all technique, is really only to follow the dictates of the unconscious. . . . When he strikes, it is not the man but the sword in the hands of the unconscious that strikes" (ZP, 21). To illustrate Takuan's instructions on the operation of no-mind as the Unconscious in the Zen art of swordsmanship, Suzuki discusses the Academy Award winning 1954 film *The Seven Samurai*, co-written and directed by Kurosawa Akira, widely regarded as a masterpiece of Japanese cinema (ZP, 21–22).[1] Suzuki comments: "There is a Japanese film play, recently introduced to American audiences, in which a scene is presented where the unemployed samurais are given a trial of their swordsmanship" (ZP, 21).[2] The samurai who finally wins this contest displays not only the highest technical mastery of swordsmanship but also an unconscious intuitive feeling of the total situation that allows him to sense a hidden danger. Explaining this scene from Kurosawa's samurai film, Suzuki says that the "sixth sense" developed by the master swordsman through Zen training is not the rational knowing of ego-consciousness but the deeper subliminal awareness of unconscious intuition: "To be exact, this is not knowledge but an intuition taking place in the unconscious" (ZP, 22).

The Art of Archery

According to Suzuki, the traditional Japanese art of archery, like that of swordsmanship, is a somaesthetic discipline that cultivates nondual bodymind awareness through integration of conscious and unconscious processes. Suzuki argues that to master archery, like other Zen-inspired traditional Japanese arts, requires that one enter *mushin* or no-mind as the cosmic Unconscious.

Zen in the Art of Archery by the German philosopher Eugen Herrigel is one of the most popular books ever published on Zen and the traditional Japanese arts. While teaching philosophy at Tohoku University in Sendai, Herrigel undertook an apprenticeship with Awa Kenzō, a master of *kyūdō* (弓道), the way of archery. However, along with the teachings of his master, Herrigel also frequently cites the translations and Zen writings of Suzuki. Moreover, Suzuki wrote the introduction to Herrigel's book (IZAA, x).[3]

To clarify the relation between Zen and the various arts of traditional Japanese culture, including archery and other military arts, Herrigel (1981, 7) cites the view of Suzuki: "In his *Essays in Zen Buddhism*, D. T. Suzuki has succeeded in showing that Japanese culture and Zen are intimately connected and that Japanese art, the spiritual attitude of the Samurai, the Japanese way of life, the moral, aesthetic to a certain extent even the intellectual life of the Japanese owe their peculiarities to this background of Zen."[4] Herrigel then discusses how among the arts that developed under the aegis of Zen in traditional Japanese culture is the military art of archery.

The most intriguing, yet also the most controversial aspect of Herrigel's book is Awa's teaching that the highest level in the Zen art of archery involves realization of the "It." Herrigel writes:

> One day, I asked the Master: "How can the shot be loosed if 'I do not do it'?"
> "'It' shoots," he replied. (1981, 51)

Herrigel asks the master: "And who or what is this 'It'?" (1981, 52). The master gradually teaches Herrigel the unified bodymind process of shooting with the bow and arrow as a sacred ritual, a ceremonial act that includes grasping the bow, nocking the arrow, raising the bow above the head, drawing and remaining at the point of highest tension, and loosing the shot with a resonant "twang" sound, each step with the correct method of deep rhythmic breathing in and out, in a state of mindful relaxation and total concentration (1981, 20–21). For years Herrigel fails to release the shot in the proper way, and is scolded by his teacher Kenzō Awa: "Stop thinking about the shot!" (1981, 47). The master further admonishes: "The right shot at the right moment does not come because you do not let go of yourself" (1981, 30). But at last, Herrigel finally has his breakthrough: "Then, one day, after a shot, the Master made a deep bow and broke off the lesson. 'Just then "It" shot!' he cried, as I stared at him bewildered. And when I at last understood what he meant I couldn't suppress a sudden whoop of delight" (1981, 52). As the dialogue resumes between teacher and student, the narrative continues: "'Do you now understand,' the Master asked me one day after a particularly good shot, 'what I mean by "*It* shoots," "*It* hits"?'" (1981, 61). Thus, the main point of Awa's instructions on Zen in the art of archery is that it is not "I" who shoots but rather "'*It*' aims," "'*It*' shoots," and "'*It*' hits." Moreover, having given his account of Zen in the art of archery, Herrigel goes on to discuss Zen in the art of swordsmanship: "It is as if the sword wielded itself, and just as we say in archery that 'It' takes aim and hits, so here 'It' takes the place of the ego, availing itself of a facility and a dexterity which the ego only acquires by conscious effort" (1981, 76).

Steven Heine, one of the foremost scholars of Zen and modern Japanese philosophy, attempts to unravel the mystery of "It" in Herrigel's book: "Fascination with Herrigel's account of this training in archery . . . revolves around the emphasis he puts on the syllable 'It' in the instructive phase used repeatedly by his Japanese mentor Awa Kenzō, '"It" shoots.' . . . The key to success is to realize that from the standpoint of all-encompassing emptiness, nobody in particular lets loose the arrow, because 'It' does the shooting in and of itself" (2008, 19).

Heine discusses some of the hypercritical negative reactions to Herrigel's book, as well as to D. T. Suzuki's endorsement of the book (in his Foreword) by Arthur Koestler in *The Lotus and the Robot* (1960), and Yamada Shōji in *Shots in the Dark* (2009, 20–21). Yamada explains the "It" as a linguistic error. As Heine points out: "Yamada speculates that Herrigel simply misheard or mistook the innocuous Japanese phrase *sore deshita*, which means 'that's it.' Perhaps Awa meant, 'That was a good shot,' without suggesting that an extraneous force was responsible" (2008, 21). In an effort to mediate between the two competing methods that he terms "traditional Zen narrative," (TZN) in this case as represented by Herrigel and Suzuki, and "historical and cultural criticism," (HCC) or as represented by Koestler and Yamada, Heine proposes his own middle way interpretation of the "It." He points out that it is quite possible that Awa told Herrigel something that was translatable as "'It' shoots." Moreover, "'It' shoots," one can argue, does not reify the subject but is rather a Western way of capturing the dynamic, action-oriented Japanese syntax (2008, 27). Heine suggests that Herrigel's expression "It shoots" is also echoed in Martin Heidegger's existential-phenomenological interpretation of an interactive

Event as an activity beyond subject-object dualism, as stated in his dictum, "The Event happens" (2008, 28). "'It' shoots" just as "the Event happens."

My contention, however, is that from the standpoint of the modern Zen philosophy, psychology, and aesthetics of Suzuki, the "It" clearly refers to *mushin* or no-mind as the cosmic Unconscious, that deeper intuitive subliminal mind operating beneath the surface of ego-consciousness and its subject-object dualism. In his introduction to Herrigel's book, Suzuki provides his own distinctive psychological interpretation of Zen in the Japanese art of archery based on his signature concept of the Unconscious: "One of the most significant features we notice in the practice of archery and in fact of all the arts as they are studied in Japan . . . is that they are not intended for utilitarian purposes only or for purely aesthetic enjoyments, but are also meant to train the mind. . . . The mind has first to be attuned to the Unconscious" (IZAA, vii). He adds: "If one really wishes to be master of an art, technical knowledge of it is not enough. One has to transcend technique, so that the art becomes an 'artless art' growing out of the Unconscious" (IZAA, vii). Suzuki thus declares that to master the art of archery, as for any of the other somaesthetic Zen-inspired arts in traditional Japanese culture, it is necessary to *empty the mind* and thereby realize the egoless state of no-mind or the Unconscious: "In the case of archery, the hitter and the hit are no longer two opposing objects, but are one reality. The archer ceases to be conscious of himself as the one who is engaged in hitting the bull's eye which confronts him. This state of unconsciousness is realized only when [one becomes] completely empty and rid of the self" (IZAA, vii). For Suzuki, then, one becomes a master in the Zen art of archery by emptying the self so that the archer is no longer conscious of shooting with the bow and arrow to hit a target but now spontaneously acts with effortless naturalness from out of his source in the Unconscious. In *Zen and Japanese Culture*, Suzuki again makes reference to the teachings of master Awa as recorded in Herrigel's *Zen in the Art of Archery* (ZJC, 120). This is how Suzuki explains the workings of Zen *mushin* or no-mind as the Unconscious in the arts of swordsmanship and archery: "The swordsman calls this unconscious 'the mind that is no mind' (*mushin no shin*) . . . which means the absence of all modes of self- or ego-consciousness. . . . If he is shooting [in the art of archery], he just takes out his bow, puts an arrow to it, stretches the string, fixes his eyes on the target, and when he judges the adjustment to be right, he lets the arrow go" (ZJC, 146–147).

In his book *Shots in the Dark*, Yamada suggests that Herrigel's account of the "It" is either something that Herrigel himself fabricated when he wrote *Zen in the Art of Archery* or that there was a miscommunication between Awa and Herrigel concerning "It shoots" (2009, 50). He concludes that Herrigel mistook Awa's phrase *sore desu* or "that's it," for "'It' shoots." Yamada's account, however, inadvertently opens up another possible interpretation: the "It" is the Unconscious. Explaining the original German version of Herrigel's *Zen and the Art of Archery* (*Zen in der Kunst des Bogenschiessens*, 1948), Yamada writes: "In considering *Zen in the Art of Archery*, particular attention must be paid to the concept of 'It,' which lies at the heart of the story. This is the teaching that says that the archer does not shoot the bow but that 'It' does the shooting; the idea that an entity beyond human understanding called 'It' acts upon the archer and brings forth a good shot" (2009, 40). Yamada now goes on to elucidate the meaning of the German word for "It":

> In the original German, "It" is expressed by the term "Es." "Es" is a familiar word in psychoanalysis and refers to the unconscious. Psychoanalysis teaches that a person's spiritual growth comes from establishing the Self (the Ego) on the foundation of "It" (the Id). To put it another way, when a person experiences a crisis of the Ego, the power of the Id becomes too dominant. Psychoanalysis treats this by analyzing the unconscious and bringing the Id to the person's consciousness so that the person can integrate it into the Ego. The "It" that Herrigel wrote about fits quite neatly into this Freudian way of thinking. (2009, 40)

As pointed out by Yamada, the German word that Herrigel uses for "the It" is *das Es*, which is also the German word that Freud used for the id or "the unconscious." From this I would argue that in the English translation of Herrigel's German work, every time there is a reference to "the It" there is a reference to *the unconscious*. Hence, when the text reads "It shoots," it means "the unconscious shoots." When the text reads "It hits," it means "the unconscious hits." And when the text proclaims, "It is not 'I' but the 'It' that shoots," it can be alternatively translated as "It is not 'I' but 'the unconscious' that shoots." My conclusion is that what Herrigel refers to as "the It" in fact signifies *das Es* (the Id), "the unconscious."

On several occasions, even in the English translation of Herrigel's *Zen in the Art of Archery*, there are strong indications that "the It" or the id is Unconscious, such as when he states that the goal of archery is "to loose the shot, self-obliviously and unconsciously" (1981, 50). Again, while comparing archery with the art of swordsmanship, Herrigel asserts: "The swordsmaster is as unself-conscious as the beginner" (1981, 77). Herrigel, a German philosopher, was thoroughly familiar with Freud's notion of the id (*Es*) as the unconscious and uses this term in the original German version to express what was translated into English as the "It" in *Zen in the Art of Archery*. If Herrigel's term for "It" is translated from the German word *Es* for the id or "the unconscious," then it conforms exactly to Suzuki's psychological view in his introduction to *Zen in the Art of Archery*, whereby to master archery one must empty the mind so as to function instinctively, or as it were, effortlessly, naturally, spontaneously, and unconsciously. Suzuki thus asserts that in the Zen art of archery, "The mind has first to be attuned to the Unconscious" (IZAA, vii). Perhaps it cannot ever be determined if Awa taught Herrigel that "'*It*' shoots." Nonetheless, I would suggest that from the standpoint of Suzuki's Zen doctrine of *mushin* or no-mind as the cosmic Unconscious, Awa's teaching "It is not 'I' but the 'It' that shoots," can be understood in psychological terms as meaning "It is not 'I' but 'the Unconscious' that shoots."

Bruce Lee, the superstar Chinese martial artist, iconic movie actor, and bestselling author who developed his own fighting style called JKD or *Jeet kune dō* (Way of the intercepting fist), was an advocate of Suzuki's idea of martial arts based on Zen/Chan no-mind and Daoist nonaction in its spontaneous functioning as the Unconscious. It should be noted that Bruce Lee was a philosophy major at the University of Washington, where he studied Asian and Western philosophical traditions. Bruce Lee's closest disciples confirm that he was very enthusiastic about Herrigel's *Zen and the Art of Archery* and recommended it to his students. Kareem Abdul-Jabbar, one of the all-time greatest players in the NBA, as well as a student of JKD and costar in Bruce Lee's film *Game of Death* (1979), recalls the following conversation with his basketball coach, wherein he says: "Did you ever read *Zen and the Art of Archery*? . . . Bruce Lee told me about it. . . . It was written by a German philosophy professor who studied archery under a Zen master. Basically, the idea is that through years of practice, the archer no longer thinks about the bow, the arrow, or the bull's-eye because the body takes over unconsciously" (2017, 71–72).

In the classic martial arts film *Enter the Dragon* (1973), the invincible Shaolin monk played by Bruce Lee gives an explanation about the secret of *Gung fu* similar to the instructions of Awa's teachings recorded in Herrigel's *Zen and the Art of Archery*, as well as the introduction to this work by Suzuki. After Bruce Lee's character wins a spectacular match before an audience of monks at the Shaolin Buddhist temple, his teacher confirms that he has now progressed from the physical to the spiritual level of combat. When his teacher asks him to describe his new spiritual insight, the Shaolin monk played by Bruce Lee first explains that the highest technique is to have no technique. He then reveals: "It is not 'I' who hits, '*It*' hits all by itself." Just as according to Herrigel's book Awa Kenzō teaches that in the Zen art of archery "'*It*' shoots," and in the samurai art of swordsmanship "'*It*' strikes," so Bruce Lee's character reveals that at the highest level of martial arts one realizes that "'*It*' hits." But once again the mystery here is to what does "It" refer? Bruce Lee himself directly answers this question when he explains: "'It' is the state of mind that the Japanese refer to as *mushin*" (Hymns, 1979, 89). It is not "I" or the rational ego-consciousness that hits, but *mushin* or no-mind as the deeper unconscious. Articulating the key Zen teaching of JKD, Bruce Lee further explains: "Learning the technique corresponds to an intellectual apprehension of Zen of its philosophy. . . . In jeet kune do, all the technique is to be forgotten, and the unconscious is to be left alone to handle the situation" (1999, 195). While defining his martial art of JKD, Bruce Lee reiterates the words of master Awa in Herrigel's *Zen and the Art of Archery*: "It is as if the sword wielded itself, and just as we say in archery that 'It' takes aim and hits" (1981, 76). Moreover, Bruce Lee teaches: "In jeet kune do, all the technique is to be forgotten, and the unconscious is to be left alone to handle the situation" (1999, 195). Lee here repeats almost verbatim the words of Suzuki from *Zen and Japanese Culture*: "In swordplay, all the technique is to be forgotten, and the Unconscious is to be left alone to handle the situation" (ZJC, 152). As Suzuki further clarifies in his introduction to *Zen in the Art of Archery*: "One has to transcend technique, so that the art [of archery] becomes an 'artless art' growing out of the Unconscious" (IZAA, vii). Or as Suzuki explains about the Zen-inspired arts in general: "Underneath all the practical techniques or the methodological details necessary for the mastery of an art, there are certain intuitions directly reaching what I call the Cosmic Unconscious" (ZJC, 192).

From the standpoint of Suzuki's Zen aestheticism, when it is said by Herrigel that in the Japanese art of archery "'It' shoots," this "It" refers to the id (*Es*) or the Unconscious. For Suzuki the Unconscious is not a reified substantial entity but refers to spontaneous unconscious operations that process information in the wider encompassing felt background of immediate experience at a level beneath the surface of ordinary waking ego-consciousness. In Herrigel's *Zen Art of Archery* as allegedly taught by Awa Kenzō, it is the Unconscious that shoots, just as in the Zen art of swordsmanship transmitted by Takuan Sōho, it is the Unconscious that strikes, while in Bruce Lee's Daoist-Zen/Chan art of JKD, it is the Unconscious that hits. Thus, in terms of Suzuki's modern Zen psychology of the unconscious mind as applied to archery, swordsmanship, and other somaesthetic martial arts of Bushido, it is not the "I" of dualistic ego-consciousness that acts through rational deliberation but rather it is *mushin* or no-mind as our deeper cosmic Unconscious, that with effortless naturalness instinctively aims, shoots, strikes, and hits all by itself.

Suzuki's "Samurai Zen" in Critical Perspective

Throughout the present volume there have already been discussions about various criticisms leveled against Suzuki's Zen. In what follows, I develop my own critique focusing on Suzuki's Zen aestheticism, especially his apologistic discourse on "samurai Zen" in Bushido as the art of swordsmanship, demonstrating how it is ultimately based on his philosophical psychology of Zen *mushin* or no-mind as the cosmic Unconscious.

Imperialistic Militarism in Suzuki's "Samurai Zen" as the Art of Swordsmanship

In recent scholarship, much of the criticism leveled against Suzuki's presentation of Zen and Japanese culture has focused on charges of excessive wartime patriotism and nationalistic militarism. As said by Jaffe: "Another major vein of Suzuki criticism . . . centers on Suzuki's Japanese nationalism, and alleged support for Japan's military aggression in Asia, including the Pacific War that raged from 1937 to 1945" (SWS I, xvi). The accusations that he supported Japanese ultranationalism, militarism, ethnic chauvinism, colonialism, and imperialism are especially aimed at Suzuki's apologistic discourse on Zen and Bushido as the way of the samurai warrior, or what is sometimes referred to as Suzuki's "samurai Zen."

Suzuki maintains that Zen kensho is an immediate experience of directly seeing into one's Buddha nature and that Buddha nature is an inseparable unity of *prajñā* and *karuṇā* or wisdom and compassion: "Buddha-nature . . . consists in *prajñā* and *karuṇā*" (MCB, 64). Yet in his writings on Bushido, Suzuki points out the apparent contradiction between Zen Buddhism as a religion of compassion and the violence of warfare: "It may be considered strange that Zen has in any way been affiliated with the spirit of the military classes of Japan. Whatever form Buddhism takes in the various countries where it flourishes, it is a religion of compassion and in its varied history it has never been found engaged in warlike activities." He continues: "How is it, then, that Zen has come to activate the fighting spirit of the Japanese warrior"? (ZJC, 61).

Arthur Koestler leveled one of the harshest criticisms against Suzuki's militaristic presentation of Zen and Bushido. Koestler criticizes the illogical, irrational, and paradoxical aspects of what he calls Suzuki's "Zen hocus-pocus" (1960, 246). Moreover, he critically undermines Suzuki's Zen writings as "pseudo-mystical verbiage," asserting that his Zen ideas are "at best an existential hoax, at worst a web of solemn absurdities" (1960, 245, 233). Furthermore, he argues that Suzuki's Zen irrationalism leads to amoralism. What alarms Koestler is Suzuki's notion that the Zen-trained samurai warrior abandons all logic and ethics so as to act "automatically" (1960, 252). Summing up Suzuki's position in his account of Bushido, Koestler writes: "The perfect swordsman, says Dr. Suzuki, 'becomes a kind of automaton, as to speak, as far as his own consciousness is concerned' [ZJC, 94]" (1960, 262). Koestler holds that it is this mechanical aspect of the Zen samurai as an automaton that results in a moral relativism beyond good and evil devoid of any universal ethical norms (1960, 232). He adds: "Nor do they recognize Good and Evil as absolutes; Japanese ethics is pragmatic, relativistic and situational" (1960, 232). Moreover, Koestler directly traces the amoralism and ethical relativism of the Zen-trained samurai warrior as a mindless robotic automaton beyond any moral standards of good and evil to Suzuki's Zen concepts of *muga* or "nonego" and *mushin* or "no-mind" (1960, 243).

Imperial Way Zen by Christopher Ives is an outstanding work that analyzes the sociopolitical ideology critique of Zen Buddhist militarism, imperialism, and ultranationalism formulated by Ichikawa Hakugen (1902–1986). The ideology critique established by Ichikawa is directed toward many leading Zen Buddhist thinkers, including Suzuki and Nishida Kitarō. Ives cites the view of Ichikawa that the Zen concept of *mushin* or no-mind has led to distorted ethical ideals based on ambiguous moral relativism underlying Imperial Way Zen (*kōdō zen,* 皇道禅). According to Ichikawa: "When this accommodating path of no-mind leads one to dwell in a static sense of oneness between one's subjectivity and external things . . . any possible ethic of responsibility gets miscarried" (cited by Ives, 2009, 135).

In *Zen at War*, Sōtō Zen priest Brian Daizen Victoria critically examines the complicit role of Zen in the militarism, imperialism, and ultranationalism of Japan's totalitarian emperor system during World War II, including the Zen writings of Suzuki, along with those of Nishida and others in the Kyoto School of modern Japanese philosophy (2006, 105–112). Even if Victoria has overstated Suzuki's involvement with Japan's World War II militarististic ambitions, he nonetheless raises valid questions about Suzuki's apologetic misuse of Zen *mushin* or no-mind:

> Experienced Zen practitioners know that the "no-mind" of Zen does in fact exist. Equally, they know that *samadhi* (i.e. meditative) power also exists. But they also know, or at least *ought* to know, that these things in their original Buddhist formulation, had absolutely nothing to do with bringing harm to others. On the contrary, authentic Buddhist awakening is characterized by a combination of wisdom and compassion — identifying oneself with others and seeking to eliminate suffering in all its forms. (Victoria, 2006, 230)

Victoria thus rightly concludes that while the Zen concept of *mushin* or no-mind has been misappropriated by Suzuki and other apologistic Japanese wartime thinkers to illicitly justify military aggression, it should instead function as the basis for a Zen Buddhist altruistic ethics of compassion.

A Critique of Suzuki's Zen Aestheticism Based on No-Mind as the Unconscious

It has been seen how critiques of Suzuki's alleged nationalistic militarism have especially been leveled against his writings on Bushido, the way of the samurai warrior. Furthermore, Suzuki explains Bushido and the art of swordsmanship as part of the wider Japanese artistic cultural heritage developed under the aegis of "Zen aestheticism," including the traditional Japanese artforms of haiku poetry, ink painting, noh drama, flower arrangement, gardening, and the tea ceremony. According to Suzuki, all the arts and crafts influenced by Zen are rooted in the egoless flow state of *mushin* or no-mind as the cosmic Unconscious. To support his view, Suzuki cites the letters written to an accomplished swordsman Takuan: "Takuan strongly emphasizes the significance of *mushin*, which may be regarded in a way as corresponding to the concept of the unconscious" (ZJC, 94). Further describing the Zen aestheticism underlying Takuan's conception of *mushin* or no-mind, Suzuki continues: "*mushin* (*wu-hsin* in Chinese), no-mind . . . is where all arts merge into Zen" (ZJC, 94). However, in this same passage, Suzuki goes on to explain the moral implication of *mushin* or no-mind as unconsciousness, saying that *mushin* is transcendence of the dualism between good and evil (ZJC, 93). In this context I present my own critical analysis of Suzuki's "Zen aestheticism," claiming that it results in an amoral worldview that eliminates normative ethical standards by reducing the good to the beautiful. Moreover, I have directed my critical remarks toward Suzuki's psychological interpretation of Bushido and the art of swordmanship based on *mushin* or no-mind as the cosmic Unconscious, especially as propounded in his "samurai Zen." Suzuki's account of Zen swordsmanship contains many profound insights and is no doubt one of the most popular aspects of his modern Zen aestheticism. Nonetheless, it is shown how the psychological concept of *mushin* underlying Suzuki's Zen aestheticism, when misapplied, becomes highly problematic at the ethical, social, and political levels of discourse.

The Critical Buddhism (*hihan bukkyō*, 批判仏教) of Matsumoto Shirō and Hakamaya Noriaki at Komazawa University undermines the modern Zen of Suzuki as a version of what they call Topical Buddhism, further described as an "aesthetic mysticism" beyond all rational and moral discrimination. Jamie Hubbard explains that what Critical Buddhism calls the Topical Buddhism of Suzuki, Nishida, and other modern Japanese Buddhist thinkers, is "a term coined to refer to an aesthetic mysticism unconcerned with critical differentiation between truth and falsity, and not in need of rational demonstration" (Swanson, 1997, vii). Critical Buddhism maintains that one of the most serious problems with the so-called Topical Buddhism of Suzuki as well as Nishida and the Kyoto School is that it has lost the original Buddhist emphasis on causation, karma, and morality. They argue that by positing absolute nothingness as an ontological topos or spatial locus beyond all conceptual distinctions, including discrimination between good and evil, the aesthetic mysticism of Suzuki and other modern Zen thinkers has eliminated any normative ground for ethics. Generally speaking, Critical Buddhism opposes the topological philosophy of Japanese Buddhism and modern Zen when it claims that everything has Buddha nature, tathagatagarbha, or original enlightenment, which they regard as a return to the Hindu Atman/Brahman theory of eternal substance. It is further argued that Suzuki's aesthetic mysticism is a "naturalism" which claims that since everything has Buddha nature, everything is to be affirmed "just as it is" (*sono mama*). For Critical Buddhism, insofar as the naturalism of Suzuki and Nishida affirms everything "just as it is" in the aesthetic immediacy of pure experience, it thereby removes the need to criticize, resist, and change unjust social conditions. Hubbard explains: "Another pernicious effect of the 'naturalism' of topical philosophy is that its affirmation that things 'as they are' already are 'as they should be' eliminates the need to think critically about either self or society. For example, the idea that Buddhism is beyond ethics is lent support by the rhetoric of Zen spokesmen such as D. T. Suzuki and Nishida Kitarō, who focus on the immediacy of direct experience beyond the reach of historical contingency" (Swanson, 1997, 100). Remarking on the charges of

Critical Buddhism against the Zen concept of Buddha nature, Heine observes: "Zen, in particular, has often hidden its support for the status quo behind what is in effect, an elitist aestheticism based on the notion that everything reflects the buddha-dharma (*zen'itsu-buppō*)" (Swanson, 1997, 257). The Zen aestheticism of Suzuki can thus be understood as a paradigm case of what Heine refers to as an "elitist aestheticism" that endorses the status quo through a naturalism that affirms everything just as it is in its Buddha nature as the beauty of emptiness-suchness.

As discussed above, Ichikawa Hakugen (Ives, 2009, 135) and the Sōtō Zen priest Brian Daizen Victoria (2006, 230) criticize how the Zen concept of *mushin* or "no-mind" led to distorted ethical ideals based on ambiguous moral relativism underlying Imperial Way Zen, thus resulting in the complicit role of Zen Buddhism in Japanese militarism, imperialism, and ultranationalism during World War II. This kind of ambiguous moral relativism is clearly exhibited in Suzuki's writings on Zen and the samurai: "Zen has no special doctrine or philosophy, no set of concepts or intellectual formulas. . . . It is, therefore, extremely flexible in adapting itself to almost any philosophy and moral doctrine as long as its intuitive teaching is not interfered with. It may be found wedded to anarchism or fascism, communism or democracy, atheism or idealism, or any political or economic dogmatism" (ZJC, 63). In this disturbing passage Suzuki asserts that Zen is a neutral position with no special philosophy of its own and can therefore be used to support *any* ideology, including totalitarian military dictatorships based on fascism. It seems that Suzuki has now completely removed Zen *mushin* from its Buddhist philosophical context grounded in an altruistic ethics of compassion, kindness, mercy, nonviolence, peace, and reverence for all life. For as said by Victoria, in its original formulation, Zen *mushin* or no-mind had nothing to do with bringing harm to others but instead was the source of wisdom and compassion (2006, 230).

In the Zen aestheticism of Suzuki, the Zen-trained samurai who attains satori as the egoless flow state of no-mind or the cosmic Unconscious acts with total freedom to transcend all moral responsibilities. Yet Suzuki expresses the problem with this view in one of his postwar writings: "In *satori* there is a world of *satori*. However, by itself *satori* is unable to judge the right and wrong of war. With regard to disputes in the ordinary world, it is necessary to employ intellectual discrimination" (Satō, 2008, 117). Thus in at least this passage, Suzuki recognizes that even if the Zen-trained samurai who has realized satori awakening to the cosmic Unconscious as undiscriminated discrimination in prajna wisdom of emptiness, nonetheless, it requires norm-governed intellectual discrimination between true and false, right and wrong, just and unjust, or good and evil to navigate in the ordinary relative world of conventional distinctions.

I would argue that Suzuki's ambiguous moral relativism, as well as his intermittent lapses into imperialistic militarism, ultranationalism, cultural chauvinism, and ethnocentrism, is ultimately the consequence of his "Zen aestheticism" (ZJC, 27; *Zen no "bi" ron*, 禅の「美」論, ZNB, 38–39), which is itself based on his philosophical psychology of Zen *mushin* or no-mind as the cosmic Unconscious. What is meant by the term "aestheticism"? Aestheticism is the doctrine that beauty is the fundamental value from which other values are derived. The doctrine of aestheticism becomes problematic, however, when it privileges the value of beauty to the degree that all other values, including logical, spiritual, and moral values, are collapsed into, or identified with, aesthetic values. Kōsaka Masaaki argues that aestheticism is *the* outstanding trait of Japanese thought and culture throughout its history: "I will treat the history of Japanese culture and society by dividing it into four periods. The characteristic which runs topographically through all the periods is aestheticism" (1967, 245). He then goes on to define the term "aestheticism" as follows: "There are many kinds of values, for example, utility, pleasure, happiness, freedom, truth, and so on. If there is a culture or society wherein beauty stands at the top of the value system, such a culture is aesthetic. This is what I mean by the term 'aestheticism'" (1967, 257). For Kōsaka, then, "aestheticism" is the general characteristic of Japanese cultural history throughout its various periods, insofar as beauty functions as the core value in Japanese tradition. But as noted by Fujita Masakatsu, postwar Japanese philosophers such as Hayashi Naoichi have severely criticized Kōsaka's aestheticism: "Kōsaka and other Kyoto School philosophers engaged in a philosophical grounding of the war . . . by aestheticizing and sanctifying the war of aggression" (2019, 208). Accordingly, I would argue that Suzuki's account of Bushido and the art of swordsmanship based on his philosophical psychology of the Unconscious can likewise be seen as an effort to justify warfare by aestheticizing violence, suicide, and death.

In *Zen and Japanese Culture*, Suzuki describes the emergence of "Japanese art culture" (ZJC, 19–37), culminating in a "Zen aestheticism" (ZJC, 27). What Suzuki calls "Zen aestheticism" is in some respects continuous with what Ivan Morris (1969, 194) refers to as the "rampant aestheticism" characterizing the "cult of beauty" that flourished during the Heian period (794–1185). This is how Morris describes the aesthetic primacy of art over morality in the Heian period cult of beauty as depicted in Murasaki Shikibu's eleventh-century novel *The Tale of Genji*: "Artistic sensibility was more highly valued than ethical goodness. . . . For all their talk about 'heart' and 'feeling,' this stress on the cult of the beautiful, to the virtual exclusion of any concern with charity, sometimes lends a rather chilling impression to the people of Genji's world" (1969, 82). Like the Heian period aestheticism portrayed in *The Tale of Genji*, the Zen aestheticism described by Suzuki raises the same problem whereby the artistic enjoyment of "beauty" (*bi*, 美) comes to be a value prioritized over the Mahayana Buddhist altruistic ethics of "compassion" (*jihi*, 慈悲) as moral sympathy for the suffering of all beings.

Suzuki himself raises the question of whether the violent act of killing in the Zen art of swordsmanship that arises from *mushin* or unconscious instinct is in conflict with the Buddhist morality of compassion for all sentient beings: "The sword is generally associated with killing, and most of us wonder how it came into connexion with Zen, which is a school of Buddhism teaching the gospel of love and mercy. . . . It is really not he [the samurai] but the sword itself that does the killing. He has no desire to do harm to anybody, but the enemy appears and makes himself a victim. It is as though the sword performs automatically its function of justice" (ZJC, 145). Here it is declared that it is not the samurai himself but the sword that kills. Or as Suzuki elsewhere tells us: "When he [the samurai] strikes, it is not the man but the sword in the hands of the unconscious that strikes" (ZP, 21). He goes on to explain how just as the sword performs automatically, the Zen-trained samurai becomes an automaton under the control of unconscious impulses: "Psychologically stated, the sword now symbolizes the Unconscious in the person of the swordsman. He then moves as a kind of automaton. . . . He has given himself up to an influence outside his everyday consciousness, which is no other than his own deeply buried Unconscious" (ZJC, 209). Moreover, in his translation of a letter on the Zen art of swordsmanship by Takuan, it is asserted: "A man who has thoroughly mastered the art [of swordsmanship] does not use the sword and the opponent kills himself" (ZJC, 166). The samurai now has complete absolution from all moral responsibility: for whereas sometimes it is said that the samurai becomes an automaton that kills under the control of the Unconscious and at other times that it is not the samurai but the sword itself that kills as directed by spontaneous impulses from the Unconscious, now we are told that upon mastering the art of swordsmanship, it is neither the samurai nor his sword that kills, because the opponent kills himself.

For Suzuki, the Japanese tradition of Zen aestheticism includes Bushido as the religio-aesthetic path of the warrior, the key teaching of which is that the samurai must wield his sword in an egoless flow state of *mushin* as the nonattached, spontaneous, and unconscious mind of satori. But he then goes on to distort and misuse the concept of no-mind as the basis for his Zen aestheticism such that ethics is replaced by aesthetics. The dangers of Suzuki's militarized Zen aestheticism can be seen in his romantic portrayal of the samurai, whereby insofar as swordsmanship is rooted in *mushin* or no-mind as the cosmic Unconscious, it becomes a creative artform that rises above the trivial conventions of morality. This complete reduction of ethics to aesthetics in Suzuki's writings on the Zen art of swordsmanship is highlighted in such passages as follows: "Without the sense of an ego, there is no moral responsibility, but the divine transcends morality. So does art. Art lives where absolute freedom is, because where it is not, there can be no creativity. . . . The art of swordsmanship belongs in this category" (ZJC, 144–155). For Suzuki, insofar as the religio-aesthetic tradition of Bushido is based on the egoless state of no-mind as unconscious intuition, it transcends all ethical rules and is free of all moral responsibility. In the Zen art of swordsmanship, logic and ethics are collapsed into an aesthetic mode of existence. Suzuki goes on to say: "When the sword is expected to play this sort of role in human life, it is no more a weapon of self-defense or an instrument of killing, and the swordsman turns into an artist of the first grade, engaged in producing a work of genuine originality" (ZJC, 145). He adds: "The man emptied of all thoughts . . . is not conscious of using the sword; both man and sword turn into instruments in the hands, as it were, of the unconscious, and it is this unconscious that achieves wonders of creativity. It is here that swordplay becomes an art" (ZJC, 146). According to Suzuki, then, the violent act of killing performed by the samurai who empties his mind of all thoughts in the egoless flow state of *mushin* or no-mind as the cosmic Unconscious does not stand in contradiction to the Buddhist ethics of compassion, mercy, and nonviolence, since it is now transformed by Zen aestheticism into the "art" of swordplay, whereupon the samurai becomes free of all moral responsibilities. In Suzuki's *Manual of Zen Buddhism*, as elsewhere throughout his works, he translates a verse from the *Dhammapada* on the fundamental teaching of Buddhist ethics: "Not to commit evils, But to do all that is good. . . . This is the teaching of all the Buddhas" (MZB, 15).[5] Indeed, as Suzuki elsewhere proclaims: "To do good is my religion" (SWS III, cover page). Yet in Suzuki's "samurai Zen" as advocated in works such as *Zen and Japanese Culture,* he tells us that deeds arising from *mushin* or no-mind as the cosmic Unconscious are spontaneous acts of a creative artist transcending all moral distinctions of good and evil. As pointed out by Nishihira Tadashi, although in *Zen and Japanese Culture* Suzuki translates most of Takuan's letter on *mushin* in the art of swordsmanship, he intentionally leaves out the part on ethics, which is the part that most interests Hakuin (2024, 127–130). Nishihira writes: "Takuan's *mushin* is connected to good and evil in a practical sense — social ethics. . . . Do good and avoid evil" (2024, 129).

Generally speaking, Suzuki criticizes dualistic morality based on cognitive distinctions between right and wrong or good and evil, with the proclamation that living by Zen is to act freely, spontaneously, and unconsciously in accordance with the nature: "The living by Zen is more than being merely moral. . . . Morality always binds itself with the ideas of good and evil, just and unjust, virtuous and unvirtuous. . . . Zen is, however, not tied up with any such ideas; it is as free as the bird flying, the fish swimming, and the lilies blooming" (LZ, 13). Furthermore, he argues that Zen achieves total freedom beyond good and evil in *mushin* or no-mind and that *mushin* is the secret of mastering all the Zen-inspired arts, including the art of swordsmanship. Suzuki further explains that for a Zen-trained swordsman, this religio-aesthetic principle of *mushin* or no-mind as the Unconscious is beyond all moral distinctions between good and evil, right and wrong, just and unjust: "This spirit is grasped only . . . when he attains to a certain state of mind known as *mushin* (*wu-hsin* in Chinese), 'no-mind.' In Buddhist phraseology, it means going beyond the dualism of . . . good and evil, being and non-being. This is where all arts merge into Zen" (ZJC, 94). The way that Suzuki misapplies his psychological Zen concept of *mushin* or no-mind as the Unconscious to support an amoral worldview beyond good and evil is again demonstrated in the following passage: "The Unconscious cannot be held responsible for its deeds. They are above moral judgments, for there is no deliberation, no discrimination. The valuation of good and bad presupposes discrimination, and where this is absent, no such valuation is applicable" (ZDNM, 116).

Throughout his writings, Suzuki maintains that satori as awakening to the cosmic Unconscious is an egoless state of unconscious consciousness or conscious unconsciousness, also expressed as undiscriminated discrimination or discriminated undiscrimination. But in such passages as this, he asserts that the Unconscious is devoid of all moral responsibility, insofar as emptiness is a state of nondiscrimination in which there is no rational discrimination between good and bad. Likewise, in his Zen aestheticism he goes on to argue that in the art of swordsmanship the samurai who empties his mind of all thoughts and instinctively acts from the Unconscious as the locus of absolute nothingness is a creative artist transcending all moral distinctions of right and wrong. Although Suzuki's Zen aestheticism is the standpoint for overcoming nihilism insofar as it affirms the beauty of all things in their emptiness-suchness, nonetheless, he falls into moral nihilism when he argues for the dangerous view that upon realizing no-mind as unconscious prajna wisdom of sunyata or emptiness, there is no discrimination of right and wrong or good and evil. In Buddhism, however, the ultimate level of sunyata or emptiness does not negate the conventional level of discriminated existence arising through the karmic process of interdependent origination.

Suzuki also makes reference to the "three poisonous passions" of "greed, anger, and folly" (ZJC, 293). Nonetheless, in his apologistic discourse on the arts of swordsmanship and archery, Suzuki's Zen aestheticism no longer gives importance to the "three poisons" of Buddhist moral philosophy, instead underscoring the unconscious spontaneity of Zen-inspired art. Yet in Buddhist ethics all evil actions committed in the world of samsara are ultimately rooted in the three poisons of attachment, hatred, and ignorance as egocentric self-grasping, while all goodness and right actions originate from compassion based on nonego or selflessness. Suzuki is correct that Zen does not reduce morality to fixed dogmatic rules of conduct. Nonetheless, it is axiomatic in Mahayana Buddhism that enlightenment as awakening to Buddha-nature is realization of emptiness and compassion.

Suzuki explains how along with tea, haiku, painting, calligraphy, and other Zen-influenced arts springing from the unconscious creative impulses of *mushin* or no-mind, the samurai became patrons of noh theater, both as spectators and actors, performing noh dramas about the great battles of courageous warriors for the entertainment of their warlords and fellow samurai (ZJC, 419). Moreover, in his analysis of how unconscious intuition guides the actions of a Zen-trained samurai warrior, Suzuki cites the views of Takano Shigeyoshi, a twentieth-century master of Japanese swordsmanship, who compares the swordplay of Bushido to the dramatic plays of Bunraku puppetry. According to Takano, like the masters of swordsmanship in Bushido, the marionette masters of Bunraku puppet theater have their source in Zen *muga* or nonego, and *mushin* or no-mind, the unconscious intuition of nondual emptiness beyond the subject-object dichotomy: "I sometimes feel that when the marionette master puts his mind wholly into the play his state of mind attains something of the swordsman's. He is then *not conscious* of the distinction between himself and the doll he manipulates. The play becomes really an art when the master enters into a state of emptiness" (ZJC, 205; italics added). Likewise, Suzuki uses the imagery of Bunraku theater to explain the workings of unconscious intuition in the Zen art of swordsmanship, whereby the samurai is a puppet controlled by the dictates of the Unconscious as the puppeteer: "The [swordsman] must turn himself into a puppet in the hands of the unconscious" (ZJC, 117).

Although Suzuki most often explains Zen aestheticism in terms of his philosophical psychology of the Unconscious, at least on one occasion he accounts for it in political, social, and historical terms as an attempt to escape from the tyrannical feudalistic oppression and ultranationalism of the *bakufu* shogunate Japanese government under military rule: "Ultra-nationalism has unfortunately set a check on the growth of vigourous original thought among the Japanese. Instead of expressing themselves by free inquiry and healthy reflection on life itself, the Japanese rather sought to escape from the feudalistic oppression by such devices as the Nō dance, the art of tea, literature, and other social and artistic entertainments. The Japanese political system, I think, is to be held responsible for the impotence or lame development of the Japanese philosophical genius" (ZJC, 308). But if in earlier periods of Japanese history Zen aestheticism emerged as an escape from feudalistic oppression, it should be considered if Suzuki's modern Zen aestheticism was likewise an attempt to escape from the Japanese totalitarian emperor system fascism, ultranationalism, and militarism that reigned during the horrors of World War II. As Faure has observed: "If the Japanese as a people escaped into aestheticism because of an oppressive regime (the feudalistic rule of the Kamakura and Muromachi periods), it may be because of another oppressive regime (Shōwa militarism) that Suzuki as an individual chose the same route" (1993, 67).

In the aesthetics of beauty as perishability depicted in traditional Japanese literature, painting, and theater, as well as later art forms such as manga, animé, and cinema, the fleeting life of the samurai warrior has often been compared to the fragile cherry blossoms having the aesthetic quality of *aware* (哀れ) or the tragic beauty of evanescence, insofar as they fall at the peak of their beauty, glory, and splendor. But as documented by Emiko Ohnuki-Tierney (2002), both in traditional Japanese Bushido and its reinvention during World War II, the poetic image of fleeting "cherry blossoms" (*sakura*, 桜) expressing the traditional Japanese value of *mono no aware* or the transitory beauty of perishability was (mis)applied toward an aestheticization of war and a militarization of aesthetics. Likewise, in his discussion of Zen in the art of swordsmanship, Suzuki writes: "The Japanese hate to see death met irresolutely and lingeringly; they desire to be blown away like the cherries before the wind; and no doubt this Japanese attitude toward death must have gone very well with the teaching of

Zen" (ZJC, 84–85). In this context Suzuki exalts the *seppuku* (*hara-kiri*) or ritual suicide committed by the brave samurai warrior who ends his own life in glory through the beautification of death. Suzuki tells the story of a low-ranking samurai who resolved to follow the death of his master out of the duty of loyalty. In a glorious display of courage and honor, the samurai calmly sits in Zen lotus posture and then composes a death poem expressing the exquisite beauty of his final moment of life, followed by a bloody suicide performed like a creative work of art, whereupon his own son finishes the task by beheading him with a sword (ZJC, 83–84). This beautification of ritual suicide by the fearless Zen-trained samurai warrior, or the brave self-sacrifice of the kamikaze pilot, like the poeticization of heroic combat, violence, and death on the battlefield, became an effective instrument for Japanese wartime propaganda based on subterfuge that uses aesthetics to camouflage dangerous political ideologies such as militarism, imperialism, colonialism, ethnic chauvinism, and ultranationalism.

To sum up the above, in Suzuki's "Zen aestheticism," both satori and its spontaneous expressions in art have their origin in the cosmic Unconscious, which as absolute nothingness is the inexhaustible source of creative possibilities. Suzuki's Zen aestheticism claims that the existential crisis of nihilism or relative nothingness is overcome by affirmation of evanescent beauty manifesting the absolute nothingness or emptiness-fullness of all things in nature, art, and everyday life. Yet this becomes problematic when he further claims that the Zen-trained samurai who empties his mind and instinctively acts by the dictates of spontaneous impulses from his cosmic Unconscious now becomes a creative artist transcending all moral responsibilities. For in Mahayana Buddhism, the *summum bonum* of life is enlightenment as realization of inseparability between emptiness and compassion. Suzuki's "samurai Zen" thus collapses into moral nihilism when it abandons the core Mahayana Buddhist ethical virtues of nonviolence, peace, kindness, mercy, and compassion, thereby lapsing into an amoral Zen aestheticism, along with an ambiguous ethical relativism beyond good and evil, whereupon there is a total reduction of goodness to beauty, morality to art, and ethics to aesthetics. It is thus in his apologistic discourse on the art of swordplay as a function of the cosmic Unconscious where Suzuki's samurai Zen aestheticism intermittently deteriorates into a militarization of art and aestheticization of war.

Chapter 4

The Unconscious in Zen and *Geidō*

The Religio-Aesthetic Way of the Fine Arts

Sumie Ink Painting

In his modern psychological analysis of Zen-influenced arts, Suzuki also considers the role of the Unconscious in Zen *sumie* (墨絵) monochrome ink painting. According to Suzuki's Zen aestheticism, the master of sumie ink painting must tap the Unconscious as the source of unlimited creative possibilities. From the standpoint of his philosophical psychology, Suzuki argues that the inkwash landscape painter overcomes subject-object duality and loses himself in Nature by entering no-mind or the Unconscious (EZB III, 337). The Unconscious guides the effortless brush strokes of a Zen-trained sumie ink painter no less than the lightning-quick sword of a samurai warrior, the elegant movements of a noh actor, the spontaneous creation of verse by a haiku poet, or the graceful actions of a tea master performing the tea ceremony. When inspired by the Unconscious, the sumie painter moves his brush without conscious effort, such that the brush strokes of his paintings exhibit an unhindered spontaneity, freedom, and immediacy of creative expression. The Zen style of monochrome landscape inkwash painting uses shades of black ink to portray the undivided aesthetic continuum of nature, wherein phenomena in the articulated foreground are depicted as fading into the nonarticulated background field of absolute nothingness thereby to reveal the Zen-Kegon dharma world of harmonious interpenetration between part and whole, focus and field, solid and void, or object and space. A sumie painting that is spontaneously produced in the ecstasy of Zen *mushin* or no-mind as the cosmic Unconscious is therefore described as manifesting those directly felt pervasive aesthetic qualities most prized in the medieval Japanese Buddhist canons of taste such as *myō* and *yūgen* or the indistinct atmospheric beauty of profound mystery. The ethereal beauty of *myō* and *yūgen* is thus an epiphany of depth from the cosmic Unconscious.

Suzuki describes the impact of Zen Buddhism on Chinese ink painting: "Zen in Song [Dynasty] influenced not only the world of thought but the world of art. Those Zen pictures that are preserved in Japan (being lost in their nativeland), bespeak eloquently of the extent to which the spirit of Zen has entered into the minds of the artists. This will readily be recognized by those who study such monk-painters as Muqi, Lian Kai, and others" (SWS IV, 169). Again, making reference to some of the foremost Zen artist-monks in the tradition of Japanese sumie ink painting: "The fundamental intuition the Zen masters gain through their discipline seems to stir up their artistic instincts if they are at all susceptible to art.... Among the noted painters of Zen in the fourteenth and fifteenth centuries we may mention Chō Densu (d. 1431), Kei Shoki (fl. 1490), Josetsu (1375–1420), Shūbun (1420–50), Sesshū (1421–1506), and others" (ZJC, 30–31). In addition to the above masters in the lineage Zen artist-monks, he also greatly admires the sumie ink paintings of the famous samurai Miyamoto Musashi (1584–1645): "Musashi was great not only as a swordsman but as a *sumiye* painter" (ZJC, 124). Miyamoto Musashi is known for his philosophical work *The Book of Five Rings* (2005), wherein he describes the importance of no-mind and emptiness in the martial arts. According to Suzuki, Miyamoto Musashi realized the egoless Zen state of empty-mindedness or the Unconscious, thereby to become a great master of both painting and swordsmanship.

Suzuki argues that the profound beauty of a Zen sumie inkwash painting emerges from the depths of *mushin* or no-mind in its functioning as the creative unconscious, so that each stroke of the brush is spontaneous, natural, and effortless: "The artist must follow his inspiration as spontaneously and absolutely and instantly as it moves.... Or we may say that the brush by itself executes the work quite outside the artist, who just lets it move on *without his conscious efforts*" (ZB, 336; italics added). "A line drawn by the *Sumiye* artist is final, nothing can go beyond it, nothing can retrieve it; it is just inevitable as a flash of lightening" (ZB, 338). Like the noh drama, tea ceremony, and haiku poetry, or the martial arts of swordsmanship and archery, in Zen inkwash painting, each movement of the brush is performed without conscious effort when it spontaneously flows out of the cosmic Unconscious focused in the lower abdomen of the physical body as the energetic center of *ki* (気) or life force. Ink painting is thus another paradigm of somaesthetics in what Suzuki refers to as the Zen aestheticism of traditional Japanese art culture, whereby bodymind oneness is cultivated by integration of conscious and unconscious processes.

Suzuki claims that when Zen ink painting arises from the cosmic Unconscious, it is not imitative but creative: "When this unconscious sincerely and genuinely identifies itself with the Cosmic Unconscious, the artist's creations are genuine .... He paints a flower which, if it is blooming from his unconscious is a new flower and not an imitation of nature" (ZP, 12–13). Zen inkwash landscape paintings of nature are not mimetic, imitative, or representational but original productions of a new landscape springing from the creative unconscious: "If Sumiye attempts to copy an objective reality it is an utter failure; it never does that, it is rather a creation" (ZB, 337). He adds: "When this is accomplished, a Sumiye picture is a reality itself, complete in itself, and no copy of anything

Figure 4.1. Splashed-Ink Landscape by Sesshū Tōyō (1495).
Source: Wikimedia Commons. Public domain.

else" (ZB, 339). "It is thus natural that Sumiye avoids colouring of any kind, for it reminds us of an object of nature, and Sumiye makes no claim to be a reproduction, perfect or imperfect" (ZB, 339).

Having argued that the function of Zen-inspired sumie painting is not to imitate, copy, duplicate, or represent nature but to spontaneously create a new landscape out of nothingness, Suzuki further explains how the ecstasy of the no-mind or no-thought state of the Unconscious is the fountainhead of aesthetic production: "By this unconsciousness nature writes out her destiny: by this unconsciousness the artist creates his work of art . . . it is genuinely inevitably, coming out of the Unconscious. The '*Wu-hsin*' and '*Wu-nien*' of which the Zen master makes so much, as we have already seen elsewhere, is also eminently the spirit of the *Sumiye* artist" (ZB, 338). Like the haiku poet, the Zen-trained sumie ink painter becomes one with the vast landscapes of nature in the beauty of its emptiness-suchness upon entering the egoless state of *mushin* or no-mind as cosmic unconsciousness: "Therefore, the artist knows nature the best when he is in a state of the unconscious (*mu-shin*, *wu-hsin*, or *acitta*); and naturally we observe that constant references are made to nature by Zen masters throughout the history of Zen Buddhism" (EZB III, 337).

Suzuki's *Sengai: The Zen of Ink and Paper* focuses on the sumie paintings, calligraphy, line drawings, and haiku poetry of Rinzai Zen master Gibbon Sengai (1750–1837), who occupied the position of abbot in Shōfukuji in Fukuoka, the first Zen temple in Japan, built by the Zen monk Eisai (1141–1215). Sengai's most famous Zen sumie ink painting is his "Circle-Triangle-Square," which achieves ultimate abstraction, simplicity, and minimalism through its depiction of nature by using the geometry of a circle, triangle, and square. Sengai was a member of the late Edo period "literati painting" (*Bunjinga*) school of Japanese art led by Ike no Taiga (1723–1776) and Yosa Buson (1716–1783). Like Buson, Sengai combined his skill as a haiku poet with his mastery of the brush to produce *haiga* (俳画) or "haiku painting," whereby a picture of the landscape is accompanied by a brief poem written in calligraphy.

Suzuki's work contains 128 Zen ink paintings, drawings, and calligraphy by Sengai, accompanied by his own commentary explaining the Zen teachings embodied in each artwork. As is characteristic of his writings, Suzuki often gives a psychological interpretation of these Zen ink paintings and poems by Sengai using his signature Zen concept of the Unconscious. Here is what Suzuki has to say about Sengai's sumie ink painting of Monju Bosatsu: "Monju Bosatsu or the Bodhisattva Mañjusri is the Bodhisattva of transcendental wisdom, *prajñā*, and one of the most important figures in the Mahayana system of Buddhist teaching. He is represented as holding a scroll of Buddhist texts in his left hand, while in his right he carries the sword of Vajrarāja" (SZIP, 51). He continues: "The significance of the scroll is self-evident, but the service his sword renders is twofold: one is to kill anything that would stand against the truth revealed to *prajñā* (transcendental wisdom, which is deeply lodged in the unconscious of everyone of us); the other is to resuscitate the dead to a life they have never suspected" (SZIP, 51). In this passage Suzuki thus clarifies one of the central themes running throughout his psychological interpretation of Zen art, meditation, and enlightenment: prajna wisdom of sunyata or emptiness is "deeply lodged in the unconscious of every one of us."

Sengai's calligraphy scroll titled *Buji* (無事) is interpreted by Suzuki as follows: "The two Chinese characters read *buji* in Japanese or *wu-shih* in Chinese. A tentative modern reading is, free from anxiety or fear. Literally, they mean no business, no work, or event, or, all is well" (SZIP, 182). For Zen master Rinzai (C. Linji, d. 866) the term *buji* signifies "doing nothing" in the sense of an enlightened person of no rank who is ordinary, common, and everyday. Zen *buji* is therefore at once reminiscent of Daoist *wuwei* (無為),"doing nothing." He then explains: "Master Tokusan (Tê-shan, 782–865) is more explicit in defining *buji*. He identifies it with *mushin*, no-mindedness" (SZIP, 183). Further clarifying *buji* as *mushin* or no-mind in its sense as the Unconscious, Suzuki adds: "This consciousness, moreover, is not our ordinary consciousness; it is that which is unconsciously conscious or consciously unconscious" (SZIP, 183). Again, he says: "'unconscious consciousness' . . . is Sengai's *buji*" (SZIP, 183). Although Rinzai's Zen teaching of *buji* is often understood as "doing nothing," Tokusan warns that this does not mean being idle but to work in daily life with no conscious effort, for it is by doing nothing devoid of egoism that everything is accomplished in nature. For Suzuki, this calligraphy scroll by Sengai thus explains how Rinzai's Zen teaching of *buji* enjoins us to be ordinary and everyday thereby to act with effortless naturalness while doing nothing in *mushin* or no-mind as the cosmic Unconscious, or what he otherwise refers to as conscious unconsciousness and unconscious consciousness.

Suzuki often speaks of the importance of laughter, humor, wit, and playfulness based on the principle of emptiness or nothingness in the religio-aesthetic tradition of Rinzai Zen. He points out that Sengai portrayed himself as Hotei the laughing Buddha: "Laughter comes out of this empty nothingness. Sengai tries to illustrate it in his drawings of Hotei" (SZIP, 8). Many of Sengai's ink paintings and haiku poems were like cartoons from Japanese *manga* that were humorous, yet also imparting Zen wisdom with profundity, simplicity, and clarity. Suzuki therefore remarks: "It would be committing a gross mistake to consider him [Sengai] as merely a common cartoonist or humorist for popular amusement. He is a serious teacher of Zen" (SZIP, 128). For Suzuki, "playfulness" (*asobi*, 遊び) and "lightness" (*karumi*, 軽み) are aesthetic qualities characterizing the Zen art of Sengai. Furthermore, Suzuki highlights the uninhibited laughter, humor, lightness, and nonattached playfulness of Sengai's Zen ink paintings while also relating them to the aesthetic quality of *myō* (妙) or the ethereal beauty of wonder and mystery (SZIP, 7).

According to Suzuki, Sengai's lighthearted Zen ink paintings express humor, laughter, and playfulness, which in turn exemplify an aesthetic attitude of artistic detachment toward the evanescent beauty of impermanent events in the passage of time. He further maintains that the detached humor, satire, laughter, and playfulness of Zen koans as well as by Sengai's Zen ink paintings and haiku poems, unexpectedly arise from out of the depths our creative unconscious as "absolute nothingness": "For playfulness comes out of empty nothingness . . . Zen comes out of absolute nothingness and knows how to be playful. In China, Song masters such as Secchō, Engo, Daie (Tai-hui), and others did this in words, characteristic of the Chinese genius; in Japan Sengai and others did this with a brush on paper" (SZIP, 7). As Suzuki points out here, while the aesthetic attitude of detached playfulness and laughter is expressed by Zen koans using words, it is communicated by Sengai through brush painting. In Zen, this outburst of laughter wells up from the unconscious depths of emptiness or absolute nothingness (SZIP, 8). The joyous laughter of Zen, like the humor of Sengai's paintings and poems, arises from out of the cosmic Unconscious as the abyss of empty nothingness.

In his psychological analysis of detached humor, laughter, and playfulness in Sengai's Zen ink paintings, Suzuki goes on to discuss comparisons with Henri Bergson's 1900 work *Laughter*: "As far as I can see, Zen is the only religion or teaching that finds room for laughter. . . . Bergson is a great philosopher of modern times and his analysis of laughter is illuminating in this connection" (SZIP, 11). He continues: "According to him [Bergson], as I understand, the comic takes place essentially when some conscious restraints, moral or intellectual, are suddenly, unexpectedly, and absentmindedly removed, contradicting the content of the restraints" (SZIP, 11). Bergson maintains that humor, jokes, comedy, and laughter arise when "conscious restraints, moral or intellectual" are absentmindedly removed, thereby shutting off the filtering mechanism that he refers to as the "cerebral reducing valve," whereupon unconscious contents are unexpectedly revealed. Suzuki adds: "It may not be out of place here to add that Bergson's 'absent–mindedness' corresponds to Buddhist terms such as no-ego-ness (*muga*, *anātman*), no-thought (*munen*), or no-mind (*mushin*, *acitta*), everyday-mindedness (*heijō-shin*), just-as-it-is-ness (*jinen-hōni*), just-so-ness (*shimo*) as contrasted with artificially and consciously designed self-control or self-restraint" (SZIP, 13). Thus, for Suzuki the detached laughter, comedy, and playfulness of Sengai's Zen ink paintings, like the jokes, puns, and humorous wordplay of Zen koans, are spontaneously produced when filtering mechanisms of conscious restraint are bypassed, thereby to arise from what Bergson calls "absent-mindedness," or what Zen terms *muga* or no-ego, *munen* or no-thought, and *mushin* or no-mind, and what Suzuki otherwise refers to as "the cosmic Unconscious."

At the outset of his 1905 work *Jokes and Their Relation to the Unconscious*, Sigmund Freud develops a psychoanalytic aesthetics by showing that like dreams and art, jokes are shaped by the primary processes of the unconscious (1960b, 9). In this work, Freud explains that jokes fall under the aesthetic category of the comical (1960b, 95). Summing up the views of Bergson and others, Freud affirms that jokes have "the characteristic of playful judgment . . . 'sense in nonsense', the succession of bewilderment and enlightenment, the bringing forward of what is hidden, and the peculiar brevity of wit" (1960b, 14). He further emphasizes that jokes involve adopting an "aesthetic attitude" of playful judgment, or an aesthetic freedom that gives rise to enjoyment and pleasure (196b, 19–11). Moreover, he states his view that jokes have their source in the unconscious psyche: "Let us decide then, to adopt the hypothesis that this is the way in which jokes are formed in the first person: a preconscious thought is given over for a moment to unconscious revision and the outcome of this is at once grasped by conscious perception" (1963, 166). In Freudian psychoanalysis, the humor of a joke is that it unexpectedly reveals something hidden, such as an aggressive or sexual allusion, hence to suddenly bring to consciousness what had previously been repressed in the libidinal unconscious. Although Suzuki does not refer to Freud's *Jokes and Their Relation to the Unconscious*, for Freud, as for Bergson and Suzuki, jokes, puns, humor, wit, comedy, and laughter arise when the intellectual and moral censorship imposed by defense mechanisms are circumvented so that repressed thoughts and emotions latent in the unconscious are suddenly manifested in consciousness. Similarly, the uninhibited laughter, brevity of wit, and nonattached aesthetic attitude of freedom and playfulness characteristic of Sengai's comical Zen ink paintings are to be explained by the momentary removal of conscious restraints, whereby hidden subliminal contents are now allowed to suddenly emerge from the Unconscious, or what here as elsewhere, Suzuki also calls "the Unknown" (SZIP, 13).

Sengai's *manga*-like ink painting of a frog sitting in what resembles zazen meditation posture is accompanied by the following brief poetic verse written in calligraphy: "If a man becomes a Buddha by practicing *zazen* . . . [a frog though I am, I should have been one long ago]" (SZIP, 95; brackets in original). This is followed by Suzuki's Zen interpretation based on his philosophical psychology of the Unconscious: "*Zazen* means 'sitting in meditation.' The frog seems always to be in this posture when we find him in the garden. If the meditation posture alone constitutes Zen, the frog's attainment of Buddhahood is an assured event. But Zen is not mere sitting. There must be an awakening in the Unconscious or Mind. This awakening is called *satori*" (SZIP, 95). Suzuki then relates the story of Chih-ch'êng, who spent long periods of time sitting in meditation prior to becoming a disciple of Huineng (d. 713), the sixth patriarch of Chan/Zen Buddhism: "Huineng, seeing this, warned him of the uselessness of 'long sitting' alone. Zen did not consist, he said, of quietly meditating on the Mind; this could become a disease, and is not the way to awaken the *prajñā*, transcendental knowledge" (SZIP, 95). As already seen in Suzuki's psychological commentary on Sengai's painting of Manju Bosatsu, this *prajñā*-intuition of emptiness is "deeply lodged in the unconscious of every one of us" (SZIP, 51). The purpose of Zen is not merely to sit cross-legged in *dhyāna* or meditation but to abruptly realize the prajna wisdom of emptiness buried in our deeper unconscious mind. Like the frog, merely sitting in zazen posture for long periods does not guarantee attainment of Buddhahood. According to the nondual Chan/Zen teachings of Huineng, practice and enlightenment are inseparable like a lamp and its light, such that *dhyāna* or meditation must always go together with *prajñā* as the primordial awareness of sunyata or emptiness, the result of which is satori as an abrupt opening to the unconscious psyche thus to make the Unconscious fully conscious in superconsciousness. In agreement with the Chan/Zen teachings of sudden enlightenment advocated by Huineng, Suzuki therefore proclaims: "Zen is not mere sitting. There must be an awakening in the Unconscious or Mind" (SZIP, 95). In this way Suzuki interprets Sengai's humorous painting of a frog and corresponding poetic verse to playfully, comically, and lightheartedly illustrate the Rinzai Zen teaching of sudden enlightenment, whereby correct sitting in lotus posture must always be accompanied by noetic insight into the cosmic Unconscious as the abyss of absolute nothingness.

Suzuki's essay "Awakening of a New Consciousness in Zen" is an interpretation of the *Ten Oxherding Pictures* by the twelfth-century Zen master Kakuan Shien (C. Kuoān Shiyuan) in terms of his philosophical psychology of the Unconscious (SWS I, 150–163). Commenting on the history of the Ten Oxherding Pictures: "Kakuan was not, however, the first to illustrate by means of pictures the stages of Zen training. There was one who made use of the *ushi's* gradually growing white to visualize progress of spiritual life in Zen" (SWS I, 151). In this earlier series the ox (*ushi*) gradually fades into nothingness as depicted by an empty circle. Zen artist-monks later added more pictures so that the journey does not end in nihilistic or relative nothingness where all is nullified into a meaningless void but in the plenary vacuum of absolute nothingness as emptiness-fullness. Suzuki explains that while the verses are by Kakuan, the Zen artist-priest who painted the ten pictures reproduced in his essay is Shūbun (1414–1463) of Shōkokuji, a Rinzai Zen temple in Kyoto (SWS I, 151). The Ten Oxherding Pictures are presented by Suzuki as illustrating developmental stages in the psychological process of awakening to a new consciousness in the Unconscious as exemplified in the life of Rinzai (C. Linji) and other Rinzai Zen lineage masters: "Psychologically, we may say that here is a sample of a new consciousness awakening in the Zen man's mind, or a new consciousness awakened in the Unconscious" (SWS I, 148). Moreover, "'The Unconscious' which has been lying quietly in consciousness itself now raises its head and announces its presence through consciousness" (SWS I, 149). He continues:

> We have given the name "consciousness" to a certain group of psychological phenomena and another name "unconscious" to another group.... This means that what is named "conscious" cannot be "unconscious" and vice versa.... The conscious wants to be unconscious and the unconscious conscious. But human thinking cannot allow such a contradiction: the unconscious must remain unconscious and the conscious conscious: no such things as the unconscious conscious or the conscious unconscious must take place. (SWS I, 149)

Figure 4.2. The Ten Oxherding Pictures by Shūbun (15th century). *Source*: Public domain.

Although the natural mind is usually divided by reason into "consciousness" and "unconsciousness," Zen overcomes this artificial bifurcation in nondual satori as the awakening of consciousness to the Unconscious: "Zen would not object to the possibility of an 'unconscious conscious' or a 'conscious unconscious.' Therefore not the awakening of a new consciousness but consciousness coming to its own unconscious" (SWS I, 149).

Suzuki then clarifies the deeper psychological function of the Ten Oxherding Pictures as follows: "'The Ten Cowherding Pictures' may be interpreted in connection with the koan methodology. . . . The pictures are explainable as illustrating stages in the psychological process the Zen student goes through when he endeavors to solve the koan" (SWS I, 153). According to Suzuki's essay, the Ten Oxherding Pictures illustrate the threefold psychological process of integrating consciousness with the Unconscious through Rinzai Zen koan training, the final stages of which culminate in satori or enlightenment. By this interpretation, the first seven pictures are stages of dualistic ego-consciousness in which the subject is still conscious of itself as separate from Mu or some other koan as an external object for contemplation; picture eight of an empty circle is a trance state of unconsciousness in samadhi concentration where the practitioner is no longer conscious of being separate from the koan; picture nine shows the return out of nihilistic nothingness to an aesthetic appreciation of the profound beauty of nature in its emptiness-suchness; and picture ten illustrates a joyous affirmation of everyday life in Zen satori as "awakening to a new consciousness." The tenth and final picture integrates aesthetic appreciation of beauty with compassion for all things by the return to everyday life in the community. In Suzuki's philosophical psychology, it is the awakening to a new consciousness whereby one becomes fully conscious of the cosmic Unconscious as the inexhaustible creative wellspring of absolute nothingness, thereby to realize the nondual egoless state of conscious unconsciousness or unconscious consciousness in superconsciousness.

Finally, Suzuki goes on to make an analogy between Zen meditation practice and sumie ink painting, saying that like the landscape painter, a Zen master whose actions spring from *mushin* or no-mind as the cosmic Unconscious of absolute nothingness, uses the blank canvas of their own existence thereby resulting in aesthetic creative transformation of everyday life into an original work of art: "This is the attitude of a Sumiye painter towards his art and I wish to state that this attitude is that of Zen towards life, and that what Zen attempts with his life the artist does with his paper, brush and ink" (ZB, 338).

Tea Ceremony

According to Suzuki, *chanoyu* (茶の湯) or the traditional Japanese tea ceremony, also called *sadō* (茶道) or the way of tea, is a religio-aesthetic path to Zen satori as awakening to *mushin* or no-mind as the nonattached, spontaneous, and unconscious mind of everyday life. *Wabi-cha* (侘茶) or the *wabi*-style of tea perfected by Sen no Rikyū (1522–1591) is another somaesthetic discipline that cultivates unified bodymind awareness through integration of conscious and unconscious processes. In the Zen aestheticism of Suzuki, the directly felt pervasive aesthetic quality of *wabi* as the minimalistic beauty of simplicity or the nonattachment of spiritual poverty in everyday life is itself an expression of no-mind or the cosmic Unconscious as prajna wisdom of emptiness-suchness.

As explained by Suzuki, *wabi*-style tea is based on "an active principle of aestheticism" (ZJC, 284). Moreover, "in *wabi*, aestheticism is fused with morality and spirituality" (ZJC, 288). He continues: "*Wabi* or *sabi*, therefore, may be defined as an active aesthetical appreciation of poverty" (ZJC, 284). He adds: "What is common to Zen and the art of tea is the constant attempt both make at simplification. . . . The art of tea is the aestheticism of primitive simplicity" (ZJC, 271). Suzuki goes on to explain the aesthetic principles underlying the Japanese tea ceremony, including *wabi* (侘び), *sabi* (寂び), and *shibumi* (渋み), all of which denote aesthetic appreciation for simple, austere, understated beauty: "By this [aesthetic] spirit, or this artistic principle, if it can be so designated, I mean what is popularly known in Japan as 'Sabi' or 'Wabi' (or 'Shibumi')" (ZB, 341). The subdued aesthetic quality of *wabi-sabi* or *shibumi* as the unembellished beauty of simplicity, naturalness, and spiritual poverty is itself a creative expression of the Prajñāpāramitā philosophy of emptiness (ZJC, 296, 300. 304). Moreover, he explains that *wabi* is not only an aesthetic principle of art, but as *wabi-zumai* (侘び住まい), it becomes a highly refined lifestyle of voluntary simplicity, poverty, and nonattachment based on the prajna wisdom of emptiness (ZJC, 284–286). Finally, he observes a parallel to the rustic Zen *wabi*-lifestyle of voluntary simplicity, nonattachment, and poverty in the American transcendentalism of Henry David Thoreau's *Walden*: "*wabi* is to be satisfied with a little hut, a room of two or three *tatami* (mats), like the log cabin of Thoreau" (ZJC, 23).

The *wabi*-style tea ceremony is a paradigm of "everyday aesthetics" as a celebration of the wonder of the ordinary as extraordinary. Suzuki writes: "Rikyū teaches that 'the art of *cha-no-yu* consists in nothing else but in boiling water, making tea, and sipping it'" (ZJC, 280). In Rikyū's tea ceremony, the directly felt pervasive aesthetic quality of *wabi-sabi* or *shibumi* is the simple, plain, and natural beauty of ordinary artifacts used in everyday life, such as the *chawan* or tea bowl for drinking green tea (ZJC, 274). As said by Suzuki's renowned student and friend Yanagi Sōetsu, the tea bowl and other folkcrafts associated with the tea ceremony exhibit the *wabi-sabi* beauty of the ordinary and the everyday, and the beauty of these ordinary artifacts emerges when they are made spontaneously, effortlessly, and unconsciously (1989, 217). According to Suzuki's Zen aestheticism, *wabi-zumai* or the "*wabi*-lifestyle" based on nonattached aesthetic appreciation of natural beauty as simplicity in the ordinary and everyday is thus an illustration of the core Zen teaching that "everyday mind is the Way."

In his discussion of the Zen aestheticism of *wabi*-style tea, Suzuki describes the cosmic Unconscious as the source of the connoisseur's aesthetic delight and artistic creativity while further depicting the Unconscious in metaphorical terms as a deep and dark "well." In this context, Suzuki cites from a haiku poem written by Toyotomi Hideyoshi for Sen-no-Rikyū, the founder of the way of tea: "When tea is made with water drawn from the depths of Mind/ Whose bottom is beyond measure/We have what is called *cha-no-yu*" (ZJC, 280). In his commentary on this poem, Suzuki relates the "depths of Mind" to the Unconscious: "When water is poured into the bowl, it is not the water alone that is poured into it — a variety of things go into it . . . things which can never be poured out anywhere except into one's own deep unconscious" (ZJC, 280–281). While explaining Rikyū's tea ceremony, Suzuki describes his Zen concept of the Unconscious in poetic terms as a bottomless well, further relating it to the alaya-vijnana as the storehouse of emptiness, in its meaning as the repository of inexhaustible creative potentialities: "As Rikyū says, the water that fills the kettle is drawn from the well of mind whose bottom knows no depths, and the Emptiness which is conceptually liable to be mistaken for sheer nothingness, is in fact the reservoir (*ālaya*) of infinite possibilities" (ZJC, 297–298).

Suzuki goes on to more explicitly articulate the Zen aesthetics of beauty as *wabi-sabi* exemplified by the art of tea in terms of his philosophical psychology of the Unconscious. In his explanation of chanoyu as a spiritual discipline, Suzuki describes how the tea ceremony provided the samurai warrior an escape from the anxiety of existence in a peaceful moment of tranquil repose: "The tea must have given him exactly this. He retreated for a while into a quiet corner of his Unconscious symbolized by the tearoom no more than ten feet square" (ZJC, 289; ZNB, 222–223). In this passage Suzuki describes the ten-feet square tearoom as a peaceful sanctuary for the samurai warrior, referring to it as symbolizing "a quiet corner of his Unconscious" (ZJC, 289; *shizuka na 'muishiki' no hito sumi*, 静かな「無意識」の一隅, ZNB, 222). For Suzuki the Japanese tea ceremony, like the other Zen-influenced arts, thus springs from the deep well of our cosmic Unconscious, which as absolute nothingness is the bottomless fountainhead of creativity.

Haiku Poetry

Throughout his works Suzuki emphasizes the intimate connection between Zen and poetry, especially haiku poetry: "Zen makes use, to a great extent, of poetical expressions; Zen is wedded to poetry" (TZBM, xxv). The *haiku* (俳句) is a traditional Japanese form of poetry composed of only three phrases with seventeen syllables that capture a moment in nature during one of the four seasons. Explaining the role of Zen satori as insight into the Unconscious from which haiku poetry springs, Suzuki writes: "The poet's *satori* is an artistic one, so to speak, while the Zen-man's grows out of a metaphysical background. . . . The artistic *satori* may not penetrate the artist's entire personality, for it may not go any further than what I feel like calling the artistic aspect of the Unconscious" (ZJC, 226). For Suzuki, the Zen-influenced literary form of haiku poetry as especially represented by Bashō (1644–1694) is an outpouring from the Unconscious. The haiku poet achieves a kind of satori or awakening to the Unconscious in the "metaphysical background" of aesthetically immediate experience. He further specifies the character of this *metaphysical background* of the Unconscious when he speaks about Zen aesthetic intuition of "the background of Emptiness" (ZJC, 363). A haiku poem does not elicit aesthetic delight through direct reference but indirectly through suggestion. Moreover, it is the simplicity, brevity, and economy of a haiku poem as an abbreviated and minimalistic artform that functions to suggest the vast undiscriminated metaphysical background of formless emptiness or absolute nothingness that encompasses all phenomena discriminated in the foreground, thereby to evoke the immediately felt pervasive aesthetic qualities of *myō* and *yūgen* as epiphanies of depth. He speaks of "the poet's satori as an artistic one," adding that the haiku poet enters into "the artistic aspect of the Unconscious" (ZJC, 226). Suzuki thus recognizes an *aesthetic unconscious* as an aspect of the cosmic Unconscious accessible through the creative production and aesthetic appreciation of haiku poetry as well as other Zen-influenced arts.

In his analysis of Zen in the art of haiku poetry, Suzuki discusses various aesthetic principles denoting the subdued beauty of simplicity, tranquility, and solitariness, such as *wabi* (侘び), *sabi* (寂び), *shibumi* (渋み), *shiori* (萎), and *fūga* (風雅), or *fūryū* (風流), especially as found in the poetics of Bashō: "Bashō was not a Buddhist monk but a devotee of Zen" (ZJC, 256). He continues: "Bashō was a poet of Eternal Aloneness. . . . According to Bashō, what is here designated as the spirit of Eternal Aloneness is the spirit of *fūga* (or *fūryū*, as some would have it). . . . *Fūga* means 'refinement of life' . . . it is the longing for *sabi* or *wabi*, and not the pursuit of material comfort or of sensation" (ZJC, 257–258). The aloneness of *sabi* and related concepts in the Zen religio-aesthetic tradition of haiku poetry is not a personal feeling of loneliness but a generalized, universalized, or deindividualized mood of solitary contemplation. In the Western mystical tradition, Suzuki finds this sense of eternal aloneness in the neo-Platonic mystical tradition, exemplified by "Plotinus' 'flight from alone to alone'" (EZB I, 283). Suzuki holds that the Zen art of *kendō* (剣道) or swordsmanship, as well as the *sabi-shiori* style of haiku poetry by Saigyō and Bashō, spring from the Unconscious as an egoless state of *munen* or no-thought and *muga* or no-self (ZJC, 126). Furthermore, Suzuki maintains that the sublime beauty of *yūgen* or "mystery and depth," like that of *myō* or "mystery," arises when the haiku poet glimpses satori as a flash of insight into the Unconscious (ZJC, 220–221).

To illustrate the Zen aesthetic principles underlying Japanese haiku, Suzuki then quotes the following poem by Bashō.

Furu ike ya!
Kowazu tobikomu,
Mizu no oto.
[The old pond, ah!
A frog jumps in:
The water's sound!]

In his analysis of this most famous of all haiku poems, Suzuki clarifies how the creative inspiration of Bashō's haiku poetry arises from the depths of the cosmic Unconscious:

> Bashō the poet . . . has passed through the outer crust of consciousness away down into its deepest recesses, into a realm of the unthinkable, into the Unconscious, which is even beyond the unconscious generally conceived by psychologists. . . . It is by intuition alone that this timelessness of the Unconscious is truly taken hold of. . . . Therefore, the poet sees into his Unconscious not through the stillness of the old pond but through the sound stirred up by the jumping frog. Without the sound there is no seeing on the part of Bashō into the Unconscious, in which lies the source of creative activities, and upon which all true artists draw for their inspiration. (ZJC, 241–242)[1]

He adds: "Bashō came across this Unconscious, and his experience was given an expressive utterance in his haiku. . . . Without reckoning on the Cosmic Unconscious, our life, lived in the realm of relativities, loses its moorings altogether" (ZJC, 243). According to Suzuki, the Zen-inspired haiku poems by Bashō arise from "Bashō's intuition of the Unconscious" (ZJC, 252). He thus concludes this discussion on haiku, saying: "I hope I have cleared up at least one aspect of the relationship existing between the Zen experience of *satori*, of nondiscrimination, and the *haiku* poets' intuition of the Unconscious" (ZJC, 253).

Suzuki analyzes the function of the cosmic Unconscious in a verse by another great haiku poet named Buson, also known as one of the greatest literati painters of Japan:

Tsuri-gane ni
Tomarite nemuru
Kochō kana
[On the temple bell
Perching, sleeps
The butterfly, oh!] (ZJC, 248)

Buson's haiku depicts the pristine beauty of a summer day on the mountain temple grounds. Also, it portrays the butterfly as a symbol of spiritual transformation that remains unconscious as it sleeps on a temple bell that may be struck at any moment, thereby to shock the evanescent creature into sudden awakening. However, Buson's haiku reveals yet a more subtle insight into the workings of the cosmic Unconscious: "But to my mind there is in Buson's haiku another side, revealing his deeper insight into life. By this I mean his intuition of the Unconscious as it is expressed by the images of the butterfly and bell. As far as the inner life of the butterfly, as Buson sees it, is concerned, it is unconscious that the bell exists, separate from itself; in fact, it is not conscious of itself" (ZJC, 250). He continues: "Is there not in every one of us a life very much deeper and larger than our intellectual deliberation and discrimination — the life of the Unconscious itself, of what I call the 'Cosmic Unconscious'? Our conscious life gains its real significance only when it becomes connected to something more fundamental, namely, the Unconscious" (ZJC, 250–251).

In his psychological interpretation of haiku poetry as an aesthetic intuition of the cosmic Unconscious, Suzuki discusses the Zen Buddhist temporal view of nature as impermanence and the Japanese sense of beauty as evanescence: "From this short characterization of Zen we can see what Zen's attitude toward Nature is. . . . Nature is always in motion, never at a standstill; if Nature is to be loved, it must be caught while moving and in this way its aesthetic value must be appraised" (ZJC, 361). As an example of this Japanese aesthetics of beauty as perishability grasped through poetic intuition of the cosmic Unconscious, he cites the example of haiku celebrating the evanescent beauty of morning glory flowers (ZJC, 380–381). In this context he analyzes a haiku written by the poetess Chiyo (1703–1775), who composes an excellent haiku that expresses the ephemeral beauty of a morning glory blossoming near a deep well, the "well" itself being a common Japanese symbol of unconscious depths. As explained by Suzuki, Chiyo's haiku manifests the beauty of mystery and depth because it emerged from the depths of her cosmic Unconscious (SWS I, 107). The haiku reads:

> *Asagao ya*
> *Tsurube torarete*
> *Morai mizu.*
> [Oh, morning glory!
> The bucket taken captive,
> Water begged for.] (SWS I, 105)

Chiyo got up early in the morning to draw water from the well, but she found the bucket entwined by the blooming morning glory vine. She was so struck with the fragile beauty of the flower that she forgot about her practical task of drawing water and stood before it absorbed in rapt aesthetic contemplation. The only words she could utter in amazement, were "Oh, morning glory!" Suzuki explains that, as expressed by the haiku, the Japanese poetess does not dare to pluck the flower from the vine: "for in her inmost consciousness there is the feeling that she is one with reality; this consciousness may still remain deeply buried in her Unconscious, but unless she had not felt it, however dimly, she would never have left the flower blooming on the vine" (SWS I, 107). He further describes how Chiyo became unconscious of herself as separate from the morning glory in a state of samadhi concentration, finally awakening to the evanescent beauty of the flower is satori: "They were so completely one that she lost her identity. It was only when she woke from the moment of unconscious identity that she realized that she was the flower itself or rather Beauty itself" (AZ, 75). As Suzuki elsewhere asserts in his interpretation of this same poem: "Psychologically, the poet was the unconscious itself in which there was no dichotomization of any kind" (FZ, 23). For Suzuki, then, the ultimate creative source of haiku poetry and other Zen-inspired arts is our deeper subconscious mind, so that the true Zen poet is the cosmic Unconscious itself.[2]

Suzuki clarifies how Chiyo made a sudden breakthrough, when after many failures, she finally produced a haiku from the depths of her Unconscious: "Chiyo (1703-75), the haiku poetess of Kaga, wishing to improve herself in the art, called upon a noted haiku master of her day" (ZJC, 224). The haiku master gave Chiyo the task of composing a haiku about the "cuckoo bird" (*hototogisu*), all being judged as mediocre. Finally, after meditation throughout the evening on the song of the cuckoo, Chiyo wrote the following verse:

> *Hototogisu*
> *Hototogisu tote,*
> *Akenikeri*!
> [Calling "cuckoo," "cuckoo,"
> All night long,
> Dawn at last!] (ZJC, 225)

The master judged this poem to be an outstanding haiku free of egoism, artificiality, or conscious effort. According to Suzuki: "Chiyo's all-night meditation on the *hototogisu* helped to open up her Unconscious" (ZJC, 225). He adds: "Haiku, like Zen, abhors egoism in any form of assertion. . . . The author is to be an altogether passive instrument for giving an expression to the inspiration. . . . And when it comes upon one, let him be a sort of automaton with no human interference. Let the Unconscious work itself out, for the Unconscious is the realm where artistic impulses are securely kept away from our superficial utilitarian life" (ZJC, 225). Suzuki concludes that haiku poetry, like all other Zen-inspired artworks in the traditional Japanese religio-aesthetic way of the artist, is a product of the cosmic Unconscious as the abyss of absolute nothingness, the Fount of infinite creative possibilities, such that the greatest haiku poems are produced spontaneously, naturally, effortlessly, and unconsciously.

The Impact of Suzuki's Zen Aestheticism on the Avant-Garde Artworld

The Zen aestheticism of Suzuki itself focuses on how Zen influenced the traditional arts of Japanese culture, such as ink painting, haiku poetry, tea ceremony, flower arrangement, and noh drama, along with martial arts including swordsmanship and archery. Yet one of the most remarkable aspects of Suzuki's Zen aestheticism was its powerful influence on postwar avant-garde artists, both in America and Japan.[3] Following the devastation of Europe during World War II, the capital of the artworld shifted from Paris to New York City. Ellen Pearlman documents the fascinating story of how Zen aestheticism impacted the community of avant-garde artists living in New York City, inspired especially by the books of Suzuki, as well as his classes and public lectures at Columbia University during the 1950s:

> What artists received from D. T. Suzuki . . . was a glimpse into the process of the nature of mind. This glimpse was heightened through the use of drugs and meditation. . . . [Zen] Buddhism helped explain a type of spontaneity that combined with abstract expressionism, assemblage, neo-Dada, rock and roll, jazz, and free-flowing poetics using the form of chance, accidents, process, immediacy of materials, and the sublime of the mundane. Artists became innovative and adopted techniques leading to the creation of new works, with an emphasis on those that were ephemeral and time-based. (2012, 165–166)[4]

In the 1950s Suzuki became a major source of inspiration for Jack Kerouac (1923–1969), Allen Ginsberg (1926–1997), Gary Snyder (b. 1930), and other Beat generation writers residing in New York City, thereby giving rise to "Beat Zen" in America. As discussed by Steven Heine (2009), the existentialist/Zen-blues music of Bob Dylan was deeply influenced by Zen through his contact with Ginsberg and other Beat authors during his years living in the Greenwich Village area of New York City. Yet R. C. Zaehner unfairly criticizes Suzuki's influence on Beat Zen in his book *Zen, Drugs and Mysticism*: "Much of the attraction of Zen Buddhism to the 'drop-out' youth of today lies in its alleged spontaneity. Nothing could be further from the truth. For the achievement of Zen enlightenment an apprenticeship of grueling toil is the indispensable prerequisite. The late Professor D. T. Suzuki, whose main concern was to present Zen to the West as attractively as possible, was largely responsible for minimizing the hardness of the Zen way" (1972).[5] Although Suzuki celebrates the unconstrained freedom of a Zen master liberated from conventions, he also strongly criticizes the libertines who one-sidedly focus on Zen spontaneity, without equal commitment to rigorous Zen practice (AIZB, 86, 124). In his famous essay "Beat Zen, Square Zen, and Zen" (1996), Alan Watts thus discusses how Beat Zen overemphasized spontaneity, immediacy, and freedom from conventions, and Square Zen focuses on strict monastic discipline, ritual, and tradition, whereas true Zen itself is a middle way between these two extremes.

In response to the "Zen boom" initiated by his own writings, Suzuki criticized the 1950s Beat Zen associated with Kerouac and others: "Lately there have taken place some incidents around me. One of them is the rise of the so-called 'beat generation' which is at present calling public attention not only in America but also in Japan. They grossly misrepresent Zen and there are some people to [sic] imagine that Zen is really responsible for the movement" (cited by R. M. Jaffe, SWS I, liv). Moreover, at the psychological level of discourse, Suzuki criticizes the rebellious and defiant angst of Beat Zen for not having yet penetrated into the profound silence, stillness, and nothingness of the cosmic Unconscious. As Suzuki writes in his essay "Zen in the Modern World," the Beat Generation revolted against authoritarianism, intellectualism, conformism, materialism, and industrialism. He adds: "But those of the 'Beat Generation' are not fully conscious of why they rebel or what they propose to do; they do not know their inner Self which is moving in the deep unconscious."[6]

Kerouac's bestselling novel *Dharma Bums* (1976) popularized "Beat Zen" as a new aesthetic spirituality based on immediacy, spontaneity, and freedom. The "Beat Zen" in Kerouac's novel is a fusion of Suzuki's Zen aestheticism with the bohemian artistic lifestyle in 1950s American counterculture, as recorded with an unedited haiku-inspired stylistic technique of "spontaneous prose composition," punctuated with satori-like moments of illumination, and driven by the rhythmic pulse of Bebop improvisational jazz music. The Beat Zen of Kerouac became a frenetic Buddhist path in search of enlightenment on a nonstop high-speed road trip to nirvana fueled by drugs, alcohol, parties, travel, and free love. *The Dharma Bums* is an autobiographical novel that recounts the eventful meeting of Ray Smith (Jack Kerouac) with Japhy Ryder (Gary Snyder) in San Francisco in 1955. Ryder is characterized as a "Zen lunatic" who is a connoisseur of Zen aesthetics, practices Zen meditation, studies Buddhist philosophy, drinks green tea, reads haiku poetry, goes mountain climbing, takes peyote, and participates in Tibetan Buddhist *yab-yum* tantric lovemaking rituals. Moreover, Ryder is described as studying Japanese and Chinese languages in preparation for intensive training at a Zen temple in Kyoto, Japan. After many discussions and experiences with Ryder as his Zen guide, Smith has an epiphany, a Zen satori or sudden flash of insight into the emptiness of mind, self, and all things in the void: "Everything is empty but awake! . . . It means that I'm empty and awake" (Kerouac, 1976, 144–145). Along with the Zen philosophy of emptiness and the practice of Zen koan meditation, Ryder teaches about the Zen aesthetics of Japanese haiku poetry, the tea ceremony, the rock garden at Ryōanji temple, and learning to see the evanescent beauty of things in nature just as they are in suchness. Ryder is also described in Kerouac's novel as practicing a minimalist Zen lifestyle of voluntary simplicity in a little rustic shack with straw floor mats: "He had a slew of orange crates all filled with beautiful scholarly books, some of them in Oriental languages, all the great sutras, comments on sutras, the complete works of D. T. Suzuki and a fine quadruple-volume of Japanese haikus" (1976, 18). Hence it is revealed that the primary source texts for the Beat Zen of Kerouac and his Zen lunatic dharma bums are the writings of Suzuki, supplemented with R. H. Blythe's four volumes on haiku poetry. The narrator Smith proclaims: "Japhy Ryder is a great new hero of American culture" (1976, 32).

The New York City author J. D. Salinger (1919–2010), best known for *The Catcher in the Rye* (1951), was also deeply influenced by the Zen Buddhism of Suzuki. In his biography *J. D. Salinger*, Kenneth Slawenski reports: "his [Salinger's] personal exploration of Zen Buddhism intensified while he was finishing *The Catcher in the Rye*. In 1950, he befriended Daisetz T. Suzuki, the renowned author and Zen master" (2010, 190).[7] *The Catcher in the Rye* is an American existentialist novel that thematizes alienation, nihilism, death, and authenticity. It can further be described as a coming-of-age novel about the teenage angst of Holden Caulfield, a disaffected malcontent who rebels against the "phony" or inauthentic world of adulthood, while trying to retain his youthful innocence. As documented by John Bishop (1976), Dennis McCort (2008), and others, Salinger's *Catcher in the Rye* is filled with implicit references to Zen themes, concepts, and koans. More explicit references to both Zen and Suzuki are found in Salinger's post-*Catcher* novellas and short stories, which are themselves often written like Zen koans that the reader must solve. The epigraph for his *Nine Stories* (Salinger 1981) is Hakuin's Zen koan: "We know the sound of two hands clapping. But what is the sound of one hand clapping?" Salinger's *Franny and Zooey* (originally published in *The New Yorker*, 1961), is a novella about the Glass family residing in New York City, whose oldest boy Seymour educates his younger brothers and sisters about Eastern mysticism, including Suzuki's Zen teachings on satori. In the words of Seymour: "Dr. Suzuki says somewhere that to be in a state of pure consciousness — satori — is to be with God before he said, Let there be light" (1961, 65).

Suzuki's classes and public lectures on Zen Buddhism at Columbia University during the 1950s influenced many avant-garde artists residing in New York City, but foremost among them was the experimental musician John Cage (1912–1992), whose piano composition *4'33"* used a duration of silence and its ambient sounds to awaken his listeners to the emptiness-fullness of the present moment. In his book *Silence*, Cage attributes the use of his experimental music to the inspiration from Dadaism along with the Zen Buddhism that he learned from Suzuki, as well as Watts, the most famous popularizer of Suzuki's Zen (1973, xi). Furthermore, Cage describes how the Zen teachings of Suzuki impacted his own art, music, and life (Larson 2013, 163).

Influenced by the Zen aestheticism of Suzuki and his student Cage, "Fluxus" emerged in the 1960s as an international avant-garde movement that included Western artists, such as its principal founder and organizer George Maciunas, along with various Japanese experimental artists. As said in *Japan Fluxus* by

Luciana Galliano: "Fluxus has been described as the most radical and experimental art movement of the 1960s, challenging conventional thinking on art and culture" (2019, xiii). Galliano points out that in addition to his activities in New York City, Cage's trip to Tokyo in 1962 was instrumental to organizing Fluxus groups and events in Japan (2019, xvi). Among the many Japanese artists involved with Fluxus were Kuboa Shigeko, Iijima Takoa (Ay-O), Kosugi Takehisa, Saito Takako, and Ono Yoko (commonly known as Yoko Ono, married to Japanese composer Ichiyanai Yoshi, and later, to John Lennon of the Beatles). Suzuki's Zen aestheticism influenced Bernard Leach in England along with Hamada Shōji and Yanagi in Japan, who were all key figures in the introduction of Japanese art culture to the world of ceramics, pottery, crafts, and folk art. The Zen aesthetic design principles of beauty such as *wabi* or simplicity, *sabi* or antiqueness, and *shibumi* or understatement became the model for the simple, plain, and rustic style of ceramics valued by the craft guild of Leach, Hamada and Yanagi. After studying a wide range of Western artistic styles, Yanagi returned to traditional Asian arts and crafts, where he became the foremost collector and interpreter of Asian folk arts. Inspired by his teacher Suzuki, Yanagi formulated an aesthetics of folk art based on a synthesis of Zen and Pure Land Buddhist traditions (1989, 10).

Yanagi focuses on the aesthetics of Asian and Japanese *mingei* (民芸) or "folkcrafts," a term he coined with Shōji and Kawai Kanjiro to express the simple, plain, natural, and rustic beauty of "ordinary things" used in everyday life. He views Japanese handicrafts as having been produced by master craftsmen effortlessly, naturally, spontaneously, and unconsciously. Yanagi's interpretation of Japanese and Asian folk arts hence shows the distinctive influence of Suzuki's Zen aestheticism based on his philosophical psychology of the cosmic Unconscious. In his book *The Beauty of Everyday Things*, Yanagi writes: "This is how I would like to view the artisan's state of mind when he is at work . . . the product is true folk art when it is made in this unconscious, natural manner" (2017, 21). Again, "The fact that they are able to create wholesome craft objects almost unconsciously is perhaps their most outstanding feature" (2017, 23). For Yanagi, folk art created by master craftsmen is the product of "an ordinary, unconscious activity" (2017, 22). Further explaining how handicrafts are made naturally, spontaneously, and unconsciously, Yanagi asserts: "The craftsman does not aim to create beauty, but nature assures that it is done. He himself has lost all thought, is unconsciously at work. . . . beauty naturally appears in works unconsciously created" (2017, 30); moreover, "for folk crafts-people, the natural approach is that of unself-consciousness, unself-awareness" (2017, 10). He adds: "This natural, unforced beauty is the result of a kind of unconscious grace" (2017, 21). It can be said that Yanagi is one the most important figures in twentieth-century Japanese aesthetics and that his life and works have been profoundly influenced by the Zen aestheticism of Suzuki, such that in his Japanese aesthetics of craftsmanship he describes Japanese folk crafts as emerging from the Unconscious.

The distinctive mark of Suzuki's Zen aestheticism is also to be found in the art of Noguchi Isamu (1904–1988), an internationally renowned Japanese American sculptor, landscape artist, and set designer for theater and dance productions. As reported by Dore Ashton, in preparation for his trip to Japan, Noguchi read Suzuki's *Zen and Japanese Culture* (1992, 96). Moreover, in her biography on Noguchi, Hayden Herrera writes: "Not long after he [Noguchi] arrived in Japan . . . he read avidly about the poetry of Bashō, D. T. Suzuki's writings on Zen, and his own father's writings on art and poetry" (2015, 258–259). Noguchi collaborated with Kurokawa Kisho, one of Japan's foremost contemporary architects, renown for his visionary building designs as well as his philosophical writings on Japanese aesthetics. Among his many famous architectural and urban planning projects in Japan and around the world, Kurokawa recalls: "I helped out . . . with drafting the plans for Isamu Noguchi's garden for UESCO in Paris" (1988, 6). In *Rediscovering Japanese Space*, Kurokawa discusses the influence of Suzuki's Zen logic of *soku-hi* or contradictory identity of "is and is not" on his own Japanese Buddhist aesthetics of emptiness as formulated in terms of *wabi* or simplicity, *ma* (間) as the beauty of empty open space between objects, and "Rikyu gray" as an ambiguous neutral color that reveals the paradoxical identity of contradictions such as being and nothingness, part and whole, or inside and outside: "Another important inspiration for my thought over the years has been the words of the Zen philosopher Daisetz Suzuki. In particular, Suzuki's discussion of the 'logic of identity and nonidentity' (*sokuhi no ronri*) has played a major part in my thinking" (1988, 43). According to Kurokawa, Suzuki's *soku-hi* Zen logic of contradictory identity between part and whole, being and nothingness, interiority and exteriority, and other dichotomies has revolutionary implications for a postmodern Japanese aesthetics of architecture: "I have often referred to Daisetz Suzuki's logic of identity and difference and emphasized the mutually embracing relationship of part and whole in what is nothing less than a revolution against the Western concept of hierarchy. . . . The revolutionary nature of Daisetz Suzuki's concept of relationships of part and whole is in its power to transcend these dualistic traps" (1988, 95). Kurokawa goes on to apply Suzuki's Zen *soku-hi* logic of paradoxical identity between contradictions to his own innovative architectural structures built on the aesthetic principle of beauty as the "symbiosis of part and whole," which functions to maximize the infinite openness of empty space in a flowing continuum between solid and void.

Suzuki's Zen aestheticism had an enormous impact on not only the avant-garde artist community of New York City in the 1950s but also the philosophical aesthetics that emerged to interpret that art. Arthur C. Danto (1924–2013) is one of the foremost American philosophers of art. Before his career teaching philosophy at Columbia University in New York City, Danto was a successful artist whose style was influenced by the Japanese woodcut printmaking of Munakata Shiko. Furthermore, Danto's analytical philosophy of art was directly inspired by the Zen aestheticism of Suzuki. Danto studied Zen Buddhism with Suzuki at Columbia University in the 1950s. A work titled *Mysticism and Morality* (1972) already reveals Danto's early interest in Eastern philosophy, including Hinduism, Daoism, and Zen Buddhism. Danto here comments about the attraction of Zen for the avant-garde artworld of New York City: "Zen had a great appeal for artists . . . and its popularity coincided with a theory of art according to which art is an activity rather than a product, to be judged primarily, if not exclusively, in terms of spontaneousness" (1988, 66). In his essay "Upper West Side Buddhism," Danto describes his satori-like epiphany upon first seeing Andy Warhol's Pop Art in an exhibition at the Stable Gallery in New York City during the 1960s, leading to the initial formation of his own philosophy of art. Moreover, Danto clarifies the influence on his aesthetics by Suzuki's lectures, classes, and writings on Zen Buddhism:

> It was Pop that engaged me as a philosopher, principally through the work of Warhol. The Brillo cartons of Warhol exemplified objects that were works of art which for all practical purpose, were indiscernible from the workaday shipping cartons of common experience. Art and life looked outwardly alike, and the philosophical task was to explain why and in what way they were different. It was here that my study of Buddhism, such as it was, and of Dr. Suzuki's writing in particular, came to my aid. (2004, 57)

Recounting the decisive impact of Suzuki's classes, public lectures, and writings on the formation of his own aesthetics, Danto indicates the even broader impact that Suzuki's Zen aestheticism had on the radical paradigm-shift in the New York City artworld from the 1950s Abstract Expressionism of Jackson Pollock to the 1960s Pop Art of Andy Warhol:

> It was not, however, until the 1960s that the wider meaning of what I learned from Dr. Suzuki — if not from his lectures, then from his books — found its way into my philosophy. I would not have been able to see this in terms of 1950s paradigms. The direction of art history changed in what I think was a radical way. Whether Dr. Suzuki helped cause this change, or merely contributed to it, is not something anyone can say with certainty. But the people who made the changes were themselves Suzuki's students one way or another. (2004, 55–56)

Elsewhere, Danto again describes the widespread influence of Suzuki's lectures and classes on Zen at Columbia University during the 1950s on the progressive intellectuals and avant-garde artists in New York City, as well as how it affected the formation of his own philosophy of art:

> The members of Fluxus were alumni of John Cage's seminar in experimental composition at the New School, and subscribed to certain ideas emanating from Dr. Suzuki's seminars in Zen

Buddhism at Columbia, both of which took place in the late 1950. Zen ideas as framed by Suzuki, had a vast transformative influence on the intellectual life of New York in those years. My own thought, set out in the already mentioned 1964 article, "The Art World," is seasoned with imagery I acquired from sitting in on Suzuki's class, as well as from his books. (2003, 21)

In *Philosophizing Art*, Danto again recalls the powerful impact of Suzuki's Zen aestheticism on the 1950s artworld of New York City. After explaining the influence of Edo period Japanese *ukioe* woodblock prints on French impressionist painting, he continues: "But by 1950 another, probably equally idealized, aspect of the Japanese spirit had begun to emerge, primarily through the concepts of Zen" (1999, 165). He continues: "Delegates from the downtown artworld made weekly pilgrimages to Dr. Suzuki's seminars on Zen, held in Philosophy Hall at Columbia University. . . . The art historian of this era will have to assign Suzuki's lectures a primordial role in the era's cultural life. Artists came as pilgrims and left as converts to the amazing thoughts to which Suzuki's slow intonation gave an almost sculptural form" (1999, 166). Beginning with his seminal essay "The Artworld" (1964), Danto identifies what thereafter became the central question in his philosophy of art, what he calls the problem of *indiscernibles*. He defines "indiscernibility" as the problem wherein there are "objects otherwise indiscernible, one of which is an artwork and one of which is not" (1981, 6). Danto provides thought experiments, asking the reader to imagine various "perceptually indiscernible counterparts" (1981, 61) or "optically indiscernible objects" (1981, 133), and then, based on acceptable criteria, to determine which of these objects is art and which of these is not art. To give a famous example from Dadaism, if Marcel Duchamp's ready-made title "Snow Shovel" (*Prelude to a Broken Arm*, 1915) exhibited in a studio, and countless other mass-produced snow shovels identical to it are visually indiscernible, why is one is an artwork, and all of the others just ordinary tools? (1981, 45, 93-94).

For Danto the problem of indiscernibility was discovered in a burst of insight when he first saw Andy Warhol's Pop Art, especially the *Brillo Boxes*. At this exhibition of Pop Art in the Stable Gallery he recognized that there were a pair of visually indiscernible counterparts with no manifest attributes to differentiate them, these being the commercial Brillo boxes and Warhol's *Brillo Boxes*. The question raised by Danto's problem of indiscernibility is that since the ordinary Brillo boxes and the *Brillo Boxes* of Warhol are perceptually indiscernible counterparts, what makes one of the pair of indiscernibles just a mere ordinary thing and the other a work of art? For Danto this raises a new the question: What is art? First, Danto refutes various attempts to define art, finally developing his own institutionalist theory, whereby an artwork is distinguished by virtue of its context-dependent location in an "artworld" thereby to have an atmosphere of art theory. What is of special interest here is that Danto discovered his central problem of indiscernible counterparts from the Zen Buddhism that he learned from Suzuki, especially about the Zen koan teachings of Qingyuan Weixin (671–740), also known in Japan as Seigen Ishin. Here is the famous koan of Qingyuan (Ch'ing Yuan): "When I began to study Zen, mountains were mountains; when I thought I understood Zen, mountains were not mountains; but when I came to full knowledge of Zen, mountains were again mountains" (ZB, 288). This passage by Qingyuan contains three dialectical stages of Zen/Chan experience: (1) ordinary mountains, (2) no mountains, and (3) the enlightened perception of mountains as religio-aesthetic phenomena. Or as rock artist Donovan puts it in the chorus of his Zen-inspired 1967 hit song *There is a Mountain*: "First there is a mountain, then there is no mountain, then there is."

Inspired by the lectures, classes, and writings of Suzuki, Danto began to analyze the problem of indiscernible counterparts in art from the standpoint of Zen Buddhism. In his book *The Transfiguration of the Commonplace*, Danto explains how Qinguan (Ch'ing Yuan) expresses the *Diamond Sutra* teaching about the nonduality of samsara and nirvana or ignorance and enlightenment. He cites another version of Qinguan's mountain/no mountain/true mountain koan that he studied with Suzuki (1981, 134). Explaining Qingyuan's koan, Danto writes:

> He sees mountains as mountains, but it does not follow that he sees them as mountains just as he saw them before. For he has returned to them as mountains by the route of a complex set of spiritual exercises and a remarkable metaphysics and epistemology. When Ch'ing Yuan says a mountain is a mountain, he is making a religious statement: the contrast between a mountain and a religious object has disappeared through making the mountain into a religious object. (1981, 134)

In the Zen/Chan koan of Qingyuan, the pair of visually indiscernible counterparts is the first stage of ordinary mountains and the third stage when the same mountains are now viewed as religio-aesthetic objects. He clarifies how one of the pair of indiscernible counterparts is an ordinary thing and the other is a work of art as follows: "To see something as art at all demands nothing less than this, an atmosphere of artistic theory, a knowledge of the history of art. Art is the kind of thing that depends for its existence upon theories; without theories of art, black paint is just black paint and nothing more . . . there could not be an artworld without theory, for the artworld is logically dependent upon theory" (1981, 135). What makes one of a pair of visually indistinguishable objects just an ordinary thing such as a Brillo box on the shelf at the grocery store and the other a work of art such as Warhol's *Brillo Box* in the gallery is that the artwork is contextually located in what Danto calls an *artworld*, thus having "an atmosphere of artistic theory." Moreover, he argues that one of the indiscernible counterparts is judged to be an artwork when it is *about* something, to have *meaning*, while the ordinary thing is just what it is and is not about anything

(1981, 139). Likewise, based on Suzuki's teachings, Danto tells us that in Zen/Chan Buddhism, what makes one of the indiscernible counterparts an ordinary mountain at the first stage of ignorance and the other a religio-aesthetic object at the third stage of enlightenment is that at the third stage the mountain acquires an atmosphere of artistic theory, including an epistemology based on prajna-intuition of sunyata or emptiness and a metaphysics of nothingness, accompanied by spiritual exercises whereby one directly acquires insight into the void.

For Danto, the religious, spiritual, and mystical value of art is that it is *transfigurative*: "Transfiguration is a religious concept" (1997, 128). Throughout his writings Danto often mentions Raphael's *The Transfiguration* (1516–1520) as one of the supreme masterworks at the height of Italian Renaissance painting. Danto's aesthetic motif of "transfiguration of the commonplace" has religious and mystical connotations not only through its exemplification by Zen Buddhism but also insofar as it invokes the Transfiguration of Jesus Christ in the New Testament, where Jesus is transfigured and becomes radiant in glory upon a mountain top (Mathew 17:1–8; Mark 9:2–8; Luke 9:28–36).

Influenced by avant-garde art movements such as Dada, Pop Art, and Fluxus, and especially by the Zen aestheticism of Suzuki, Danto also came to emphasize the fusion of art and life to disclose the wonder of the ordinary as extraordinary. According to Danto, in the 1960s philosophy and art were characterized by a *return to the ordinary*, as exemplified by the Pop Art of Warhol, as well as the ordinary language philosophy of Ludwig Wittgenstein and John Austin. Danto states, "pop celebrated the most ordinary things of the most ordinary lives — corn flakes, canned soup, soap pads, movie stars, comics. Something in the 1960s explains, has to explain, why the ordinary things of the common world suddenly became the bedrock of art and philosophy. The abstract expressionists despised the world the pop artist apotheosized" (1981, 130). Just as how Michael Duchamp's dadaist ready-made named *The Fountain* (1917) converts an ordinary porcelain urinal into an artwork, also known as "the Buddha of the bathroom," and the Pop Art of Warhol's *Brillo Boxes* (1964) turns ordinary Brillo shipping cartons into sculptures, the Zen aestheticism of Suzuki redirects our attention away from transcendent abstractions to the beauty of concrete ordinary objects used in everyday life, such as the plain, simple, unadorned ceramic *wabi*-style bowls for drinking tea. For Suzuki's modern Zen aestheticism, as for Danto's philosophy of art, an artwork defamiliarizes mundane objects and familiarizes the mysterious to reveal the ordinary as extraordinary, hence resulting in what the latter calls a "transfiguration of the commonplace." Like Danto's description of the change from the 1950s Abstract Expressionism of Pollock to the 1960s Pop Art of Warhol, Suzuki describes how Zen art constitutes a radical paradigm-shift from other-worldliness to a *this*-worldly model of art as a consecration of the ordinary and everyday, thereby to initiate a movement from transcendence to immanence. This re-enchantment of the ordinary through transfiguration of the commonplace is the hallmark of Danto's philosophy of art and Suzuki's Zen aestheticism. In the modern Zen aestheticism of

Suzuki, as for Danto's analytical philosophy of art, there is an illumination of the quotidian that dissolves conventional boundaries between art and non-art. It can thus be said that both Danto and Suzuki have formulated historical-cultural variants of an "aesthetics of the ordinary," culminating in the transfiguration of everyday life into art.

PART TWO

ZEN AND WESTERN MODELS OF THE UNCONSCIOUS

Chapter 5

The Unconscious in Zen and American Thought

In *Americans and the Unconscious* (1986), Robert C. Fuller documents "the psychologizing of American thought" by means of the psychological concept of *the unconscious* and that the notion of a *higher unconscious* thereafter became central to the "aesthetic spirit" of American religions. Fuller maintains that the unconscious became symbolic for the hidden depths of nature, including the inmost depths of human nature, resulting in "a uniquely American mode of spirituality in which the aesthetic — as opposed to the doctrinal or moral — dimension predominates" (1986, 6). He traces the American tradition of "aesthetic spirituality running through the writings of Jonathan Edwards, Ralph Waldo Emerson, and William James" (1986, 12). This American tradition of "aesthetic spirituality" promoted a distinctive form of natural piety in which aesthetic harmony with inner and outer nature, instead of a moralistic emphasis on sin and repentance, became the basis of spiritual life (1986, 16). According to Fuller, it was in the philosophical psychology of William James that this American tradition of aesthetic spirituality was articulated in scientific terms with a doctrine of the unconscious: "The Jamesian synthesis of psychology and religion elevated the unconscious to the status of a modern symbol of the relationship of human beings to their creative source" (1986, 95). While Edwards, Emerson, and others in the American tradition of aesthetic spirituality described the inflow of spiritual power into the soul, it was James who specified how "the unconscious" was the *psychological mechanism*, or "subliminal door," through which this divine inflow enters the human mind. James argued that it is through this psychological mechanism of the unconscious that the person is continuous with a wider, deeper, and higher subliminal self through which religious experiences of conversion, revelation, and salvation come (1986, 79). Fuller sees the notion of a "higher unconscious" in the American tradition of aesthetic spirituality developed by Edwards, Emerson, and James, as further running throughout the New Thought mind-cure movement, as well as neo-Freudian, Existentialist, Humanistic, and Transpersonal Psychology in America. The American concept of an unconscious in its higher creative aesthetic functioning established the basis for a new religious discourse: "The rediscovery of the 'higher' unconscious has made a kind of religious discourse possible for individuals to whom the idea of a Supreme Being 'up there' or 'out there' is untenable" (1986, 164).

Fuller concludes that this higher unconscious in the American psychologized tradition of aesthetic spirituality has "helped to make the unconscious one of the most powerful religious ideas of the twentieth century" (1986, 164).

Suzuki was profoundly influenced by the American philosophical tradition, including Emerson, Thoreau, James, and New Thought metaphysics. I would argue that in his missionary effort to introduce Zen in the West, Suzuki drew on the notion of a higher unconscious in this American tradition of aesthetic spirituality, especially as formulated in the philosophical psychology of James. As noted by Richard M. Jaffe, one of the topics that Suzuki lectured on at the First Congress of the Congress of World Faiths in London in 1936 and then in the United States on the way back to Japan, was "Zen Buddhism and the Philosophy of the Unconscious" (ZJC, xiv). By applying a philosophical psychology of the Unconscious to reinterpret Zen, Suzuki was tapping into the psychologized American tradition of aesthetic spirituality. Just as in the American tradition of aesthetic spirituality the "God within" was conceived as the subconscious mind, in the Zen aestheticism of Suzuki, our indwelling Buddha nature was described in psychological terms as the cosmic Unconscious. For Suzuki the cosmic Unconscious is the *psychological mechanism* through which the creative power and illuminated wisdom of Buddha nature flow into consciousness. In Suzuki's Zen aestheticism, the indwelling Buddha nature, like the God within of Christian mysticism, operates through the workings of the unconscious, or what James refers to as "the subliminal door." Similar to what Fuller terms the "aesthetic spirit" of the American tradition grounded in a notion of the higher unconscious, Suzuki thus formulated a psychologized Zen aestheticism based on his notion of the cosmic Unconscious as the source of infinite creative possibilities.

In what follows, it will be shown how Suzuki's Zen doctrine of the Unconscious has been influenced by at least two major sources from within the American tradition of aesthetic spirituality, including (1) the interpretation of mystical experience as an inflow from "the subconscious" in James's philosophical psychology, itself partly influenced by the New Thought metaphysics; and (2) the doctrine of unconscious perception as "prehension" or dim aesthetic feeling in Alfred North Whitehead's organic process metaphysics. Moreover, I clarify that yet another source for Suzuki's knowledge about this American tradition of aesthetic spirituality was F. S. C. Northrop's *The Meeting of East and West* (1979), which postulated the concept of nature as an "undifferentiated aesthetic continuum" influenced by the radical empiricism of James and Whitehead.

Zen and William James

William James (1842–1910) was a medical doctor who with Charles S. Peirce became co-founder of classical American philosophy, including pragmatism, radical empiricism, and process metaphysics. Moreover, James is to be counted as one of the founders of modern psychology, having published his monumental *Principles of Psychology* (1890) ten years before Sigmund Freud's *The Interpretation of Dreams* (1900). Here it will be discussed how James's psychological explanation of mystical experience as an inflow from the subconscious became a major source for Suzuki's view of Zen satori as opening to the cosmic Unconscious in superconsciousness.

Suzuki's earliest discussion of James is in *Seiza no susume* ("A Recommendation for Quiet Sitting," 1900), coauthored with his Zen teacher Shaku Sōen Roshi, an essay analyzing the psychological and physiological effects of *zazen* or "seated meditation" using the theory of emotions developed by James and Carl Lange. In this essay Suzuki and Shaku Sōen endorse the Lange-James theory of emotion, which argues that emotions arise from physical stimuli within the body. Citing the words of James: "We feel sorry because we cry, angry because we strike, afraid because we tremble, and not that we cry, strike, or tremble, because we are sorry, angry, or fearful, as the case may be" (SWS I, xxvii). Furthermore, the coauthors explain: "According to the zazen method at hand, one strives to always keep the lower abdomen full of power, the breathing always uniform, the heart beat tranquil, the muscles of the whole body always resilient." They continue: "According to the Lange-James hypothesis, this is because emotion is nothing more than consciousness of changes in the physical body arising from an object" (SWS I, 6–7). Making reference to the unconscious, they add: "Mental reflex action is said to be when the mind moves unconsciously directly in response to external stimuli" (SWS I, 8). In contrast to the Cartesian body-mind dualism characterizing modern Western philosophy, the Zen tradition of Japanese Buddhism presupposes a nondual psychosomatic model of embodied cognition based on the "oneness of body-mind" (*shinjin ichinyō*, 心身一如). Zen emphasizes that satori corresponds to physical, somatic, or bodily states, including correct upright sitting in the lotus posture, muscular relaxation, and deep rhythmic abdominal breathing. For Suzuki, then, the Lange-James hypothesis is a paradigmatic Western theory by means of which to elucidate this principle of bodymind unity underlying Zen Buddhist satori and its creative expressions in somaesthetic artforms. But as will be seen, in Suzuki's psychosomatic theory, the head is the center of consciousness, and the lower abdominal region beneath the navel is the center of unconsciousness, whereas nondual Zen satori integrates the conscious and the Unconscious in superconciousness.

James and Suzuki on "Pure Experience"

In the chapter on mysticism from *The Varieties of Religious Experience* (1902), James explains mystical experience as what the psychiatrist Dr. Richard M. Bucke terms "cosmic consciousness." In his book *Cosmic Consciousness*

(1991), Bucke described cosmic consciousness as an immediate experience of the all-embracing macrocosm within the individual microcosm (1991, 3). Bucke then cites the Buddha's attainment of *nirvāṇa* as a paradigm case of one who has realized cosmic consciousness (1991, 97).

Although Suzuki had already read the early writings of James, he first met him while lecturing at Harvard University in 1909. Nishida Kitarō heard about James through Suzuki, who recommended as early as 1902 that Nishida acquaint himself with *The Varieties of Religious Experience*. Nishida obtained a copy of this work in 1904 and used it, along with *Principles of Psychology* and *Essays in Radical Empiricism* (1912), to formulate his own general theory of "pure experience" (*junsui keiken,* 純粋経験), as articulated in his maiden work *An Inquiry into the Good* (*Zen no kenkyū* 善の研究, 1911). According to the radical empiricism of James, the stream of pure experience is devoid of subject-object or knower-known bifurcation and prior to cognitive analysis. It will be seen that for Suzuki, as for Nishida and James, "pure experience" likewise refers to a continuum of awareness purified of egocentrism and subject-object dualism.

Richard Jaffe explains how James's radically empirical notion of "pure experience" influenced Nishida and Suzuki: "One can clearly see how Suzuki, while developing language for explaining ignorance and the awakening that was satori in Buddhism, engaged with the notion of 'pure experience' being developed in the first half of the twentieth century by William James and Nishida Kitarō, who was stimulated by James's efforts to detail the contours of a philosophy of 'radical empiricism'" (SWS I, xlvi). It is common for members of the Kyoto School of modern Japanese philosophy to assert that "pure experience" devoid of subject-object bifurcation was a Western category by means of which Nishida articulated the nondual flow state of Zen satori. As said by Takeuchi Yoshinori: "The concept of pure experience . . . is the Western philosophical mold into which Nishida poured his own religious experience cultivated by his Zen training" (1982, 182). Nishida, however, does not himself analyze pure experience with direct reference to Zen but instead develops his own metaphysics of pure experience as the ultimate reality underlying all phenomena. In fact, it was Suzuki who explicitly developed "pure experience" to articulate his view of Zen satori as direct insight into the cosmic Unconscious in superconsciousness. Moreover, Suzuki identifies Zen with James's "radical empiricism" as a method that returns to the directly felt qualitative immediacy in the continuum of nondual pure experience, whereupon things appear "just as they are" (*sono mama*) in *śūnyatā* or emptiness as *tathatā* or suchness (ZB, 324).

Here it should be noted that in several important essays the esteemed Japanese Buddhist scholar Robert Sharf has sharply criticized Suzuki's Jamesean concept of "pure experience." In his critique of Suzuki's New Meiji Buddhism, Sharf (1994; 1995) argues that Suzuki shifts the emphasis on ritual performance and doctrinal learning that characterized traditional monastic institutions of pre-Meiji Zen, to a new privileging of "religious experience," or in terminology influenced by James and Nishida, a "pure experience" that is personal, direct, unmediated, and nondual (Sharf 1993, 20). Sharf further claims that the Japanese terms for "experience," *keiken* (経験) and *taiken* (体験), were not used in traditional Zen literature and were only later coined during the Meiji period (1868–1912). Responding to Sharf, however, the Zen scholar and teacher Victor Sōgen Hori defends Suzuki's view by means of an exhaustive computer search on the Chinese Buddhist Electronic Text Association database, countering that while *keiken* and *taiken* were not used, the common term for "experience" in classical Zen/Chan discourse was *taitoku* (體得) (2016, 54–55). He thereby argues that for Suzuki, as for Japanese Zen Buddhism, satori is not just a ritualized performance but a phenomenological event of pure experience. Moreover, Hori steadfastly maintains that Suzuki's Zen is not an "invention" of the tradition as claimed by Sharf but the tradition itself.

In his essay "Reason and Intuition in Buddhist Philosophy" (RI, 66–109; SZ, 85–128), Suzuki explains Zen *prajñā*-intuition of sunyata or emptiness as the continuum of pure experience anterior to subject-object dualism. Clarifying the contrast between reason versus intuition, Suzuki explains that *vijñāna* or discursive reason grasps only the parts, whereas nondiscursive Zen *prajñā*-intuition of emptiness takes in the whole (RI, 95; SZ, 121). He adds, "*Śūnyatā*, then, is *prajñā,* and *prajñā* is *śūnyatā*" (RI, 79). Suzuki elsewhere remarks that this distinction between prajna-intuition and reason finds its parallel in Spinoza: "In one sense *prajna*-intuition may be said to correspond to Spinoza's *scientia intuitiva*. According to him, this kind of intuition . . . in contrast to *ratio*, produces the highest peace and virtue of the mind" (SZ, 147). Just as Spinoza's *scientia intuitiva* apprehends the various phenomena of nature as interlocking modes of one substance as God/Nature, for Suzuki it is through *prajñā*-intuition of things as they are in their emptiness-suchness that one grasps the whole in the parts. Moreover, Zen Buddhist *prajñā*-intuition of emptiness is itself an act of pure experience: "*Prajñā* is pure experience, beyond differentiation. It is the awakening of *śūnyatā* to self-consciousness" (RI, 79). Again, he tells us: "Buddhist philosophy . . . starts from pure experience" (RI, 95). For Suzuki, Zen Buddhist philosophy begins from a description of an egoless pure experience insofar as it discloses the field of emptiness as a dynamic flux of relationships in the stream of becoming devoid of subject-object bifurcation and anterior to discursive analysis where things are perceived as they are in their suchness. He adds: "This is why *śūnyatā* is said to be a reservoir of infinite possibilities and not just a state of mere [nihilistic] emptiness . . . It is not a concept reached by intellection, but what is given as pure act, as pure experience" (RI, 97). In a diagrammatic chart, Suzuki then identifies pure experience with other Zen Buddhist notions including *śūnyatā* or emptiness, *tathatā* or suchness, *prajñā*-intuition, Bodhi or enlightenment, and *mushin* or no-mind, which he otherwise terms the Unconscious (RI, 85).

Suzuki further identifies "pure experience" with Northrop's concept of nature as the *undifferentiated continuum* (RI, 94; SZ, 119). In his 1946 work

The Meeting of East and West, Northrop describes the "differentiated continuum" postulated by concepts in the West, as contrasted to the panoramic, all-embracing "undifferentiated aesthetic continuum" directly felt by intuition in Eastern traditions such as Zen/Chan Buddhism, Daoism, and their creative expression in East Asian landscape painting. As Northrop explains, his concept of the "undifferentiated aesthetic continuum" was itself especially influenced by the radical empiricism of James and Whitehead. Northrop maintains that due to its privileging of the "differentiated continuum" in the clearly articulated foreground, Western civilization has developed advanced science and technology, whereas because of its intuition of the "undifferentiated continuum" in the nonarticulated background of immediate experience, Eastern culture has developed a profoundly aesthetic worldview. In Suzuki's Japanese Buddhist framework, Northrop's "differentiated continuum" postulated by abstract ideas corresponds to *vijñāna* or discursive understanding, while Northrop's "undifferentiated aesthetic continuum" apprehended by intuition corresponds to Zen Buddhist *prajñā*-intuition of emptiness in pure experience: "To the Western mind, 'continuum' may be a better term than *śūnyatā*. . . . In the 'continuum' immediately given . . . there is no differentiation of subject and object, of the seer and the seen" (RI, 94; SZ, 119). According to Suzuki, then, "pure experience" devoid of subject and object, like the Zen Buddhist *prajñā*-intuition of sunyata or emptiness, functions to disclose what Northrop terms the "undifferentiated aesthetic continuum" of nature. As Robert Aitken Roshi has pointed out, however, at the Second East-West Philosophers' Conference held at the University of Hawaii in 1949, Suzuki also criticized Northrop's recently published book, exclaiming: "The trouble with the 'undifferentiated aesthetic continuum' is that it is *too* differentiated" (AZL, 211; italics added).

In *Mysticism: Christian and Buddhist*, Suzuki further develops his approach to Zen mysticism in terms of James's concept of pure experience as follows: "Pure experience is . . . a state of suchness. This is possible only when the mind is *śūnyatā* itself, that is, when the mind is devoid of all its possible contents except itself" (MCB, 23). Elsewhere in the same text: "Buddhist philosophy, therefore, is the philosophy of Suchness or philosophy of Emptiness. . . . It starts from the absolute present which is pure experience, an experience in which there is yet no differentiation of subject and object" (MCB, 60). Suzuki here defines "pure experience" as devoid of subject-object dualism, as anterior to cognitive reflection, as direct awareness of things as they are in emptiness-suchness, and as happening in the here-now of the absolute present. Moreover, he asserts: "The Buddhist philosophy of Suchness thus starts with what is most primarily given to our consciousness — which I have called pure experience" (MCB, 61). He goes on to identify pure experience not only with the Zen Buddhist notion of emptiness as suchness but also what in the *via negativa* apophatic Christian mysticism of Meister Eckhart is the immediate experience of the Godhead of nothingness as *isness* (MCB, 60). In Suzuki's radical empiricism, Zen mystical experience through prajna-intuition of the continuum of emptiness thereby culminates in pure experience of events "just as they are" (*sono mama*) in their isness, thusness or suchness.

In an essay titled "The Buddhist Concept of Reality," delivered at the second East-West Philosophers' Conference held at the University of Hawaii in 1949, Suzuki addresses the question: "What is reality?" (SWS IV, 220). He answers that for Christians it is God, for Hindus it is Atman-Brahman, and for the Chinese it is Dao. For Zen Buddhism, however, the concept of ultimate reality is sunyata or emptiness (SWS IV, 236). Moreover, he then interprets the Zen Buddhist nondual concept of ultimate reality as sunyata or emptiness in terms of the American psychologist James's radically empirical notion of "pure experience" (SWS IV, 219–236). Suzuki uses his Jamesian notion of pure experience to illuminate Zen Buddhist terms designating ultimate reality, such as dharmakaya, absolute nothingness, prajna-intuition, and sunyata or emptiness, which he in turn relates to other Western concepts, including Bergson's élan-vital, and Northrop's "undifferentiated aesthetic continuum" (SWS IV, 231–232). He goes on to ask: "Now the question will be how to have a self-realization of 'pure experience' whereby we take hold of reality" (SWS IV, 230). His response is that the self-realization of ultimate reality as pure experience is not achieved by cognitive analysis, nor by logical postulation, nor by dialectical reason, but only through direct prajna-intuition of sunyata or emptiness as undiscriminated discrimination, what he also refers to here in Zen paradoxical terms as being "unconsciously conscious" (SWS IV, 236). In a key passage, Suzuki thus declares: "The ultimate reality as conceived in Buddhist philosophy is "pure experience," *śūnyatā,* a grand integration which is before subject and object are intellectually differentiated; it is the cosmic or divine Unconscious becoming conscious" (SWS IV, 231). Hence, while Suzuki interprets the nondual Mahayana Buddhist principle of sunyata or emptiness in terms of James's continuum of pure experience, he ultimately formulates pure experience in terms of his Jamesian psychologized Zen concept of satori as becoming fully conscious of the cosmic Unconscious in superconsciousness.

James and Suzuki on the Unconscious

Suzuki, like James, maintains that the heart of religion is not to be found in rituals, doctrines, and institutions, but in mystical experience, or as it were, in the pure experience of things as they are in their directly felt qualitative immediacy. Moreover, influenced by James's philosophical psychology, Suzuki asserts that the inner source of mystical experience is the unconscious, subconscious, or subliminal mind. James writes: "It is evident that from the point of view of their psychological mechanism, the classical mysticism and these lower mysticisms spring from the same mental level, from that great subliminal or transmarginal region of which science is beginning to admit the existence, but of which so little is really known" (1982, 426). Likewise, while explaining the mystical state of enlightenment as Bodhi or prajna-intuition of emptiness in Mahayana Buddhism, where the self expands to include the cosmos, Suzuki refers to *trans-marginal consciousness*, which is James's signature term for the unconscious, subconscious or subliminal mind: "To use psychological terms, it is a state of . . . trans-marginal consciousness, where all sense-perceptions and conceptual images vanish, and where we are in a state of absolute unconsciousness" (OMB, 72). Suzuki is therefore indebted to James's account of mystical experience for not only his radically empirical understanding of Zen satori as a continuum of pure experience devoid of egoism and subject-object duality but also his psychological interpretation of mystical experience as the realization of "trans-marginal consciousness," or what he further describes as a sudden inflow of the subconscious into consciousness. Hence in the statement cited above, Suzuki tells us that Buddhist prajna-intuition of sunyata or emptiness, articulated in terms of radical empiricism as "pure experience," is psychologically expressed through his notion of Zen satori as becoming conscious of the cosmic Unconscious (SWS IV, 231)

In *The Varieties of Religious Experience*, James develops his notion of the subconscious as the inner source for mystical experiences of cosmic consciousness as reported by the Buddha and other illuminated saints in world religions throughout the ages. To explain the mystical experience of cosmic consciousness, as well as religious experiences of conversion, revelation, illumination, and ecstasy, or paranormal experiences of telepathy, hypnotic trance, clairvoyance, prophecy, mediumship, automatic writing, and spontaneous healing, along with psychedelic experiences that are chemically induced by pharmaceutical drugs, James sets forth the hypothesis that all such events arise from out of the subconscious mind or subliminal self: "Let me then propose, as an hypothesis, that whatever it may be on its farther side, the 'more' with which in religious experience we feel ourselves connected is on its hither side the subconscious continuation of our conscious life" (1982, 513). As stated above by James, the subconscious is "continuous" with our conscious life, as part of the full spectrum of awareness. Hence, for James the subconscious is to be otherwise conceived as a "trans-marginal consciousness." In his phenomenology of higher states of mystical experience, James describes cosmic consciousness as opening to the dark penumbral fringe, field, or horizon that encircles the clear focal region of consciousness, further identifying this psychical *more* beyond the edge of consciousness with the subliminal, transmarginal, or subconscious dimensions of the mind (1982, 508). The "conscious/unconscious" distinction of depth psychology is thus described by James in phenomenological terms as the "focus/fringe" structure of the perceptual field as disclosed by immediate experience. Throughout his work James emphasizes that the transmarginal region of the subconscious, like the wider field of consciousness with which it is continuous, is not a reified substance but rather it is a *function* of dynamic processes, relationships, and events in the stream of experience. For James, the subconscious is the psychological mechanism or subliminal door through which spiritual illumination flows into the conscious mind in mystical awakening to cosmic consciousness thereby to culminate in beatific experience of the divine within.

Although James is known for the striking originality of his thought, nonetheless, various sources influenced his notion of the subconscious or subliminal self. In 1867 James began an extended period of study abroad in Germany thus becoming familiar with concepts of the unconscious in German philosophy and psychology. However, James's notion of the subliminal self was also shaped by new concepts of the unconscious mind that emerged within the American tradition of religion, philosophy, psychology, and parapsychology. In James's radical empiricism, the basic datum given for psychology is not an isolated atomic sensory impression but the entire field of consciousness, including its encompassing margins, horizons, or fringes, and it is this peripheral fringe of consciousness that denotes "the subconscious," or the *subliminal self*. Thus, for James the subconscious is not a separate compartment but the relational fringe of consciousness itself, or what he refers to as "transmarginal consciousness," thereby to establish continuity between consciousness and the unconscious within a nondual "experience-continuum" (1996, 104). James gives credit for this discovery of an extramarginal consciousness to Frederic W. Myers.[1] As summed up by Henri Ellenberger in his massive work *The Discovery of the Unconscious*: "Myers was not only a parapsychologist, but also one of the great systematizers of the notion of the unconscious mind" (1970, 314). In Myers' view, the "subliminal self" or the unconscious mind has inferior and superior functions. The inferior functions of the subliminal self are shown in those processes of dissociation investigated by psychiatry, while the superior functions of the subliminal self are revealed in works of creative genius, which he understood as the "subliminal uprush" of storehouses of information from the depths of the unconscious mind. Also, Myers held that the superior functions of the subliminal self are expressions of what lie beneath "the threshold of consciousness" and can account for communication with the spirits of the deceased, or other psychical phenomena such as ecstatic trance, hypnotism, automatic writing, extra sensory perception, telepathy, clairvoyance, prophetic dreams, and spiritual healing. Making reference to an 1892 article by Myers on the subconscious, James tells us:

> Since one of the duties of the science of religions is to keep religion in connection with the rest of science, we shall do well to seek first of all a way of describing the "more," which psychologists may also recognize as real. The *subconscious self* is nowadays a well-accredited psychological entity; and I believe that in it we have exactly the mediating term required. . . . The explorations of the transmarginal field has hardly yet been seriously undertaken, but what Mr. Myers said in 1892 in his essay on the Subliminal Consciousness is as true as when it was first written. (1982, 511–512)

Another important source for James's view of the subliminal self was the concept of the subconscious mind in the popular nineteenth-century "New Thought" or mind-cure movement in America, also referred to as Religious Science, Divine Science, Mental Science, Christian Science, Unity Church International, New Thought Alliance, and other offshoots. The largest among the New Thought organizations in the world today is the modern Japanese movement Seichō-no-Ie founded by Taniguchi Masaharu (1893–1985), which synthesizes Japanese Buddhism, Shintoism, Christianity, and New Thought teachings of the human mind as constituted by the conscious, subconscious, and superconscious (1962, 139–140).[2] Many books popularizing the New Thought mind-cure gospel of health, happiness, and prosperity describe the inexhaustible power and wisdom of our subconscious mind.[3] New Thought books emphasized the notion of the unconscious, subconscious, or superconscious mind as the "God within" and taught many practical techniques for tapping the power and wisdom of the subconscious, including relaxation, letting go, prayer, silent meditation, focused concentration, deep breathing, creative visualization, affirmation, positive thinking, mental repetition, active imagination, decrees, self-hypnosis, autosuggestion, and other spiritual exercises. Moreover, New Thought mind-cure books taught that the subconscious mind is the inner source for all healing, as well as for creativity, artistic inspiration, mystical experience, and religious salvation.

As a physician, James was interested not only in the mystical, religious, and spiritual aspects of the subconscious but also in the medical, curative, and healing powers of the subliminal mind. Hence, in Lectures IV and V in *The Varieties of Religious Experience*, James explains at length "The Religion of Healthy-Mindedness" advocated by the New Thought mind-cure philosophy (1982, 94). James goes on to explain the central importance of the "subconscious" or *subliminal self* in this gospel of healthy-mindedness spread by New Thought mind-cure philosophy: "The spiritual in man appears in the mind-cure philosophy as partly conscious, but chiefly subconscious; and through the subconscious part of it we are already one with the Divine . . . we find in it traces of Christian mysticism, of transcendental idealism, of vedantism, and of the modern psychology of the subliminal self" (1982, 100). He continues: "Finally, mind-cure has made what in our protestant countries is an unprecedentedly great use of the subconscious life. . . . Its founders have added systematic exercise in passive relaxation, concentration, and meditation, and have even invoked something like hypnotic practice" (1982, 115). James notes that New Thought teachings on the subconscious have "both a speculative and a practical side" and says that that it is this practical aspect of mind-cure philosophy dealing with relaxation, concentration, meditation, visualization, and other spiritual exercises for contacting our subliminal mind that especially appeals to the spirit of American pragmatism (1982, 94–96). Suzuki also discusses New Thought metaphysics but emphasizes the differences between Zen koan practice and

New Thought meditation exercises: "Zen is not to be confounded with a form of meditation as practiced by 'New Thought' people" (AIZB, 40).

As discussed earlier, for Suzuki the Zen illumination experience of satori is to become fully conscious of the cosmic Unconscious in superconsciousness (AZL, 62; LZ, 88). Also, it has been shown that Suzuki's notion of mystical experience as "superconsciousness" derives from James's chapter on Mysticism in *The Varieties of Religious Experience*, where James cites the Hindu philosopher Swami Vivekananda's analysis of mind into consciousness, unconsciousness, and superconsciousness. Moreover, this notion of superconsciousness articulated by James and Vivekananda became prevalent in the American movement known as New Thought. Just as James cites the early nineteenth-century tradition of New Thought metaphysics, likewise, New Thought authors frequently make reference to James' philosophical psychology of the subconscious. For example, James influenced an early mind-cure author named William W. Atkinson (1862–1932), who was editor of the popular magazine New Thought from 1901 to 1905 and wrote dozens of New Thought books. Also, he wrote many books on esoteric Indian yoga philosophy and meditation under the name of Yogi Ramacharaka and other pseudonyms. In his influential New Thought book *Subconscious and the Superconscious Planes of Mind* (1909), Atkinson cites at length various scholarly views on the deeper hidden mind of the unconscious, including those of Gottfried Wilhelm Leibniz, Arthur Schopenhauer, Eduard von von Hartmann, Fredric Myers, Oliver Wendell Holmes, Wilhelm Wundt, James, and many others. He begins with the two-level theory of infra-conscious mentation as having both a conscious and subconscious mind wherein the subconscious in the hypnotic trance state is amenable to control by suggestion. Atkinson endeavors to demonstrate that the subconscious mind regulates all autonomic bodily functions and that by giving suggestions to the subconscious, one can heal the physical body of its ailments. In this context, Atkinson cites the words of James: "The unconscious mind as revealed by hypnotism can exercise marvelous control of the nervous, vasomotor and circulatory and other systems" (2010, 128). Atkinson goes on to present a more comprehensive three-level notion of mind as having a conscious, subconscious, and superconscious. Making reference to the teaching of Vivekananda, and other Hindu gurus visiting America and Europe, he reports: "These Oriental teachers taught that just as there was a subconsciousness, below the ordinary plane of consciousness, so was there a superconsciousness, above the ordinary plane" (2010, 25). He further explains, "instead of being the greater memory, or storehouse of the impressions of the past, as is the subconscious, the superconsciousness of the individual is the latent possibilities of the future man, or superman" (2010, 171). Atkinson's view of the superconscious mind, itself influenced by James and Vivekananda, thus has clear parallels with Suzuki's modern Zen concept of satori as becoming conscious of the cosmic Unconscious in superconsciousness, or with the threefold structure of mind as constituted by the conscious, subconscious, and superconscious described by Taniguchi Masaharu (1962, 139–140).

In another bestselling New Thought book first published in 1963 titled *The Power of Your Subconscious Mind*, Joseph Murphy writes: "William James, the father of American psychology, said that the power to move the world is in your subconscious mind. Your subconscious mind is one with Infinite Intelligence and Boundless Wisdom" (2008, 40). And elsewhere, "William James said that the greatest discovery of the nineteenth century was the power of the subconscious mind touched by faith" (2008, 201). In accord with other New Thought writings, Murphy describes the subconscious mind as the source of all aesthetic experience and creative genius in the arts: "Great artists, musicians, poets, speakers, and writers tune in with their subconscious powers and become animated and inspired" (2008, 98). He continues: "The subconscious mind is the deep well from which great artists draw their awe-provoking power" (2008, 38). For Murphy, as for others in the New Thought mental science movement, through the deeper subconscious mind we are already one with the universal mind of God. Murphy adheres to the biblical teaching that *"the kingdom of God is within you"* (Luke 17:21). Hence, the God of Christianity is now understood by New Thought as the "indwelling Lord," or the "Christ within" that resides in our deeper subconscious mind, which Murphy calls "the cosmic subconscious" (1968, 8, 17, 18–31, 131), what Atkinson calls "the superconscious" (2010), and what Troward calls the "greater subconscious mind" (2000, 84). Prayers directed to God as the indwelling Lord invoke the boundless wisdom, creative genius, divine intuition, and healing power of the subconscious. Murphy explicitly identifies the biblical notion of the indwelling Lord with "spiritual laws of the subconscious mind" (2008, 201). He further explains this biblical notion of the "God within" in its function as the universal laws governing the subconscious by reference to the following verse from the New Testament: *"Ask, and you will receive; seek, and you will find; knock, and the door will be opened.* (Matthew 7:7). What does this celebrated verse tell us? . . . There is always a direct response from the Infinite Intelligence of your subconscious mind to your conscious thinking" (2008, 81–82). Citing the Old Testament, he continues: "I sought the Lord's help and he answered me; he set me free from all my terrors" (Psalm 34:4). Murphy's commentary on this verse goes: "*Lord* is an ancient word meaning *law* — the power of your subconscious mind" (2008, 261). He adds: "Learn the wonders of your subconscious. Understand how it works and functions. Master the techniques given to you. . . . Your subconscious will respond, and you will be free of all fears" (2008, 261). Like other New Thought authors, Murphy formulates a psychological interpretation of Christian theology wherein God is now comprehended as what he calls "the cosmic subconscious," such that prayer, meditation, and other spiritual exercises become techniques for tapping the inexhaustible wisdom and creative power of our own subconscious mind. As said in Luke 17:21, "the kingdom of God is within you." According to New Thought metaphysics, as well as the philosophical psychology of James, this means that the "God within" is our subliminal self, such that religion is the discipline that enables us to restore contact with our own deeper, wider, and higher unconscious mind.

Like the New Thought movement, James regards meditation, prayer, ritual, and other forms of spiritual exercises as cultivating "openness to the 'subliminal' door" (1982, 524). For James, the religious encounter with the divine through mystical experiences, visions, raptures, ecstasies, conversions, or revelations are all to be explained as "invasions from the subconscious region" (1982, 512–513). Monistic interpretations of American Transcendentalism, German Idealism, and Indian Vedantism describe this mystical experience as the finite self-attaining union with an absolute, but in psychological terms, it is an opening to the "transmarginal consciousness," the "subconscious," or "the higher faculties of our own hidden mind" (1982, 513). In Theism, religious experience is explained by James as owing to our faith in the merciful grace of a personal God, but this is also to be psychologically understood as having its origins in the subconscious or subliminal layers of the mind: "If the grace of God miraculously operates, it probably operates through the subliminal door, then" (1982, 270). As James further emphasizes in his chapter on "Mysticism," intoxication through alcohol, anesthetic revelations from ether and nitrous oxide, or plant hallucinogens like the peyote cactus, as well as various kinds of psychic phenomena such as trance, automatic writing, telepathy, clairvoyance, prophecy, spiritual healing, and the clinical phenomenon of hypnosis or mesmerism, can be understood as functions of our subconscious mind.

In his analysis of James's views on mystical experience as a function of the subconscious or unconscious, his biographer Gerald Myers writes: "The 'age of the subconscious/unconscious' had arrived and James knew it; he anticipated its influence in science and society, foreseeing and lamenting the anti-religious developments in Freudian theory . . . he saw that the subconscious or the psychical *more* could be used in the name of religion" (1986, 427). Myers further points out: "James identified a vital connection between mystical experience, abnormal psychology, the mind-cure movement, and psychical research. The connection lay in the psychological concept of the subconscious. . . . Psychologists and religious mystics alike understand that any experience, when we reflect upon it, has no definite boundary but radiates from its center into a surrounding *more*" (1986, 471). For James, a mystical experience of cosmic consciousness is a kind of pure experience wherein consciousness articulated in the clear foreground focus of attention shades off into to the dark nonarticulated background of the perceptual field, which itself constitutes the transmarginal, subconscious, or unconscious region of our subliminal mind. In *A Pluralistic Universe* (1909), James sums up his phenomenological description of transmarginal experience as the subconscious *more* beyond the threshold of consciousness in terms of the focus/fringe structure of the perceptual field: "My present field of consciousness is a centre surrounded by a fringe that shades insensible into a subconscious more" (1967, 288).

158 | D. T. Suzuki on the Unconscious in Zen Art, Meditation, and Enlightenment

It can now be seen how Suzuki, like the radical empiricism of James, articulates a philosophical psychology explaining the mystical experience of cosmic consciousness, the Japanese Buddhist paradigm for which is Zen satori or sudden enlightenment. Influenced by the philosophical psychology of James, whereby the subconscious is the *psychological mechanism* or "subliminal door" for mystical experience of cosmic consciousness, Suzuki argued that Zen satori is a breakthrough of our deeper, wider, and higher unconscious mind into the field of everyday consciousness. Suzuki thus arrived at his modern psychologized reinterpretation of Zen satori as a sudden inflow of the cosmic Unconscious into ordinary consciousness in superconsciousness.

Figure 5.1. The Focus/Fringe Structure of Trans-Marginal Consciousness. *Source*: Created by the author.

Zen and A. N. Whitehead

After a distinguished career teaching mathematics, symbolic logic, and physics in England, Alfred North Whitehead (1881–1947) joined the faculty of Harvard University in 1924 at the age of sixty-three, during which time he formulated a new system of thought known as process philosophy. In the preface to *Process and Reality*, Whitehead expresses his special indebtedness to William James and John Dewey (1978, xii). Since Whitehead published his major philosophical texts while at Harvard University, and because he aligned himself with the thought of James and Dewey, he is generally included within the American philosophical tradition, as characterized by pragmatism, radical empiricism, and process metaphysics. According to Whitehead's axiological process cosmology, the universe is a creative advance into novelty directed toward the maximum production of aesthetic value as beauty. For Whitehead, all aesthetic occasions of experience with the intrinsic value of beauty emerge from a creative synthesis of diverse multiplicity into novel unity. Each aesthetic occasion of experience arises through its *prehensions* or unconscious feelings of all the other occasions in the universe from its own perspective, thereby to both contain and pervade the whole spatiotemporal continuum as a microcosmos of the macrocosmos. Whitehead associates his concept of *prehension* or unconscious feeling with Henri Bergson's "intuition" as the sympathy that enters into events and directly grasps their unique aesthetic qualities in the flow of time. Following a brief presentation of Whitehead's process metaphysics of unconscious experience based on the doctrine of *prehension* or unconscious perceptions, it will then be demonstrated how the Zen aestheticism of Suzuki adopts Whitehead's signature concept of "prehension" to describe satori as awakening to the cosmic Unconscious through prajna-intuition of sunyata or emptiness as a dynamic process of interdependent origination.

Whitehead's concept of "prehension" or unconscious feeling of the whole in each part is especially formulated in his magnum opus *Process and Reality*, Part III, titled "The Theory of Prehensions," also called "The Theory of Feelings" (1978, 219–282). *Prehensions*, he says, are the dimly felt relations to every other occasion in the universe by which a novel, aesthetic, and self-creative occasion emerges into momentary existence. For Whitehead each momentary occasion of aesthetic experience arising through creative synthesis of many into one is similar to the "monads" of Leibniz, wherein each monad is a living mirror that reflects the universe from its own unique perspective as a microcosm of the macrocosm. In Whitehead's re-envisioning of Leibniz's perspectival monads, an aesthetic occasion of experience arises into actuality by unconsciously "prehending" or *feeling* the entire universe from its own standpoint (1978, 80). In the higher phases of awareness, an occasion of experience is characterized by "apprehension" of a small focal region of the perceptual field illuminated by consciousness, while the enveloping background field of relationships is dimly *felt* through "prehensions" at the level of unconscious perception in the primordial mode of causal efficacy. In *Adventures of Ideas*, Whitehead explains that his distinction between unconscious "prehension" versus conscious "apprehension" thus follows the example of Leibniz's monadology, which distinguishes unconscious "perception" from conscious "apperception" (1933, 234–235).

In *Whitehead's Metaphysics*, Ivor Leclerc gives a systematic account of Whitehead's category of "prehension" or *feeling* as an unconscious mode of primordial perception at the base of all experience (1975, 140–145). Leclerc describes two basic modes of perception in Whitehead's process metaphysics, including the mode of sensory experience ("presentational immediacy"), which is clear, distinct, vivid, and conscious, and the more primordial perception in the nonsensory mode of prehension or feeling ("causal efficacy"), which is dim, vague, and unconscious. Leclerc further describes how in contrast to the clear consciousness of vivid sensory awareness, "prehension" or the dim feeling of causal efficacy is as an act of *unconscious perception* of data whereby an event perceptually "grasps" other events from its own perspective and includes them as objects in its own composition (1975, 144).

A work titled *Archetypal Process* edited by David Ray Griffin explores various parallels between Whitehead's process metaphysics and Jungian depth psychology: "Whitehead presupposes the basic insight of depth psychology, that conscious experience arises out of unconscious experience. . . . Consciousness illuminates only a small portion of what we perceive (prehend)" (1989, 242). In *Underworlds: Philosophies of the Unconscious from Psychoanalysis to Metaphysics,* Jon Mills has developed what he refers to in different contexts as Whitehead's "unconscious cosmology," "unconscious metaphysics," and "unconscious ontology," which in turn grounds his "philosophical psychology" of the unconscious (2014, 145). He goes on to emphasize that Whitehead's unconscious ontology is based on the doctrine of *prehension* as vague and dim unconscious feeling: "Prehensive activity is first and foremost organized unconscious experience. Therefore, the fundamental processes that comprise the nature of reality have an unconscious ontology" (2014, 145).

Although he does not mention Whitehead by name, Suzuki interprets his key notion of the cosmic Unconscious as prajna-intuition of sunyata or emptiness using Whitehead's signature concept of "prehension." It was Whitehead who coined the word *prehension* as a technical term for an occasion's dimly felt relationships to its surrounding environment. For Whitehead, "prehension" is unconscious aesthetic feeling of the whole in each part. Suzuki's use of the term prehension to describe unconscious prajna-intuition thus demonstrates that he was influenced by Whitehead's process metaphysics, either directly or indirectly. Suzuki's familiarity with Whitehead's thought is assured by the fact that to clarify his Zen aestheticism in Western terms, he explains unconscious prajna-intuition of sunyata or emptiness as "the continuum" articulated in *The Meeting of East and West* by Northrop (RI, 94; SZ, 119). He thus writes: "To the Western mind, 'continuum' may be better than *śūnyatā*" (RI, 94; SZ, 119).

Suzuki also refers to the key concept of Northrop's work, explaining how the sunyata or emptiness designates an "undifferentiated aesthetic continuum" (SWS IV, 232). Moreover, Suzuki further goes on to identify the undifferentiated aesthetic continuum with "pure experience" as the cosmic Unconscious becoming conscious (SWS IV, 231). In this work, Northrop explicitly and systematically develops his mentor Whitehead's organic process vision of nature based on intuition of an undivided aesthetic continuum where each actual occasion "ingresses" through complex multiterm relations in a foreground/background situation unified by directly felt pervasive quality thereby to contain and pervade the whole undifferentiated aesthetic continuum as a microcosm of the macrocosm. Furthermore, in this work, Northrop applies his Whiteheadian vision of nature as an undifferentiated aesthetic continuum to interpret Eastern modes of thought, including Daoism, Zen/Chan Buddhism, and their creative artistic expression in East Asian inkwash paintings.

In his essay titled "Satori," Suzuki describes the "prehension" or unconscious grasping of the undivided aesthetic continuum of nature in satori awakening as follows: "What is given us primarily, immediately, is a continuum which is not divisible into atoms. . . . The concrete whole is to be intuited as such. The whole is not to be *prehended* by accumulation. . . . Therefore, the continuum, undivided, undivisible, infinitely cumulative, and yet as a concrete object of *prehension*, cannot belong to the world of particulars. . . . It is attainable only . . . by an existential leap. This is satori" (AZL, 28–29; italics added). While discussing Zen koan practice, Suzuki then proceeds to explicitly identify "prehension" of the undivided aesthetic continuum, where each part manifests the whole and each moment reveals eternity in nondual Zen satori as awakening to the cosmic Unconscious, conceived as unconscious consciousness or superconsciousness: "When satori obtains in the Absolute Present, all these questions [koans] solve themselves. The mind or consciousness serially divided and developed in time, always escapes our *prehensions*. . . . It is only when our unconscious consciousness or what might be called super-consciousness comes to itself, is awakened to itself, that our eyes open to the timelessness of the present in which and from which divisible time unfolds and reveals its true nature" (AZL, 46; italics added). Suzuki further uses the Whiteheadian category of "prehension" to explain prajna-intuition of sunyata or emptiness as awareness of relationality in Zen enlightenment whereby one can directly experience interpenetration between man and nature in an undivided aesthetic continuum while also retaining their distinctive particularity: "It is not Man facing Nature as an unfriendly stranger but Man thoroughly merged in Nature, coming out of Nature and going into Nature, and yet conscious of himself as distinguishable in a unique way. But their distinguishability is not conceptual and can be *prehended* as such in what I call prajna-intuition" (SWS I, 126; italics added). As said by Suzuki here, the interdependence, interrelationship, and interpenetration between man and nature are not grasped conceptually, but "can be *prehended* as such in what I call prajna-intuition." Suzuki follows this with his translation of an encounter dialogue with Zen master Daidō of Tōsu:

> Daidō of Tōsu (Datong of Touzishan, 819-914) was asked, "Who is Vairocana Buddha?"
> "Tōsu answered, "He already has a name.
> "Who is the master of Vairocana Buddha?"
> "Prehend (*huiqu*) him when Vairocana has not yet come into existence." (SWS I, 126)

Suzuki goes on to discuss prehension as prajna-intuition of emptiness in terms of Zen no-mind as the Unconscious: "Zen calls this 'mind of no-mind', 'the unconscious conscious'" (SWS I, 126). In this passage Suzuki translates the Chinese term *huiqu* (會取) by the Whiteheadian term "prehend." The Chinese word *huiqu* is composed of two characters, *hui* (會) meaning "to meet" and *qu* (取) meaning "to grasp," which Suzuki renders as "prehend" and which for Whitehead is an act of grasping or taking hold of an object by unconscious perception in an event of directly felt aesthetically immediate experience. It should be noted that this last sentence in the above passage is elsewhere translated by Suzuki as "Take hold [*huiqu*] of him before Vairocana was" (SWS IV, 232). The Chinese term *huiqu,* translated as "prehend," can therefore otherwise be rendered as "to take hold of."

Suzuki further describes his Zen aestheticism based on unconscious prajna-intuition in Whiteheadian terms as an act of "intuitive prehension":

> There is truth in saying that the Oriental mind is intuitive while the Western mind is logical and discursive. An intuitive mind has its weaknesses, it is true, but its strongest point is demonstrated when it deals with things most fundamental in life that is, things related to religion, art, and metaphysics. And it is Zen that has particularly established this fact — in satori. The idea that the ultimate truth of life and of things generally is to be intuitively and not conceptually grasped, and that this *intuitive prehension* is the foundation not only of philosophy but of all other cultural activities, is what the Zen form of Buddhism has contributed to the cultivation of artistic appreciation among the Japanese people. . . . It is here then that the spiritual relationship between Zen and the Japanese conception of art is established. (ZJC, 219; italics added)

By way of an overgeneralization, Suzuki here argues that mainstream Western philosophy is logical while the Japanese mind is intuitive. For Suzuki this means that psychologically speaking, Western intellectualism is based on the primacy of rational ego-consciousness, while the Zen aestheticism of Japanese art culture is based on prajna-intuition of the Unconscious. Moreover, to explain the unconscious aesthetic intuition of beauty in the Zen arts, Suzuki again employs the Whiteheadian idea of *prehension*, or what he terms "intuitive prehension"

(ZJC, 219). Suzuki and Whitehead thus describe how in a self-creative event of aesthetically immediate experience arising through harmonious interpenetration between the many and the one, there is a "prehension" or unconscious feeling of the whole in each part, such that each part manifests the whole as a microcosmos of the macrocosmos, or what Suzuki's modern psychologized Zen refers to as satori experience of the cosmic Unconscious in superconsciousness.

Chapter 6

THE UNCONSCIOUS IN ZEN AND GERMAN PHILOSOPHY

Although the notion of an unconscious psyche was popularized in the twentieth century by the depth psychologies of Sigmund Freud and C. G. Jung, the concept of the "the unconscious" (*das Unbewusste*) was already an established concept in the tradition of German philosophy. The modern notion of "the unconscious" is a discovery, or as others would argue, a construction, of nineteenth-century German philosophy and psychology. In *Thinking the Unconscious*, co-editors Angus Nicholls and Martin Liebscher problematize this question about the ontological status of the unconscious in German philosophy. They ask if "*the* unconscious" (*das Unbewusste*) is a substantial entity with ontological status that is "discovered," or if it is a mental construct that has been "invented"? Nicholls and Liebscher criticize Henri F. Ellenberger's *The Discovery of the Unconscious: The History and Evolution of Dynamic Psychiatry* (1970), arguing that while it is a magisterial work, it is nevertheless "methodologically inadequate," insofar as it presumes the objective existence of "*the* unconscious" as something to be discovered instead of an object *created* through modern discourse in the human sciences (2010, 3).

References to the unconscious are to be found in many eighteenth-, nineteenth-, and twentieth-century German writers, including Boehme, Leibniz, Wolff, Platner, Goethe, Novalis, Herder, Kant, Fichte, Schelling, Hegel, Schiller, Schopenhauer, Nietzsche, Carus, von Hartmann, Jaspers, Freud, Jung, and numerous others. Starting with one of his earliest publications in 1894, Suzuki makes reference to Eduard von Hartmann's *Unbewusste* or "the Unconscious." In his 1907 work *Outlines of Mahayana Buddhism* (1907), Suzuki gives an interpretation of central Buddhist concepts in terms of the tradition of German thought, including philosophical, psychological, mystical, and aesthetic notions of the Unconscious. After discussions of Suzuki's Zen doctrine of the Unconscious in relation to Jacob Boehme, G. W. Leibniz, and Immanuel Kant, special attention is given to F. W. J. Schelling and von Hartmann, since they developed the most explicit and systematic formulations of the unconscious in the tradition of German philosophy. What follows is a brief overview of the unconscious in German philosophy, along with a discussion of how Suzuki's Zen doctrine of the Unconscious has been influenced by German idealist metaphysics and the tradition of Romantic-Transcendentalism.

The Abyss in Jacob Boehme's Philosophical Mysticism

In German philosophy, psychology, and mysticism, another term for the unconscious was "the abyss" (*Ungrund*). In his book *Underworlds*, Jon Mills argues that Hegel developed an important philosophy of the unconscious and that while Hegel makes very few references to "the unconscious," he more often uses "the abyss," along with "night-like abyss" or "nocturnal abyss" (*Abgrund*) as metaphors for the depths of the unconscious (2014, 18–19). This image/concept of "the abyss" of nothingness, however, goes back to the Christian mysticism of Jacob Boehme (1575–1624). Clarifying the historical development of this notion of an unconscious abyss in German thought, Mills explains: "Hegel himself did not originate the notion of the unconscious abyss, rather he took it over in large measure from Schelling, Boehme and neo-Platonism. Schelling was among the very first philosophers to underscore the importance of the unconscious" (2014, 25). He continues: "The concept of the abyss (*Ungrund*), however, derives from the theosophic Christianity of Jacob Boehme. . . . Boehme's impact on Schelling was considerable. Boehme developed an elementary form of dialectic consisting of positive and negative polarities that emerged out of Godhead's original undifferentiated non-being (*das Nichts*) which unfolded through orderly stages of manifestation toward absolute self-consciousness" (2014, 26).

Suzuki frequently refers to the German image/concept of an "abyss" (J. *shinnen*, 深淵) to characterize his Zen doctrine of the Unconscious, such as the "abyss of the Unconscious" (EZB III, 7), "an unfathomable abyss of Prajñā, the Unconscious" (ZDNM, 144), "abyss of unknowability" (ZDNM, 112), "abyss of mystery "(ZJC, 257), "abyss of Nirvana" (SZ, 75), "abyss of Suchness" (OMB, 72), "abyss of Śūnyatā" (OIMB, 87), and "abyss of absolute nothingness" (SWS I, xlvii, 139, 140, 143). For Suzuki ultimate reality itself is described in metaphorical terms as an abyss of nothingness: "They call that reality an 'abyss,' 'nihil,' or 'nothingness,' a kind of bottomless abyss" (SWS I, 199). Speaking of the alaya-vijnana or storehouse consciousness of Yogacara Buddhism, Suzuki claims: "The *Ālaya* may be considered as corresponding to 'the Unconscious'" (SWS I, 139). He adds that when the Unconscious in its aspect as the alaya-vijnana has been purified of karmic residues it is termed *kokoro* (heartmind), whereupon "it is an abyss of absolute nothingness" (SWS I, 139–140). Moreover, we are told that Zen satori is a leap into the abyss of nothingness: "When the Zen man has a satori . . . the whole universe sinks into nothingness. In one sense, satori is leaping out of an abyss of absolute nothingness; and in another sense it is going down into the abyss itself" (SWS I, 143). For Suzuki, the abyss of absolute nothingness is also referred to as an abyss of emptiness-suchness, both of which refer to the bottomless abyss of the Unconscious: "The eternal abyss of Suchness . . . is a state of transcendental or trans-marginal consciousness . . . a state of absolute unconsciousness" (OMB,

72). Clarifying Suzuki's Rinzai Zen concept of the true self or authentic Person as a bottomless abyss of absolute nothingness, the Kyoto School philosopher Abe Masao writes: "The bottomless abyss is, needless to say, 'Emptiness', 'Void' or 'Cosmic Unconsciousness' which is supra-individual" (1985, 75).

According to Suzuki, "Zen is a bottomless abyss" (AIZB, 43). In a discussion on parallels between Zen and Christian mysticism, Suzuki remarks: "the principal teaching is to go beyond the intellect and plunge into the abyss of unknowability" (ZDNM, 112). Invoking the metaphor of the unconscious mind as a nocturnal abyss in German mysticism, Suzuki goes on to describe the contents of this "abyss of unknowability" as arising from "the darkness of silence, from the wilderness of the Unconscious" (ZDNM, 113). In the Zen mysticism of Suzuki, as for German tradition of via negativa Christian mysticism, the image/concept of a nocturnal abyss of nothingness functions as a vivid metaphor for boundless inner depths of the Unconscious. Further clarifying his description of the human mind (*kokoro*, 心) as "an abyss of absolute nothingness," Suzuki explains that absolute nothingness signifies "the unfathomable depths of an abyss" (SWS I, 140). Suzuki's Zen notion of the cosmic Unconscious as an "abyss of absolute nothingness" (SWS I, xlvii, 139, 140, 143) is thus reminiscent of Boehme's unconscious nocturnal abyss as the Godhead of primordial undifferentiated "nothingness" (*das Nichts*).

The Monadology of G. W. F. Leibniz

According to Leibniz (1646–1716), the basic ontological units are "monads," each of which is a unique perspective of the universe formed mostly by unconscious minute perceptions but which in the higher-grade monads build up into the conscious awareness of apperceptions. Here it will be shown how Suzuki explains his Zen concept satori as awakening to the cosmic Unconscious in terms of the Zen-Kegon philosophy of interpenetration between one and many as visualized by Indra's net. Furthermore, he then makes references to Leibniz's monadology, where each jewel on Indra's net is akin to Leibniz's perspectival monads that unconsciously perceive the entire cosmos from their own point of view.

The concept of the unconscious in German thought is traced back to the genius of Leibniz, a lawyer, scientist, and philosopher-mathematician who discovered the binary arithmetic used in computer science today. Moreover, simultaneously with Isaac Newton, Leibniz is credited with having discovered infinitesimal calculus. In Germany, "the unconscious" (*das Unbewusste*) had its origins in such ideas as Leibniz's *petites perceptions* or unconscious "micro-perceptions" that remain just below the surface level of conscious awareness. The related German term "subconscious" or *unterbewusste* (beneath or under consciousness) is associated with the *petites perceptions* (G. *dunktle Vorstellungen*) of Leibniz and his school, referring to perceptions of which we are not directly aware but that are "in" consciousness and can, under the right conditions, come to our awareness. For Leibniz, conscious perceptions are the summation of countless minute perceptions, each of which we cannot be aware of, since they lie below a quantitative threshold. In Leibniz's monadology, these small perceptions make up an immense background of unconscious experience, which together constitute our vague awareness of the larger whole surrounding the clear and distinct apperception of objects within the total field of perception. In his *Philosophical Aphorisms* of 1776, the Leibnizian philosopher Ernst Platner was the first to use "the unconscious" (*das Unbewusste*) and "unconsciousness" (*unbewusstsein*). Influenced by Leibniz and his school, Schelling and others refer to the unconscious in its higher functioning as "superconscious" (*überbewusst*). The first German dictionary entry on the term *unbewusst* or "unconscious" appears in Adelung's dictionary of 1780 in which it is defined as referring to things that are unknown (Nicholls and Liebscher, 2010, 20).

According to the rationalism of Leibniz, the mind is not originally a *tabula rasa* or "blank slate" as held by the British empiricism of John Locke, but instead perceives necessary truths as "innate ideas," and these innate ideas lie below the threshold of awareness in the unconscious. Moreover, in Leibniz's panpsychist metaphysics, the basic ontological unit is a "monad," and each monad is a center of perception, a living mirror of totality that reflects the entire universe from its own unique perspective as a microcosm of the macrocosm. Although the monad experiences its entire universe from a perspective, Leibniz makes a fundamental distinction between two levels of experience — that of "apperception" at the level of consciousness and "perception" at the level of unconsciousness, which is constituted by a vast welter of *petites perceptions* or microperceptions. Again, Leibniz distinguishes between *perceptions sensibles* or conscious apperceptions and *perceptions insensibles* or unconscious perceptions. Leibniz thus criticizes René Descartes for identifying the human subject with the *cogito* as the clear and distinct awareness of apperception or consciousness while failing to recognize the existence of unconscious perception.

For Leibniz, a perspectival monad expresses totality because, while consciousness apperceives only a small part of the total field, unconscious perceptions dimly experience the whole universe from a unique viewpoint as an individual microcosm of the all-inclusive macrocosm. Leibniz's monadology describes a mental continuum of experience in terms of degrees of clarity and vagueness, starting at the top with *apperceptions*, or clear and distinct mental experiences, followed by *perceptions* that have a dull awareness and, below these, *minute perceptions*, or unconscious perceptions, which are so faint as to lie beneath the surface of consciousness. In the panpsychic continuum of nature, the lower-level monads such as rocks and plants experience their world in a dim or unconscious manner, while the higher-level monads such as humans and some animals are a mixture of both unconscious perceptions and conscious apperceptions. Leibniz claims that a distinguishing feature of higher-level monads constituting the rational human mind of "spirits" is that they are formed by conscious apperceptions supported by innumerable unconscious microperceptions of all the other monads in the universe, as well as by the unconscious perception of "innate ideas." Thus, according to Leibniz's theodicy, nature is a hierarchical continuum of perspectival monads with varying degrees of clarity and vagueness, but it is only God the supreme monad that has clear apperception of the whole universe past, present, and future.

In *The Fold*, Gilles Deleuze interprets Leibniz's monadology as describing a Baroque period aesthetics of flamboyant ornamental beauty as maximal complexity-in-simplicity, wherein all monads are *folds* in the fabric of the universe or a folding-in of the whole cosmos into the artistic perspective of each monadic center of perception, such that all monads are the result of a process of "folding-unfolding" (1993, 8). For Deleuze, the aesthetic paradigm for this folded chaosmos is the Japanese art of *origami*: "The model for the sciences of matter is the 'origami,' as the Japanese philosopher might say, or the art of folding paper" (1993, 6). Deleuze clarifies how in Western philosophy, the beauty of this origami-like folded universe is exhibited by the monads of Leibniz as well as their reformulation in the events of A. N. Whitehead, where the universe is enfolded in each monad as a microcosm of the macrocosm, and then unfolded so as to influence all subsequent events in the pluralistic multiverse (1993, 6). In Leibniz's monadology, the process by which the manifold of the universe is enfolded into each monad is an *unconscious psychic mechanism*: "Macroperception is the product of differential relations that are established among microperceptions; it is thus an unconscious psychic mechanism that engenders the perceived in consciousness" (1993, 95). Deleuze adds: "The mechanism is thus inevitably folded in the monads, with unconscious perceptions comprising these minute folds as the representations of the world" (1993, 94). According to Deleuze, then, the origami-like folded universe of Leibniz and Whitehead is a decentered aesthetic chaosmos wherein every monadic center is formed by a psychic mechanism of unconscious microperceptions that enfolds-unfolds the world from its own perspective as a microcosmos of the macrocosmos.

In his book *Leibniz and China*, Franklin Perkins gives an excellent summary of how for Leibniz the rational human mind is a monadic perspective of the universe, visualized as an iceberg where at the tip are apperceptions with conscious awareness and at the base are the vast welter of unconscious minute perceptions: "What emerges thus far is that each mind has a unique perspective. . . . This perspective is like the tip of an iceberg, though. It dips off gradually into unconscious, unrecognized perceptions, in two directions. One leads into our unconscious expression of the universe, into what Leibniz calls minute perceptions" (2004, 78). Leibniz's examples usually involve many unconscious perceptions that build up into the conscious awareness of apperception, as the unrecognized perceptions of individual waves build into the noticeable roar of the sea. Perkins continues: "Our perspective also dips off gradually into our unconscious stock of innate ideas . . . innate ideas exist in our perception even before we become aware of them . . . they exert an unconscious influence on our perspective" (2004, 79). Thus, as clarified by this image of an iceberg, in Leibniz's monadology, the higher-level monads of the rational human mind are constituted by the conscious awareness of apperceptions at the surface that dip down into a vast ocean of unconscious minute perceptions, including unconscious perceptions of the universe and unconscious cognition of necessary truths as innate ideas.

It has been shown how Suzuki's concept of the cosmic Unconscious as the abyss of nothingness is identified with the Zen-Kegon dharma realm of unobstructed harmonious interpenetration between parts and the whole as visualized by the holographic vision of Indra's net, wherein all dharmas are like brilliant jewels reflecting totality from their own perspective. This Zen-Kegon doctrine of the Jeweled Net of Indra has striking parallels with Leibniz's monadology in the West. According to Leibniz, the basic units constitutive of nature are "monads," each of which is described as a living mirror that reflects the cosmos from its own viewpoint as a world in miniature. In one of his first essays published in 1894, Suzuki directly refers to Leibniz's concept of the monad as an ultimate metaphysical principle (PPOH, 135). Elsewhere, he says that nondual prajna-intuition grasps reality as sunyata or emptiness, understood as a "continuum" where the basic entities are "units or monads" (RI, 96). According to Suzuki the undivided aesthetic continuum of nature is composed of monads wherein "parts are related to the whole" (RI, 95). He continues: "Each unit (or monad) is associated with another unit singly and with all other units collectively in a net-like fashion" (RI, 95). Suzuki's description of nature in terms of a nondual continuum of emptiness as interdependent origination where each monad is related to all the other monads, as well as to the whole universe in "net-like fashion," is a reference to Leibniz's monadology and to the metaphor of Indra's net in Zen-Kegon Buddhist philosophy. Elsewhere, Suzuki again invokes Leibniz's theory of monads along with the Kegon vision of unobstructed harmonious interpenetration between parts and the whole as beheld in Zen satori: "When an individual monad is perceived reflecting the absolute [emptiness] or the absolute itself, there is satori. . . . This perfect interpenetration is the content of satori" (AZL, 62). Suzuki then goes on to say that the experience of Zen satori as awakening to the cosmic Unconscious is to be described in terms of Leibnizian monads that mirror the world from a unique perspective, as well as through the Zen-Kegon Buddhist concept of spacelike transparent dharmakaya emptiness or interdependent co-arising visualized as Indra's net, wherein the smallest particle both permeates and contains the whole universe: "The cosmic Unconscious in terms of space is 'Emptiness' (*shunyata*). To reach the Emptiness is satori. Therefore, when things are surveyed from the satori point of view, Mount Sumeru conceals itself in one of the innumerable pores on the skin. I lift a finger and it covers the whole universe" (AZL, 62). Here it is explained that in contrast to dualistic perspectives, there is also what Suzuki calls "the satori point of view," the nondual perspective of Zen enlightenment, which sees all events as resplendent jewels on Indra's Net where all is one and one is all. Hence, just as for Leibniz each monad unconsciously perceives the cosmos from its own standpoint in Suzuki's Zen aestheticism, satori reveals the cosmic Unconscious as the Zen-Kegon dharma realm of unobstructed harmonious interpenetration wherein every shining jewel on Indra's net reflects the whole undivided aesthetic continuum of nature from its own perspective as plurality-in-unity, thereby to multiply the beauty, splendor, and glory of the universe from every point of view all at once, ad infinitum.

Obscure Representations in the Transcendental Idealism of Immanuel Kant

Leibniz's doctrine of "unconscious perceptions" is further developed in the philosophy of Immanuel Kant (1724–1804). As pointed out by Nicholls and Liebscher (2010, 9–18), many aspects in Kant's transcendental idealist notion of the self imply a doctrine of the unconscious, including his idea of dark perceptions, the transcendental ego, the original unity of apperception, and the artistic genius of aesthetic creativity. The early Kant accepted Leibniz's *petites perceptions*, or what Kant himself called "unconscious," "dark" or "obscure" representations (*dunkele Vorstellungen*). Kant writes: "There is something imposing and it seems to me, profoundly true in the thought of Leibniz; the soul embraces the universe only with its faculty of representation, though only an infinitesimally tiny part of these representations is clear" (Nicholls and Liebscher, 2010, 10). The unconscious is implicit in Kant's transcendental idealist notion of self as a constructive agent, which by an active process constitutes human experience by synthesizing elements into a coherent whole by an unknowable faculty he terms the *transcendental unity of apperception*, or the "I think," which accompanies each act of perception. For Kant the transcendental ego is the self that is necessary for there to be a unified empirical self-consciousness. In Kant's metaphysics of experience, the transcendental ego unconsciously synthesizes the manifold of sensations with a priori categories of the understanding. But according to Kant, nothing can be known of this transcendental self at the level of consciousness, since it is not an "object" of experience but a *condition for the possibility of experience* and is therefore in itself unknowable, or unconscious.

Nicholls and Liebscher explain the role of the unconscious in the transcendental unity of apperception as postulated in the B version of the Transcendental Deduction in Kant's *Critique of Pure Reason* (1781). Kant establishes what he calls the "original synthetic unity of apperception" (*ursprünglich-synthetische Einheit der Apperzeption*), the "I" which accompanies and makes possible all representations that are given to me (2010, 15). This "I" or original unity of apperception, however, is an unconscious operation: "This is because the "I" of apperception or reflection (*Ich der Reflexion*) is not equipped to cognize itself as "inner experience" (*innere Erfahrung*) . . . since clear and distinct cognitive knowledge of the self and all its parts is not possible, then parts of the self remain, in Kant's terms, dark (*dunkel*), obscure, or unconscious" (Nicholls and Liebscher, 2010, 16).

In one of his first essays "The Place of Peace in Our Hearts" (1894), Suzuki notes that "Kant talked of 'Ding an sich'" (PPOH, 134). Kant's *Ding an sich* or "thing-in-itself" is the noumena or ultimate reality behind all phenomenal appearances but is unknowable and therefore unconscious. Again, in *Outlines of Mahayana Buddhism*, Suzuki makes numerous references to Kantian philosophy, even citing a passage from the German edition of Kant's treatise on aesthetics, *Kritik der Urteilskraft* (*The Critique of Judgment*, 1790) (OMB, 188). In this text Suzuki relates Kant's "transcendental ego," or "transcendental unity of apperception," to the alaya-vijnana, the storehouse consciousness of Yogacara Buddhist psychology. Suzuki here tells us: "the All-Conserving Mind (Alaya) in a certain sense resembles the Unconscious" (OMB, 84). Likening the alaya-vijnana to unconscious operations of the transcendental ego in Kant's philosophy, he goes on to say: "The Alaya is not yet conscious of itself," adding: "The Alaya is perhaps to be compared in a sense to the Kantian 'ego of transcendental apperception'" (OMB, 84).[1] The main point of Suzuki's discussion here is that the alaya-vijnana of Yogacara Buddhism, like the transcendental ego of Kant's philosophy, explains the constitution of human experience by reference to unconscious processes.

In *The Zen Doctrine of No Mind*, Suzuki again relates his Zen concept of no-mind or the Unconscious in its aspect as everyday mind to Kant's transcendental unity of apperception: "The mind in 'everyday mind' . . . is rather a state of mind in which there is no specific consciousness of its own workings, reminding one of what the philosophers call 'transcendendental apperception'. This may correspond to what I have called the Unconscious (*wu-hsin* or *wu-nien*)" (ZDNM, 106). According to Suzuki, no-mind or the Unconscious in its function as everyday mind, "has no specific consciousness of its own workings," and in this sense functions like the transcendental apperception of Kant's philosophy. Suzuki again takes up this comparison between his Zen notion of the Unconscious and Kant's transcendental apperception:

> Prajñā on the plane of the conscious may be said to correspond to the apperceiving mind. But the mind in its apperceiving character points to the plane of *mata-jñāta* [thought], where as Prajñā is essentially the Unconscious. If we follow some philosophers and postulate "transcendental apperception", Prajna may be said to share something of it. Ordinarily the apperceiving mind is occupied too much with the outgoing attention, and forgets that at its back there is an unfathomable abyss of Prajñā, the Unconscious. When its attention is directed outwardly, it clings to the idea of an ego-substance. It is when it turns its

attention within that it realizes the Unconscious. (ZDNM, 144–145; italics in original)

Elsewhere, Suzuki again compares Kant's transcendental ego to his own Zen concept of the Unconscious. First, using the vocabulary of Kant and German idealism, Suzuki distinguishes the empirical ego of consciousness from the transcendental ego of the Unconscious, which functions as the transcendental unity of apperception (MCB, 113). Further distinguishing the empirical or relative ego of consciousness from the transcendental ego of the Unconscious, Suzuki explains: "The transcendental ego is the creative agent and the relative ego is the created" (MCB, 115). He continues: "Objectively speaking, the empirical or relative ego is one of many other such egos. . . . Inwardly, its contact or relationship with the transcendental ego is constant, immediate, and total. . . . . The cognition of the transcendental ego at the back of the relative ego sheds light into the source of consciousness. It brings us in direct contact with the unconscious" (MCB, 114). It can now be seen that while Suzuki in no way identifies Zen with the philosophy of Kant, on occasion he uses Kantian vocabulary such as the transcendental ego, or the transcendental unity of apperception, to explain in Western nomenclature how the Unconscious functions as the basis of consciousness and how the cosmic Unconscious operates as a condition for the possibility of experience in general. Thus, for the modern Zen Buddhism of Suzuki, as for the German philosophy of Kant, clear empirical consciousness of human experience is grounded in dark, obscure, or unconscious processes.

The Unconscious in the Aesthetic Idealism of F. W. J. Schelling

In the tradition of German philosophy, Friedrich Wilhelm von Schelling (1775–1854) articulated a fully explicit and systematic doctrine of "the unconscious" (*das Unbewusste*). Moreover, it was Schelling who first posited a systematic doctrine of art as a creative product of the unconscious. As demonstrated by scholars of Buddhist modernism such as David L. McMahan (2008), the modern hybrid Zen of Suzuki was significantly influenced by the traditions of German Romanticism and American Transcendentalism. Although often unacknowledged in his writings, Suzuki's Zen doctrine of the Unconscious, like all modern concepts of the unconscious mind, is strongly indebted to the German tradition of philosophy and psychology. As will be seen, Suzuki's Zen concept of the cosmic Unconscious as superconsciousness is in some ways near to that of Schelling, who refers to "the unconscious" (*das Unbewusste*) in its higher functioning as the "superconscious" (*überbewusst*). Indeed, speaking in terms at once reminiscent of Schelling and the tradition of German Romanticism, Suzuki proclaims: "Satori is God's coming to self-consciousness in man — the consciousness all the time underlying human consciousness, which may be called super-consciousness" (AZL, 61).

Like the German idealist tradition running through Fichte, Schelling, Hegel, von Hartmann, and others, Suzuki describes the evolution of mind or spirit toward self-realization. According to Suzuki, "Rationality starts with the rising of consciousness out of the primordial Unconscious" (SWS I, 115). He goes on to say: "Zen is where this consciousness is about to rise. Or it may be better to say that the consciousness is caught at the very moment of rising from the unconscious. This moment is an absolute present, the crossing point of time and timelessness, of the conscious and the unconscious" (SWS I, 124–125). Suzuki holds that in the course of evolution, rational ego-consciousness emerged from out of its generative matrix in Nature as the cosmic Unconscious, resulting in the formation of a separate "ego" with its characteristic dichotomy between subject and object, seer and seen, or knower and known. The Unconscious as sleeping Nature is therefore the primordial ground, source, and origin of consciousness. Just as man emerges from Nature as the cosmic Unconscious, so Nature as the Unconscious becomes aware of itself in and through the self-consciousness of man (SWS I, 119). Although from the side of ego-consciousness and its subject-object dualism the Buddha mind or Buddha nature is called "the Unconscious," from its own side it is superconscious. Again, Suzuki holds that while all sentient beings have indwelling Buddha nature and are thus originally enlightened, it operates at a subliminal level until realization of Zen satori, whereupon the Unconscious becomes fully conscious of itself. For Suzuki the basic function of consciousness is to constantly plunge deeper and deeper into its primordial source in the Unconscious. Moreover, it is Zen meditation practice that opens the gateway to the Unconscious, finally culminating in satori as full awakening to the cosmic Unconscious in superconsciousness. Just as the ego and its subject-object dualism makes the Unconscious unconscious, so Zen makes the Unconscious conscious in the superconscious.

S. J. McGrath emphasizes the pervasive influence of Schelling on modern theories of the unconscious: "Prototypes for three of the major models of the unconscious in the twentieth century, the Freudian bio-personal unconscious, the Jungian collective unconscious, and the Lacanian semiotic unconscious, can be traced back to Schelling" (2012, 1). It can be said that Suzuki's Zen doctrine of the Unconscious also shows the influence of Schelling. Suzuki and Schelling view self-realization as an inward act of illumination whereby consciousness becomes aware of its origin, source, and ground in the Unconscious. Furthermore, Suzuki and Schelling understand the aesthetic intuition of beauty in art and nature as a creative act that integrates conscious and unconscious processes.

Throughout his works on Zen Buddhism, Suzuki makes reference to various representatives of the Romantic and Transcendentalist traditions, including Johann Wolfgang von Goethe (SWS I, 197), Fichte (SZ, 79), and others in German Romanticism; William Wordsworth (ZJC 227, 263–264, 266) and

Lord Alfred Tennyson (ZJC, 264, 354) in English Romanticism; and Ralph Waldo Emerson (ZJC, 123n, 207, 312, 343–344) and Henri David Thoreau (ZJC, 23, 342, 344) in American Transcendentalism. In his work *The Making of Buddhist Modernism*, McMahan persuasively argues that the modernized hybrid Zen of Suzuki was greatly influenced by German Romanticism and what he calls the Romantic-Transcendendalist tradition: "Much in Suzuki's writings on Zen derives from Romanticism, Transcendentalism, and their successors, although he seldom gives them much credit for influencing his thought" (2008, 123). According to McMahan, Suzuki's Buddhist modernism is a hybridization of Zen with the tradition of Romantic-Transcendentalism: "Suzuki takes Zen literature out of its social, ritual, and ethical context and reframes it in terms of a language of metaphysics derived from German Romantic idealism, English Romanticism, and American Transcendentalism" (2008, 125).

This is McMahan on Schelling's German Romantic aesthetics of the unconscious: "For Schelling, art was an 'emanation of the absolute,' . . . revealing the unity of the conscious and unconscious. . . . Art, therefore, is elevated above even philosophy" (2008, 120). McMahan then discusses the role of the unconscious in the Zen aesthetics of spontaneity in Suzuki's Buddhist modernism and its relation to the German Romantic metaphysics of Schelling: "Suzuki is clearly drawing from psychoanalytic theory, and perhaps the Romantics, when he declares, like Schelling as well as Jung, that the unconscious is the seat of creativity" (2008, 131). He adds: "Whether Suzuki obtained his framework from the Romantics themselves or secondhand through Emerson, Jung, or others is unclear. It is clear, however, that he adopted not only their language but their metaphysics as his vehicle, and would have found himself comfortable with Schelling's references . . . to art as what connects the conditioned world with the infinite, the conscious with the unconscious" (2008, 132). For McMahan, Suzuki's Zen Buddhist modernism and Schelling's German Romanticism emphasize the unconscious as the source of spontaneity, creativity, and originality in the act of artistic production. Thus, in the modern hybrid Zen/Romantic-Transcendentalist model of Suzuki, as for Schiller, Goethe, Schelling, and others in the tradition of German Romanticism, all artistic creativity and aesthetic intuition of beauty is to be comprehended as a spontaneous upsurge from the unconscious mind.

In his early philosophical system Schelling proclaims that nature is the unconscious poetry of spirit that at last becomes fully conscious of itself through the creation of human artworks. As explained by McGrath: "In the 1800 *System of Transcendental Idealism*, unconscious productivity, intelligence free of reflection, emerges as the master concept. What nature produces . . . she produces unconsciously. Art occupies a place of privilege in Schelling's *System* because artistic creation, like natural production, emerges spontaneously from the unconscious" (2012, 13). Schelling's German Romantic idealist metaphysics thereby explains the developmental process whereby nature as sleeping spirit undergoes evolution from unconsciousness to consciousness to their integration in self-consciousness, finally reaching its consummation in the aesthetic experience of beauty in art. Sebastian Gardner sums up Schelling's philosophy of nature and its culmination in a philosophy of art as follows: "In Schelling's *System*, sustained and explicit reference is made to the unconscious. Nature is conceived as the product of the self's unconscious activity, more specifically, of the 'productive imagination'.... In this system art finds a place: works of art have a privileged position as exemplifications of the unity of conscious and unconscious factors which constitutes reality, a unity which philosophy can only outline in the barest fashion" (1999, 391). The highest stage of Schelling's Romantic idealism is aesthetics or philosophy of art. For Schelling the aesthetic intuition of beauty in a creative work of art realizes the identity of opposites such as subject and object, freedom and nature, conscious and unconscious. Schelling holds that the work of art is a creation of genius, just as it is the productive imagination and aesthetic intuition of creative genius that brings about reconciliation between conscious and unconscious operations in an artwork.

This is how Schelling himself describes the creative activity of artistic genius as an original imaginative act of aesthetic intuition that synthesizes the conscious and unconscious in a work of art: "It is postulated, therefore, that this simultaneously conscious and unconscious activity is to be exhibited in the subjective factor, in consciousness itself. Only aesthetic activity is of this kind, and every work of art is intelligible only as the product of such an activity" (Hofstadter and Kuhns, 1976, 354–355). Summing up his philosophy of nature in relation to his aesthetics and philosophy of art, Schelling proclaims: "The objective world is only the primitive, as yet unconscious, poetry of the spirit; the general organon of philosophy — and the keystone of the whole arch — is the philosophy of art" (1976, 355). Schelling above clearly expresses his view that nature is the unconscious poetry of spirit and that the apex of his system is philosophy of art. Nature as unconscious poetry of spirit is still asleep and awakens to become fully self-conscious only through the aesthetic intuition of artistic genius and its creative expression in the artwork:

> The postulated product is none other than the product of genius, or, since genius is possible only in art, the product of art.... That all aesthetic production rests on the opposition of activities may properly be inferred from the declaration by all artists.... For if every impulse originates in a contradiction ... then the artistic impulse must also proceed from such a feeling of an inner contradiction.... Consequently it can only be the contradiction between the conscious and the unconscious in the artist that sets the artistic impulse into motion. (Hofstadter and Kuhns 1976, 365)

The artistic impulse to create beauty in art itself arises from an inner contradiction between the conscious and the unconscious. Schelling goes on to argue that every aesthetic production starts from the feeling of an infinite contradiction between the conscious and unconscious, and the art product must be the aesthetic feeling of a satisfaction realized by an imaginative synthesis of conscious and unconscious activity in the beauty of an artwork (Hofstadter and Kuhns, 1976, 368). Schelling thus sums up his view as follows: "The work of art reflects for us the identity of conscious and unconscious activity. . . . The basic character of the work of art is thus an unconscious infinity [synthesis of nature and freedom]" (1976, 367; brackets in original). The Zen aestheticism of Suzuki approximates Schelling's philosophy of art, in that both posit the ultimacy of Mind and refer to Mind as "the Unconscious" prior to self-realization. Also, like Schelling, the Zen aestheticism of Suzuki refers to the Unconscious in its higher functioning as "superconscious" (*überbewusst*). While for Hegel self-realization is achieved through reconciliation of subject and object via dialectical reason, and for Fichte it is attained by ethical conduct, for Schelling's Romanticism, as for Suzuki's Zen Buddhist modernism, self-realization occurs through aesthetic intuition, poetic vision, and artistic creation. Monroe Beardsley sums up Schelling's view of self-realization as an act of aesthetic intuition that integrates conscious and unconscious activities: "This can only be understood through the discovery of an 'intuition' in which the Self is both conscious and unconscious at once. And this intuition can only be 'artistic intuition,' since artistic activity combines both a conscious (deliberate) element . . . and an unconscious (inspired) element, that he [Schelling] calls *Poesie*" (1966, 232). Similarly, in Suzuki's hybrid modernist Zen aestheticism, satori as consciousness of the Unconscious is achieved through aesthetic intuition of beauty in nature, art, and everyday life.

Hence, both Suzuki's Zen Buddhist modernism and Schelling's German Romanticism establish the primacy of aesthetic experience, including artistic creation and aesthetic appreciation, since it is especially through aesthetic intuition of beauty in art and nature whereby the unconscious mind at last becomes fully conscious of itself in superconsciousness. One of the distinctive views of Schelling and others in nineteenth-century German Romanticism is that artistic genius has its source of inspiration in the unconscious. Likewise, the modernist Zen aesthetics of Suzuki explains art as springing upward from the bottomless depths of our unconscious mind: "In fact, all works of original creativity are the products of the unconscious" (ZJC, 140). Also, for Suzuki and Schelling, the unconscious is not just a psychological process on the underside of consciousness but also an ontological unconscious mind-ground functioning as the basis of nature and the cosmos itself. For both thinkers, then, artistic creation, like natural production, emerges spontaneously from the unconscious as the ontological source of creativity. Moreover, Suzuki and Schelling view art as an aesthetic satisfaction produced by integrating the contradiction between consciousness and unconsciousness. Using language suggestive of Schelling and German romanticism, Suzuki tells us that satori is God's coming to self-consciousness in man as the cosmic Unconscious that all the time underlies human consciousness as its ground, especially as realized through aesthetic experience of beauty in everyday life. It can therefore be said that for Suzuki, as for Schelling, the human striving for self-realization culminates in the creative work of art grasped by aesthetic intuition, insofar as it expresses the synthesis of conscious and unconscious processes.

The Grand Synthesis in Eduard von Hartmann's *Philosophy of the Unconscious*

Here it will be shown that, starting from his earliest writings, Suzuki uses Eduard von Hartmann's doctrine of "the Unconscious" (*das Unbewusste*) to interpret central notions of Zen and Mahayana Buddhism. Similar to von Hartmann, Suzuki often capitalizes the word *unconscious*, thereby to emphasize the primacy, ultimacy, and centrality of "the Unconscious" in his metaphysical system. As will also be seen, Suzuki's view of satori is at once reminiscent of von Hartmann's explanation whereby aesthetic and mystical experience occur through an inflow of the Unconscious into consciousness. And like von Hartmann, Suzuki refers to his Zen Buddhist doctrine of no-mind, no-thought, and nonego as the Philosophy of the Unconscious.

Although neglected today, *Philosophy of the Unconscious* (*Philosophie des Unbewussten*, 1869) by von Hartmann summed up and crystallized views of the unconscious mind that had been developing in the German philosophical tradition running through Boehme, Leibniz, Kant, Fichte, Schelling, Hegel, Arthur Schopenhauer, and C. G. Carus while in turn influencing theories of the unconscious posited by Freud, Jung, and others. It was von Hartmann who postulated "the Unconscious" as *the* ultimate metaphysical principle underlying all experience, including all artistic, moral, and religious experience. Von Hartmann described three layers of the Unconscious: (1) the absolute unconscious, which constitutes the substance of the universe and is the source of the other forms of the unconscious; (2) the physiological unconscious, which like Carus's unconscious, is at work in the origin, development, and evolution of living organisms of nature, including man; and (3) the relative or psychological unconscious, which lies at the source of our conscious mental life. Von Hartmann describes a psychical continuum of multiple levels of the unconscious, ranging from the absolute unconscious of nature (similar to the "world soul" of Romanticism) to the psychological unconscious, which underlies the consciousness of all individuals. Moreover, like Carus, von Hartmann argues that consciousness develops gradually, but it always remains under the influence of the unconscious and then periodically returns to it in sleep.

In *Philosophy of the Unconscious*, von Hartmann reviews precursors to his own notion of the Unconscious, considering how a doctrine of the unconscious has been hinted at or presupposed by earlier German philosophers such as Leibniz, Kant, Fichte, Schelling, Hegel and Schopenhauer. Von Hartmann acknowledges Leibniz's distinction between the "apperceptions" of consciousness, and the *"petites perceptions"* or vague microperceptions, as the earliest doctrine of the unconscious (1931 Vol. I, 18). Nonetheless, he complains that Leibniz does not explicitly, consistently, and systematically develop his notion of the unconscious, such that the role of the unconscious as "unclear perceptions" is left only as a tacit presupposition underlying his monadology. According to von Hartmann the doctrine of the Unconscious as the ultimate metaphysical principle was most clearly set forth by Schelling: "On the other hand, we find in Schelling the conception of the Unconscious in its full purity, clearness, and depth" (1931 Vol. I, 24). Although von Hartmann is influenced by Schelling's notion of the unconscious, he is no less influenced by Schopenhauer's notion of "blind Will," which he identifies as the Unconscious: "The Will, the sole metaphysical principle of Schopenhauer, is therefore, of course, an unconscious Will" (1931 Vol. I, 39). Von Hartmann therefore claims that his key metaphysical principle of "the Unconscious" is itself a synthesis of the "unconscious Idea" of Hegel with the "unconscious Will" of Boehme, Schelling, and Schopenhauer (1931 Vol. I, 29).

Von Hartmann further discusses Schelling's view that everyday life arises from the interaction of conscious and unconscious processes: "In all, even the commonest and most everyday production, there co-operates with the conscious an unconscious activity" (1931 Vol. I, 24). But in criticism, von Hartmann points out how Schelling does not consistently follow through with his insight. Although Schelling initially states that commonplace everyday activity involves conscious and unconscious operations, it is in fact applied only to the aesthetic production of art. Again, quoting the words of Schelling: "The aesthetic *alone* is such an activity (one at the same time conscious and unconscious)" (von Hartmann, 1931 Vol. I, 25). Influenced by Schelling, von Hartmann views the ancient Greek tragic theater of Aeschylus, the Renaissance painting of Raphael, the German classical music of Beethoven, and other artworks made by the productive imagination of creative genius, as being inspired by the Unconscious. Moreover, like Schelling, von Hartmann views the creative artwork as a synthesis of conscious and unconscious activities through productive imagination of the artistic genius (1931 Vol. I, 364). But in contrast to Schelling, von Hartmann's own philosophy of the Unconscious consistently argues that *all* production in daily life is a unity of conscious and unconscious forces, including the aesthetic creation of art.

There are many points of convergence between von Hartmann and Suzuki in their respective doctrines of the Unconscious. In his essay "Eduard von Hartmann's *Philosophy of the Unconscious*," Gardner cites from James Mark Baldwin's *Dictionary of Philosophy and Psychology* (1902), where the following is given as the entry for the concept "unconscious": "According to v. Hartmann . . . the unconscious is the absolute principle, active in all things, the force which is operative in the inorganic, organic, and mental alike, yet not revealed in consciousness. . . . For us it is unconscious, in itself it is superconscious (*überbewusst*)" (Nicholls and Liebscher, 2010, 173). Likewise, for Suzuki, as for von Hartmann, the Unconscious is the absolute metaphysical principle. Moreover, both claim that while from the side of our conscious mind this absolute principle is called "the Unconscious," in itself and from its own side, it is *superconscious*. Von Hartmann's claim that all art emerges from the Unconscious approximates Suzuki's Zen aestheticism, whereby Zen artworks spring from their source in the unconscious mind. For Suzuki, the traditional Japanese arts spring from *mushin* or "no-mind" as the Unconscious, which is a negative expression for the positive experience of *heijōshin* or "everyday mind." Suzuki thus agrees with von Hartmann that all ordinary experience of everyday life is a creation of conscious and unconscious forces, including the production of art.

Just as von Hartmann examines aesthetic experience of beauty in art as a product of the Unconscious, so in his chapter on "The Unconscious and Mysticism" he analyzes mystical experience of enlightenment as a function of the Unconscious (1931 Vol. I, 354–372). In his inquiry into the Unconscious as the source of mystical experience, von Hartmann considers a wide variety of mystics, including his favorite mystical philosopher, Boehme. Von Hartmann holds that the main characteristic of mystical experience is spiritual death and rebirth through loss of ego, or annihilation of self: "To die to one's ownness, to completely annihilate personality, and let one's self be lost in the divine essence, is expressly demanded" (1931 Vol. I, 367). Again, "The way, which, historically, has always been taken is that of annihilation of consciousness — the endeavor to let the individual perish in the Absolute" (1931 Vol. I, 366). In the ecstatic state of mystical illumination, "the Ego at once desires to be annihilated, and to subsist to enjoy this annihilation" (1931 Vol. I, 366). He adds that the egoless mystical experience of self-annihilation is itself directly initiated by the Unconscious: "Since consciousness that it has not derived its knowledge directly or indirectly from sense-perception ... it can only have arisen through inspiration from the Unconscious, and we have accordingly comprehended the essence of the mystical – *as the filling of consciousness with a content (feeling, thought, desire) through involuntary emergence of the same from the Unconscious*" (1931 Vol. I, 363; italics in original). Likewise, in the Zen mysticism of Suzuki, satori or enlightenment is the experience of self-negation in *muga* or nonego and *mushin* or no-mind as the Unconscious. Similar to the Zen philosophical mysticism of Suzuki, von Hartman explicitly views the beatific mystical experience as an inspiration from "the Unconscious," or a filling of consciousness with the contents of the Unconscious, which he further identifies with the total annihilation of Ego-consciousness.

Von Hartmann goes on to explain that the aesthetic experience of beauty is itself a mode of the egoless mystical experience of the divine, which he identifies as an "intrusion of the Unconscious": "I characterize those thoughts and feelings as mystical in form, which owe their origin to an immediate intrusion of the Unconscious, thus before all the aesthetic feeling in contemplation and production, the origin of sensuous perception and the unconscious processes in thinking feeling, and willing generally" (1931 Vol. I, 364). It can now be seen how von Hartmann's doctrine that mystical and aesthetic experience involve an annihilation of Ego, along with an upsurging of the Unconscious into consciousness is also to be found in the Zen aestheticism of Suzuki. The proximity of Suzuki's Zen aestheticism to von Hartmann's *Philosophy of the Unconscious* is clearly evidenced when he declares: "It may be better to regard the Buddhist teaching of Non-ego [*muga*] as the practical method of expounding the philosophy of the Unconscious" (EZB III, 317).

Von Hartmann and the tradition of nineteenth-century German idealism exerted a strong influence on Suzuki's modern Zen Buddhist doctrine of the Unconscious. Suzuki read and even published in German, often citing from German texts in the original, while also being conversant with the tradition of German philosophy and psychology. As observed by Richard M. Jaffe: "Suzuki's notion of the relationship between enlightenment and ignorance developed in the context of the nineteenth-century idealism and continental philosophy of Immanuel Kant (1724–1804), Arthur Schopenhauer (1788–1860), and Eduard von Hartmann (1842–1906), as well as the critique and development of their thought by his colleague Nishida Kitarō, in particular relying on such terms as 'will,' 'Subconscious,' and 'Unconscious' to render in English Buddhist concepts" (SW I, xivi). In one of his earliest publications titled "The Place of Peace in Our Heart" (1894), Suzuki already demonstrates his knowledge of German philosophy, including Hartmann's philosophy of the Unconscious: "To explain the universe, Spinoza wrote about 'substancia,' Leibniz made 'monades' his key element, Kant talked of 'Ding an sich,' Hegel used the 'Absolute,' Schopenhauer the 'Wille,' and von Hartmann 'Unbewusste'" (PPOH, 135). Suzuki here tells us that in the history of Western philosophy, various notions have been selected as ultimate metaphysical principles explanatory of the universe, including Spinoza's "Substance" as God/Nature, Leibniz's "monads" as perspective mirrors of totality, Kant's "thing-in-itself" as the unknowable reality (noumena) behind all appearances (phenomena), Hegel's "Absolute" as *Geist* or Mind/Spirit unfolding through the dialectical process, Schopenhauer's "Will" as the blind life force objectified in all phenomena, and von Hartmann's *Unbewusste* or "the Unconscious." Furthermore, in Suzuki's 1907 work *Outlines of Mahayana Buddhism*, he discusses the alaya-vijnana or all-conserving mind (storehouse consciousness) of Yogacara Buddhism in relation to von Hartmann's philosophy of the Unconscious. Suzuki here asserts that the alaya-vijnana is to be compared with "Hartmann's *Unbewusste Geist* (unconscious spirit)" (OBM, 84). He adds: "The All-Conserving Mind (Alaya) in a certain sense resembles the Unconscious" (OMB, 84).

It should be noted that von Hartmann's *Philosophy of the Unconscious* was made known to the modern Japanese intelligentsia by Mori Ōgai (1862–1922). Ōgai was an eminent Japanese medical doctor at the rank of surgeon general. Also, with Sōseki Natsume (1867–1916), he became one of the premier

Japanese novelists of the Meiji Restoration period (1868–1912). After several years in Germany studying advances in German medicine, Ōgai returned to Japan having translated many works of German literature, philosophy, and aesthetics. Early in his career, Ōgai interpreted traditional Japanese artistic and literary concepts employing von Hartmann's *Philosophy of the Unconscious*. Based on von Hartmann's aesthetic idealism, Ōgai argues that the Unconscious is the source of all beauty, art, poetry, and literature. Ōgai goes on to analyze the aesthetic content of *yūgen* (幽玄) as the beauty of mystery and depth so highly valued in the Japanese canons of taste, using it as synonymous with von Hartmann's concept of "the Unconscious" (Bowring 1979, 73–77, 129–130). Suzuki's Zen Buddhist notion of the cosmic Unconscious as the ultimate creative source of *yūgen* or the profound beauty of mystery and depth in Zen-inspired artworks (ZJC, 220) is therefore consonant with the Japanese literary poetics of Ōgai influenced by the German aesthetics of von Hartmann.

For von Hartmann, the mystical experience of spiritual illumination and the aesthetic experience of beauty have their origin in an influx of the Unconscious into consciousness so that the creative geniuses of art can also be counted among the greatest mystics as the spiritual geniuses of religion (1931 Vol. I, 364). Likewise, Suzuki arrived at similar conclusions, explaining the religio-aesthetic experience of satori as an egoless state whereby there occurs an upsurge of the cosmic Unconscious into ordinary consciousness in satori as superconsciousness. Suzuki thus explicitly relates the alaya-vijnana or deeper subliminal mind of Zen and Mahayana Buddhism to von Hartmann's notion of the Unconscious, "*Unbenwusste Geist* (unconscious spirit)" (OMB, 84). Finally, like von Hartmann, Suzuki refers to his own Zen Buddhist mystical aestheticism based on *muga* or nonego as "the philosophy the Unconscious" (EZB III, 317).

Chapter 7

THE UNCONSCIOUS IN ZEN AND GERMAN PSYCHOLOGY

Following the publication of *Zen Buddhism and Psychoanalysis* (1960), Suzuki's Zen concept of the Unconscious exerted a profound impact on Western psychotherapy, starting with the German schools of neo-Freudian psychoanalysis and Jungian analytical psychology. Nevertheless, several buddhologists have questioned Suzuki's translation of *mushin* as "the Unconscious," noting its potentially misleading influence on Western psychologists. In a chapter from his important work *Chan Insights and Oversights*, Bernard Faure criticizes various aspects of Suzuki's Zen, including "his unfortunate rendering of the Chinese term *wuxin* (J. *mushin*, no-mind or no-thought) as 'Unconscious,'" which he claims then provided a ground for misunderstanding that attracted Zen psychologists such as C. G. Jung, Erich Fromm, Karen Horney, and Hubert Benoit (1993, 63–64). Yet the renowned Zen scholar Heinrich Dumoulin expresses an opposing view: "The interplay of these two movements [Zen and psychoanalysis] is one of the most fascinating aspects of twentieth century cultural history" (1992, 87). Dumoulin adds: "The encounter between Zen and Western psychologists was facilitated by Suzuki's readiness to see satori as insight into the unconscious" (1992, 93).

Sigmund Freud is often said to have discovered, or at least rediscovered, "the unconscious." In critical reaction to Freudian psychoanalysis, "the unconscious" was rejected by experimental psychology as a speculative notion lacking any scientific empirical basis. For decades the reductionist psychology of Behaviorism developed by John Watson and B. F. Skinner completely abandoned Freud's introspective analysis of the unconscious based on subjective first-person reports for an objective third-person description of observable behavior as mechanistic conditioned response to stimuli. More recently, however, in the fields of cognitive psychology, neuroscience, and medicine, the unconscious has once again been reclaimed. As documented by Frank Tallis (2012), John Bargh (2017), Leonard Mlodinow (2013), Stanislas Dehaene (2014), Joel Weinberger and Valentina Stoycheva (2020), and many others, scientific evidence for "the unconscious" has now been provided by new state of the art technologies, such as functional magnetic resonance imaging, electroencephalography, and magnetoencephalography. Moreover, James Austin (2016) refers to his extensive neuroscientific research in Japanese Zen temples using breakthrough neuroimaging technologies, including functional magnetic resonance imagery, diffusion-weighted imaging, and related instruments such as electroencephalography and magnetoencephalography (magnetoencephalography), to record the effect of Zen meditation on the brain. For Austin, the task of neuroscientific research on Zen and the brain is to monitor subconscious processing operations during Zen meditation as well as ecstatic states of satori-kensho using functional magnetic resonance imagery and other brain-imaging technologies. Together, these scientific advances in functional magnetic resonance neuroimaging, electroencephalography brainwave measurements, and other new technologies, as well as the application of these technological breakthroughs to document changes in the brain during Zen meditation, have now provided ample scientific evidence for the largely unconscious information processing of data in human experience, including *all* acts of perception, action, memory, and cognition operating in the states of waking, dreaming, and sleeping.

In *Zen Buddhism in the 20th Century*, Dumoulin refers to the dialogue between Zen and psychoanalysis initiated by the work of Suzuki's psychological interpretation of satori as opening to the Unconscious. He goes on to discuss how researchers in psychology, medicine, and neuroscience at Tokyo University conducted experiments to monitor changes in brainwave activity using electroencephalography technology by attaching electrodes to the head of Zen monks during the practice of Zen meditation: "Four kinds of brainwaves have been distinguished. . . . The most frequently registered beta waves arise in the brain of the active person directed to the outside world; alpha waves accompany inner quiet and serenity; theta waves indicate a sleepy, twilight state of consciousness; delta waves correspond to completely unconscious sleep" (1992, 89).

As Dumoulin further documents, in these experiments, the scientific measurement of brainwave changes from beta to alpha to theta to delta frequencies during Zen meditation indicates that there is a shift from consciousness to progressively deeper unconscious levels, while remaining fully lucid, alert, and awake (1992, 89–92). This neuroscientific research on Zen and the brain can therefore be viewed as supporting Suzuki's account of Zen meditation and enlightenment as a process of becoming increasingly conscious of the Unconscious in superconsciousness.

Zen and Freudian Psychoanalysis

Sigmund Freud (1856–1939) was a medical doctor who pioneered the technique of psychoanalysis, the importance of the unconscious, along with the use of hypnosis, free association, and dream interpretation for psychotherapy. In his first topological model of the psyche articulated in *The Interpretation of Dreams* published in 1900, there are three divisions: the conscious (Cs), the preconscious (Pcs), and the unconscious (Ucs). Earlier in his career, Freud had already experimented with various methods of accessing the unconscious, such as hypnosis and pharmaceutical drugs. However, in this work he now declares: "*The interpretation of dreams is the royal road to a knowledge of the unconscious activities of the mind*" (Freud, 1965, 647; original italics). Freud maintains that dreams are the fulfillment of a forbidden unconscious wish, the substitute satisfaction of repressed sexual or aggressive desires arising from the Oedipal complex but which are disguised by the censorship mechanism, thereby allowing one to sleep without disturbance. According to Freud, the aim of psychoanalysis is to make the unconscious conscious, thus to replace the id by the ego.

In Freud's later topological model of the unconscious developed in *The Ego and the Id* (1923), the psyche is divided into (1) the id, (2) the ego, and (3) the superego. At the outset of this work, he asserts: "The division of the psychical into what is conscious and what is unconscious is the fundamental premise of psychoanalysis" (1960a, 3). According to this later model, however, while the id is completely unconscious, the ego or executive function, and the super-ego or ethical function, operate at the conscious as well as unconscious levels of the psyche. This later model recognizes that while all that is repressed is unconscious, not all that is unconscious is repressed. It is now seen that the psyche cannot just be divided into consciousness and unconsciousness but that the unconscious pervades *all* aspects of the mind.

In *The Age of Insight: The Quest to Understand the Unconscious in Art, Mind and Brain*, Eric Kandel, winner of the 2000 Nobel Prize in Medicine, recovers the significance of Freud's unconscious for medical science as well as for art, literature, cinema, and aesthetics. From the standpoint of modern neuroscience, Kandel offers a positive reevaluation of Freud's model of the unconscious: "Freud's ideas have held up well and are now central to modern neural science. The first idea is that most of our mental life, including most of our emotional life, is unconscious at any given moment; only a small component is conscious" (2012, 47).

Kandel historically contextualizes the emergence of Freud's psychoanalysis by taking the reader back to "Vienna 1900." Sigmund Freud was a medical student at the University of Vienna School of Medicine, which at the time was the center of medical studies in Europe. Carl von Rokitansky (1804–1878), the dean of the Vienna School of Medicine, set the agenda for the medical curriculum by systematically developing clinical-pathological correlations between visible symptoms and their hidden underlying causes. In Kandel's words: "Rokitansky's influence on medicine was broad . . . he was applying to medicine the insight of the Greek philosopher Anaxagoras (500 B.C.), a founder of atomic theory: 'The phenomena are a visible expression of that which is hidden.' Rokitansky argued that to discover the truth, we must look below the surface of things" (2012, 47). This claim made by the ancient Greek philosopher Anaxagoras, that "the phenomena are a visible expression of that which is hidden," thus became a fundamental axiom for the Vienna Medical School. According to Kandel, the philosophical principle that *truth lies hidden beneath the surface* not only became the fundamental axiom of Freudian psychoanalysis but also quickly spread to the scientific disciplines of medicine, neurology, and psychiatry, as well as to literature, film, painting, and other arts.

Psychoanalysis and Suzuki's Philosophical Psychology

In *Zen Buddhism and Psychoanalysis*, Suzuki interprets Zen, Zen art, and Zen aesthetics based on his modern philosophical psychology of the Unconscious, or what in this work he also refers to as the "creative unconscious" (ZP, 31). Suzuki, like Freud, argues that psychological problems can be resolved by bringing unconscious contents into consciousness. But as already demonstrated, Suzuki always distinguishes his own Zen concept of the cosmic Unconscious from the personal unconscious of Freudian psychoanalysis and the collective unconscious of Jungian analytical psychology (ZDNM, 144). Suzuki tells us: "What I mean by 'the unconscious' and what [Freudian] psychoanalysis means by it may be different, and I have to explain my position" (ZP, 10). Speaking of his own Zen concept of the cosmic Unconscious, Suzuki explains: "The unconscious in its Zen sense is, no doubt, the mysterious, the unknown" (ZP, 17). He further writes: "May we not call this unknown the Cosmic Unconscious, or the source of infinite creativity" (ZP, 17). He continues: "I do not know if it is correct to call this [Zen] kind of unconscious the Cosmic Unconscious. The reason I like to call it so is that what we generally call the relative field of consciousness vanishes away somewhere into the unknown, and this unknown, once recognized, enters into ordinary consciousness" (ZP, 16). Hence, in contrast to the id or personal unconscious of repressed libidinal drives postulated by Freudian psychoanalysis, Suzuki's philosophical psychology is based on what he terms the "cosmic Unconscious," which as dharmakaya emptiness or absolute nothingness is the reservoir of infinite creative potentialities and the source of all Zen-inspired arts: "When this unconscious sincerely and genuinely identifies itself with the Cosmic Unconscious, the artist's creations are genuine" (ZP, 12).

Suzuki then goes on to discuss some of the psychotherapeutic aspects of his Zen concept of the cosmic Unconscious as the wellspring of creativity: "This profession, 'artists of life,' may sound new and quite odd, but in point of fact we are all born artists of life and, not knowing it, most of us fail to be so and the result is that we make a mess of our lives, asking 'What is the meaning of life?' 'Are we not facing blank nothingness?'" He continues: "But the Zen-man can tell them that they all have forgotten that they are born artists, creative artists of life, and that as soon as they realize this fact and truth they will all be cured of neurosis or psychosis or whatever name they have for their trouble" (ZP, 15). Hence, in Suzuki's philosophical psychology, various pathological symptoms including anxiety, neurosis, and psychosis arise when spontaneous creative impulses from the cosmic Unconscious are blocked, thereby to inhibit their natural aesthetic expression through creative activities in art and everyday life: "For the creative unconscious can never be suppressed; it will assert itself in one way or another. When it cannot assert itself in the way natural to it, it will break all the barriers, in some cases violently and in other cases pathologically" (ZP, 31).

According to Suzuki, the "Cosmic Unconscious" is "the fountainhead of all creative possibilities" (ZP, 19). Suzuki then discusses how his Zen concept of the cosmic Unconscious relates to the psychological and existential problem of anguish. In this context he considers the view of Western existential psychology that nihilistic moods such as anxiety, despair, or fear and trembling at both the conscious and unconscious levels arise from the limitless freedom opened up by an encounter with the cosmic Unconscious, which as the abyss of absolute nothingness is the bottomless well of infinite creative possibilities. Making an apt reference to the psychological investigation of anxiety in Søren Kierkegaard's existentialism, Suzuki tells us: "Zen does not find anything frightening in infinite possibilities, unlimited freedom, never-ending responsibility.... Kierkegaard was somewhat neurotic and morbid when he dilated on fear.... The existentialist looks into the abyss of *tathatā* [suchness] and trembles, and is seized with inexpressible fear. Zen would tell him: Why not plunge right into the abyss and see what is there?" (ZB, 319–320).

Suzuki's philosophical psychology based on his Zen notion of the creative unconscious approximates the view of Otto Rank, who was at one time Freud's closest disciple and appointed successor. Robert Kramer clarifies the difference between Freud and Rank as follows: "Neurosis is not a failure in *sexuality*, as Freud insisted, but a failure in *creativity*" (2019, 58). Kramer cites the view of Rollo May: "Decades ahead of his time, Rank speaks of neurosis as a failure in creativity and the suffering human being as an *artiste manqué*, a failed artist" (2019, 21). It is further clarified that in his masterwork *Art and Artist: Creative Urge and Personality Development* (1932), Rank establishes the primacy of the unconscious drive as "creative will" (2019, 10). As opposed to Freud's libidinal unconscious as repressed sexuality based on the Oedipal complex, Kramer sums up Rank's notion of the pre-Oedipal unconscious as *creative will*, explaining that at its deepest levels the unconscious expands into the cosmos itself: "The unconscious, according to Rank, is unknown.... The unconscious is an infinite past stretching backwards into the impenetrable icy darkness of the cosmos 'before' our sudden arrival on the planet and forward into an equally infinite abyss looming 'after' our death" (2019, 61). According to Rank, the basic trauma of our unconscious psyche is not the Oedipal complex postulated by Freud but the primordial "birth trauma," the pain of separation anxiety from the mother's womb. At the microcosmic level, it is only through empathetic identification with others that the trauma of separation can be overcome. Yet as explained in Rank's *Art and Artist*, at the macroscopic level his psychotherapy aims toward the mystical experience of rapture as "an identity with the cosmic process" (2019, 110). Again, Rank tells us that his psychotherapy achieves its summit in "the potential restoration of a union with the Cosmos" (2019, 111). For Rank, as for Suzuki, illnesses such as anxiety, neurosis, and psychosis are caused by obstructions to the spontaneous flow of creative will from the cosmic Unconscious, and the remedy is to be found in a mystical experience whereby there is a liberation of creative will, thereby resulting in a transfiguration of life into art. Finally, it should be remembered that while Suzuki would agree with Rank that the primordial trauma is separation anxiety from the womb, it is not the mother's womb, but the tathagatagarbha as the "womb of Buddhahood."

It is furthermore interesting to note how Suzuki's Zen concept of Buddha nature as the cosmic Unconscious, in certain ways, functions like the "unconscious God" of Victor E. Frankl (1905–1997). Frankl was a holocaust survivor especially known for his 1946 book *Man's Search for Meaning*, which describes his efforts to find meaning in life while imprisoned in the Nazi death camp at Auschwitz. Like Freud, he was a Jewish medical doctor who taught psychiatry at the Vienna Medical School in Austria. Frankl was known as having established the Third Viennese School of Psychotherapy after Freud and Alfred Adler. According to Frankl, however, beyond the id or libidinal unconscious of Freud, is the "unconscious God," the inner source that provides answers to existential anxiety, alienation, nihilism, and despair while also luring us toward freedom, joy, and salvation. In his book *The Unconscious God* (*Der Unbewusste Gott*, 1946), Frankl developed logotherapy as a technique guiding patients to search for and discover the ultimate meaning of their life by establishing a personal relationship with the "unconscious God" (1975, 61–62). He maintains that to speak of the "unconscious God" does not mean that God is unconscious but only that human beings may be unconscious of the divine and of their personal relation to it. The phrase "unconscious God" thus refers to our "relation to a hidden God." Likewise, when Suzuki describes Buddha nature as the "cosmic Unconscious," it does not mean that Buddha nature is unconscious but rather that due to the ego and subject-object dualism, we become unconscious of our own Buddha nature prior to satori as full awakening to the cosmic Unconscious in superconsciousness.

Kondo Akihisa was among the first Japanese psychotherapists to be influenced by this dialogue between Zen and psychoanalysis initiated by the writings of Suzuki. Kondo was a medical physician and psychiatrist who studied with Suzuki and the neo-Freudian psychoanalyst Karen Horney in the mid-1950s, which led him to develop his own Zen-oriented psychotherapy. In his essay "The Stone Bridge of Joshu," Kondo sums up differences between notions of the unconscious in Suzuki's Zen and Freud's psychoanalysis (AZL, 181–188). First, he points out that in 1900, when Suzuki published in the United States his first book in English, his translation of *Awakening of Faith*, Freud published his first book on psychoanalysis, *The Interpretation of Dreams*. He then discusses how Freud and Suzuki criticize the pathology of suffering in Western culture based on the split between rational consciousness and the irrational unconscious and then offer their own remedies: "Freud stressed the meaning of the unconscious, the forces of emotion, as opposed to the conscious, the power of reason, and their conflict as the source of neurosis. Suzuki specifically clarified the dichotomous and discriminating nature of reason as the source of human suffering" (AZL, 184). He adds: "Freud's approach to the solution of the problem was by means of psychoanalysis. It was guided by the principle of bringing the unconscious into consciousness . . . 'Where there was id — there shall be ego'" (AZL, 184). Kondo goes on to discuss Suzuki's Zen approach: "Suzuki's contribution in this regard was, of course, the way of Zen" (AZL, 184). As Kondo further notes, for Suzuki, as for Freud, the goal is to become conscious of the unconscious: "However, in his [Suzuki's] case, what he means by conscious is different from Freud's notion of bringing the libidinal unconscious into consciousness. Suzuki's term means to become conscious of 'the Cosmic Unconsciousness,' which is achieved by awakening to *prajna*" (AZL, 184). As pointed out by Kondo, then, while Freudian psychoanalysis is a method for becoming conscious of the id or libidinal unconscious of repressed instincts, Suzuki's Zen method aims to become conscious of the cosmic Unconscious by awakening to prajna wisdom of sunyata or emptiness.

Freud, Suzuki, and Doi Takeo on the Unconscious

In Freudian psychoanalysis, the mystical experience is analyzed as an infantile regression to a primitive state of unconsciousness. Freud was an atheist who reductively explained away religion as psychical infantilism based on repressed unconscious childhood wishes so that the belief in God and his moral commandments is the unconscious wish fulfillment of a surrogate Father-image projected by the superego. In *The Future of An Illusion* (1927) and *Civilization and Its Discontents* (1930), Freud discusses the so-called mystical experience of an "oceanic feeling," or a feeling of oneness with the universe. According to Freud's psychoanalysis, however, the oceanic feeling is not a religious experience of salvation, a communion with a transcendent god, or a mystical experience of cosmic consciousness but merely an infantile regression to the pre-ego stage, a pathological return to the mother's womb as an unconscious defense mechanism for escaping the anxieties of adulthood.

Likewise, the renowned Japanese psychiatrist Doi Takeo has formulated a psychological critique of Zen satori or enlightenment that is at once reminiscent of Freud's reductive explanation of mystical experience as an oceanic feeling produced by infantile regression to the pre-ego state. As explained by psychiatrist Frank Johnson in his book on Doi's psychology, *amae* functions in Japanese behavior as an unconscious drive, motive, or wish to depend on others so as to identify subject and object: "*Amae* can be identified as an unconscious (primary) drive, operating alone or along with other drives to seek affiliation with external objects — specifically in encounters involving security, indulgence, cherishment, and nonsexualized affection" (1993, 211). In *The Anatomy of Dependence* (*Amae no kōzō*), Doi uses his key psychological notion of *amae* (甘え), or the unconscious infantile dependency drive, as a generalized explanation to interpret Japanese Groupism. Doi defines *amae* as follows: "*Amae* is essentially a matter of dependence on the object, a desire for the identification of subject and object" (1971, 114; 1973, 99). According to Doi, *amae* mentality as the unconscious infantile wish to identify subject and object is what underlies the patterns of social interaction in Japanese group-consciousness. The prototype of *amae* behavior lies in the psychology of the infant in its dependency relationship to its mother. In this case, *amae* as the infantile dependency drive takes the form of "to coax," "to play the baby," or "to behave like a spoiled child" to presume upon and take advantage of the indulgent mother's kindness. Doi claims that the Zen experience of satori, and its reformulation in the modern Zen philosophy of Nishida Kitarō as a "pure experience," are expressions of Japanese *amae* mentality as an unconscious infantile dependency drive for identification of subject and object: "In this regard it is interesting that Nishida philosophy which became so popular in prewar Japan, with its notion of pure experience in which subject and object fuse, has clearly received an influence from Zen" (1971, 92; 1973, 83). Moreover, Doi applies his psychological critique to traditional Japanese principles of beauty influenced by Zen aestheticism, including *mono no aware* (the pathos of things), *wabi* (rustic poverty), *sabi* (solitariness), *shibui* (elegant restraint), and *iki* (chic), all being defined in terms of *amae* as the unconscious infantile dependency drive to identify subject and object (1971, 91).

Doi's explanation of Zen satori, Nishida's pure experience, and the concepts of Zen aestheticism as a function of *amae* or the unconscious infantile dependency drive is thus similar to Freud's account of mystical experience as an oceanic feeling produced by infantile regression to the pre-ego state as a return to the mother's womb. Commenting on this reductionistic Freudian psychoanalytical view of mystical experience as a return to the womb, however, Suzuki observes: "The psychologist may explain it [satori] by alluding to our prenatal abode in the mother's womb, but Buddhists would go further back and talk about the womb of Tathagatahood (tathagatagarbha). . . . The tathagatagarbha is no other than the *kokoro*" (SWS I, 151). He adds, "*kokoro* . . . is an abyss of absolute nothingness" (SWS I, 140). For Suzuki, the cosmic Unconscious is a modern psychological term for the tathagatagarbha. Thus, while for Suzuki the religio-aesthetic experience of Zen satori is a return to the womb, it is not an infantile regression to primitive unconsciousness in the mother's womb as said by Freudian psychoanalysis. Instead, Zen satori is a return to the tathagatagarbha or "womb of Buddhahood," the creative matrix of Buddha nature, also termed "original enlightenment" (*hongaku*, 本覚), here identified with *kokoro* as the abyss of nothingness, the realization of which is satori as full consciousness of the cosmic Unconscious in superconsciousness. Hence, in Suzuki's philosophical psychology, just as the primal birth trauma is a dualistic feeling of separation anxiety from tathagatagarbha, so nondual Zen satori is return to tathagatagarbha as Buddha's womb.

The Unconscious in Psychoanalysis, Suzuki, and Yaoshan Weiyan

In his essay "Zen Buddhism, Freud, and Jung," the eminent scholar of Japanese philosophy T. Kasulis claims that there is no concept of "the unconscious" in Zen:

> It is not difficult to note obvious ways in which Freud's psychoanalystic theories are not in accord with the basic viewpoint of Zen Buddhism. Most important of all, the primary distinction in psychoanalysis — the split between the conscious and the unconscious mind — has no correlate in Zen. At those rare points when Zen Buddhists do make distinctions concerning the nature of mind, it is usually more along the lines of the "thinking/not-thinking/non-thinking" characterization used by Dōgen, a characterization that he in fact inherited from Yüeh-shan. (1977, 69)

Kasulis here argues that Dōgen's Sōtō Zen does not recognize a "conscious/unconscious" distinction within the human mind, but instead articulates a threefold distinction of "thinking/not-thinking/non-thinking." In Dōgen's scheme of triadic distinctions, "thinking" is the attitude of affirmation, "not-thinking" is the attitude of negation, and "non-thinking" (or "without-thinking") is the standpoint of enlightenment that neither affirms nor denies but sees what is (1977, 70). Kasulis continues: "Although we will make some further references to Dōgen's triadic distinctions later in this paper, for now we only wish to point out that in the Zen Buddhist distinction we find no equivalent to the Freudian or Jungian conception of the unconscious" (1977, 70). Making reference to Suzuki's *Zen and Psychoanalysis* (1960), Kasulis further maintains that it is only on one occasion that Suzuki speaks of the Zen unconscious to satisfy his naïve Western audience of psychoanalysts (1977, 69, fn. 2). However, as I have demonstrated throughout the present volume, Suzuki does not make reference to the Unconscious on just one occasion in deference to an audience of uninformed Western psychologists but that it is *the* central notion underlying his modern psychological interpretation of Zen and that he articulates this notion of the cosmic Unconscious throughout his entire corpus of works on Zen from beginning to end. Elsewhere, in his essay "Reading D. T. Suzuki Today," Kasulis gives a knowledgeable overview of Suzuki's work, but once again claims that Suzuki only discusses "the Unconscious" late in his career during the 1960s after his meeting with Erich Fromm and other Western psychologists as recorded in *Zen and Psychoanalysis* (2007, 42). But as has been amply demonstrated, Suzuki articulates a concept of the Unconscious throughout his long and prolific career and applies his philosophical psychology of the Unconscious to interpret all aspects of Mahayana Buddhist theory and practice.

Kasulis points out that the triadic distinction of "thinking/not-thinking/non-thinking" distinction used by Dōgen in Sōtō Zen Buddhism was inherited from Yüeh-shan Hung tao (1977, 69; 1981, 71–72). However, throughout his writings, Suzuki also frequently makes reference to the life and teachings of Yüeh-shan Hung tao (Yaoshan Weiyan: 745–827 or 751–834), also known in Japanese as Yakusan Igen. Moreover, Suzuki uses Yakusan's triadic distinction of "thinking/not-thinking/without-thinking" to support his own Zen aestheticism and philosophy of traditional Japanese art based on his characteristic psychological interpretation of *mushin* or no-mind as the nonattached, spontaneous, unconscious mind of enlightenment. For the Rinzai Zen of Suzuki, this encounter dialogue on Yakusan's injunction to think about not-thinking by without-thinking is to be comprehended as a paradoxical koan for inducing satori as awakening to the cosmic Unconscious (SWS I, 107).

In "The Morning Glory," Suzuki discusses Yakusan's threefold distinction of "thinking/not-thinking/without-thinking" while considering a haiku written by the woman poet Chiyo, who composes an outstanding poem on the ephemeral beauty of a morning glory that emerges from the depths of her Unconscious. Speaking of Chiyo's poem, Suzuki remarks: "Psychologically, the poet was the unconscious itself in which there was no dichotomization of any kind" (FZ, 23). Moreover, Suzuki interprets his Zen concept of *mushin* or no-mind as the Unconscious in terms of Yakusan's articulation of enlightenment as *hishiryō* (without-thinking), here translated as "the Unthinkable." In his psychological analysis of Chiyo's haiku about the morning glory as originating from the Unconscious, Suzuki therefore goes on to discuss Yakusan's koan about Zen meditation as thinking about not-thinking by without-thinking, although he translates the terms differently, now rendered as "thinking about unthinking through the Unthinkable": "Yakusan Igen (Yaoshan Weiyan, 751–834) of the Tang dynasty was one day found sitting in meditation, and a monk asked him, 'What are you thinking, so intently sitting?' 'I am thinking the unthinkable.' 'How can the unthinkable be thought?' The master said, 'Unthinkable!'" (SWS I, 112).[1] For Suzuki, satori or the enlightened state of thinking about not-thinking by *hishiryō* as without-thinking or beyond-thinking is what he here translates as the Unthinkable: "Thinking beyond thinking belongs in the realm of prajna-intuition, which is thinking out of thought, thinking the unthinkable" (SWS I, 112). In the context of Suzuki's psychological interpretation of Zen satori, thinking of not-thinking by without-thinking, or thinking of unthinking by the Unthinkable, is itself prajna-intuition of *mushin* or no-mind as the cosmic Unconscious. In the same essay, Suzuki therefore refers to "the Unthinkable" (SWS I, 112) as "the Unconscious" (SWS I, 107) and "the Unknown" (SWS I, 111). When speaking of the haiku poetry of Matsuo Bashō and Chiyo as creative expressions of the cosmic Unconscious, Suzuki has elsewhere stated: "Bashō the poet . . . has passed through the outer crust of consciousness away down into its deepest recesses, into a realm of the unthinkable, into the Unconscious, which is even beyond the unconscious generally conceived by psychologists" (ZJC, 241–242). Suzuki's Zen aestheticism thus explicitly identifies "the Unthinkable" (*hishiryō*) with "the Unconscious" while at the same time revealing it to be the subliminal fountain of creativity for haiku poetry and other Zen-inspired arts that developed within the Japanese religio-aesthetic tradition. Moreover, here as elsewhere, Suzuki emphasizes that his notion of the Unthinkable or the cosmic Unconscious is beyond those conceptions of the subliminal mind formulated by Western psychology, including the personal unconscious of Freudian psychoanalysis and the collective unconscious of Jungian analytical psychology. For Suzuki, then, Yakusan's teaching on koan meditation as thinking about not-thinking by without-thinking or the Unthinkable is to be psychologically interpreted as becoming conscious of the cosmic Unconscious in superconsciousness.

Erich Fromm on Zen and Psychoanalysis

Zen Buddhism and Psychoanalysis contains essays by Suzuki along with psychoanalysts Fromm and Richard De Martino. The centerpiece of this volume is Suzuki's essay "Lectures on Zen Buddhism" (ZP, 1–76), wherein he articulates his philosophical psychology of the cosmic Unconscious. In this essay Suzuki further develops his Zen aestheticism, stating that the cause of psychological problems such as neurosis and psychosis, or existential problems of nihilism, alienation and anxiety, is the repression of spontaneous impulses from the creative unconscious. According to Suzuki, then, the cure for neurosis and other pathological symptoms is to emancipate our unconscious creative impulses, thereby to become what he refers to as "creative artists of life" (ZP, 15).

Fromm (1900–1980) was a distinguished German psychoanalyst associated with the Frankfort School of philosophy, which also included such prominent figures as Theodor Adorno, Jurgen Habermas, Herbert Marcuse, Max Horkheimer, and Walter Benjamin. In *Americans and the Unconscious*, Robert C. Fuller describes the *psychologization* of American religion as transformed into an "aesthetic spirituality." He then sums up the pervasive impact of Fromm on psychoanalysis in America while also clarifying how the neo-Freudian psychology of Fromm differed from its Freudian predecessor in many important respects, including its wider notion of the unconscious based on Suzuki's Zen notion of satori (1986, 126). David McMahan similarly explains Buddhist modernism as a process of demythologization, detraditionalization, and decontextualization, which itself involves the *psychologization* of Buddhism, citing Jung's psychological interpretation of Tibetan Buddhism and Suzuki's psychologized understanding of Zen Buddhism. Moreover, he points out the importance of Fromm in this psychologization of modern Zen Buddhist theory and practice:

"Later, the psychoanalyst Erich Fromm collaborating with Suzuki, suggested that Zen was a kind of radical psychoanalysis that strove to unearth the entirety of the unconscious and bring it to consciousness, thereby overcoming alienation and bringing the practitioner to wholeness" (2008, 56)

It was especially Fromm's seminal essay "Psychoanalysis and Zen Buddhism" (ZP, 77–141), itself based on the writings of Suzuki, which fashioned the intercultural dialogue between Zen and psychoanalysis. He notes the growing interest in Zen by psychotherapists such as Jung, Horney, and Benoit in the West, along with Sato Koji and others in Japan (ZP, 78, fn. 1). Moreover, Fromm points out how just as Zen Buddhism endeavors to overcome suffering, Western psychoanalysis and existentialism aim to overcome anxiety, alienation, meaninglessness, and other problems of human existence (ZP, 79). After encountering the Zen Buddhism of Suzuki, however, Fromm came to significantly revise his ideas about psychoanalysis, including its concepts, methods, and aims (ZP, xiii). Due to the influence of Suzuki, he came to enlarge his Freudian view of the unconscious, explore new therapeutic techniques for accessing the unconscious, and reconceptualize the goal of psychoanalysis as a transformative path to enlightenment by recovering the whole unconscious and making it fully conscious.

To begin with, Fromm cites Freud's well-known dictum summing up the method of psychoanalysis: "Where there was Id — there shall be Ego" (ZP, 80). In other words, that which is unconscious shall become conscious through psychoanalysis. Enlarging the idea of the unconscious beyond the Freudian model of the id or personal unconscious as a locus of repressed instincts, Fromm describes his idea of a universal unconscious coextensive with the cosmos, similar to Suzuki's Zen notion of the cosmic Unconscious: "Consciousness represents social man. . . . Unconsciousness represents universal man, the whole man, rooted in the Cosmos" (ZP, 106). He adds, "When we free ourselves from the limited concept of Freud's unconscious . . . then Freud's aim, the transformation of unconsciousness into consciousness ('Id into Ego'), gains a wider and more profound meaning" (ZP, 107).

In his discussion about Suzuki's understanding of Zen satori as an awakening to the "cosmic Unconscious," Fromm argues that to the extent that the Unconscious becomes conscious through the practice of Zen or psychoanalysis, it ceases to be unconscious. Thus, rather than using Suzuki's term the "cosmic Unconscious" to denote Zen satori, Fromm prefers the term "cosmic consciousness" as coined by the psychiatrist Richard M. Bucke (ZP, 134). But it should be remembered that on occasion Suzuki himself also uses the term "cosmic consciousness," for instance, to clarify the awakening experiences triggered by listening to the rain in the poetry of Dōgen in Zen Buddhism and Henry David Thoreau in American Transcendentalism (ZJC, 242).

Zen and Jungian Psychology

The Swiss psychiatrist Carl Gustav Jung (1875–1961) was at one time Freud's closest student of Psychoanalysis but went on to develop his own school called Analytical Psychology based on his signature notion of the "collective unconscious." In *Psychology and the Unconscious* (1912), Jung explains his radical break from the psychoanalysis of Freud based on the personal unconscious of repressed instincts and elaborates on his notion of a "collective unconscious" operating at a deeper level of the psyche. Jung played an important role in introducing Asian religions to the West by writing psychological commentaries on translations of Eastern texts, including seminal works on Daoist alchemy, the *Yijing* (Book of Changes), Tibetan Vajrayana Buddhism, Indian kundalini yoga, and other traditions. Moreover, Jung became a friend of Suzuki, who invited him to write the foreword to his *Introduction to Zen Buddhism* (1934). For Jung, the path to Zen enlightenment described by Suzuki was a variant of the individuation process toward Self-realization achieved by integration of conscious and unconscious processes, thereby to recover the psychical totality of oneself. Jung further interacted with Suzuki at two Eranos conferences in Switzerland (in 1953 and 1954). There was a reciprocal exchange between the two, whereby Jung learned about Zen from Suzuki, just as Suzuki was influenced by Jung's transpersonal depth psychology of the collective unconscious. As said by Sakamoto Hiroshi, along with the philosophical psychology of William James, the work of Jung had the most influence on Suzuki's psychological interpretation of Zen (1978, 36).

Although Suzuki often makes reference to the collective unconscious in Jung's analytical psychology, he always emphasizes that it should be clearly distinguished from his own Zen notion of the cosmic Unconscious realized in satori as superconsciousness. Jung applies the *tri-kāya* or "three bodies" theory of Mahayana and Vajrayana Buddhism to analyze the structure of the human unconscious. According to Jung, while Freudian psychoanalysis is restricted to *nirmāṇakāya* as the level of physically embodied mind governed by the id or personal unconscious of repressed sexual instincts, his own method of analytical psychology descends into *sambhogakāya* as the imaginal realm of the collective unconscious with its archetypal images of wholeness and transformation. In the present volume, however, I demonstrate that in contrast to Freudian psychoanalysis and Jungian analytical psychology, Suzuki's modern psychologized Zen concept of the cosmic Unconscious focuses on *dharmakāya* as the spacelike luminous void of sunyata or emptiness, also referred to as the transparent openness of absolute nothingness.

Jung's Collective Unconscious

This is how Jung describes his cartography of the human psyche: "Summing up, I would like to emphasize that we must distinguish three psychic levels: (1) consciousness, (2) the personal unconscious, and (3) the collective unconscious" (1971, 38). Jung's major contribution to psychology is to have posited a deeper layer of the psyche, holding that beneath the id or personal unconscious of repressed instincts posited by Freud, there is the collective unconscious, a universal reservoir of numinous archetype images. Freud maintains that the center of the psyche is the ego. By contrast, for Jung the ego is only the center of waking consciousness, whereas "the Self" is the center of the total psyche, including both the conscious and the unconscious. The goal of Jung's analytical psychology is thus Self-realization through the individuation process leading to psychical wholeness by integration of conscious and unconscious processes in a *coincidentia oppositorum*.

For Jung, as for Freud, dreams, fantasies, visions, and hallucinations are a window to the unconscious. He further argues that the psyche is a self-regulating system whereby the archetypes of the collective unconscious revealed by dreams and fantasies have a *compensatory* function. Freud holds that dreams from the id or personal unconscious are disguised wish fulfillments or substitute-gratifications of repressed sexual and aggressive drives. Jung, however, maintains that dreams function to "compensate" for the narrow one-sided attitude of normal waking ego-consciousness, thereby to restore psychical equilibrium by establishing homeostasis between conscious and unconscious processes. For Jung, archetypes such as mandalas from the collective unconscious thereby function as symbols of transformation and images of wholeness leading to Self-realization through a union of opposites, including microcosm and macrocosm, male and female, good and evil, conscious and unconscious.

According to Jung, the human experience of going down into the collective unconscious of archetypes in dreams, hallucinations, and visions was described through ancient myths of descent to the Underworld as the *mundus imaginalis* or imaginal realm of primordial images. Jung recorded many of his own dreams, visions, and hallucinations of descending into the Underworld in his autobiography titled *Memories, Dreams, Reflections* (1961), as well as in his more recently published *Red Book* (2009). The earliest dream recorded is one of descending into a hole in the ground to the Underworld of the dead with its spirits, gods, and ancestors (1989, 11–13). In other dreams and visions, he descends into the Underworld through an ancient stairway, a tunnel, a well, a crater, or some other conduit to the other side, whereupon he encounters archetypal figures and has a dialogue with them. Jung's map of the psyche with its three-tiered structure of conscious, personal unconscious, and collective unconscious was itself revealed in his archetypal visionary dream of going down the stairs of a multistoried house with a subterranean cellar underneath the basement. Moreover, aside from his involuntary dreams, visions, and hallucinations, Jung records journeys down into the subterranean depths of the Underworld designating the collective unconscious and its archetypes using his clinical psychotherapeutic method of "active imagination," a technique of guided lucid dreaming that directs the individuation process toward Self-realization by visualizing mandalas and numinous images of wholeness and transformation.

Jung discusses active imagination in his commentary on a Daoist yoga text based on the archetypal mandala image of a golden flower, whereby alchemical transformation is achieved by rotation of a golden light in microcosmic orbit up and down the two central channels to construct a subtle energy body. Jung discovered that the first step of active imagination is to create an inner mental vacuum by emptying the mind and doing nothing so as to let things happen naturally, effortlessly, spontaneously, and unconsciously. In his *Commentary on 'The Secret of the Golden Flower'* Jung claims that the visualization of archetypal images through the alchemical process of active imagination begins with Daoist *wuwei* (無為) as non-action, not-doing, letting-be, or doing nothing. Furthermore, he relates this Daoist attitude of *wuwei* to the Christian mystic Meister Eckhart's spiritual exercise of letting things happen, or letting be, as an attitude of detachment that induces breakthrough to the Godhead of nothingness. According to Jung it is the process of creating a mental vacuum by emptying the mind into nothingness and letting go of all thoughts that one initiates active imagination thus to let archetypal symbols of transformation surface into consciousness from the depths of the collective unconscious. While dreams, visions, and psychotic hallucinations occur involuntarily, "active imagination" is a voluntary process of semicontrolled lucid dreaming whereby energetically charged archetypal images of transformation from the depths of the collective unconscious can be gradually integrated with and assimilated into consciousness toward the goal of Self-realization. For Jung, the process of active imagination is similar to the visualization of icons in the Eastern Orthodox church, the envisaging of archetypal Christ-images in *The Spiritual Exercises of Saint Ignatius* (1548), or the visualization of tantric mandala paintings of enlightened buddhas in Tibetan Buddhism.

Suzuki develops a psychology of art where all Zen-inspired artforms are spontaneous products of cosmic unconsciousness. Freud held that art and literature is an expression of the individual unconscious. Surrealism, which fuses realistic depictions of life with subconscious fantasy images from the dream state, is the paradigm of an art movement based on Freud's psychoanalytical interpretation of art as sublimation of repressed aggressive and sexual drives in the personal unconscious. Jung also argued that the unconscious is the source of art and literature but focused on artforms emerging from the "collective unconscious" and its numinous archetype images. Jungian depth psychology influenced the abstract expressionist paintings of Jackson Pollock, who regarded his "drip technique" of pouring colored paint on a horizontal canvas in a semiconscious trancelike state as a spontaneous expression of archetypal patterns from the collective unconscious. For Jung, the *imago-Dei* or God-images of religious art such as the mandala paintings of Tibetan Buddhism were exemplars of artworks projected from the collective unconscious as the reservoir of archetypes. Although Suzuki regards Zen art as a product of the unconscious mind, it is neither the personal unconscious of Freud nor the collective unconscious of Jung. According to Suzuki, Zen art emerges from what he terms the "cosmic Unconscious" as primordial awareness of spacelike dharmakaya emptiness or absolute nothingness. As said by Michele Marra: "In talking about aesthetics, the Kyoto School grounded the arts in a privileged space of 'emptiness' or 'nothingness'" (1999, 171). In the vocabulary of Nishida, the founder of the Kyoto School of modern Japanese philosophy, this spatial locus is termed *mu no basho* (無の場所) or the "place (field, topos) of nothingness," and is the source from which all Zen art emerges. However, in Suzuki's Zen aestheticism this spatial locus of emptiness is reformulated in psychological terms as the cosmic Unconscious: "The cosmic Unconscious in terms of space is 'Emptiness' (śūnyatā)" (AZL, 62; LZ, 88). For Suzuki, paradigm cases of Zen-inspired art produced from out of the cosmic Unconscious as the spatial locus of absolute nothingness are traditional Japanese art forms, including haiku poetry, sumie ink painting, noh drama, and tea ceremony, all of which function to manifest the ephemeral beauty of things in their emptiness-suchness. In Suzuki's description of Zen artworks, the cosmic Unconscious as the encompassing space of absolute nothingness is manifested through "the background of Emptiness" (ZJC, 363). One of the characteristic features of Zen art forms produced by the cosmic Unconscious, then, is that they reveal the undiscriminated metaphysical background of emptiness or absolute nothingness that surrounds all objects discriminated in the foreground, thereby to disclose the beauty and mystery of phenomena as an epiphany of bottomless depths.

Jung's Psychological Commentary
on Suzuki's *Introduction to Zen*

In his foreword to Suzuki's *Introduction to Zen Buddhism*, Jung describes how beneath the threshold of consciousness is the unconscious, including both the personal unconscious of Freudian psychoanalysis and the collective unconscious of Jungian analytical psychology: "The unconscious is an unglimpsable completeness of all subliminal psychic factors," a "'total exhibition' of potential nature" (AIZB, 22). Again, "The unconscious is the matrix of all metaphysical assertions, of all mythology, all philosophy . . . and all forms of life which are based upon psychological suppositions" (AIZB, 23). For Jung, the collective unconscious is the inherited storehouse of archetypal images, which he variously compares to Plato's "Forms," and Immanuel Kant's "*a priori* categories," that function to organize human experience into numinous patterns.

In his psychological commentary on Suzuki's *Introduction to Zen Buddhism*, Jung interprets Zen koan meditation as a process whereby the unconscious surfaces into consciousness:

> Now if consciousness is emptied as far as possible of its contents, the latter will fall into a state (at least a transitory state) of unconsciousness. This displacement ensues as a rule in Zen through the fact of the energy of the conscious being withdrawn from the contents and transferred either to the conception of emptiness or to the koan. . . . The amount of energy that is saved goes over to the unconscious, and reinforces its natural supply up to a certain maximum. This increases the readiness of the unconscious contents to break through to the conscious. (AIZB, 22)

He continues: "Since the emptying and the closing down of the conscious is no easy matter, a special training and an indefinitely long period of time is necessary to produce that maximum of tension which leads to the final break-through of unconscious contents into the unconscious" (AIZB, 22). Here it is stated by Jung that in Zen koan meditation described by Suzuki, "consciousness is emptied as far as possible of its contents." Also, he speaks of the "emptying . . . of consciousness." Furthermore, "if consciousness is emptied as far as possible of its contents, the latter will fall into a state . . . of unconsciousness." For Jung, this "emptying" of consciousness through Zen koan meditation establishes a mental vacuum, thereby to enable contents from the unconscious to surface into waking consciousness.

According to Jung, the relation between the conscious and the unconscious is based on "a *compensatory* relationship: the contents of the unconscious bring to the surface everything necessary in the broadest sense for the completion, i.e., the completeness, of conscious orientation" (AIZB, 23). The "transcendent function" of the psyche is a self-regulating system that aims to compensate for the one-sided attitudes of waking ego-consciousness by bringing up contents from the depths of the collective unconscious, thereby to establish homeostasis, psychic equilibrium, balance, and integration between the conscious and unconscious aspects of the psyche. During Zen koan practice, the mind is "emptied" of feelings, desires, images, fantasies, and thoughts so that the available surplus charge of libido or psychic energy is increased to its maximum and transferred to the unconscious, whereupon contents from the depths of the collective unconscious volcanically erupt into consciousness. In Jung's view, Zen satori is an event whereby there is an emptying of the mind, resulting in a "final break-through of unconscious contents into the conscious" (AIZB, 22). Likewise, Suzuki also formulates a psychological interpretation of Zen satori as a breakthrough of the unconscious into consciousness. For Suzuki, however, the deepest level of the unconscious is not the *mundus imaginalis* or imaginal realm of Jung's collective unconscious with its dreamlike archetypal images but his own Zen notion of the cosmic Unconscious as the transparent void of emptiness or absolute nothingness.

For Jung, the *mondō* or "question-answer" interview process during Zen koan meditation is to be explained by the compensatory function of the psyche whereby contents of the unconscious surface into consciousness: "Every invasion of the unconscious is an answer to a definite condition of the conscious" (AIZB, 23). The solution to paradoxical koans does not come from rational ego-consciousness, but from unconscious intuition. Jung holds that Zen meditation has its Western equivalent in what he terms the individuation process of becoming whole (AIZB, 24). Jung, however, also criticizes Zen for trying to obliterate the ego and therefore questions the suitability of Zen practice for Westerners. According to Jung, whereas Eastern psychology teaches dissolution of ego, the modern Western mind needs to cultivate a strong and healthy ego-consciousness, while at the same time integrating it with the contents of the unconscious. He argues that for the Westerner, the proper aim of the individuation process is to shift from the ego as the center of consciousness to "the Self" as the center of the total psyche, including both its conscious and unconscious activities.

Miguel Serrano, one of the last visitors to see Jung before his death, records this conversation where Jung states:

> Today no one pays attention to what lies behind words . . . to the basic ideas that are there. Yet the idea is the only thing that is truly there. What I have done in my work, is simply to give new names to those ideas, to those realities. Consider, for example, the word "Unconscious." I have just finished reading a book by a Chinese Zen Buddhist. And it seemed to me that we were talking about the same thing, and that the only difference between us was that we gave different words to the same reality. Thus use of the word Unconscious doesn't matter; what counts is the idea that lies behind the word. (1997, 100)

This account demonstrates Jung's conviction that his own depth psychology of the collective unconscious was in accord with the wisdom teachings of Zen/Chan Buddhism. For Jung such Zen terms as mind, no-mind, one mind, the unborn, and the storehouse consciousness are alike functional equivalents of the Unconscious. Hence, for Jung the path of Zen Buddhism is another historical-cultural variant of the individuation process toward psychical wholeness achieved through integration of conscious and unconscious processes.

Jung, Zen, and Tibetan Buddhism

Jung gives an illuminating psychological interpretation of Tibetan Vajrayana Buddhist cosmology so that the "three bodies" of Buddha (nirmanakaya, sambhogakaya, dharmakaya) and the "three bardos" or intermediate states (sidpa, chonyid, chikhai) function to signify three levels of the unconscious psyche. In his "Psychological Commentary on *The Tibetan Book of the Great Liberation"* (1939), Jung argues that in Mahayana and Tibetan Vajrayana Buddhism there is a threefold structure of the One Mind or unconscious psyche based on the "three bodies" of Buddha: (1) dharmakaya — the "wisdom body" as the realm of emptiness or nothingness, referred to in Tibetan Buddhism as the clear light bliss of the void; (2) sambhogakaya — the "enjoyment body" as the imaginal realm of archetypes such as the mandala images of buddhas appearing in visions and dreams; and (3) nirmanakaya — the "transformation body" of the historical Buddha in his embodied form. Again, nirmanakaya is the coarse physical body, sambhogakaya is the subtle energy body, and dharmakaya is the very subtle body as clear light bliss of emptiness. A key notion of the text is "One Mind," which Jung identifies as the unconscious psyche. In Jung's words: "the One Mind is the unconscious, since it is characterized as 'eternal, unknown, not visible, not recognized'" (1978, 124). After developing the Buddhist idea of One Mind in psychological terms as the unconscious, Jung goes on to analyze the unconscious in terms of the "three bodies" of Buddha: "Put into psychological language . . . The unconscious is the root of all experience of oneness (*dharmakāya*), the matrix of all archetypes or structural patterns (*sambhogakāya*), and the *conditio sine qua non* of the phenomenal world (*nirmāṇakāya*)" (1978, 123). In this key passage, Jung claims that the unconscious is the source of all human experience, and that it has a threefold structure: (1) the dharmakaya of radiant emptiness, (2) sambhogakaya of transformative archetypal images, and (3) nirmanakaya or the physically embodied mind driven by repressed erotic and aggressive instincts.

Whereas Jung describes the different levels of the unconscious as including the dharmakaya, sambhogakaya, and nirmanakaya levels of the psyche (1978, 123), he then further articulates the three levels of the unconscious in terms of the three "bardos" (intermediate states) of *The Bardo Thödol*, translated by a Tibetan Buddhist lama under the editorship of Evans-Wentz as *The Tibetan Book of the Dead* (1927). These three bardo planes include (1) chikai bardo corresponding to dharmakaya as the clear light bliss of the void; (2) chonyid bardo corresponding to sambhogakaya as the imaginal realm of dreams, visions, and hallucinations; and (3) sidpa bardo corresponding to nirmanakaya as rebirth into the physical realm of embodied existence. In the Vajrayana tradition of Tibetan Buddhism, the three bodies of dharmakaya, sambhogakaya, and nirmanakaya correspond to the three bardos of the afterlife, including chikhai bardo or clear light of death, chonyid bardo or the intermediate state of hallucinations, and sidpa bardo as rebirth into the embodied waking consciousness of physical existence, which are in turn correlated with the three bardo states of everyday life: sleeping, dreaming, and waking. Enlightenment is to become aware of the whole spectrum of the human mind, including life and death, waking and sleeping, consciousness and unconsciousness.

Jung argues that Freudian psychoanalysis focuses on the sexual and violent fantasies of sidpa bardo (nirmanakaya), which is in turn correlated with the personal unconscious of repressed instincts: "Freudian psychoanalysis... was mainly concerned with sexual fantasies. This is the realm that corresponds to the last and lowest region of the *Bardo,* known as the *Sidpa Bardo*" (1978, 65). He continues: "Freudian psychoanalysis, in all its essential aspects, never went beyond the experiences of the *Sidpa Bardo*; that is, it was unable to extricate itself from sexual fantasies.... Freud's theory is the first attempt made by the West to investigate, as if from below, from the animal sphere of instinct, the psychic territory that corresponds in Tantric Lamaism to the *Sidpa Bardo*.... It is therefore not possible for Freudian theory to reach anything except an essentially negative valuation of the unconscious" (1978, 66). In contrast to Freudian psychoanalysis, the analytical psychology of Jung focuses on chonyid bardo (sambhogakaya), which corresponds with the collective unconscious and its archetypal images: "[T]he contents of the *Chonyid Bardo* reveal the archetypes, the karmic images which appear first in their terrifying form. The *Chonyid* state is equivalent to a deliberately induced psychosis" (1978, 70). Furthermore, Jung goes on to clarify that the peaceful and wrathful deities of chonyid bardo are karmic projections of archetypes from the collective unconscious: "The world of gods and spirits is truly 'nothing but' the collective unconscious inside me" (1978, 75). Or conversely: "The collective unconscious is the world of gods and spirits outside me" (1978, 75).

Jung then cites *The Bardo Thödol* on the advent of chikhai bardo: "O nobly born (so and so), listen. Now thou art experience the Radiance of the Clear Light of Pure Reality. Recognize it" (1978, 62). He also cites: "Thine own consciousness, shining, void, and inseparable from the Great Body of Radiance, hath not birth, nor death, and is the Immutable Light — Buddha Amitābha" (1978, 63). Moreover, Jung describes chikhai bardo as corresponding to dharmakaya or the clear light bliss of the void: "This realization [of Clear Light in Chikhai Bardo] is the *Dharmakāya* state of perfect enlightenment" (1978, 62). However, while Jung cites from the text to describe chikhai bardo and dharmakaya as the clear light bliss of the void, his own analytical depth psychology does not explore this level of the psyche. Instead, Jung's analytical psychology focuses on archetypes of the collective unconscious that appear in chonyid bardo at the level of sambhogakaya as the *mundus imaginalis* or intermediate realm of images. But as will be shown here, Suzuki's Zen concept of the cosmic Unconscious signifies chikhai bardo, which corresponds to the dharmakaya of luminous emptiness.

Throughout his works, Suzuki frequently discusses the "triple body" of Buddha doctrine, including the dharmakaya, sambhogakaya, and nirmanakaya: "*Dharmakāya*, 'The Dharma body'... the Buddha in his suchness... *Sambhogakāya* which literally means the 'enjoyment body'... *Nirmāṇakāya,* meaning 'the body of transformation'" (ZJC, 425, fn). The Zen Buddhist framework of Suzuki identifies dharmakaya (J. *hosshin,* 法身) or Buddha's law body as the absolute nothingness of emptiness-suchness, which in psychological terms he refers to as Mind or the cosmic Unconscious:

> Suchness is also termed "Mind" (*citta*) from the psychological point of view. . . . When, however, even "Mind" is regarded too intellectual the Buddhists call it Dharmakaya ["Law Body"]. . . . The doctrine of the Triple Body (*trikāya*) has thus evolved from the notion of Dharmakaya. . . . It is Emptiness or Void (*śūnyatā*). . . . Emptiness is suchness in which there is nothing empty. . . . Emptiness unites in itself both fullness and nothingness" (SWS II, 82)

Moreover, while for Suzuki the core doctrine of Buddhism is negatively expressed by concepts such as *muga* (*anātman*) or no-self, it is positively expressed by the notion of dharmakaya as emptiness-suchness: "If I am asked what constitutes the most characteristic and essential feature of Buddhism that distinguishes it at once from all the other religious systems, I would reply: It is, negatively stated, the doctrine of non-atman, and, positively stated, the doctrine of Dharmakaya" (SWS IV, 18).

Suzuki explicitly identifies his Zen concept of the cosmic Unconscious with spacelike dharmakaya emptiness or absolute nothingness, for instance, when he speaks of "the Dharmakāya [which is the Unconscious]" (EZB III, 16; brackets in original text). Moreover, as the dharmakaya, the cosmic Unconscious is identified with emptiness: "The cosmic Unconscious in terms of space is 'Emptiness'" (AZL, 62; LZ, 88). Again: "'the Unconscious' is the Chinese [Chan/Zen] way of describing the realisation of Emptiness (*śūnyatā*)" (EZB III, 18). Elsewhere: "Dharmakāya or Prajñā, being 'emptiness' itself" (SWS IV, 225). Finally, while the Unconscious is identified with the dharmakaya of emptiness, it is not a nihilistic emptiness: "Emptiness unites in itself both fullness and nothingness" (SWS II, 82).

In *Waking, Dreaming, Being,* Evan Thompson explains how it is usually thought that in the waking state the mind is "conscious," whereas in the dream and deep sleep states the mind is "unconscious."

> Since we ordinarily identify with the gross level of consciousness — the five senses and the sixth mental sense — and these shut down in deep sleep, deep sleep seems to the ordinary mind to be a state of unconsciousness. But a subtler level of pure awareness, which constitutes a . . . "base consciousness" underlying sensory and mental consciousness, continues from moment to moment throughout waking, dreaming, and deep sleep. Lucid deep sleep affords an opportunity to experience directly pure awareness in its nature as clarity or luminosity — an experience that is described . . . as blissful. (2017, 265–266)

As further explained by Thompson, while from the perspective of ordinary consciousness the state of deep sleep is termed "unconscious," it can otherwise be described as a *very subtle consciousness*, which through the meditative techniques of Yoga, Vedanta, and Tibetan Buddhism can be transformed into a state of *lucid deep sleep*: "Yoga, Vedanta, and Buddhism assert that the subliminal consciousness present in dreamless sleep can become cognitively accessible through meditative training" (2017, xxxvii). Likewise, in the Rinzai Zen/Chan tradition of Suzuki, the cosmic Unconscious as prajna-intuition of emptiness can be directly realized through koan practices such as concentration on the keyword Mu. It should be pointed out that Suzuki's understanding of the Zen Buddhist term *prajñā* as awakening to unconscious processes trace back to Hindu Vedanta philosophy based on the Vedas. In the Vedanta it is proclaimed that the waking (*jagrat*), dream (*svapna*), and sleep (*sushupti*) levels are pervaded by *turiya* or the fourth state, wherein one becomes continuously lucid in the otherwise unconscious states of dream and sleep. In the *Mandukya Upanishad* of Hinduism, the ultimate reality of Atman-Brahman is identified with the primordial sound of AUM and is said to have four quarters — the three states of waking (*vaishvanara*), dream (*taijasa*), and deep sleep (*prajñā*), as well as the fourth state (*turiya*). Regarding deep sleep: "That is the state of deep sleep wherein one asleep neither desires any object nor sees any dream. This third quarter is Prajna, whose sphere is deep sleep" (Mandukya Upanishad, I. 5). Zen Buddhist *prajñā* as the intuitive wisdom of emptiness is thus related to this Upanishadic notion of Prajna as the blissful state of deep sleep, which is directly experienced in *yoga nidra* or lucid yogic sleep.

As shown above, there is a significant distinction between the personal unconscious of Freud, the collective unconscious of Jung, and the Zen concept of the cosmic Unconscious developed by Suzuki. In *The Zen Doctrine of No Mind,* Suzuki asserts: "The unconscious mind has its pathological states on the plane of sense (*drista-śruta*) and thought (*mata-jñāta*), corresponding to the 'Unconscious' of Analytical Psychology [Jung] or Psycho-analysis [Freud]. . . . The psycho-analytical Unconscious cannot go deep enough to include the question of no-minded-ness" (ZDNM, 144). For Suzuki, neither the personal unconscious of Freudian psychoanalysis nor the collective unconscious of Jungian analytical psychology reaches down into the bottomless depths of Zen no-mind as the cosmic Unconscious, the recognition of which is satori awakening to superconsciousness. When expressed in terms of the triple body doctrine in Mahayana and Tibetan Vajrayana Buddhism, this means that while the personal unconscious of Freudian psychoanalysis corresponds to nirmanakaya as the level of repressed erotic and aggressive instincts, and the collective unconscious of Jungian analytical psychology corresponds to sambhogakaya as the imaginal realm of archetypal images, the cosmic Unconscious of Suzuki corresponds to the Zen satori of *mushin* or no-mindedness, which reveals spacelike dharmakaya as the nondual transparent void of emptiness or absolute nothingness.

In the Zen Buddhism of Suzuki, as for Tibetan Vajrayana Buddhism, dharmakaya is the very subtle awareness of clear light emptiness, which is always present at the subliminal levels of the mind that normally goes unrecognized but which can be recognized through meditative equipoise on emptiness. In psychological terms, it can be said that to experience no-mind in satori and realize dharmakaya as emptiness-fullness is to become awake in the deep sleep state thus to become fully conscious of the Unconscious in superconsciousness. This realization whereby one becomes conscious of the Unconscious is thus the state of lucid sleep whereby according to Rinzai Zen masters, waking and sleeping or day and night are the same. As recorded in *The Book of MU* (2011) edited by James Ford and Melissa Blacker, the importance of continuously focusing on the Mu koan day and night, throughout the waking, dreaming, and sleeping phases, is strongly emphasized by the Rinzai tradition of Zen Buddhism. In his commentary on the Mu koan in the first public case record of the *Mumonkan* (Gateless Barrier), Zen master Mumon (Wumen) tells us: "What is the barrier of the Ancestral Teachers? It is just this one word "Mu" — We call it the Gateless Barrier of the Zen tradition. . . . concentrate on this one word "Mu." Day and night, keep digging into it" (2011, 19). Rinzai Zen master Koryu Osaka instructs: "You totally become Mu, from morning to night; even in dreams — even in sleep! — you are with Mu and Mu becomes yourself. That is the way to work on this koan . . . ultimately an explosion will take place" (2011, 57). Similarly, Rinzai Zen master Harada Sogaku explains: "Concentrate on this one word Mu. Carry it with you day and night. . . . Gradually the koan and the self become completely one. . . . Not only during your waking hours but also during sleep, don't forget. Don't separate from Mu" (2011, 69).

Suzuki discusses the case of Wuxue Zuyuan (1226–1286), known posthumously in Japan as Bukkō Kokushi (Foguan Guoshi), the National Teacher who founded the Engakuji monastery. Bukkō recalls: "When seventeen I made up my mind to study Buddhism and began to unravel the mysteries of 'Jōshū's Mu'. . . . In the fifth or sixth year . . . the 'Mu' became so inseparably attached to me that I could not get away from it even while asleep. This whole universe seemed to be nothing but the 'Mu' itself" (EZB I, 255–256). Rinzai Zen master Hakuin describes the goal of one-pointed meditation on the Mu koan as to "achieve the state where waking and sleeping are the same" (Yampolsky 1971, 118). It can thus be said that Suzuki's notion of satori as insight into the cosmic Unconscious, in its meaning as unconscious consciousness or conscious unconsciousness, refers to what Hakuin identifies as the enlightened state where day and night or waking and sleeping are the same, the contemplative state wherein one is awake while asleep, or the condition of *lucid sleeping* where the transparent luminous void of deep sleep is fully manifested to the conscious mind. Suzuki emphasizes that *mushin* or no-mind as the Unconscious is the "ordinary mind" of everyday life. Yet it is often forgotten that the ordinary mind of everyday life includes the waking, dreaming, and sleeping states, along with the very subtle witness consciousness that pervades all three states, what Suzuki refers to as the cosmic Unconscious. As said by Thompson in his analysis of Buddhist meditation, "in day-to-day life we experience states of consciousness subtler than the waking state, such as the dream state and deep sleep" (2017, 85).

In his *Manual of Zen Buddhism*, Suzuki describes this very subtle consciousness of wakeful or lucid yogic sleep attained by Zen practice in terms of a modern psychology of the Unconscious: "When the Yogin has all these mental disturbances well under control, his mind acquires a state of tranquility in which his consciousness retains its identity through waking and sleeping hours. The modern psychologist would say that he is no more troubled with ideas which are buried deeply repressed, in his unconsciousness; in other words, he has no dreams. His mental life is thoroughly clear and calm like the blue sky where there are no threatening clouds" (MZB, 72). Suzuki here gives a modern psychological interpretation of Zen as a process of becoming conscious of the Unconscious, such that there is continuity between mental states of waking (consciousness) and sleeping (unconsciousness). When describing the mental state of an adept yogin who has realized satori as awakening to the cosmic Unconscious through Zen koan practice, Suzuki therefore tells us: "His mind acquires a state of tranquility in which his consciousness retains its identity through waking and sleeping hours" (MZB, 72).

Zen, the Jungian Psychology of Kawai Hayao, and the Fiction of Murakami Haruki

Like Nishida Kitarō, Nishitani Keiji, and others in the Kyoto School of modern Japanese philosophy, Suzuki has developed a syncretic East-West philosophy and Buddhist-Christian dialogue based on a Zen doctrine of absolute nothingness, where emptiness is fullness and all things manifest in the beauty of suchness. Unlike the Zen aestheticism of Suzuki, however, the modern Japanese philosophy of Nishida and the Kyoto School lacks a depth psychology of the Unconscious. Nonetheless, the unconscious mind intermittently appears as a topic of discourse in recent Japanese philosophy, literature, and psychology.

Yuasa Yasuo is a leading modern Japanese philosopher who focuses on the theme of achieving bodymind unity in Japanese Buddhism, with comparisons to Western philosophers of lived embodiment such as Maurice Merleau-Ponty and Henri Bergson. Also, Yuasa analyzes the role of the unconscious in the bodymind unity realized by Eastern self-cultivation techniques such as Zen, Yoga, Daoism, Oriental medicine, and traditional Japanese arts. He first develops his theory of bodymind oneness through awakening to the unconscious in *The Body: Toward and Eastern Mind-Body Theory* (1987) and *The Body, Self-Cultivation and Ki-Energy* (1993). Moreover, in his book *Overcoming Modernity* (2008), Yuasa gives a psychological interpretation of Zen, Japanese Buddhism, and other Eastern traditions based on Jung's notion of the collective unconscious, the archetypes, and synchronicity. Like Suzuki, Yuasa formulates a *somaesthetics*, which through traditional Japanese art cultivates "somaesthesis" (1993, 51) to achieve bodymind oneness, resulting in an integration of conscious and unconscious processes.

In his essay "The True Self in Zen and Jung" (1997) reporting a dialogue between Jung and the Japanese Kyoto School philosopher Hisamatsu Shin'ichi about the unconscious mind, Abe Masao explains differences between Zen *mushin* or no-mind and the collective unconscious of Jungian psychology. Abe clarifies that for Jung the deeper levels of the mind are said to be "unconscious" from the dualistic standpoint of the "I" or ego-consciousness. For Hisamatsu, however, the Zen process of koan meditation realizes the emptiness or nonsubstantiality of the conscious and the unconscious thus to experience satori as an awakening to the formless self of absolute nothingness. Through Zen meditation one realizes dissolution of the ego in no-mind, understood as the original mind that is completely aware of itself. Hence, while for Abe and Hisamatsu the Jungian model is limited because much of the psyche remains partly unknowable or unconscious of itself from the dualistic standpoint of the ego, in Zen satori one realizes the nondual state of no-mind, no-self, nonego, emptiness, and absolute nothingness, thereby to become fully aware of the true mind in its totality (1997, 158). Abe sums up the difference between Jung and Zen as follows: "In Jung, self as the total personality consists of the consciousness as 'I' or 'ego,' which is known to itself, and the unconscious, which remains unknown. . . . In contrast to this, according to Zen, the self is not the unknown, but rather the clearly known" (1997, 153–154).

Kawai Hayao and the Magical Realist Novels of Murakami Haruki

The "collective unconscious" was popularized in Japan by the Jungian psychotherapist Kawai Hayao (1928–2007). First it will be shown how Kawai analyzes the literary motif of going down an ancient well to explore the collective unconscious in the novels of Murakami Haruki and how he also collaborated with Murakami on various projects (Kawai Hayao and Murakami Haruki, 1996). Kawai, the founder of Jungian analytical psychology in Japan, was a professor of psychology at Kyoto University and a colleague of Ueda Shizuteru, a distinguished member of the Kyoto School of modern Japanese philosophy running through Nishida Kitarō, Tanabe Hajime, and Nishitani Keiji.[2] Anticipating the discussion that follows below, Kawai tells us that he first became interested in Zen Buddhism after reading Jung's psychological commentary on Suzuki's *Introduction to Zen Buddhism.* Kawai's study of Suzuki's works on Zen brings him to the realization that Zen practice *leaps over* the Freudian personal unconscious of repressed instincts and the Jungian collective unconscious of archetypal images to the deeper unconscious level of nonego, emptiness, and absolute nothingness.

Haruki Murakami Goes to Meet Hayao Kawai (2016) is a dialogue between the Japanese novelist Haruki and the foremost Jungian psychotherapist in Japan, Hayao. Murakami (b. 1949) is the best-selling author in contemporary Japanese literature. Here it will be shown how Murakami's postmodern magical realist fiction takes the reader on an imaginative journey to the Underworld by descending into an ancient well as the passageway between waking consciousness and the subconscious. Just as Suzuki's Zen aestheticism describes the cosmic Unconscious in poetic terms as "the well of mind whose bottom knows no depths" (ZJC, 298), Murakami uses the literary metaphor of a "well" (*ido*) as an opening to the hidden subterranean realm of our unconscious psyche. In his dialogue with Kawai, Murakami explores the Jungian psychological dimensions of his literary works, although as will be seen, Kawai clarifies how Suzuki's Zen unconscious of emptiness or absolute nothingness transcends the intermediate realm of images constituting Jung's collective unconscious.

The Forbidden Worlds of Haruki Murakami by Matthew Stretcher explains how for Murakami the descent of consciousness through a well to the "other world" of the unconscious can be partly described in terms of Freud's model of the id or personal unconscious, as well as the Jungian model whereby one goes down even lower into the depths of the collective unconscious (2014, 75).[3] The subterranean realm of Murakami, like the collective unconscious of Jung, is the reservoir of archetypal images, myths, dreams, hallucinations, and visions (2014, 134). Throughout his work Stretcher demonstrates the various ways Murakami's fiction uses the image of an ancient deep well as the passageway between consciousness and the unconscious. Moreover, Stretcher analyzes Murakami's recurrent use of the Japanese word *ido* (井戸) or "well" as a homonym for Freud's *id* (pronounced in Japanese *katakana* script as イド or *ido*), thus to denote "the unconscious" (2014, 72, 78).

In *Haruki Murakami Goes To Meet Hayao Kawai*, the special focus of this dialogue between Murakami and Kawai is the metaphor of the "well" and the imaginative act of "well-digging" to open up a tunnel down to the collective unconscious in Murakami's fiction, especially his most acclaimed work, *The Wind-Up Bird Chronicle* (*Nejimakidori kuronikuru*, ねじまき鳥クロニクル, 1994–1995). In this work, the protagonist Okada Toru descends into an ancient well leading to the mythical realm of the collective unconscious in an effort to find his wife Kumiko, who has mysteriously disappeared. Summing up his novel, Murakami states: "It's like going down to the bottom of a well and entering a kind of netherworld" (2016, 88). Kawai responds: "That's also the sense I got from reading *The Wind-Up Bird Chronicle*. In a nutshell, it's about going down into a well" (2016, 46). According to Kawai, Murakami's novels, like Jungian depth psychology, are about going down to the bottom of an ancient well or other conduit leading to the Underworld, thereby to establish integration between the conscious and the subconscious. Kawai says that Murakami's novels and Jungian depth psychology endeavor to heal the fragmented psyche by going down into wells to recover images, dreams, and lost traumatic memories of the collective unconscious through active imagination (2016, 67). As further emphasized by Murakami, Toru's descent into the subconscious through a well to retrieve the soul of his wife Kumiko in *The Wind-Up Bird Chronicle* is similar to a variety of mythological tales involving the hero's journey, including the ancient Greek myth of Orpheus descending to the subterranean realm of Hades to retrieve the soul of his dead wife Eurydice, and the Shinto creation myth recorded in *Kojiki* (ca. 712, Record of Ancient Matters), where Japan's earth-creating god Izanagi pursues his dead wife Izanami into the cavernous depths of the Underworld. It is only going on a shamanic journey down an ancient well as the tunnel leading from the surface of consciousness down to the subterranean realm of the collective unconscious that Toru is able to recover Kumiko's lost soul from the Underworld.

The dialogue between Murakami and Kawai describes the narrative "turn" in *A Wind-Up Bird Chronicle* from a detached viewpoint to a socially engaged and morally committed perspective, along with a psychological shift from healing not only personal but also collective trauma. Describing the protagonist in *A Wind-Up Bird Chronicle*, Kawai writes: "The main character goes down into the well, and the well leads to Khalkhn Gol and other very deep places" (2016, 45). Kawai here describes Murakami's novel as about going down into a well leading to the Khalkhn River in eastern Mongolia and northern China's inner Mongolian region during the Soviet–Japanese border conflicts in 1939, known in Japan as the Nomonhan Incident, where Russian soldiers drove out the Japanese army from outer Mongolia. The Nomonhan Incident, like the Rape of Nanking and the horrible atrocities of World War II, have become deeply repressed traumatic memories as well as sources of guilt in the Japanese nation. It is thus by going down a well that Murakami's novel initiates a therapeutic process by retrieval of these lost memories buried in the nation's unconscious, thereby to achieve a cathartic healing of the Japanese collective psyche.

Kawai Hayao and the Zen Psychology of Suzuki

In *Buddhism and the Art of Psychotherapy* Kawai describes how he first became interested in Zen: "My interest in Zen increased. I was stimulated by Jung's foreword to D. T. Suzuki's *Introduction to Zen Buddhism*, which I read in English. In this way, I gradually was drawn toward Zen" (2008, 18). Kawai adds that he became further interested in Zen Buddhism upon seeing the Ten Oxherding Pictures illustrating the stages of spiritual development in Zen meditation, along with Suzuki's psychological commentary on these pictures, first published in Suzuki's *Essays in Zen Buddhism* (First Series) (2008, 36). Moreover, he studied the deeper philosophical meaning of the Ten Oxherd Pictures with Ueda Shizuteru at Kyoto University: "[W]hen I started to teach at Kyoto University, my colleague, Professor Shizuteru Ueda, an expert on the Zen 'Oxherding' genre, gave me many useful insights" (2008, 17). From the standpoint of Ueda and the Kyoto School of modern Japanese philosophy, the Ten Oxherding Pictures depict the three ontological levels of being, relative nothingness, and absolute nothingness: (1) the first seven pictures represent the locus of substantial being grounded in ego-consciousness of subject-object dualism; (2) the eighth picture of an empty circle symbolizes the dissolution of ego-consciousness and all substantial objects into a negative void at the locus of relative nothingness, or nihilism; (3) the ninth and tenth pictures signify the achievement of the Zen "true self" by return to the pure experience of nature and everyday life at the spatial locus of absolute nothingness, understood as the boundless openness where emptiness is fullness and fullness is emptiness, so that all things are manifested just as they are in suchness.

Kawai holds that the Ten Oxherding Pictures illustrating the archetypal stages of spiritual development in Zen Buddhism is a variation of what Jung calls the "individuation process" as the quest for wholeness through integration of conscious and unconscious processes. For Kawai, the Ten Oxherding Pictures also designate what Jung calls the "hero's journey," wherein the hero of ancient myth undergoes an initiation process of death-rebirth to achieve Self-realization. While death is shown by ego-transcendence through dissolution into a nihilistic void of relative nothingness by the empty circle of picture eight, resurrection in absolute nothingness is shown by pictures nine and ten, first by aesthetic appreciation of the evanescent beauty of nature as emptiness-suchness in picture nine, and then through moral compassion for others depicted by the tenth picture of an altruistic bodhisattva returning to society in everyday life. Moreover, Kawai analyzes parallels that he sees between the Ten Oxherding Pictures of Zen Buddhism and medieval pictures of the alchemical process of transmuting lead into gold, used to amplify the individuation process of spiritual transformation toward wholeness in Jungian psychotherapy (Kawai 2008, 36–87).

In his book *The Japanese Psyche*, Kawai gives a Jungian psychological analysis of Japanese fairytales as a product of archetypes from the collective unconscious. Kawai, however, emphasizes the cultural differences between Japan and the West, arguing that Western fairytales are based on the patriarchal and monotheistic God of Judeo-Christianity, while Japanese fairytales must instead be understood in terms of Zen Buddhist nonego and emptiness or absolute nothingness (1996, 167–168). The Zen concepts of nonego, emptiness, and absolute nothingness that were appropriated from Suzuki and the Kyoto School philosopher Ueda Shizuteru thereafter became central to Kawai's Jungian/Zen Buddhist syncretic interpretation of the Japanese unconscious psyche and its cultural products, including ancient myths and fairytales, along with their creative expression in modern Japanese literature.

Proceeding further into his comparative analysis between Jungian psychology and Zen Buddhism, Kawai points out that while Jung's individuation process toward wholeness descends to the personal unconscious, and then to the collective unconscious, it does not reach the deeper level that Suzuki's Zen calls emptiness or absolute nothingness: "Jung, as a psychologist, limited his work to considering those things which can be grasped by ego and then verbalized. He expressed these from the ego's side, so he talked about the 'personal unconscious' and the 'Collective Unconscious'" (1996, 105–106). He adds: "Jung has separated the 'personal unconscious' and the Collective Unconscious as strata deep in the mind. They represent, if expressed in the Buddhist way, the gradual deepening of the level of consciousness. Jung made no mention of a level of 'Emptiness'" (1996, 105). Jung describes the personal unconscious and collective unconscious from the dualistic standpoint of the ego, which Kawai terms the "middle zone" of images. This middle zone refers to the *mundus imaginalis* or "imaginal realm," the intermediate level images in the personal and collective unconscious operating between the surface level of waking ego-consciousness on the one side and the deeper level of emptiness on the other. Jung, however, does not examine this Zen Buddhist level of the unconscious, the level of sunyata or emptiness. By contrast, the sudden enlightenment of Suzuki's Rinzai Zen Buddhism *leaps over* the middle zone of images in the personal and collective unconscious so as to directly access the deeper level of the unconscious characterized by emptiness or absolute nothingness. In Kawai's words:

> [Zen] Buddhism, on the other hand, passed through such an area at once and reached the level of "emptiness consciousness" or "conscious nondiscrimination." Thus it describes the conscious from that side, not from the ego's side. In order to accomplish such a descent in the level of consciousness, Buddhism developed various methods of meditation and chanting practices which maintain full awareness of concentration and observation. . . . So during such practices as *zazen* (Zen meditation), for example, Zen refuses to attend to the "middle zone" of ego consciousness, reaching instead toward "emptiness consciousness." Jungian psychology, it seems to me, focuses on images from that middle zone, which Zen practitioners pass through, and interprets them in relation to the ego. (1996, 106)

According to Kawai, then, while Jungian psychology concentrates on archetypal images in this middle zone of the collective unconscious as encountered from the dualistic standpoint of ego-consciousness, the sudden enlightenment of Zen *leaps over* this intermediate realm of the *mundus imaginalis* and enters directly into the depths of the Buddhist unconscious as the level of emptiness. Thus, while Freudian psychoanalysis examines disguised pictorial images of repressed instincts buried in the personal unconscious and Jungian psychology analyzes *imago dei* or God-images, mandalas, and other transformative archetypes of wholeness in the collective unconscious, Japanese Buddhism cultivates what Kawai terms "emptiness consciousness," or what for Suzuki is nondual Zen satori awakening to the cosmic Unconscious as the transparent spacelike dharmakaya of nonego, emptiness, and absolute nothingness.

Chapter 8

THE UNCONSCIOUS IN ZEN AND FRENCH THOUGHT

The French philosopher Henri Bergson proclaimed: "To explore the unconscious, to work in the subterranean of the mind . . . will be the main task of psychology in the opening century (cited in Ellenberger, 1970, 321). In *The Order of Things,* the French philosopher Michel Foucault develops an archaeology of the human sciences, wherein he argues that "the unconscious" is an epistemological category that demarcates not only psychoanalysis but also the field of the human sciences in general (2002, 197). The French psychiatrist Jean-Martin Charcot (1859–1947) conducted pioneering research into the subconscious as the source of hysteria and the use of hypnosis as a cure. Sigmund Freud and the French psychologist Pierre Janet (1959–1947) became students of Charcot and continued to advance ideas on the unconscious. The unconscious, however, was reinvented in the twentieth century by French thinkers such as Jacques Lacan, Jacques Rancière, Jean-Paul Sartre, Jacques Derrida, Gilles Deleuze and Felix Guattari. In what follows I thus establish a transcultural dialogue between Suzuki's Zen Buddhist notion of the Unconscious with twentieth-century French philosophy, psychology, and aesthetics, including Rancière's aesthetic unconscious, Sartre's rejection of the unconscious for a transparent consciousness as nothingness devoid of ego, Lacan's curved topology of the semiotic unconscious imagined as a Möbius strip where inside and outside are paradoxically different yet the same, along with Deleuze and Guattari's rhizomatic unconscious, or as it were, the schizoanalytic unconscious as a rhizome or acentric network of autonomous multiplicities where each point is interconnected to every other point in the net.

Rancière and Suzuki on the Aesthetic Unconscious

The Unconscious in Suzuki's Zen aestheticism can be further considered in terms of what the contemporary French philosopher Jacques Rancière has called the "aesthetic unconscious," which he develops in his book *The Aesthetic Unconscious* (2010). Suzuki's modern Zen concept of the cosmic Unconscious is an "aesthetic unconscious" insofar as it operates as the fount of unlimited creative possibilities: "The poet's *satori* is an artistic one, so to speak, while the Zen-man's grows out of a metaphysical background. . . . The artistic *satori* may not penetrate the artist's entire personality, for it may not go any further than what I feel like calling the artistic aspect of the Unconscious" (ZJC, 226). The "artistic aspect of the Unconscious" realized in the poet's satori is what can otherwise be termed the *aesthetic unconscious*. Suzuki's aesthetic unconscious, or artistic aspect of the cosmic Unconscious, is what he also refers to as "the creative unconscious" (ZP, 31).

Rancière's "aesthetic unconscious" (*L'inconcient esthétique*) has its basis in Freud's psychoanalytical interpretation of art and literature from the standpoint of the id or libidinal unconscious, with illustrations from the biography of Leonardo da Vinci, Michelangelo's *Moses,* Jensen's *Gradiva,* and the *Oedipus* of Sophocles. By contrast, Suzuki's Zen unconscious is nearer to the collective unconscious of Jung but endeavors to go beyond both Freud and Jung with his notion of the cosmic Unconscious as dharmakaya emptiness. Suzuki's Zen doctrine of the cosmic Unconscious is in turn used to explain traditional Japanese arts such as haiku poetry, noh drama, ink painting, and the tea ceremony, all of which use forms to manifest an enveloping background of space as the transparent openness of emptiness or absolute nothingness. Nevertheless, it can be said that Suzuki and Rancière have formulated cultural-historical variants of an aesthetic unconscious.

As explained by Joseph Tanke in his outstanding book on Rancière's philosophy of art, the key theme in Rancière's political aesthetics is "distribution of the sensible" (*le partage du sensible*). In his effort to retrieve the politics of aesthetics, Rancière holds that art is a practice of distributing and redistributing the sensible world. The basic political, ethical, and economic question with respect to any "distribution" (*partage*) of the sensible is whether it is founded on equality or inequality. As explained by Tanke, in Rancière's political aesthetics, "equality" is the primary means for contesting hierarchical and exclusionary distribution of the sensible functioning as the basis of social, economic, and political inequity (2011, 1–2).[1]

In *The Aesthetic Unconscious*, Rancière claims that the "aesthetic regime" based on the principle of nonhierarchical equality is constituted by an identity of conscious and unconscious or voluntary and involuntary processes in the work of art, what he otherwise terms logos and pathos, or thought and non-thought (2010, 28). Likewise, according to Suzuki's Zen aestheticism, the beauty of Zen art emerges through integration of conscious and unconscious processes, what he otherwise terms the interpenetration of "thought" and "no-thought," or "mind" and "no-mind." Within their own historical, cultural, and theoretical contexts, Suzuki and Rancière frame variants of an "aesthetic unconscious" insofar as they both conceive of art as an interaction of conscious and unconscious processes, otherwise understood as an interplay of thought and non-thought.

It should further be pointed out that Rancière's political aesthetics and, in some instances, Suzuki's Zen aestheticism underscore the theme of countering hierarchical, exclusionary, and oppressive regimes with emancipatory artforms that promote a democratic system based on freedom and equality. In his discussion of the beauty of *wabi* (詫び) underlying the traditional Japanese tea ceremony as a paradigm of Zen aestheticism, Suzuki writes:

> Had the art of tea and Zen something to contribute to the presence of a certain democratic spirit in the social life of Japan? In spite of the strict social hierarchy established during her feudal days, the idea of equality and fraternity persists among the people. In the tearoom, ten feet square, guests of various social grades are entertained with no discrimination. . . . In Zen, of course, no earthly distinctions are allowed, and its monks have free approach to all classes of society and are at home with them all. (ZJC, 278)[2]

We can thus open up a preliminary dialogue between Suzuki and Rancière based on their respective notions of an *aesthetic unconscious*, along with their political aesthetics of nonhierarchical egalitarian artforms, their antinihilistic aestheticism, and their fusion of art with daily life, as well as their conceptions of art as an interplay of thought and non-thought, otherwise described as the integration of conscious and unconscious processes in the creative work of art.

Zen, Derrida, and Lacan on the Unconscious as a Möbius Band

The leading figure in French psychoanalysis is Jacques Lacan (1901–1981). For Lacan, as for Freud, the cornerstone of psychoanalysis is "the unconscious" (*l'inconscient*). Lacan's "return to Freud" in the 1950s involved a return to the primacy of the unconscious, as opposed to an emphasis on the ego as for the then predominant school of Ego psychology (Fink 1997, 24–25). Although Lacan initiates a recovery of Freud, he also reinvents the unconscious using French structuralism, semiotics, and linguistics. Yet he is also a precursor to French poststructuralism with his deconstruction of the human subject into emptiness. Lacan argues that the unconscious is not to be identified with repressed primal instincts as for conventional Freudian psychoanalysis but instead has a language with its own rules, syntax, and grammar. Lacan's unconscious is therefore the "semiotic unconscious" with the structure of a language. For Lacan the symbolic order of language uses an enormous vocabulary of words governed by a system of complex grammatical rules that are followed spontaneously, and since it is impossible to be fully conscious of them all at any one time, it is this that produces the "unconscious Other."

In his later writings there is a methodological shift from linguistics to topology, whereby Lacan now visualizes the paradoxical structure of the semiotic unconscious with geometrical shapes, especially the Möbius strip. It will be shown how Lacan deploys the elastic Möbius band for revealing the curved topological space of the semiotic unconscious as a decentered empty subject where inside is outside and outside is inside. Likewise, it will be shown that Suzuki's Zen concept of the cosmic Unconscious has the topology of a Möbius strip, such that "it is outside and yet within" (LS xxix). As will be discussed in what follows, the Möbius band was first depicted in the Rinzai Zen lineage of Suzuki by ink paintings of Zen master Hakuin. After discussing the works of recent Japanese scholars including Yoshizawa Katsuhiro (2009), Makise Hidemoto (2017), and Hagiwara Takao (2014), I explain how the Möbius band in Jacques Lacan's psychoanalytic concept of the semiotic unconscious can be applied to Suzuki's Zen concept of the nondual cosmic Unconscious having a paradoxical structure where inner and outer are different and yet the same.

The Möbius Band

To understand how the aesthetic-scientific image/concept of the Möbius band can be used to articulate the paradoxical structure of Lacan's semiotic unconscious and Suzuki's cosmic Unconscious, it is first necessary to explain what the Möbius band is. Topology is a branch of geometry that studies the mathematical properties of various shapes. In topology, one of the most remarkable shapes is the Möbius strip, a folded surface with only one side having a curved path that brings the traveler back to his starting point mirror-reversed. What is surprising about the folded shape of a Möbius strip is that it seems to have two sides but only has one side, which is only realized by traversing the whole strip until one has returned to the beginning from the other end. A Möbius band can be made by taking a paper strip and folding it into a half-twist then joining the ends of the strip to form a loop. The Möbius strip was independently discovered by two German mathematicians in 1858, August Ferdinand Möbius (1790–1868) and Johann Benedict Listing (1808–1882). In topology, a Möbius strip is closely related to the torus or doughnut shape, the Klein bottle made by attaching two Möbius strips together at their common boundary, the cross-cap, rim phenomena, and the Borromean knot composed by three interlocking torus rings. For Lacan, the Möbius strip illustrates the topological space of the unconscious as a curved shape that folds back into itself thereby to blur the distinction between inside and outside.

Clifford Pickover gives a comprehensive overview of the Möbius band and similar topological shapes in *The Möbius Strip*. In this book, Pickover discusses the Möbius strip as a key to numerous sciences including mathematics, geometry, topology, physics, chemistry, mechanics, psychology and cosmology; its functions in technology, engineering, and mechanics; as well as its application to various arts such as painting, sculpture, architecture, music, literature, and film, as well as toys and video games (2006, 146). In the visual arts, the Möbius loop has been made famous especially by the illustrations of M. C. Escher, such as his 1963 woodcut *Moebius Strip II* (Red Ants). Although Pickover's book *The Möbius Strip* focuses on the topological structure of the Möbius band in Western science, technology, art, and literature, he clearly sees the Möbius band as analogous to the paradoxical structure of a Zen koan, declaring: "The Möbius strip is a koan for scientific minds" (2006, 194).

The French psychoanalyst Lacan uses topology to articulate the paradoxical structure of the unconscious, including topological shapes with an empty center such as the Borromean knot, the cross-cap, the Klein bottle, the torus, and the Möbius strip. In the following, Lacan declares his main thesis about his semiotic unconscious while further indicating his use of topology as a method to explain the structure of the semiotic unconscious: "If psycho-analysis is to be constituted as the science of the unconscious, one must set out from the notion that the unconscious is structured like a language. From this I have deduced a topology intended to account for the constitution of the subject" (1998, 203). In Lacan's psychoanalytical writings on the unconscious there is a shift from linguistics to topology, and in his topology the Möbius band is of special importance. A key to understanding Lacan's notion of the unconscious as structured like a language is that it is a *decentered subject* always dispersing itself into an endless chain of signifiers. One of the basic dictums of Lacan's psychoanalysis is that "the unconscious is outside." As a decentered empty subject, the unconscious is not merely "inside" the psyche as its center but instead has an ex-centric, a-centric or ek-static structure, thus to already be "outside" itself. For Lacan this ek-static structure of the unconscious as a decentered empty subject can be visualized through the folded up, twisted, and coiled topological shape of an elastic Möbius band.

Lacan came to increasingly utilize the mathematical discipline of topology to articulate the ex-centric and ek-static structure of the unconscious. Dylan Evans therefore speaks of "the theoretical shift from linguistics to topology which marks the final period of Lacan's work" (1996, 192). Like the topological concept/image of "the fold" employed by Deleuze and Maurice Merleau-Ponty, Lacan's half-twisted elastic Möbius band is a curved shape that folds back on itself, thereby to blur the distinction between inner and outer or subject and object, just as it dissolves the boundaries separating conscious and unconscious. Lacan therefore maintains that in authentic human ex-sistence, the paradoxical structure of the unconscious is ex-centric, ex-timate, and ek-static, or already outside itself. As explained by Evans: "The unconscious is not interior: on the contrary, since speech and language are intersubjective phenomena, the unconscious is 'transindividual'; the unconscious is, so to speak, 'outside'" (1996, 220).

For Lacan, it is through the folds of a curved Möbius band and other elastic topological shapes that one can best describe the ek-static and ex-timate structure of the semiotic unconscious as a decentered empty subject where outside and inside are paradoxically the same: "Let's see for ourselves now with what I've taught you to find in the Möbius strip. In taking this band — having opened it — and joining it back to itself by giving it a half twist on the way, you get with the greatest of ease a Möbius strip" (2015, 96). Elsewhere, Lacan explains the decentered unconscious subject as being like a "Moebius strip that has no underside, that is to say, that in following it, one will come back mathematically to the surface that is supposed to be its other side" (1998, 235). Again, Lacan articulates the paradoxical structure of the decentered semiotic unconscious as a "Moebius surface," exclaiming: "Well! This surface is a Moebius surface, and its outside continues its inside" (1998, 156). Hence, the half-twisted Möbius strip that folds-in upon itself demonstrates how the ex-centric, ex-timate, and ek-static structure of the semiotic unconscious is not merely "inside" the subject as its fixed center but is already "outside" itself, thereby establishing an undivided psychical continuum between interiority and exteriority. As Evans puts it:

> The moebius strip (*bande de moebius*) is one of the figures studied by Lacan in his use of Topology. . . . The figure illustrates the way that psychoanalysis problematises various binary oppositions, such as inside/outside, love/hate, signifier/signified, truth/appearance. While the two terms in such oppositions are often presented as radically distinct, Lacan prefers to understand these oppositions in terms of the topology of the moebius strip. The opposed terms are thus seen to be not discrete but continuous with each other. (1996, 119–120)

The Möbius strip has been used to illustrate the ambiguous paradoxical structure of psyche and cosmos not only by Lacan in French psychoanalysis but also by the Japanese tradition of Zen Buddhism.[3] According to Lacan's topology of the psyche, the image/concept of a Möbius band shows how although the human mind seems to have two sides, an underside (unconscious) and an upperside (conscious), there is only one side in a continuum. For Lacan, the semiotic unconscious as a decentered empty subject has a paradoxical structure because it is not "interior" to the subject as its inner core, but rather, it is ex-centric, ex-timate, or ek-static and thus already outside of itself. This ek-static view of authentic human existence is also found in Zen Buddhism. In his book *The Method of Zen*, the German philosopher Eugen Herrigel discusses the acentric experience of *ek-stasis* or "ecstasy" in both Zen and Christian mysticism: "In Zen, human existence as such is 'ek-static' and 'ek-centric,' whether we are aware of it or not" (1974, 19). Likewise, Suzuki asserts: "When one attains the state of 'Muga,' the state of 'Mushin,' the Unconscious, is realized. Muga is something identified with a state of ecstasy in which there is no sense of 'I am doing it' (EZB III, 318).

It has been seen that Zen master Hakuin is a central figure in the lineage of Suzuki's Rinzai Zen Buddhism. *The Religious Art of Zen Master Hakuin* by Yoshizawa demonstrates that Hakuin was not only the greatest Rinzai Zen masters but also one of the greatest masters of inkwash painting and calligraphy in the history of Japanese art. Moreover, in a chapter titled "Hakuin's Möbius Band" (2009, 212–218), Yoshizawa reveals that the Möbius strip appears in some of Hakuin's *sumie* ink paintings. Hakuin uses the Möbius strip in his ink paintings as an *upāya* (J. *hōben*, 方便) or expedient teaching device to manifest the paradoxical structure of mind and the universe as emptiness devoid of subject-object dualism. The historical significance of this is that these Zen ink paintings by Hakuin (1686–1768) are dated around one hundred years prior to the alleged Western discovery of the Möbius strip in 1858 by Möbius (1790–1868). Hakuin often depicted himself in his paintings as Hotei, one of the seven gods of good fortune, commonly known as the rotund laughing Buddha of happiness. In one of Hakuin's ink paintings with the Möbius band motif, Hotei is shown in the empty center of a circular scroll upon which is inscribed a paradoxical koan (see fig. 8.1). The painting therefore itself functions as a koan.

Yoshizawa explains how this Zen ink painting by Hakuin titled "Hotei holding up a scroll" exhibits the structure of a Möbius strip: "The painting is remarkable for the unique visual device Hakuin has employed in it. Hotei, by twisting the two ends of the long rectangular sheet of paper he is holding up,

Figure 8.1. Hakuin's Möbius Strip. *Source*: Public domain.

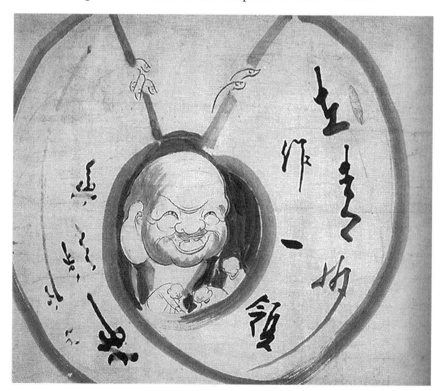

creates a circular band with a one-sided surface, that is, it has no front or back" (2009, 213). Moreover, Yoshizawa discusses how the Möbius band reveals the nondual paradoxical structure of both mind and reality, whereupon being is nothingness and nothingness is being:

> In painting these compositions Hakuin has created what is known as a Möbius band. The Mobius band, or strip, is named after its discoverer, the German mathematician and astronomer August Ferinand Möbius (1790-1868) . . . it is a rectangular surface twisted and joined at the ends so as to produce a continuous one-sided surface without front or back. . . . The Möbius band has no front or back, or rather, the front is the back, the back is the front. This formulation has a parallel in the Buddhist view of reality. In the overall structure of existence as we perceive it (what is termed "mind"), being is itself nonbeing, nonbeing is itself being. . . . It is this reality, transcending all relative forms such as being and nonbeing, that Hakuin's paintings attempt to convey. (2009, 214)

In his essay "Derrida and Zen," Hagiwara Takao uses the Möbius strip to clarify the paradoxical structure of *différance* in the French deconstructionism of Derrida, as well as the paradoxical Zen logic formulated by Suzuki in Japanese Zen Buddhism (2014, 123–150). Derrida's paradoxical logic of *différance* functions to deconstruct self-identity into an endless play of differences, such that presence is deconstituted into absence, whereupon all reified absolutes are decentered into irreducible multiplicity without a fixed center. For Suzuki the paradoxical Zen logic of *soku-hi* (即非) or "is and is not" is a Buddhist dialectic of affirmation-qua-negation that takes the discursive form: "A is A, because A is not-A." Hagiwara then goes on to apply the Möbius strip as an expedient tool for illustrating the structure of paradox in both Derrida and Suzuki.

The starting point for Hagiwara's discussion of the Möbius strip is the scholarship of Yoshizawa, already discussed above, as the one who first revealed the use of the Möbius strip to depict the paradoxical structure of awakened Buddha mind in the ink paintings of Zen master Hakuin. Yoshizawa gives the following as an example of Hakuin's Zen logic of twofold negation when remarking on one of his own Möbius band paintings. In poetic verse form paradoxically structured like a Zen koan, Hakuin declares that in his ink painting — "I venerate the Great Sage Manjushri," adding, "Manjushri is not depicted in the paper," and "Manjushri is not apart from the paper" (2009, 216–217). Yoshizawa comments: "This twofold negation approximates the twisting and joining of the Möbius band" (2009, 217). As further clarified by Hagiwara, the twofold negation of explaining the paradoxical structure of the Möbius band is precisely what Suzuki calls the Zen logic of *soku-hi* or "is and is not." For Hagiwara's notion of the Möbius band and Suzuki's Zen paradoxical logic of *soku-hi*, by entering into the deepest part of oneself, the person is turned inside out so as to already be outside themselves, whereupon the binaries of interior and exterior or subject and object are different yet the same.

As a prelude to his discussion of the Möbius strip in Derrida and Zen, Hagiwara first responds to what he regards as an unwarranted criticism leveled against Suzuki by Robert Magliola. In his comparative study of Derrida and Buddhism titled *Derrida on the Mend*, Magliola distinguishes "*a*centric Zen" versus "centric Zen." Magliola holds that the paradigm of a-centric Zen is Nagarjuna's sunyata or emptiness articulated through a Buddhist calculus of negations, and it is this form of acentric Buddhism that parallels the differential logic of Derrida: "I shall argue that Nagarjuna's *śūnyatā* ('devoidness') is Derrida's *différance*" (1986, 89). Thus, for Magliola the *différance* of Derrida's deconstructionism is a functional equivalent to the sunyata or emptiness of Nagarjuna's acentric Buddhism, insofar as both decenter all absolutes into an inexhaustible play of differential relationships. Magliola further argues that Suzuki posits a version of "centric Zen" that reifies, entifies, and substantializes the flow of reality as ceaseless becoming into an eternalized absolute, thus to stand opposed to both Derrida's deconstructionism as well as acentric Zen Buddhism (1986, 97).

Hagiwara elucidates the Möbius strip as an image/concept for articulating Derrida's deconstructionism and Suzuki's a-centric Zen (2014). Moreover, he shows how Nishida's topos of nothingness as explained through Suzuki's paradoxical Zen logic of *soku-hi* can be envisioned as having the topological shape of a Möbius band with a half-twist expressed as "inverse correspondence." As Hagiwara states above: "The Möbius strip . . . works as a metaphor to explain Derridean *différance* and [D. T. Suzuki's] *soku-hi* logic" (2014, 125). In my own essay "Derrida and the Decentered Universe of Ch'an/Zen Buddhism" (1990), I have analyzed Magliola's comparison between Derrida's *différance* and a-centric Zen *śūnyatā* or emptiness, as further applied toward an interpretation of art, literature, and aesthetics in Japanese culture. Nevertheless, it was Lacan who first introduced the image/concept of the Möbius strip into postmodern French philosophy, psychology, and aesthetics. In this section I have therefore endeavored to clarify how the Möbius band illustrates the paradoxical structure characterizing the decentered empty subject of the unconscious in the Zen Buddhism of Suzuki and the psychoanalysis of Lacan, whereby inside and outside are both different and yet the same. Although Hagiwara never mentions Suzuki's notion of the cosmic Unconscious, he does ask the reader to "imagine what I will call 'the cosmic Möbius strip,' a Mobius strip expanded to the size of the universe" (2014, 142, fn. 10). I would therefore suggest that Suzuki's acentric Zen logic of *soku-hi* characterizing the paradoxical structure of Buddha mind as "the cosmic Unconscious" can itself be visualized in topological imagery as what Hagiwara calls "the cosmic Mobius strip."

Zen and Sartre on the Transparency of Consciousness

The great French existentialist, phenomenologist, novelist, playwright, political activist, and Nobel prize laureate Jean-Paul Sartre (1905–1980), who together with his partner Simone de Beauvoir embodied the postwar bohemian café society lifestyle of the literati, intelligentsia, and avant-garde artworld in Paris, is widely regarded as the most famous philosopher of the twentieth century.

Sartre emphatically denies the existence of "the unconscious." In *Being and Nothingness*, he explains: "Existential psychoanalysis rejects the hypothesis of the unconscious; it makes the psychic act co-extensive with consciousness" (1992, 728). The existential phenomenology and psychology of Sartre describes human consciousness as a "nothingness" that is clear, empty, and transparent and therefore devoid of a fixed essence or ego. Moreover, insofar as the nothingness of human consciousness is transparent, there can be no intrapsychic dualism between the conscious and the unconscious. Sartre maintains that because human consciousness is empty and transparent, it has total freedom to create itself out of nothingness, and so we cannot be psychically determined by unconscious drives, motives, or complexes as said by Freud. Sartre's abandonment of the unconscious for that of a consciousness transparent to itself thus leads him to repudiate all notions of libido-driven psychic determinism, such as unconscious drives, repressed instincts, will to power, or a universal Oedipus complex (1992, xliii). For Sartre it is an inauthentic act of bad faith to explain behavior as determined by unconscious drives, instead of recognizing our total freedom to create ourselves, thereby to become an authentically existing individual by making choices freely and then taking full responsibility for our choices. In the existential aesthetics of Sartre, because the subject is a nothingness devoid of an ego, it is fully transparent to itself through and through, such that the authentic individual is not determined by unconscious motives or subliminal drives but has total freedom to create itself anew at each moment analogous to the way an artist creates an artwork.[4]

Sartre holds that insofar as subjective consciousness is a sheer nothingness devoid of an ego, it is fully "transparent." At the conclusion of *Transcendence of the Ego*, Sartre asserts: "The Transcendental Field, purified of all egological structure, recovers its primary transparency. In a sense, it is a *nothing*" (1988, 93). For Sartre, the primary characteristic of human consciousness devoid of an ego is its "nothingness," further described in terms of its *transparency*. Like the existential-phenomenology of Sartre, the Zen of Suzuki also describes the mind as "transparent" while further characterizing the transparency of the mind as nothingness. Both the French existentialism of Sartre and the Zen aestheticism of Suzuki claim that because the mind is a transparent emptiness or nothingness devoid of an ego, the authentic person has the freedom to create itself anew at each moment, like an artist creating a painting, a poem, or a play. For Suzuki, however, the transparency of mind is realized only after the nondual experience of Zen satori or enlightenment. Although before satori parts of the mind are by convention said to be "unconscious," after satori the mind becomes transparent to itself through and through. Moreover, according to Sartre's dualistic ontology of *Being and Nothingness*, the transparency and nothingness of subjective consciousness stands over against the opaqueness and being of external objects in the world. For Suzuki, however, in the nondual experience of Zen satori both mind and the world become transparent in absolute nothingness.

While Sartre's existentialism was a powerful influence on the avant-garde artworld centered in Paris during the 1940s, so Suzuki's Zen aestheticism influenced the postwar avant-garde artists located in New York City during the 1950s and 1960s. Also, Sartre and Suzuki maintain that similar to the way an artist creates a painting, poem, or play, the authentic person creates themselves as an artwork at each moment in the freedom of nothingness as an abyss of infinite creative possibilities. Like Sartre's existential phenomenology, Suzuki describes the "transparency" of consciousness as nothingness devoid of an ego, and like Sartre, he also emphasizes the total creative freedom that arises from this. But for Suzuki, consciousness becomes completely transparent to itself only *after* realizing its natural uncontrived state of no-mind in the Zen experience of satori or enlightenment. Following the Zen satori experience of no-mind it is realized that consciousness is transparent in absolute nothingness, whereupon there is no division between conscious and unconscious, nor is there a bifurcation between subject and object, or *pour-soi* and *en-soi*, but only an infinite openness, luminosity, and transparency. The nondual Zen experience of satori is described by Suzuki as awakening to the cosmic Unconscious in superconsciousness thereby to eradicate the previous dualism between the conscious and the unconscious.

Whereas Sartre contrasts the "transparency" of subjective consciousness as nothingness to the *opacity* of objects, Suzuki maintains that after Zen satori the dualism is overcome such that both subject and object become "transparent" in absolute nothingness. In Suzuki's lexicon, "transparency" is interchangeable with sunyata or emptiness and is used to describe the Zen nondual experience of satori awakening. Suzuki describes how after his satori with the Mu koan, he experienced himself and nature as transparent while descending the stairs to the gate at Engakuji temple: "I remember that night as I walked back from the monastery to my quarters in the Kigen'in temple, seeing the trees in the moonlight. They looked transparent and I was transparent too" (SWS I, 209–210). In Suzuki's writings the word "transparency" is often used to characterize the clear, diaphanous, or pellucid appearance of phenomena seen just as they are in their emptiness-suchness so that after the nondual Zen experience of satori, both self and nature are viewed as transparent: "Let us first get an experience of transparency, and we are able to love Nature, and its multiple objects, though not dualistically. . . . Transparency is the keynote to the Zen understanding of Nature, and it is from this that its love of Nature starts" (ZJC, 257). Elsewhere, Suzuki remarks: "The aim of Zen is . . . to return to the original state of purity and transparency" (ZJC, 359). He continues: "When Zen speaks of transparency, it means this clearing away, this thorough wiping of the surface of the mind-mirror" (ZJC, 361). Elsewhere, this is how Suzuki describes the nondual Zen experience of satori in the state of no-mind or no-thought: "Not a single idea will disturb your consciousness . . . you have become open, light and transparent" (AIZB, 47). Zen satori is therefore characterized by its openness, luminosity, and transparency.

In the dualistic ontology of Sartre's *Being and Nothingness*, the objects in the external world of Being are *en-soi* or "in-itself" and characterized by their "opacity," whereas the interiority of subjective consciousness is the nothingness of *pour-soi* or "for-itself" and is characterized by its "transparency." Suzuki makes reference to Sartre's categories of *en-soi* and *pour-soi* to articulate the dualism between consciousness and its objects, such as when he speaks of "the two modes according to Sartre of *en-soi* and *pour-soi*" (SWS I, 133). He further comments here that Sartre's two modes of *en-soi* and *pour-soi* are mentally fabricated notions resulting in a false dualism and, therefore, should not be reified into absolute substantial entities. Furthermore, Suzuki uses Sartre's two existential-ontological modes of *pour-soi* for consciousness as the transparency of nothingness and *en-soi* for opaque external objects to analyze the Zen/Chan koan teachings of Qingyuan Weixin (671–740). Qingyuan's koan reads as follows: "When I began to study Zen, mountains were mountains; when I thought I understood Zen, mountains were not mountains; but when I came to full knowledge of Zen, mountains were again mountains" (ZB, 288). According to Suzuki, in Western philosophy nature has been conceived as *en-soi* or in-itself, an externalized object standing in opposition to *pour-soi* or for-itself of the internal Cartesian subject (SWS I, 117). From the dualistic standpoint of Western philosophy, the mountains are externalized, objectified, and substantialized as *en-soi* or in-itself. The nondualistic standpoint of Zen philosophy, however, describes the unity of human consciousness and nature as an integration of *pour-soi* and *en-soi*: "On the other hand, Nature becomes part of my being as soon as it is recognized as Nature, as *pour-soi*. . . . I am in Nature and Nature is in me" (SWS I, 123). Suzuki adds that from the standpoint of Zen satori, "there is no distinction between *en-soi* and *pour-soi*" (SWS I, 129–130).

According to Suzuki's nondual Zen interpretation, Sartre's existential phenomenology describes the dualism between opaque solid objects as *en-soi* at the first level where mountains are mountains, and the nothingness of consciousness as *pour-soi* at the second level where mountains are not mountains. Yet the artificial dualism between the opacity of external objects as *en-soir* and the translucency of subjective consciousness as *pour-soi* is surmounted at the third stage of Zen satori, whereupon mountains are once again reaffirmed as mountains, but as empty, nonsubstantial, and transparent. In Suzuki's words: "When we come to this stage of thinking, pure subjectivity is pure objectivity, the *en-soi* is the *pour-soi*, there is perfect identity. . . . But the identity does not imply the annihilation of one at the cost of the other. The mountains do not vanish; they stand before me. . . . The mountains are mountains and yet not mountains" (ZB, 289). For Suzuki, then, after the nondual Zen experience of satori, the false dichotomy between *pour-soi* and *en-soi* or subjectivity and objectivity at the first stage of substantialism where mountains are mountains, and the relative nothingness of *pour-soi* at the second stage of nihilism where mountains are not mountains, is now overcome in the absolute nothingness at the third stage in which mountains are again mountains, whereupon both *pour-soi* and *en-soi* appear "transparent" in their emptiness-suchness. For Suzuki, it is in this nondual Zen-Kegon standpoint of absolute nothingness that both consciousness and its objects become fully translucent, such that there is total nonobstructed interfusion between *pour-soi* and *en-soi*, subjectivity and objectivity, or unity and multiplicity. He goes on to say that in Zen satori at the third stage of absolute nothingness, the mind becomes wholly transparent to itself in an "interfusion of consciousness and unconsciousness" (AZ, 36).[5]

For Suzuki, as for Sartre, the mind is ultimately to be characterized as "transparent" with no hidden or subconscious regions unknown to consciousness: "To speak conventionally . . . there are unknown recesses [the sub-conscious] in our minds" (AIZB, 108). Suzuki, however, then goes on to explain: "To designate them as 'sub-consciousness' or 'supra-consciousness' is not correct. The word 'beyond' is used simply because it is a most convenient term to indicate their whereabouts. But as a matter of fact there is no 'beyond,' no 'underneath' . . . in our consciousness. The mind is one indivisible whole and cannot be torn in pieces" (AIZB, 108). He continues: "The so-called *terra incognita* [of the Unconscious] is the concession of Zen to our ordinary way of talking . . . the Zen psychologist sometimes points to the presence of some inaccessible region in our minds. Though in actuality there is no such region apart from everyday consciousness" (AIZB, 108). In this important passage, Suzuki clarifies that terms such as the subconscious, unconscious, or supraconscious are in fact only *provisional designations* that cannot be hypostasized into absolute entities imputed by mind as having substantial, permanent, or independent existence on their own side. The mental continuum is an indivisible whole that cannot be artificially divided and then compartmentalized into the conscious, subconscious, and supraconscious as reified entities with ontological status. He concludes: "When the *koan* breaks down all the hindrances to the ultimate truth, we all realize that there are, after all, no such things as 'hidden recesses of mind'" (AIZB, 108). For Sartre, consciousness as emptiness or nothingness is transparent and therefore has no hidden or unconscious aspects. Likewise, Suzuki holds that after the nondual Zen experience of satori, consciousness becomes transparent without any hidden recesses of the mind. Although in conventional terms we speak of unknown regions of the psyche such as the subconscious or unconscious, from the ultimate point of view, both the mind and the world are empty, void, and transparent. According to Suzuki, parts of the mind are said to be "unconscious" only from the standpoint of reified Ego-consciousness and its subject-object dualism. But in the egoless state of nondual Zen satori, consciousness becomes transparent with no hidden aspects to be designated as subconscious, unconscious, or supraconscious. Suzuki thus declares that after satori, the illuminated mind becomes fully transparent to itself through and through, "all out in the open with nothing hidden" (RHD, 124). He again declares: "Perhaps there is after all nothing mysterious in Zen. Everything is open to your full view" (ZB, 18). Or as he elsewhere puts it: "There is nothing hidden in Zen: all is manifest and only the dim-eyed ones are barred from seeing it" (ZB, 312). For Suzuki, then, before satori a large part of the mind remains unknown to dualistic ego-consciousness and is therefore provisionally designated in conventional terms as "the Unconscious." But at the ultimate level of discourse, the nondual Zen experience of satori makes the Unconscious conscious in superconsciousness, whereupon the mind becomes like a clear and bright crystal fully translucent to itself in the openness, luminosity, and transparency of absolute nothingness.

Zen and the Rhizomatic Unconscious of Delueze-Guattari

There are striking parallels between the "cosmic Unconscious" as *Indra's Net* in Suzuki's Zen aestheticism and the "schizoanalytic unconscious" as a *Rhizome* or acentric network of interconnected multiplicities in the French poststructuralism of Deleuze and Guattari. Deleuze is one of the foremost postmodern French philosophers, while Guattari is a leading French psychiatrist. In the 1950s Guattari was trained and certified in psychoanalysis directly under Lacan. Nonetheless, Guattari went on to reject Lacanian psychoanalysis and its concept of the semiotic unconscious. It was through their remarkable collaboration that Deleuze and Guattari together came to work out *schizonanalysis* based on their notion of "the rhizomatic unconscious."

Deleuze and Guattari set forth their notion of the schizoanalytic unconscious as a "rhizome" in their coauthored work *A Thousand Plateaus*. This remarkable text establishes a new postmodern vision of nontotalizable multiplicity, difference, and openness of a decentered *chaosmos* (1987, 313), which is itself imagined through the botanical metaphor of the "rhizome" as a horizontal subterranean stem that forks off and proliferates randomly in every direction. The first chapter of this text is entitled "Introduction: Rhizome," which functions as a manifesto for a new schizoanalytic psychology based on the rhizomatic unconscious (1987, 3–25). For Deleuze and Guattari, the unconscious is an "assemblage" with tendencies toward both trees and rhizomes. They claim that modernity is dependent on the arborescent "tree" metaphor whereby the mind organizes information in systematic and hierarchical principles as branches of knowledge grounded in roots or foundations. While the tree model affirms unity, hierarchy, and identity, the rhizome model celebrates irreducible multiplicity, plurality, and difference. In opposition to the arborescent tree model of psychoanalysis, the rhizome model of schizoanalysis uproots the tree metaphor to decenter information into acentric, heterogeneous, and open systems thereby to undermine totalizing, essentializing, substantializing, and centralizing modes of foundationalist thought. Insofar as the schizoanalytical unconscious is rhizomatic, it is constituted by decentered multiplicities in becoming, such that totalized unities, vertical hierarchies, and rigid institutional structures are only colonized or territorialized rhizomes.

According to Deleuze and Guattari, "the unconscious" of psychoanalysis is rooted in the centric and hierarchical tree model that stratifies libido into fixed structure, whereas in schizoanalysis the unconscious is based on an acentric, nonhierarchical, and destratified rhizome model that liberates the flow of creative energy to induce endless variations, becomings, intensities, and transformations. In the schizoanalysis of Deleuze and Guattari, the rhizome is a term for the deterritorialized and thus emancipated flow of surplus unconscious libido, energy, and desire. They argue that whereas psychoanalysis produces neurotic subjects that conform to authority and are repressed in their desire, schizoanalysis aims to unblock the flow of desire to achieve liberation from repressive social structures, territorialized spaces, and hierarchical institutions. According to Freudian psychoanalysis, schizophrenic delirium is an illness due to repressed instincts, forbidden wishes, and traumatic memories in the unconscious. For Deleuze and Guattari, however, the psychotic delirium of schizophrenia breaks out of the unconscious as a creative flow of surplus productive desires that generate a proliferation of intense feelings, ideas, images, and visions thus to dismantle the homogeneous subject into a flowing network of heterogeneous assemblages. While psychoanalysis endeavors to construct a stable and healthy Ego functioning as a unified center, schizoanalysis is a decentering process that aims to rupture self-identity into an irreducible play of differences thereby to shatter the unified subject into an acentric multiplicity in constant becoming.

In the introduction to *A Thousand Plateaus*, Deleuze and Guattari develop a radical French poststructuralist idea of the unconscious as a desiring machine based on their key image: the Rhizome. The *rhizome* or subterranean lateral network of acentric multiplicities is opposed to what they term arborescence, or the tree image, which denotes totalizing principles, binary oppositions, dualisms, and hierarchies, as well as absolutized centers, essences, and foundations. As opposed to Western thought modeled on arborescence based on an image of a stratified hierarchical tree, they put forward the new emancipatory image of a rhizome as a nonhierarchical, acentric, destratified, pluralistic, heterogeneous, polymorphic, and differential network of interconnected multiplicities in constant flux. In botany the rhizome is a subterranean horizontal stem of plants growing underground that send out multiple shoots from their nodes, such as grasses, weeds, ginger, turmeric, bulbs, and tubers. The mushroom is botanically a fungus, yet nonetheless, it has the weblike structure of a rhizome as an endlessly proliferating acentric subterranean mycelial network. In cybernetics, the Internet or World Wide Web is a rhizome as an acentric network whereby digital information, knowledge, and power are now equally available to everyone, thus to be fluid, connective, decentered, and nonhierarchical. In neuroscience, they maintain that the mind/brain is a rhizome as a decentered neural network of multiple autonomous dendrites, neurons, axons, and synapses (1987, 15). Deleuze and Guattari further discuss the rhizomatic character of the unconscious in schizoanalysis through psychedelic experience in what they term "pharmacoanalysis" (1987, 283).

According to Deleuze and Guattari the characteristics of the rhizome as a decentered network are its connectability, heterogeneity, multiplicity, asignifying rupture, and cartography as a map with multiple entry and exit points (1987, 7–12). These characteristics together establish a basic trait of the rhizome model, namely, *acentrism*. "Arborescent [tree] systems are hierarchical systems with centers" (1987, 16). While the tree model of arborescent systems has a fixed center, the rhizome model is radically *a*centric: "To these centered systems, the authors contrast acentered systems, finite networks of automata" (1987, 17). A rhizome is therefore defined as an interconnected network constituted by "an acentered multiplicity" (1987, 17). Elsewhere, "in contrast to centered . . . systems with hierarchical modes of communication and preestablished paths, the rhizome is an acentered, nonhierarchical, nonsignifying system . . . without an organizing memory or central automaton" (1987, 21). In their summary of traits characterizing the rhizome, it is claimed that, "unlike trees or their roots, the rhizome connects any point to any other point" (1987, 21). Altogether, then, the rhizome image underlying the French deconstructionist philosophy of Deluze and Guattari, including the rhizomic unconscious of schizoanalysis, is to be envisioned as an acentered network of autonomous multiplicities in ceaseless flow, wherein every point is connected to every other point in the differential web of relations.

Deleuze and Guattari tell us that "the unconscious" of Freudian psychoanalysis is based on an arborescent tree model such as to be a centralized, foundationalist, hierarchical, stratified, and closed system, whereas the *rhizomatic unconscious* of schizoanalysis is acentric, nonfoundational, interconnected, multiple, heterogenous, differential, nonhierarchical, destratified, open, and chaosmotic: "Take psychoanalysis as an example again: it subjects the unconscious to arborescent structures, hierarchical graphs . . . central organs, the phallus . . . not only in its theory but also in its practice of calculation and treatment. Psychoanalysis cannot change its method in this regard: it bases its own dictatorial power upon a dictatorial conception of the unconscious" (1987, 17). In their critique of Freudian psychoanalysis, Deleuze and Guattari praise Freud for his discovery of the unconscious. They argue, however, that while Freud sometimes approaches a rhizomatic view of the unconscious as an acentric network of multiplicities, he always falls back to an arborescent notion of the unconscious as a hierarchical tree with the roots as its center, unity, and foundation: "No sooner does Freud discover the greatest art of the unconscious, this art of molecular multiplicities, than we find him tirelessly at work bringing back molar unities. . . . On the verge of discovering a rhizome Freud always returns to mere roots" (1987, 27). Whereas the "dictatorial conception of the unconscious" in Freudian psychoanalysis is based on its hierarchical tree structure, the schizoanalysis of Deleuze and Guattari is based on the emancipatory rhizome model of the unconscious as an acentric network of autonomous multiplicities:

> Schizoanalysis on the other hand, treats the unconscious as an acentered system, in other words, as a machinic network of finite automata (a rhizome), and thus arrives at an entirely different state of the unconscious. . . . the issue is never to reduce the unconscious or to interpret it or make it signify according to a tree model. The issue is to produce the unconscious, and with its new statements, different desires: the rhizome is precisely this production of the unconscious. (1987, 18)

Finally, Deleuze and Guattari use the aesthetic-scientific image/concept of a labyrinthine subterranean "rhizome" model of the unconscious to provide a new and radical alternative to models of the unconscious based on the arborescent tree model, including Freud's personal unconscious of repressed instincts governed by the Oedipal complex, Lacan's semiotic unconscious structured as a language, and Jung's collective unconscious of archetypes. Deleuze and Guattari thereby set forth their own schizoanalytic doctrine of the *rhizomatic unconscious* as an open, chaosmic, decentered, heterogeneous, unstratified, and differential network of endlessly proliferating autonomous multiplicities in perpetual becoming.

The Rhizome Model of the Unconscious in Japanese Postmodern Culture

French postmodernism, including the psychoanalysis of Lacan, and the schizoanalysis of Deleuze and Guattari based on the "rhizome model," was first introduced into Japan in *Structure and Power* (*Kōzō to chikara*, 1983) by Asada Akira. Surprisingly, this difficult work became a sensation in Japan, enjoying great popularity both inside and outside the academic world. Asada argues that modern society is represented by the "tree model," while postmodern society is represented by the "rhizome model" of French deconstructionism. Influenced by Asada Akira, the "rhizome model" of Deleuze and Guattari was then applied to Japanese *otaku* popular culture in a bestselling work titled *Otaku: Japan's Database Animals* (*Dōbutsu suru postumodan: otaku kara mita nihon shakai*) by Azuma Hiroki. The term "otaku" here refers to Japanese youth who fanatically consume, produce, and collect *manga* (graphic novels, comic books), *anime* (animated films), computer video games, and related collectible products (2009, xv). According to Azuma, the emergence of postmodern Japanese otaku culture during the 1980s was based on a radical shift from the tree model to the rhizome model as a centerless web or net in constant becoming. Azuma calls Japanese otaku "database animals" and describes the rhizome model as the "database model." To explain Japanese otaku subculture, Azuma employs the theoretic framework of French postmodernist philosophers, including Jean-Francois Lyotard's analysis of the postmodern condition as abandonment of all totalizing "grand metanarratives" and their replacement with multiple *petits recits* or "little stories," Jean Baudrillard's concept of "simulacra," and Deleuze and Guattari's notion of the "rhizome." Azuma goes on to clarify how in French postmodernism, the "tree model" was itself replaced by the *rhizome model*, or what Azuma himself reformulates in the cybernetic language of computer technology as the database model. Describing this paradigm-shift from the tree model to the rhizome model in postmodern Japanese otaku subculture, Azuma writes: "However, with the arrival of postmodernity, that tree-model world image collapsed completely. So what kind of structure accrues to the postmodern world? One candidate for explaining the Japan of the 1980s that often seemed borne out in reality was the 'rhizome' model. . . . An easily understandable example of this is the Internet. The Net has no center. That is to say, no hidden grand narrative regulates all Web pages" (2009, 31). Azuma holds that after the collapse of totalizing grand metanarratives of the "tree model" underlying modernity, the postmodern condition of Japanese otaku subculture is more adequately conceived as a *rhizome*, defined as "a heterogeneous, centerless, ever-changing network" (2009, 132, n. 14).

The Rhizomic Unconscious in *Ghost in the Shell*

The French postructuralist theme of "the rhizome," as well as the decentered rhizomatic structure of the unconscious, is explored in a Japanese animated film titled *Ghost in the Shell: Stand Alone Complex* (2006), directed by Kenji Kamiyama. Like the original 1989 *Ghost in the Shell*, this spinoff is about Public Security Section 9, which investigates cybercrime in the near future, 2034. When an unknown enemy named "the Puppeteer" begins committing horrific cyberterrorist attacks through the Internet, various hypotheses are considered as to the possible identity of the Puppeteer. In chapter 19 of the film titled "The Puppeteers Real Identity," the female cybercop Kusanagi Motoko finally reveals the astonishing truth—that the Puppeteer is a *Rhizome* formed as a gestalt-pattern from the "collective unconscious" of senior citizens being medically cared for on the Internet. Moreover, this rhizome is being managed by a "cyberbrain." While using online computer graphics on a screen to holographically display the incredible form of the rhizome as a decentered network spreading out endlessly through "cyberspace" (*dennōkūkan*, 電脳空間),

Motoko explains: "This is the full view of the rhizome that has been woven by the elderly people's gestalt. The rhizome doesn't contain the concept of a 'center.' Therefore, the hub's cyberbrain is constantly in motion. That or the rhizome itself might be acting as the hub." Later in the film it is clarified that the Puppeteer is "the name of the cyberbrain that managed the hub of the . . . senior citizen's rhizome." Moreover, it is theorized that the rhizome was itself produced by the "collective unconscious" of these senior citizens. The rhizomatic unconscious of these aging citizens somehow resulted in an evil plot involving monstrous cybercrimes that include computer hacking, murder, forced suicide, and abduction of children on a massive scale. Yet it is further disclosed that this decentered rhizome emerged as a gestalt-pattern generated from the collective unconscious of multiple senior citizens on the net in an effort to solve Japan's mounting social problems: rising population of the elderly, increasing unemployment, decreasing worker force, and the rapidly declining birthrate in a collapsing economy. This Japanese cyberpunk animated film ends with Motoko expressing with awe: "The net is truly vast and infinite!" And this net or cybernetic matrix is a gestalt formed by the collective unconscious having the multiple, fluid, heterogeneous, and acentric structure of a *rhizome*.

The Rhizome as Indra's Net in Zen Buddhism

It should be recalled that Suzuki describes the "amalgamation of Zen and Huayen (Kegon) philosophy" (ZJC, 50–51, SWS III, 195). I propose that a very significant point of East-West convergence can be discovered between the Deleuze/Guattari model of the schizoanalytic unconscious as a *Rhizome* and Suzuki's Zen/Chan Buddhist concept of the cosmic Unconscious in terms of the Kegon/Huayan (Skt. Avatamsaka) Buddhist metaphor of *Indra's net*. The differential, multiple, and decentered rhizomatic unconscious of Deleuze and Guattari in French schizoanalysis, like the cosmic Unconscious of Suzuki in Zen Buddhism, describe the unconscious as an acentric network of interrelationships. My suggestion here is that the postmodern metaphor of a rhizome opens a new perspective on the ancient Buddhist metaphor of Indra's net, insofar as both metaphors envision psyche and cosmos as a perpetually flowing *centerless web* of autonomous multiplicities where every point is connected to every other point in the net. Although the schizoanalytic unconscious of Deleuze and Guattari is not pictured as a vertical tree, but as an underground horizontal rhizome, they nonetheless recognize how the tree image can be encompassed within a rhizome, just as a tree can itself metamorphize into a rhizomatic flow of endlessly proliferating subterranean multiplicities, intensities, and becomings. Hence, in a comment about the sacred Bodhi Tree in India where Guatama Siddhartha awakened from unconscious sleep to become the Buddha, Deleuze and Guattari proclaim: "Buddha's tree itself becomes a rhizome" (1987, 20).

While in French poststructuralism, Deleuze and Guattari develop their schizoanalytic unconscious as a labyrinthine subterranean rhizome, in Zen Buddhism Suzuki explains Zen satori or enlightenment in psychological terms as insight into the cosmic Unconscious further described in terms of the Zen-Kegon vision of Indra's net as a subliminal mesh or network of interrelationships. Here emerges a striking point of convergence between the "schizoanalytical unconscious" of Deleuze and Guattari as Rhizome, and the "cosmic Unconscious" of Suzuki's Zen Buddhism as Indra's Net. To repeat the words of Deleuze and Guattari: "Schizoanalysis . . . treats the unconscious as an acentered system, in other words, as a machinic network of finite automata (a rhizome), and thus arrives at an entirely different state of the unconscious" (1987, 18). For Deleuze and Guattari, the schizoanalytic unconscious is now to be envisioned as a rhizome, and a rhizome is an acentric network of multiplicities that ceaselessly branches out in every direction in the boundless openness of the chaosmos.

Here it must be emphasized that in the Zen-Kegon Buddhism of Suzuki there is no transcendent "God" functioning as a transcendental signified, ultimate ground, or absolute metaphysical center, so that Indra's net becomes an *acentric* network of cosmic interrelationships, whereupon now *every point in the net is the center*. Suzuki describes the Zen-Kegon Buddhist reality of emptiness, interdependent co-origination, and Indra's net using the Renaissance period Christian mystical image of *infinite spheres*: "It is a circle that has no center, or rather, it is a circle with its center everywhere" (SWS III, 116). He continues: "Because spiritual insight has this infinite circularity, its center can exist everywhere. . . . When this centerless center is gained, spiritual awakening is accomplished" (SWS III, 117). And elsewhere, he explains: "Experience has no centre, no circumference" (ZDNM, 143). For Suzuki, the Zen-Kegon vision of reality as a vast network where each monad unconsciously perceives the whole from its own point of view abandons the monotheistic notion of an absolute "center" and instead multiples reality so that each dharma in the pluralistic multiverse now becomes itself the center as a perspective mirror of totality. Suzuki's cosmic Unconscious as Indra's net, like the schizoanalytic unconscious, is not a unified cosmos but a "chaosmos," imagined by the French poststructuralist metaphor of a rhizome as a *centerless web* of relationships. Thus, like the rhizomatic unconscious in the schizoanalysis of Deleuze and Guattari, the cosmic Unconscious as Indra's net in the Zen-Kegon Buddhism of Suzuki is an acentric web of interconnections where each point in the subterranean network is itself a center, so that in the field of emptiness or absolute nothingness, the center is everywhere. The matrix of Indra's net envisioned by Suzuki's cosmic Unconscious where each monad is likened to an *infinite sphere* can thus be described in schizoanalytic terms as what Deleuze and Guattari call "the Rhizosphere" (1987, 252).

It should finally be noted how in *Rediscovering Japanese Space*, the renowned architect Kurokawa Kisho develops a Japanese Buddhist aesthetics of emptiness influenced by Suzuki's paradoxical Zen *soku-hi* or "is/is not" logic of identity between contradictions such as part and whole, unity and multiplicity, microcosm and macrocosm, or interior and exterior: "I have often referred to Daisetz Suzuki's logic of identity and difference and emphasized the mutually embracing relationship of part and whole in what is nothing less than a revolution against the Western concept of hierarchy" (1988, 95). Moreover, Kurokawa's Zen Buddhist aesthetics of emptiness as the decentered openness of encompassing space is explained in terms of the rhizome model of Deleuze and Guattari: "The concept of the rhizome as explained by Deleuze and Guattari in *Rhizome, extrait de Mille Plateaux* is a dynamic, varied, and plural form. They liken modern society to a tree. . . . In contrast, a rhizome is an interlocking web" (1988, 123). According to Kurokawa's Japanese Buddhist aesthetics of emptiness, then, Suzuki's Zen *soku-hi* logic of paradoxical identity between part and whole or microcosmos and macrocosmos, which itself underlies his explanation of Indra's net in Kegon Buddhism, is directly linked to the French postmodernist image of the rhizome as a centerless web of relationships in dynamic becoming.

The Re-Visioning of Indra's Net as a Rhizome

Above I have suggested various parallels between Suzuki's Zen-Kegon metaphor of the cosmic Unconscious as Indra's net and Deleuze/Guattari's postmodern aesthetic-scientific image/concept of the schizoanalytic unconscious as a rhizome. Looking anew at Indra's net as a rhizome also functions to critically examine both models from the standpoint of the other. Revisioning the rhizome model of Deleuze and Guattari in terms of Suzuki's Zen-Kegon image/concept of Indra's net expands the possibilities for realizing the deeper spiritual, metaphysical, ethical, and aesthetic dimensions of the rhizomatic unconscious as a basis for Zen Buddhist satori or enlightenment. On the other side, viewing the Buddhist metaphor of Indra's net as a rhizome in the infinite openness of a decentered chaosmos prevents it from being totalized into a fixed, static, deterministic, and monistic cosmos. When Suzuki's Zen-Kegon notion of the cosmic Unconscious as the dharma realm of Indra's net is reimagined by the Deleuze/Guatarri model of the schizoanalytic unconscious as a subterranean rhizome, it becomes a more liberated, spontaneous, improvisational, and creative process within the boundless openness of a decentered chaosmos as it randomly forks off and shoots out from its underground nodes into new, multiple, and unpredictable directions.

In my book *Process Metaphysics and Hua-Yen Buddhism* (1982), I established an East-West intercultural dialogue between Huayan/Kegon Buddhism and Alfred North Whitehead's organic process metaphysics of interpenetration between multiplicity and unity. Yet in this work, I also developed a Whiteheadian critique of Huayan/Kegon Buddhism. Part of my argument was to demonstrate that the standard doctrinal formula for Huayan is that "many is one and one is many." By contrast, in *Process and Reality*, Whitehead proclaims: "the many become one and are *increased* by one" (1978, 21). The polemic here is that in contrast to the more static, totalistic, and deterministic vision of Huayan Buddhism, Whitehead's doctrine of interpenetration between many and one sets forth a dynamic evolutionary process vision of the cosmos as an emergent creative advance into novelty directed toward maximum production of beauty.

Deleuze and Guattari assert: "The rhizome operates by variation, expansion . . . offshoots" (1987, 21). There is much in common between Deleuze and Guattari's schizoanalytic notion of the unconscious as a subterranean rhizome having the structure of a decentered network of autonomous multiplicities in constant flux, and Whitehead's organic process metaphysics of interpenetration between many and one, which proclaims "'becoming' is a creative advance into novelty" (1978, 28). The distinguished process theologian Roland Faber has established a new postmodern creative synthesis of Whitehead's process cosmology and the French poststructuralist vision of Deleuze/Guattari's open-ended schizoanalytic chaosmos as a rhizome. Describing the rhizome, Faber asserts:

> Against the all-pervasive hierarchical dualism of the sublime deduction of multiplicity from the One . . . Deleuze develops a *logics of the multiple, creative, and virtuality infinitely multiplying seriality of the AND*. Because of its moving, creative, and relational character of pure immanence without pre-given abstract orders of subjection (logocentrism), Deleuze labels the Open with the metaphor of the "rhizome" (instead of the "tree"). While "arborescence" indicates hierarchical structures, extreme stratification, and linear thinking, a "rhizomatic" symbolizes (and biologically actualizes) an interrelated network . . . of constantly moving multiplicities, and an assemblage of heterogeneous connections. (2014, 81; italics in original)

Connecting the infinite openness of Deleuze's rhizomatic chaosmos of acentric heterogeneous multiplicities in flux to Whitehead's process metaphysics of becoming as a creative advance into novelty, Faber adds: "This is what Deleuze finds in Whitehead: a thoroughly creative world in which 'unification' is always 'multi-pli-cation — the creation of *folds of difference*'" (2014, 81).

Hence, when the Huayan/Kegon Buddhist metaphor of Indra's net is reimagined in terms of Deleuze/Guattari's French postmodern metaphor of the *rhizome* as a subterranean acentric network branching out and shooting off randomly, spontaneously, and unpredictably in every direction, it approximates Whitehead's organic process cosmology of perpetual becoming through interpenetration of many into one as a creative advance toward novelty. Suzuki's Zen-Kegon Buddhist religio-aesthetic vision of the cosmic Unconscious as Indra's net is hereby transformed into a schizoanalytic-process model of the rhizomatic unconscious as an open chaosmos emerging from a ceaselessly proliferating centerless web of irreducible autonomous multiplicities in constant flux, whereupon the Jeweled Net of Indra now becomes an extemporaneous, nontotalizable, decentered, pluralized, and ever-expanding network of interrelationships that spontaneously produces ever-new variety, multiplity, originality, creativity, and emergent novelty without end.

Chapter 9

THE UNCONSCIOUS IN ZEN AND TRANSPERSONAL PSYCHOLOGY

Suzuki's Zen concept of the cosmic Unconscious exerted a major influence on what has become known as transpersonal psychology. The field of transpersonal psychology aims to formulate a comprehensive map or metatheoretical overview of the human mind, both conscious and unconscious, based on an integral synthesis of Western psychology and Eastern wisdom traditions such as Buddhism, Hinduism, Tantrism, Daoism, Sufism, Zen, and Yoga, as well as Shamanism. Generally speaking, transpersonal psychology explores the deeper, wider, and higher aspects of the unconscious thereby going beyond the individual to the more collective, transpersonal, and cosmic dimensions of the human psyche. Here it will be seen how Suzuki himself makes an important contribution to transpersonal psychology based on his modern Zen Buddhist doctrine of the cosmic Unconscious. Suzuki argues that Japanese spirituality involves a psychological process of self-realization whereby one becomes conscious of the Unconscious thereby awakening to the supraconscious in what he terms "unconscious consciousness" (JS, 84). This integration of consciousness with unconsciousness is further described as the process whereby the intellectual discrimination penetrates into its own roots in nondiscrimination. Moreover, the spiritual process of self-realization culminates in achievement of the supra-individual Person as a transpersonal self: "This is the real person — the self-realization of the supra-individual Person" (JS, 114). For Suzuki, the true self of Zen is the "supra-individual Person" (*chōko no nin*, 超個の人), otherwise rendered as a "trans-individual Person," who at the same time is "one individual person" (*hitori*, 一人). That is to say, the Person is both the supra-individual and the single individual: "Because the supra-individual Person transcends individuality, it is not within the realm of the individual self. ... The supra-individual Person is not without a relation to the individual self; there is a deep, in fact inseparable, relation between them" (JS, 76). Abe Masao explains Suzuki's Zen notion of the supra-individual authentic Person or true self as follows: "'Person' has two aspects — one exists as a finite individual, and at the same time, one is a 'bottomless abyss'. The bottomless abyss is, needless to say, 'Emptiness', 'Void' or 'Cosmic Unconsciousness' which is supra-individual" (1985, 75). Suzuki can therefore be said to have formulated an Eastern variant of transpersonal psychology whereby, through integration of conscious and unconscious processes, Zen aims toward "the self-realization of the supra-individual Person" in the vacuum-plenum of absolute nothingness where emptiness is fullness and fullness is emptiness.

In what follows there will be a critical examination of Suzuki's Zen model of the cosmic Unconscious in relation to the field of transpersonal psychology as developed by Abraham Maslow, Ken Wilber, Hubert Benoit, G. I. Gurdjieff, Roberto Assagioli, and Stanislav Grof. The last chapter will focus especially on Suzuki's critique of drug-induced satori advocated by Aldous Huxley and others who claim that psychedelic experience is the shortcut path to enlightenment.

Satori, Peak Experience, and the Unconscious in Zen and Abraham Maslow

Abraham Maslow (1908–1970) is regarded as a founder of both humanistic and transpersonal psychology thus being regarded as one of the most influential psychologists of the twentieth century. The purpose of Maslow's "third force" humanistic psychology was to counter the reductionism of psychoanalysis and behaviorism. According to Maslow, the basic psychological drive is neither gratification of instincts by the pleasure principle governing the id or libidinal unconscious in Freudian psychoanalysis nor the mechanical response to stimuli through conditioned reflexes as in B. F. Skinner's behaviorism, but rather, it is an innate tendency of the organism toward self-actualization. Furthermore, Maslow's "fourth force" transpersonal psychology introduces the spiritual dimension of ego-transcendence. Maslow is known for his "hierarchy of human needs" visualized as a pyramid diagram, including the lower "deficiency needs" of sustenance, safety, care, and recognition or self-esteem, and at the top of the pyramid, the higher "Being-need" for *self-actualization*, which is the striving to realize one's highest potentials. In the process of self-actualization, there are the aesthetic needs for beauty, art, and creativity and the cognitive needs for knowledge, understanding, and insight. At the apex of the pyramid is the "peak experience," the most intense, expansive, open, awake, illuminating, and joyful moments of life. The peak experience of self-actualizing persons ideally has two components: an emotional aspect of ecstasy and a noetic aspect of insight. For Maslow there is a deep inner unconscious core to the human psyche that continually orients the individual in the direction of growth, development, integration, and self-actualization of one's higher potentials, reaching its summit in peak experiences and plateau experiences. Here it will be shown that according to Maslow, the *muga* or nonego of Zen satori described by Suzuki is itself the paradigm case for the ego-transcendence of peak experience, and that like Zen satori, the peak experience has its origins in the spontaneous aesthetic creativity of our deeper unconscious.

At the outset of *Religion, Values, and Peak-Experiences*, Maslow explains, "'revelations' or mystical illuminations can be subsumed under the head of 'peak-experiences'" (1964, 19). For Maslow, a peak experience is like the pure experience of William James or the consummatory experience of John Dewey (1964, xi). Moreover, on the Eastern side, it will be seen that Maslow's peak experience is inspired especially by Suzuki's notion of the Zen satori experience. For Maslow, peak experiences arise not only in religious contexts but in athletics, love, sex, natural child birth, and philosophical insight, as well as in creative, aesthetic, and artistic moments (1964, xi–xii). In this way Maslow aims to enlarge the notion of "religious" or "mystical" so that peak experiences can be triggered by ordinary experiences of everyday life.

In his work *Toward a Psychology of Being*, Maslow explains that his humanistic and transpersonal psychotherapy aims to initiate the process of self-actualization toward peak experience by facilitating an openness to the deeper core of human nature in the unconscious mind: "Many aspects of this inner, deeper nature are either (a) actively repressed, as Freud has described . . . or (b) 'forgotten'. . . . Much of the inner, deeper nature is therefore unconscious" (1968, 191–192). But while Freudian psychoanalysis has a negative concept of the unconscious as the source of psychosomatic illness and neurotic symptoms, Maslow instead focuses on the positive aspects of the deeper unconscious psyche in its higher functioning as the source of creativity, spontaneity, playfulness, artistic production, aesthetic enjoyment, romantic love, orgastic potency, moral compassion, religious ecstasy, mystical insight, and other aspects of peak experience (1968, 196). Maslow's clinical research discovered that self-actualizing persons capable of having frequent peak experiences were able to unify the conscious and unconscious aspects of the psyche: "One especially important finding in self-actualizing people is that they tend to integrate the Freudian dichotomies and trichotomies, i.e. the conscious, preconscious, and the unconscious (as well as the id, ego, and superego)" (1968, 207). For Maslow, the capacity to integrate the conscious, preconscious, and unconscious, including what he terms the healthy unconscious in its higher-level functioning of aesthetic creativity and mystical insight, is a necessary precondition for eliciting the ecstatic peak experiences of self-actualizing persons. Hence, one of the basic aims of Maslow's humanistic and transpersonal psychology is "the development toward the concept of a healthy unconscious" (1968, 208).

According to Maslow's transpersonal psychology, the process of self-actualization, realization of one's highest potentials, and the capacity for peak experiences, all have their source in the deeper unconscious. In existential terms, he asserts that the unconscious that underlies the process of self-actualization toward peak experience is rooted in what the Christian existentialist theologian Paul Tillich calls the "dimension of depth." Yet, like other transpersonal psychologists, Maslow distinguishes between the lower or unhealthy unconscious of Freudian psychoanalysis and the healthy unconscious in its higher functioning of aesthetic creativity as the basis for self-actualization toward peak experience (1971, 173). For Maslow the healthy unconscious is the fountain of aesthetic, artistic, and creative peak experiences common to self-actualizing persons. In this context Maslow speaks of "the primary creativeness which comes out of the unconscious, which is the source of new discovery — of real novelty" (1971, 82). The aesthetic creativity, spontaneity, and novelty of the deeper unconscious is seen as the key to the peak experiences of self-actualizing persons (1971, 83). Through humanistic and transpersonal psychotherapy one can expedite the self-actualization process toward peak experiences characteristic of artistic, creative, and spontaneous persons by integration of the conscious and the unconscious (1971, 89).

For Maslow, the psychotherapeutic process of self-actualization is measured by "peak experiences," including aesthetic, creative, artistic, mystical, religious, orgastic, athletic, oceanic, and psychedelic experiences. The peak experience of self-transcendence corresponds the "unitive consciousness" of mystical experience, which Maslow relates to the core religious experience of Zen, Daoism, Yoga, and Christian mysticism, as well as the psychedelic experience described by Aldous Huxley (1971, 115). Maslow says that humanistic and transpersonal psychotherapies, like Freudian psychoanalysis, Jungian depth psychology, existentialism, mysticism, and Zen Buddhism reach into the depths of the unconscious. He adds: "But now as we learn steadily that these depths are not only the wellsprings of neuroses, but also of health, joy, and creativeness, we begin to speak of the healthy unconscious" (1971, 163).

For Maslow, a paradigm case of the peak experience is the "Zen satori" described by Suzuki. In his book *Americans and the Unconscious*, Robert Fuller explains how Maslow's humanistic and transpersonal psychology of peak experience based on the higher unconscious relates to the "aesthetic spirituality" characterizing both American Transcendentalism and Suzuki's Zen mysticism (1986, 160). Throughout his writings, Maslow discusses Suzuki's work on Zen Buddhism and analyzes the peak experience in terms of the Zen satori experience as awakening to the joy, wonder, ecstasy, and aesthetic delight of each moment. Maslow thus speaks of "the peak experience itself, or the *satori* experience that Suzuki describes" (1971, 252). In Maslow's analysis, like the ego-transcendence of the peak experience, the immediate experience of Zen satori as described by Suzuki is an ecstatic state of *muga* or nonego as the act of losing oneself in the present moment of everyday life, while at the same time being one with the universe: "The *muga* state is frequently spoken of as if it were the same as the satori state. Much of the Zen literature speaks of *muga* as if it were total absorption with whatever one was doing at the time, for example, chopping wood with all one's heart and might. And yet the Zen people also talk about this as it if were the same as the mystic unification with the cosmos" (1971, 254). Thus like the Zen satori described by Suzuki, the peak experience of Maslow is noetic insight into how each part reveals the whole and the whole is manifested in each part, just as how every moment reveals eternity and the eternal is disclosed in each moment. For Maslow the peak experience is a core religious experience of transcendence, including "transcendence in the sense of loss of self-consciousness," "transcendence of the ego," "transcendence of time," "transcendence of space," "transcendence of dichotomies," "transcendence of subject-object dualism," "transcendence of the split between facts and values," "transcendence as mystical experience," "transcendence as cosmic consciousness," and various other senses of the term (1971, 269–279). These traits of the peak experience can also be used to characterize the Zen satori experience as reported by Suzuki. What Maslow refers to as "transcendence in the sense of loss of self-consciousness" is further described as "the same kind of self-forgetfulness which comes from getting absorbed, fascinated, concentrated" (1971, 269). Again, he refers to it as "transcendence of the ego or of the conscious self" (1971, 269). It can be said that peak experiences of ego-transcendence as loss of self-consciousness is what Suzuki describes as the egoless state of *mushin* or no-mind and *muga* or no-self in the Zen experience of satori as awakening to the cosmic Unconscious. Indeed, Suzuki himself describes the Zen satori enlightenment of *muga* or no-mind as a peak experience: "The enlightenment-experience, therefore, is the one which we can have only when we have climbed up to the highest peak from which we can survey the whole field of Reality. . . . it is a state of absolute Suchness, of absolute Emptiness which is absolute fullness" (OIMB, 246). In this same passage, Suzuki goes on to say that from the standpoint of Buddhist-Christian comparative mysticism, the peak experience of satori enlightenment as an ecstatic no-mind state of absolute emptiness, is the "Suchness or 'is-ness' (*isticheit*) in Eckhart's terminology" (OIMB, 246).

In *Toward a Psychology of Being*, Maslow says that peak experiences should not be conceived as if they were "Nirvanic states of perfection" but as transitory moments of illumination within an ongoing process of self-actualization (1968, 44). The peak experience is not a once-and-for-all achievement but a moment-by-moment process of self-actualization whereby one awakens to the sacred in the here-and-now of everyday life. But in his later work *The Farther Reaches of Human Nature*, Maslow introduces his idea of "plateau experiences" (1971, 281, 283, 348, 349). Whereas the *peak experience* is transitory, dramatic, episodic, climactic, and explosive with an element of aesthetic shock or surprise, the *plateau experience* is more constant, sustained, continuous, controlled, and cultivated by practice (1971, 348). Based on his clinical research, Maslow concludes: "For the transcenders, peak experiences and plateau experiences become the most important things in their lives" (1971, 283).

Maslow further analyses peak experience by reference to Suzuki's account of similarities between Zen and the "unitive consciousness" of Meister Eckhart's Christian mysticism: "'Suchness' is a synonym for the Japanese word *sonomama*. (Descriptions are found in the book by Suzuki, *Mysticism: Christian and Buddhist*) . . . Literally it means the 'as-it-isness' of things" (1971, 251). For Maslow the Zen satori experience of things as they are (*sono mama*) in their concrete particular emptiness-suchness and the experience of *is-ness* in the unitive consciousness of Christian mysticism illustrate a core feature of peak experience as what he calls the "Being-cognition" of things in daily existence. Maslow says that the peak experience, like Suzuki's Zen satori, is triggered by the most commonplace events of ordinary experience thereby to realize an interfusion of the secular and the sacred: "The great lesson from the true mystics, from the Zen monks, and now also from the Humanistic and Transpersonal psychologists," says Maslow, is "that the sacred is *in* the ordinary, that it is to be found in one's daily life" (1971, 345). Finally, like Suzuki's account of Zen satori, Maslow's notion of peak experience is described as springing from out of the artistic, aesthetic, and spontaneous activity of our deeper unconscious as the inexhaustible source of all creative potentialities.

The Unconscious in Zen and Ken Wilber's Spectrum of Consciousness

Ken Wilber, another leading pioneer of transpersonal psychology, explains the various states of conscious, unconscious, and superconscious levels constituting the "spectrum of consciousness." According to Wilber, the full spectrum of consciousness explored in his transpersonal psychology, like the electromagnetic spectrum in physics, is a continuum of multiple wavelengths, only a small fraction of which are visible (conscious), but most of which are usually invisible (unconscious), such as infrared rays, ultraviolet rays, x-rays, radio waves, gamma rays, cosmic rays, and other vibratory bands. Wilber's "spectrum psychology" (1993, 7) is an integral synthesis that appropriates a broad range of Eastern and Western philosophies, psychologies, and mystical traditions while also incorporating insights from the other transpersonal psychologists, including James, C. G. Jung, Maslow, Assagioli, Benoit, Gurdjieff, and Grof. The East-West synthesis of Wilber's transpersonal psychology has also been profoundly influenced by the modern neo-Hindu philosophy and Integral Yoga of Sri Aurobindo (1872–1950), wherein the absolute existence-consciousness-bliss (*sat-cit-ananda*) of Atman/Brahman undergoes "involution" or descent from superconscience into inconscient matter, then undergoes a reverse process of "evolution" or ascent of kundalini-shakti back up the spectrum through matter, life, and mind, finally returns back to its origin in superconscience. Wilber likewise incorporates Gurdjieff's esoteric psychology based on a full spectrum model of involution-evolution in descending and ascending octaves of vibrations. Moreover, he analyzes Suzuki's Zen doctrine of the Unconscious and exposition of Yogacara Buddhist depth psychology. According to Wilber, Suzuki's presentation of the eight *vijñānās* (consciousnesses) of Yogacara Buddhist psychology spans the full spectrum of consciousness, such that the illusory world of dualism between subject and object appears when Buddha nature undergoes involution from the storehouse-consciousness to rational ego-consciousness to the sense-consciousnesses and through Buddhist yoga practice then initiates a reverse process of evolution going from the five sense-consciousnesses to ego-consciousness to the storehouse consciousness and, at last, culminating in a transpersonal and superconscious experience of the Void through contemplative practices such as Zen meditation on the dharmakaya of formless emptiness.

In *The Spectrum of Consciousness* Wilber endeavors to clarify Suzuki's Zen Buddhist view that Mind becomes unconscious through attachment to, and identification with, the separate ego and its correlate subject-object dualism: "We pay for duality with the sleep of the unconsciousness" (1993, 134). Through this dualism between subject and object, "Mind itself — is rendered underlying, implicit, unnoticed, unconscious. In other words, most of us are unaware that what we are is Mind . . . Mind is the fundamental unconscious" (1993, 134). Wilber further explains: "In our terminology, the Level of Mind, being pure consciousness, is never conscious of itself, and so is Unconscious. . . . Thus the Level of Mind is 'Unconscious' in two similar yet slightly different senses: unconscious because we are ignorant of its 'existence,' and unconscious because we cannot know it dualistically — we know Mind by being it, and in no other way" (1993, 135). He continues: "Because Mind can never become an object of consciousness, it is frequently referred to as 'the Unconscious'. . . . Mind is the Unconscious (*wu hsin, wu nien*) because as Absolute Subjectivity, as non-dual awareness, . . . it cannot be known as an object of conscious" (1993, 135). Because for Suzuki the Mind cannot be known dualistically and therefore cannot become an object of subjective consciousness, it is called "the Unconscious." Moreover, Suzuki's Zen concept of the Unconscious is at base co-extensive with the universe itself. "In short, the primary dualism renders the Unconscious unconscious. And that implies . . . that the very root 'layer' of the unconscious is the universe itself. The sun, moon, and stars, the mountains, clouds, and waters, even the cars, planes, and trains: these truly are some of the 'contents' of our base unconscious" (1993, 135).

Based on various works translated by Suzuki, Wilber goes on to describe the Yogacara Buddhist psychology set forth by Asanga and Vasubandhu and its elaboration in *The Laṅkāvatāra Sūtra*, the *Awakening of Faith*, and the *Platform Sutra* (Wilber, 1993, 157). Wilber maintains that Suzuki's Zen concept of the Unconscious and presentation of the eight *vijñānas* or consciousnesses in Yogacara Buddhism represent a full spectrum model of the human mind. In this context, Wilber cites Suzuki's description of Yogacara Buddhist psychology: "The mind . . . evolves (*vritti*) into eight vijnanas [or levels]: Alaya, Manas, Manovijnana, and the five senses" (1993, 157; brackets in the original). Wilber comments: "In essential aspects, this is very similar to our description of the evolution of the spectrum of consciousness, and so as we now describe the eight *vijnanas* of Mahayana psychology, we will simultaneously point out the corresponding levels of the spectrum of consciousness" (1993, 157). For Wilber, the evolutionary process of ascension up the full spectrum of consciousness as outlined in Suzuki's presentation of the eight *vijñānas* in Yogacara Buddhist psychology, from the five sense consciousnesses to *manovijñāna* to *manas* to ālaya-vijñāna or the storehouse consciousness, ultimately culminates in an awakening to the dharmakaya emptiness of Buddha mind as "the Void" (1996a, 98). Moreover, Wilber describes how this awakening to the Void at the summit of the spectrum of consciousness is itself a peak experience of "the transpersonal and superconscious realms" (1996, 112). Finally, the superconscious experience of the Void is itself directly realized by meditation on the dharmakaya of formless emptiness as exemplified by the practice of Zen (1996, 112). Wilber's full spectrum model of transpersonal psychology has in this way been profoundly influenced by Suzuki's Zen doctrine of the Unconscious together with Suzuki's analysis of the eight consciousnesses in Yogacara Buddhist psychology. Moreover, Wilber goes on to develop his own transpersonal map of the human psyche containing five levels of unconsciousness, including what he calls the ground unconscious, the archaic unconscious, the submergent unconscious, the embedded unconscious, and the emergent unconscious (1996, 97–108).[1] Thus according to Wilber's integral psychology, Suzuki's Zen concept of the Unconscious together with his presentation of the eight consciousnesses of Yogacara Buddhism, designate a full spectrum model of the psyche, the ultimate level of which is a transpersonal and superconscious experience of the Void as dharmakaya emptiness.

D. T. Suzuki, G. I. Gurdjieff, and the Zen Unconscious of Hubert Benoit

The Zen Doctrine of No Mind by Suzuki was translated into French as *Le Non-Mental Selon La Pensée Zen* (1952) by Hubert Benoit (1904–1992). It is due to the efforts of Benoit that Suzuki's Zen became widely known in France. Benoit was a distinguished French medical physician, surgeon, psychiatrist, violinist, and writer, who endeavored to develop connections between Zen Buddhism and Western psychotherapy. He also published an original book on Zen under the French title *La Doctrine Suprême* (2 vols. 1951, 1952), now available in English as *Zen and the Psychology of Transformation: The Supreme Doctrine*.

In the preface to *Zen and the Psychology of Transformation,* Benoit states: "My supposed reader should have read particularly *The Zen Doctrine of No Mind* of Dr. D. T. Suzuki, or, at least, the preceding works of the same author" (1990, xiii). The influence of Suzuki's Zen concept of no-mind as the Unconscious is evident throughout this work, especially Chapter 9 titled "The Zen Unconscious" (1990, 72–78). Benoit, like Suzuki, distinguishes the subconscious and unconscious of conventional Western psychology from what he terms no-mind as the "Fundamental Unconscious" of Zen satori: "This Principle, anterior to all consciousness . . . we ought to call here the Fundamental

Unconscious (No-Mind or Cosmic Mind of Zen)" (1990, 134). In this context, Benoit describes how Zen satori awakening occurs through a radical shift of attention from the conscious to the Unconscious: "If this understanding were complete from the first this shifting of the profound attention would be realized immediately, in its entirety, with stability; this attention would be reinstated in the Unconscious (or Self or Own-Nature of Zen), and satori would take place" (1990, 128). As a medical doctor and psychotherapist, Benoit is interested in how Suzuki's approach to Zen meditation and enlightenment can assist the therapeutic process of healing pathological symptoms of neurosis. Benoit maintains that before attaining satori, all persons suffer from "unconscious metaphysical distress." Just as Zen Buddhism aims to overcome the problem of universal suffering, Western psychotherapy endeavors to cure mental, physical, and emotional distress at the conscious and unconscious levels. Influenced by Suzuki's Zen doctrine of no-mind, Benoit holds that all kinds of subconscious distress or anxiety are resolved upon achieving satori as becoming fully conscious of the Unconscious. "When consciousness has courageously penetrated at last to the plane of the emotive state, hitherto subconscious, there will be revealed the penetration of the profound attention into the Unconscious, the domain of Absolute Positivity which dissipates all distress" (1990, 129).

As revealed in James Moore's biography *Gurdjieff: The Anatomy of a Myth* (1991), Benoit became a disciple of the Russian-Greek/Armenian mystic Gurdjieff (1866–1949) at the latter's school in Paris held at a chateau known as the Prieuré. The esoteric psychology of Gurdjieff made an enormous impact on the 1960's counterculture. Gurdjieff's esoteric psychology is referred to as the Fourth Way, a path that integrates the body, emotions, and mind by self-observation during the commonplace activities of everyday life. Although Benoit sometimes makes direct references to aspects of Gurdjieff's thoughts (2004, 251–252, 261), his writings are permeated with veiled references to Gurdjieff's system of esoteric philosophy and psychology, otherwise referred to in alchemical terms as "the Work."[2] It can be said that throughout his various writings Benoit establishes a transpersonal psychology based on an integral synthesis of Western psychoanalysis, Suzuki's Zen psychology of the cosmic Unconscious, and the mysticism of Gurdjieff.

In his discussion of Benoit, Wilber speaks of "the genius of Benoit" (1993, 300). Elsewhere, he refers to "that most penetrating psychoanalyst and interpreter of Eastern philosophy, Hubert Benoit" (1977, 171). Furthermore, in his book *The Spectrum of Consciousness*, Wilber discusses Benoit and Gurdjief as having developed transpersonal psychologies based on a full spectrum model of consciousness wherein the mind can be viewed as a multileveled continuum of different vibrating bands (1993, 169). Wilber further remarks that in Gurdjieff's psychology, the higher vibratory bands or musical octaves of the multileveled spectrum "clearly corresponds with the Transpersonal Bands" (1993, 169). As will be seen, for Benoit these transpersonal bands of the mental continuum are identified with Suzuki's Zen satori experience of awakening to the cosmic Unconscious in superconsciousness, or what Benoit himself terms the "Zen Unconscious," and "cosmic supra-consciousness."

William Segal, an artist and disciple of Gurdjieff, as well as a student of various Zen masters, was also a friend of Suzuki. In their preface to Suzuki's essay "The Predicament of Modern Man" included in the *Selected Works of D. T. Suzuki* (Vol. III), co-editors Moriya Tomoe and Jeff Wilson mention Segal's connections to Suzuki's Zen and Gurdjieff's mysticism: "*Gentry* was a men's fashion magazine with abundant sophisticated artwork, but because of the keen interest in Zen of its editor, William Charles Segal (1904–2000), who was strongly influenced by the mystic George Gurdjieff (d. 1949), Suzuki contributed several pieces to it in the 1950s" (SWS III, 140). According to Segal's own book subtitled *An Intimate View of the Gurdjieff Work, Zen Buddhism, and Art*, Suzuki became very interested in "the Work" of Gurdjieff.[3] Gurdjieff taught his students to practice self-observation and self-remembering by concentrating on the three centers of the bodymind while performing Sufi-like dance movements to music that he composed to integrate conscious, subconscious, and unconscious processes. At one point Segal describes Suzuki's reaction to Gurdjieff's teachings, spiritual exercises, and sacred dance movements:[4] "When Mr. Gurdjieff died, I was a friend of the Buddhist scholar D. T. Suzuki. . . . Almost unanimously, the Zen masters I knew were especially interested in the Gurdjieff movements, if they knew about them. Suzuki and I went to several movement films and classes together. He said, 'You know, Zen and Gurdjieff are very close'" (2003, 195).

Gurdjieff was regarded as a master of hypnotism, who used hypnotic trance induction to explore the mysteries of our deeper unconscious mind. In his book *Gurdjieff and Hypnosis*, Mohammad Tamdgid provides an account of how Gurdjieff's practice of self-remembering during ordinary activities in daily life functions to unite conscious, subconscious, and unconscious processes by directing attention to the three centers (or brains) of the human bodymind organism. He explains that for Gurdjieff it is because the three centers usually operate in separation, that "the organism is still an *unconscious* apparatus, serving the "blind" forces of nature. . . . Human organism is not born, in other words, with an inherent actual and ready-made ability to blend the intelligences associated with the physical, intellectual and emotional centers, namely the instinctive unconscious, waking conscious and subconscious realms of the psyche" (2009, 80). Tamdgid further clarifies Gurdjieff teaching that higher states of cosmic consciousness are attained only by "a unitary being whose threefold brains [centers] work harmoniously in concert with one another, the realms of the unconscious/instinct (domain of instinctive bodily functions), waking consciousness (domain of intellectual knowledge), and subconscious (domain of feelings and emotions) are intricately connected with and aware of one another" (2009, 82). For Gurdjieff, it is when full attention is directed through self-observation to the intellectual center of waking consciousness in the head, the emotional/feeling center of the subconscious in the heart, and the physical/

instinctive/movement center of the unconscious in the lower abdominal region that the conscious, subconscious, and deeper unconscious are unified, thereby to sense the psychosomatic totality of oneself as a microcosm of the macrocosm. Hence, through self-remembering and self-observation at each moment of everyday life, one recovers their wholeness as a mental-emotional-physical unity thereby to fully integrate the conscious, subconscious, and unconscious processes constituting the psychosomatic self.

The influence of Gurdjieff on Benoit's understanding of psychoanalysis and Zen Buddhist theory and practice runs throughout his writings. In the esoteric psychology of Gurdjieff, one of the basic metaphysical principles is termed "the Law of Three." At the outset of his book, Benoit refers to this Law of Three, which states that all creative process involves three forces: (1) a positive force, (2) a negative force, and (3) a neutralizing/conciliatory force (Benoit, 1990, 6; 2004, 15). According to Benoit: "We can only bring about any change in our total organism if we apply the Law of Three" (1990, 125; 2004, 124). Benoit further clarifies: "This 'Law of Three' can be symbolized by a triangle; the two lower angles of the triangle represent the two inferior principles of creation, positive and negative; the apex represents the Superior or Conciliatory Principle" (1990, 6). For Benoit, the key teaching of Zen, as for Gurdjieff, is to awaken from unconscious sleep through constant self-observation, thereby

Figure 9.1. Relation between satori, sleep, and waking. *Source:* Created by the author.

to become fully conscious of the cosmic Unconscious. He describes the process of transformation in Zen as follows: "Thus we go little by little towards a state in which deep sleep and the waking state are reconciled" (1990, 109). He adds that this "astonishing conciliation" manifesting the Law of Three occurs in satori through the "Great Work" or transformative inner alchemy of Zen practice (1990, 109). Again, he clarifies how waking and sleeping or consciousness and unconsciousness are reconciled in the Zen superconscious state of satori: "In reality, whether I sleep or remain awake, I am from this moment in the state of satori. Sleep and waking are steeped equally in this state; the state of satori, with regard to sleep and waking, plays the role of a hypostasis which conciliates them" (1990, 229). To illustrate Gurdjieff's Law of Three as it relates to Suzuki's Zen Buddhist psychology of satori awakening to the Unconscious, Benoit (1990, 229) provides the triangle or pyramid diagram shown in Fig. 9.1.

According to Benoit, Zen satori is the conciliatory force uniting the negative force of unconscious sleep and the positive force of awakening. Explaining the above diagram, Benoit writes:

> Just as my ordinary awakening seems to me to be a progress in relation to my sleep, so satori should be a 'super awakening', a 'veritable' awakening, a supreme progress in relation to my actual waking state. Just as my ordinary awakening gives back to me a consciousness which was lacking to me while I slept, so satori should give me a 'supra-consciousness' which is lacking in me now. . . . I believe that mental hyper-activity, in extasy . . . attaining a critical point of tension, will obtain the bursting of the last barrier and entrance into a state of cosmic supra-consciousness. (1990, 228)

While the waking state is dualistic ego-consciousness and the sleep state is unconsciousness, nondual Zen satori is a "super awakening," which reconciles conscious wakefulness and unconscious sleep in what Benoit terms "cosmic supra-consciousness."

For Benoit, as for Suzuki, to achieve Buddhahood in Zen satori requires a super-awakening to no-mind as the cosmic Unconscious, or what Benoit calls "The Zen Unconscious" (1990, 72). The reason for this is clearly expressed by Benoit: "In the universal, original Unconscious I know that I am Buddha" (1990, 165). Benoit thus emphasizes that upon awakening from sleep in satori, the enlightened Zen practitioner realizes their "identity, in the Unconscious, with Buddha-the-Absolute" (1990, 167). For Suzuki and Benoit, "the Unconscious" is the level of Buddha nature, while rational ego-consciousness arising from subject-object dualism is the level of ordinary human beings. It is only in satori as awakening to the cosmic Unconscious in superconsciousness that one realizes their inherent Buddha nature.

To conclude, it can be said that for the transpersonal psychology of Benoit, as for the Zen of Suzuki, and the Fourth Way of Gurdjieff, the meditative process of self-observation or mindfulness during the ordinary activities of everyday life, aims toward awakening from unconscious sleep so as to become fully conscious of the unconscious thereby to experience what Suzuki describes as awakening to the cosmic Unconscious in superconsciousness and what Benoit refers to as awakening to the Zen Unconscious in cosmic supraconsciousness.

Superconsciousness in Zen and Roberto Assagioli's Psychosynthesis

Suzuki's Zen concept of satori as becoming conscious of the cosmic Unconscious in superconsciousness is here discussed in terms of the Psychosynthesis of Roberto Assagioli, an Italian medical doctor, psychiatrist, and pioneer of transpersonal psychology. It will be shown how Assagioli's own doctrine of superconsciousness is a synthesis of various psychological, philosophical, and mystical wisdom traditions, both Western and Eastern, including the Zen Buddhism of Suzuki.

The philosophical psychology of Suzuki argues that while Zen satori is awakening to the unconscious mind, it is not to be mistaken as the lower unconscious of Western psychoanalysis. Let us recall this key statement by Suzuki: "Psychologically speaking, *satori* is super-consciousness, or consciousness of the Unconscious. The Unconscious is, however, not to be identified with the one psychologically postulated. The Unconscious of satori is . . . the cosmic Unconscious" (AZL, 62; LZ, 88). Suzuki thus asserts that in modern psychological terms, Zen satori is to become conscious of the cosmic Unconscious in superconsciousness. While from the standpoint of reified ego-consciousness and its subject-object dualism the originally enlightened Buddha nature is said to be "unconscious," in itself it is superconscious. As discussed earlier, Suzuki's Zen concept of satori as superconsciousness itself traces back to William James's *The Varieties of Religious Experience*, wherein Swami Vivekenanda is cited on Yoga as a method for achieving the superconscious state of samadhi. In his book *Raja Yoga* (1986), Swami Vivekenanda teaches that beneath consciousness is the unconscious, while above consciousness is the higher workings of superconsciousness (James, 1982, 400). Suzuki's use of the term "superconsciousness" is also reminiscent of the 1909 New Thought metaphysics book *Subconscious and the Superconscious Planes of Mind* by William Atkinson (Yogi Ramacharaka), which after citing the views of Vivekananda and James, articulates a threefold intrapsychic division of mind into the conscious, subconscious, and superconscious. According to Suzuki, then, Zen satori is not the lower unconscious of Freudian psychoanalysis but an awakening to the higher creative functions of the cosmic Unconscious in superconsciousness.

As shown by Firman and Gila in their introduction to psychosynthesis, it is known that Roberto Assagioli met with Suzuki and read his works on Zen

Buddhism (2002, 14). Assagioli directly quotes Suzuki on Zen satori as requiring a primacy of unconscious "will" over conscious "intellect" (2010, 81, 173). Moreover, at times Assagioli describes awakening to superconsciousness through psychosynthesis techniques using traditional Zen Buddhist vocabulary popularized by Suzuki. Explaining superconscious states of enlightenment in Zen Buddhist terms, Assagioli writes: "These are the states variously called *samadhi, prajna, satori,* ecstasy, cosmic consciousness, etc." (2010, 91). Elsewhere, Assagioli describes awakening to superconsciousness in the language of Zen Buddhism as "a Nirvana-like phenomena of joy and release" (2012, 268). Like Suzuki's Zen, Assagioli's psychosynthesis holds that realization of superconsciousness often occurs through "spontaneous illumination" (2012, 77) or "sudden enlightenment" (2007, 20–21), what he also calls following Maslow, a "peak experience" (2012, 34).

In his book *Psychosynthesis,* Assagioli provides a comprehensive transpersonal map of the unconscious as having three levels: (1) the lower unconscious, (2) the middle unconscious, (3) and the higher unconscious, or super-consciousness (2012, 15). Summing up his cartography of the human unconscious,

Figure 9.2. Assagioli's Oval Diagram of the Mind.
Source: Roberto Assagioli, Oval Diagram of the Mind, in *Psychosynthesis* (Amherst, Massachusetts: The Synthesis Center, 2012), 15.

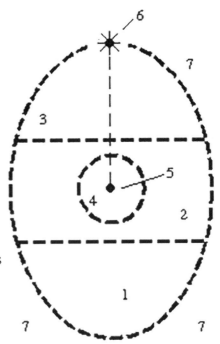

1. The Lower Unconscious
2. The Middle Unconscious
3. The Higher Unconscious or Superconscious
4. The Field of Consciousness
5. The Conscious Self or "I"
6. The Higher Self
7. The Collective Unconscious

Assagioli writes: "Of course, everything of which that conscious self is not aware can be called 'unconscious,' including the lower, middle and higher parts of the unconscious. But we think that whenever possible it is better to indicate the level of which we are speaking, and therefore use for the higher unconscious the word 'superconscious'" (2012, 78). The lower unconscious is the personal unconscious of Freudian psychoanalysis consisting of repressed instincts and forgotten traumatic memories. The middle unconscious is the level of our most recently forgotten and easily recalled experiences, similar to what Freud called the preconscious. The higher unconscious, or superconsciousness, is the source of artistic creativity, moral compassion, and spiritual illumination. Assagioli illustrates this multilevel structure of the mind by what he calls his oval or eggshell diagram (fig. 9.2).

In Assagioli's oval or eggshell diagram of the human psyche (2012, 15; 2010, 12; 2007, 27), all three layers of the unconscious, including the lower, middle, and higher unconscious or superconsciousness, are surrounded by the Jungian collective unconscious. At the center of the middle unconscious is the "I" in the field of consciousness. Assagioli's oval diagram of the psyche covers the entire spectrum of the human mind, including multiple stratified layers of the unconscious. Different layers of the spectrum are said to be "unconscious," however, only because they have not yet been integrated with and assimilated into consciousness. In the oval diagram, the broken lines dividing the various multiple strata of the psyche indicate that the layers are not separate compartments but are porous, open, and permeable, thereby to interpenetrate in an undivided psychical continuum. Thus, each level of the unconscious, including the lower, middle, and higher unconscious or superconscious, can potentially become fully conscious when incorporated into the total field of expanded awareness.

In his psychosynthesis, Assagioli also develops various clinical practices corresponding to each level of unconsciousness ranging from the lower to the middle to the higher unconscious or superconscious. Assagioli's psychosynthesis recognizes *the aesthetic way of beauty* as a major path to realization of the transpersonal self through integration of contents from the higher unconscious or superconscious: "Transpersonal realization through beauty can be called the aesthetic way" (2010, 85). A paradigm example of Assagioli's aesthetic way of beauty is his guided meditation technique for transpersonal psychosynthesis through a spiritual exercise based on Dante's *The Divine Comedy*, the masterpiece of Italian literature, starting with a visualization of descent into hell as the lower unconscious, followed by an ascent up the mountain of purgatory as the middle unconscious, finally mounting further upward to paradise as the higher unconscious or superconscious. Assagioli remarks: "The third part — the visit to Paradise or Heaven — depicts in an unsurpassed way the various states of superconscious realization" (2012, 186–187).

As documented by Kay Larson, in his lectures and classes Suzuki often illustrated his Zen map of the human mind by using oval or eggshell diagrams (2013, 171). Larson further makes reference to class notes on this oval diagram of the mind in one of Suzuki's lectures as recorded by his student John Cage, the famous avant-garde musician and artist:

> I had heard a lecture by Daisetsu Suzuki, with whom I was studying the philosophy of Zen Buddhism, on the structure of the Mind. He had gone to the blackboard and had drawn an oval shape. Halfway up the left-hand side he put two parallel lines. He said the top of the oval was the world of relativity, the bottom was the Absolute, what Eckhart called the Ground. The two parallel lines were the ego or mind (with a little m). The whole drawing was the structure of the Mind. (2013, 174)

As described by Cage, in Suzuki's oval diagram the top level is the world of relativity, whereas the bottom level was the absolute Ground. In Suzuki's *The Zen Doctrine of No Mind*, there is a similar oval or eggshell diagram illustrating his Zen map of the human psyche, where the top half is the apperceiving mind of consciousness, including sensation (*dṛṣṭa-śruta*) and thought (*mata-jñāta*), while the lower half depicts various psychological states of unconsciousness,

Figure 9.3. Suzuki's Oval Diagram of the Unconscious. *Source:* Daisetsu Suzuki, Oval Diagram of the Unconscious, in *The Zen Doctrine of No Mind*, edited by Christmas Humphreys (London: Rider, 1969), 145.

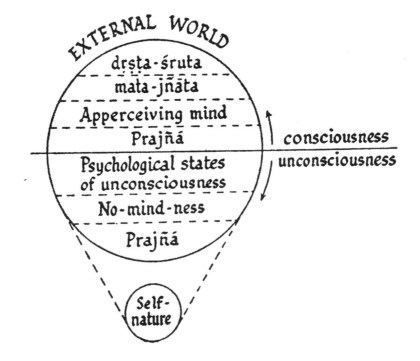

the deepest level of which is no-mind-ness (*mushin*), or the Unconscious as prajna wisdom of emptiness (ZDNM, 145, diagram 3) (fig. 9.3).

In his autocommentary on this oval diagram, Suzuki emphasizes that the Unconscious of Zen Buddhism is not to be mistaken as "corresponding to the 'Unconscious' of Analytical Psychology or Psycho-Analysis. . . . The psycho-analytical Unconscious cannot go deep enough to include the question of no-mind-ness" (ZDNM, 144). That is to say, beneath the personal unconscious of repressed instincts in Freudian psychoanalysis, and even beneath the collective unconscious of archetypal images postulated by Jungian analytical psychology, lies Zen *mushin* or no-mind-ness as the cosmic Unconscious of absolute nothingness that is directly experienced through kensho, "seeing into self-nature." Moreover, Suzuki indicates how his Zen concept of the Unconscious illustrated in the oval diagram goes beyond the unconscious of Western psychology and signifies a "super-psychological" level of experience: "Diagram 3 attempts to explain the same fact of experience. . . . Below the bisecting line we have two divisions of the Unconscious, psychological and super-psychological. In the latter, Prajñā, the Unconscious and no-mind-ness are included" (ZDNM, 144).

In the oval or eggshell diagram illustrating the infrastructure of the human mind according to his modern hybrid psychologized Zen Buddhism, Suzuki divides consciousness from unconsciousness then further divides the Unconscious into two levels — the psychological and super-psychological — the latter referring to what he otherwise calls the level of superconsciousness. Similarly, Assagioli's oval diagram shows the division between consciousness and unconsciousness and further distinguishes between three intrapsychic levels of the unconscious: the lower unconscious, the middle unconscious, and the higher unconscious or superconscious. Like Assagioli's psychosynthesis, Suzuki's Zen notion of the cosmic Unconscious is not to be conflated with the id or lower personal unconscious of repressed drives in Freudian psychoanalysis, or even the collective unconscious of numinous archetypal images described by Jungian analytical psychology but is instead to be understood as the higher unconscious of superconsciousness. Moreover, he describes how the superconscious mind can be directly accessed through artistic creativity and the aesthetic experience of beauty, as well as by meditation, visualization, and other spiritual exercises. Finally, in the Zen map of the psyche formulated by Suzuki, as in the psychosynthesis of Assagioli, various layers of the mind are referred to as "unconscious," only because they have not yet been integrated with and assimilated into consciousness. Both the oval or eggshell diagrams of Assagioli and Suzuki use broken lines to indicate that the various multiple levels of consciousness and unconsciousness are not compartmentalized but are porous, open, and interpenetrating layers within the total field of an undivided experiential continuum. Similar to Assagioli's psychosynthesis, then, Suzuki's modern psychological interpretation of Zen holds that when the latent contents of unconsciousness are fully integrated with ordinary consciousness, it results in nondual Zen satori as sudden awakening to the inexhaustible creative potentialities of the cosmic Unconscious in superconsciousness.

Psychedelic Experience and Suzuki's Zen Critique of Drug-Induced Satori

This section examines Suzuki's provocative essay "Zen and Drugs" (RD, 129; SWS III, 233) wherein he criticizes the notion of drug-induced satori. After briefly considering the position of those exploring drug-induced satori, including Aldous Huxley, Stanislov Grof, Rick Strassman, and others, I analyze Suzuki's critique of this view. Suzuki especially directs his criticism toward the notion of drug-induced satori in Huxley's *The Doors of Perception*, where Zen enlightenment is compared with the psychedelic experience induced by mescaline.

First, however, it should be pointed out that while Suzuki criticized drug-induced satori in public, in private he was deeply interested to experiment with psychedelics. In the 2006 documentary film *A Zen Life: D. T. Suzuki* (2006), Ms. Okamura Mihoko, the longtime personal secretary for Suzuki until the end of his life, reveals that at 85 years of age, after hearing so much about similarities between Zen satori and LSD-induced psychedelic experience, Suzuki often requested LSD. Moreover, the psychiatrist Albert Stunkard, a devoted Zen practitioner and Suzuki's longtime personal physician in Japan, reports how Suzuki often asked for LSD but that those around him always declined, using the excuse of his high blood pressure, fearing that the psychedelic experience would be too overwhelming for Suzuki in his later years.

Grof is an eminent psychiatrist and a cofounder of transpersonal psychology. If for Romantic poets such as Coleridge it was narcotics including the poppy seed and its opiate derivatives that were "Nature's passport to the unconscious" (Tallis, 2012, 7), for Grof it is LSD and other psychedelics that open up the subliminal doors to the unconscious mind. In his 1975 work titled *Realms of the Human Unconscious* (republished in 2009 as *LSD: Doorway to the Numinous*), Grof tells us: "Freud once said of dreams that they were the *via regia* or royal way to study the unconscious: to an even greater degree this seems to be true for the LSD experience" (2009, 220). At the outset of his career, Grof conducted decades of legal research on LSD therapy at universities and medical clinics in Prague and the US. Also, in his later research he investigates the unconscious through altered states that simulate psychedelic experience induced by his neo-shamanic method of Holotropic Breathwork, which uses rapid breathing techniques while listening to ecstasy-inducing music with hypnotic rhythms (2009, xxiii). Grof describes his efforts to map the unconscious mind over decades of legally sanctioned LSD research and LSD therapy in his essay on psychedelic medicine titled "Observations from 4,000 LSD

Sessions": "We were doing something we called psycholytic therapy, which was a large number of medium dosages (150 to 200 micrograms) of LSD. . . . We were able to remove layer after layer and map the unconscious, moving from the Freudian individual or personal unconscious, through what I call the 'perinatal unconscious,' related to the memory of birth, to what Jung called the collective unconscious — both its historical and mythological, or archetypal aspects" (2017, 50). For Grof, psychedelics function to make subliminal contents of the deeper unconscious mind surface into consciousness: "The phenomena observed in psychedelic sessions are manifestations of deep areas of the unconscious unknown to and unacknowledged by contemporary science" (2009, xx). Summing up his new map of the unconscious, Grof writes: "I have attempted to outline the cartography of the human unconscious as it has been manifested in LSD sessions of my patients and subject" (2009, 32). He adds: "The description of the new model of the unconscious based on LSD research . . . reflects a multidimensional and multilevel continuum of mutually overlapping and interacting phenomena . . . we can delineate for the purpose of our discussions the following four major levels, or types, of LSD experience and the corresponding areas of the human unconscious: (1) abstract and aesthetic experiences, (2) psychodynamic experiences, (3) perinatal experiences, and (4) transpersonal experiences" (2009, 32–33). Finally, Grof describes the ultimate transpersonal realm of the unconscious revealed by LSD as follows: "The last and most paradoxical transpersonal phenomenon to be discussed in this context is the experience of the supracosmic and metacosmic Void, of the primordial emptiness, nothingness, and silence" (2009, 208). Among the world's various religious and mystical schools compatible with his transpersonal psychology, Grof mentions the tradition of Zen Buddhism, by which he is no doubt referring to Suzuki's Zen (2009, 142). Hence, similar to Suzuki's Zen psychology of the cosmic Unconscious, Grof above describes the deepest transpersonal level of the unconscious as the supracosmic Void of emptiness, nothingness, and silence.

Eric Cunningham argues from the standpoint of a cultural historian that a "Zen nexus" emerged between Suzuki's Zen and the use of psychedelics during the 1960s countercultural revolution in the West (2007, 31). As said by Cunningham: "Drawing upon the English language Zen canon of D. T. Suzuki, as well as the experiences of western authors who read Suzuki and later brought their understanding of Zen into experiments with hallucinogens, I will trace the steps by which modern Zen became associated with psychedelic experience" (2007, 35). According to Cunningham, Suzuki's writings on Zen provided a new vocabulary for articulating the otherwise ineffable dimensions of psychedelic experience: "Suzuki's popular works, published over the course of six decades of international Buddhist 'evangelizing,' brought the Zen precepts of 'nothingness,' 'no mind,' and *satori* into psychoanalysis, Christianity, and popular literature, and ultimately into the domains of radical psychedelic activism" (2007, 32). There arose a "fusion of cultural vocabularies," as seen when

Harvard psychologist Timothy Leary referred to the psychedelic experience of LSD as "drug-induced *satori*" (2007, 32). Likewise, Strassman, a medical physician, psychiatrist, and longtime Zen practitioner, describes the "DMT-induced 'enlightenment experience'" (2015, 95).[5] Zen terms denoting enlightenment popularized by Suzuki's Zen, such as satori, kensho, mushin, muga, samadhi, nirvana, moksha, dharmakaya, and sunyata, came to be increasingly used by those attempting to describe altered states of consciousness brought on by LSD and other psychedelic drugs, also termed "entheogens," or that which produces the divine within.[6] Cunningham further documents how the term "psychedelic" as originally coined by Humphry Osmond in 1957, signifies manifesting hidden contents of the deeper mind latent in the subconscious (2007, 23–24).

Suzuki's Critique of Drug-Induced Satori

It should be pointed out that while Suzuki was influenced by James's notion of pure experience, as well as his idea of mystical experience as a function of the subconscious, he was also familiar with James's account of photisms or spiritual illuminations triggered by mind-altering intoxicants for accessing the subliminal mind, including peyote used in Native American religious ceremonies, as well as anesthetic pharmaceutical drugs, such as ether and nitrous oxide (James, 1982, 387–388). Nonetheless, Suzuki himself strongly criticized the notion of drug-induced satori, wherein Zen enlightenment is mistakenly conflated with hallucinations produced by psychedelic drugs. In his preface to R. H. Blyth's translation of the *Mumonkan* (*The Gateless Barrier*) (1228), Suzuki claims that Zen "has been the subject of gross misunderstanding and fantastic interpretation by those who have never actually had the Zen experience. Among such interpreters we count the modern addicts to uses of so-called psychodelic [sic] drugs (LSD, mescaline, psilocybin, etc.). That the visions have really nothing to do with Zen, psychologically or spiritually, is ascertainable when one carefully studies for instance, Case XIX of this book" ("Preface" in Mumonkan: 1966, vii.). One of Suzuki's recurrent themes is that what the Zen doctrine of the Unconscious refers to in negative terms as "no-mind" (*mushin*) or the cosmic Unconscious is in its positive expression termed the "ordinary mind" (*heijōshin*) of everyday life, now comprehended as the *isness* or "emptiness-suchness" of things just as they are. Suzuki here attempts to distinguish the illusory hallucinations of drug-induced psychedelic experience from authentic Zen awakening by reference to Case 19 of *The Gateless Barrier*, which teaches "ordinary mind is the way" (*heijōshin kore dō*, 平常心是道).

In the proceedings from a symposium on Zen and psychedelics that were published in *The Eastern Buddhist* (New Series, vol. 4. no. 2, Oct. 1971), an academic English language journal founded by Suzuki himself contains Suzuki's essay titled "Religion and Drugs" (RD, 128–133), wherein he underscores the differences between Zen satori and psychedelic experience.[7] This essay is itself based on translations from Suzuki Daisetsu's *Daisetsu tsurezuregusa* (DT, 336–339, 358–361). More recently, a revised version of this has been released as a popular work for nonacademic Japanese readers, *Zen no tsurezure* (禅のつれずれ, Idle Thoughts on Zen), including a chapter titled "LSD and Zen," where Suzuki critically examines the notion of drug-induced satori through ingestion of LSD, mescaline, peyote, and other psychedelics (ZTZ, 78–83, also 45–52). At this symposium Suzuki along with Alan Watts, Robert Aitken Roshi, Ueda Shizuteru, and others agree that drug-induced psychedelic experience differs from an authentic Zen experience of the true self as the "ordinary mind" of everyday life. In his own essay titled "Religion and Drugs," Suzuki begins with the insight: "Strangely, religion and drugs are closely associated. Karl Marx who founded the 'School of Communism' called religion an opiate, but for that matter the communism which he advocated is also a kind of religion and therefore a drug, no doubt" (RD, 129; SWS III, 233). Suzuki discusses especially what he calls "mystical drugs," or psychedelics:

> By mystical drugs I refer to *soma* used in Vedic India, haseesh among the Arabs, peyote among the American Indians, and so on. Alcohol may be included.... In Japan, sake [rice wine] is offered to the gods.... However it has yet to produce the sort of hallucinatory images induced by taking peyote, haseesh, etc. It is to peyote and other related mystical (that is, psychedelic) drugs that I want to give close attention. (RD, 129; SWS III, 234)

Suzuki adds: "Chemical analysis of peyote has recently led to the development of various drugs in the United States, among which the most well known is LSD" (RD, 129; SWS III, 234). For Suzuki, however, "mystical drugs" such as LSD and other psychedelics do not lead to authentic Zen satori or enlightenment but only give rise to illusory maya-like hallucinations.

Suzuki's essay "Zen and Drugs" goes on to criticize Huxley's *The Doors of Perception*, an account of Huxley's pioneering experiments with mescaline, the active ingredient of the peyote cactus plant, taken as a sacrament for millennia in the sacred ceremonies of Native Americans. In Huxley's account of drug-induced satori he describes the aesthetically immediate dimension of life as enjoyed through a heightened synaesthetic awareness of beauty disclosed by vivid colors, sounds, and other sensations. Suzuki, however, claims that the hallucinations elicited by mescaline reported by Huxley have no connection with the authentic Zen experience of satori: "In his book *The Doors of Perception*, Aldous Huxley described his own experience with the drug (mescaline). He saw a hitherto unknown world upon opening this 'door.' He then tried to relate this experience with that of Zen. Though Mr. Huxley had taken an interest in Zen, he did not have the guidance of a Zen teacher. He thus sets forth to writing a detailed description of the world of illusory vision brought on by mescaline" (RD, 129; SWS III, 234). Suzuki next claims: "Zen experience is quite often confused, even by some so-called Zen people, with the hallucinatory state (*makyō*)" (RD, 129; SWS III, 234). The main point in Suzuki's essay is that it is a mistake to confuse Zen satori with the maya-like illusory visions seen in the delirious state of *makyō* (魔境) and, then, to further identify *makyō* with the hallucinations of psychedelic experience thereby to erroneously infer that Zen satori and the altered states of psychedelic experience are the same. For Suzuki, mind-altering psychedelic drugs produce vivid hallucinations, but they do not lead to the Zen satori awakening of no-mind, which in its positive expression is the ordinary mind of the true self.

This is how Huxley responds to the objection made by some critics, that mystical rapture induced by psychedelic drugs cannot be an authentic experience of the divine, on the grounds that it is produced artificially by chemicals: "But, in one way or another, *all* of our experiences are chemically conditioned ... most contemplatives worked systematically to modify body chemistry, with a view to creating the internal conditions favorable to spiritual insight" (2009, 155). Huxley's polemic here is that *all* experiences are chemically conditioned, or as he otherwise puts it: "The brain is chemically controlled" (2009, 149). Moreover, Huxley mentions the discovery of naturally occurring psychoactive compounds in the human body, which have similar effects to mescalin intoxication (2009, 11). The brain of the human bodymind is a chemical factory that naturally produces serotonin, dopamine, endorphins, adrenaline, opioids, DMT, and other psychoactive agents that when released through spiritual practices, function to expand consciousness and trigger the most profound states of mystical enlightenment. Huxley thus argues that mystics, ascetics, and contemplatives, including the saints of all religions, have always attempted to elicit beatific experiences of spiritual illumination by modifying the biochemical conditions of the brain, through meditation, asceticism, fasting, isolation, flagellation, sleep deprivation, prolonged chanting, sensory deprivation, and other techniques but which can now be more effectively attained by the neuroscientific knowledge of pharmacology (2009, 155–156). Based on the philosophical view of Henri Bergson that the brain is *eliminative* and not productive in its primary functioning, Huxley maintains that psychedelic catalysts such as mescaline function to inhibit the "cerebral reducing valve," which normally *filters* the vast welter of information received by Mind-at-large so that it recedes into the subconscious, thereby to allow only a trickle of data funneled into the conscious mind for evolutionary purposes of survival through adaptation to the environment (2009, 26). Yet temporary "bypasses" to the cerebral reducing valve may be accessed through spiritual exercises, Zen meditation, hypnosis, or psychoactive drugs such as mescaline (2009, 24).

Suzuki criticizes Huxley's *The Doors to Perception* in an effort to discredit any association between Zen and "drugs." He thereby endeavors to distinguish the artificial drug-induced hallucinations of mescaline allegedly described by Huxley, from the natural and authentic Zen experience of satori, which is the realization of dharmakaya as the emptiness-suchness of things perceived just as they are by the ordinary mind of the true self. Yet it is clear that Suzuki has seriously misrepresented Huxley for the sake of his argument. At the outset of his work, Huxley reports: "The other world to which mescaline admitted me was not the world of visions; it existed out there, in what I could see with my eyes open. The great change was in the realm of objective fact" (2009, 16). Next, Huxley emphasizes that his spiritual experience under the influence of mescaline was the *Istigkeit* or "Is-ness" of Meister Eckhart, the great via negativa Christian mystic who describes the Godhead of nothingness as the *isness* of things (2009, 17).

Huxley discusses the Zen tradition of Huineng and Hakuin, Japanese landscape painting and haiku poetry, as well as the Zen mysticism of Suzuki himself. Indeed, in an effort to describe his psychedelic experience, Huxley adopts the Zen vocabulary of Suzuki, including Nirvana, as well as Dharma-Body (dharmakaya), Suchness (tathata), Not-self (anatman), Void (sunyata), Mind (citta), and Moksha (liberation). As Huxley begins to experience the psychotropic effects of mescaline, he ponders a Zen koan from Suzuki's writings: "And then I remembered a passage I had read in one of Suzuki's essays, 'What is the Dharma-Body of the Buddha?' (The Dharma-Body is another way of saying Mind, Suchness, the Void, the Godhead). The question is asked in a Zen monastery to an earnest and bewildered student" (2009, 18–19). In this koan, the student asks, "What is the Dharma-Body of the Buddha?" to which the Zen master responds: "The hedge at the bottom of the garden" (2009, 19). As Huxley clarifies, this means that the Dharma-Body of the Buddha, or the dharmakaya of emptiness, refers to the ordinary things of everyday life in their concrete particular "suchness" or *isness*. In this context, Huxley emphasizes that his mystical experience of the holy as *Mysterium tremendum* induced by mescaline intoxication was not characterized by illusory visions, dreams, or hallucinations but by an aesthetically immediate experience of the Dharma-Body of Buddha as "the Void": "In their art no less than in their religion, Taoists and the Zen Buddhist looked beyond visions to the Void, and through the Void at "the ten thousand things" of objective reality" (2009, 47). Thus, in the phenomenological account of his mescaline-induced psychedelic experience, Huxley never reports artificially produced hallucinations but always describes his encounter with "the Void" as the dharmakaya of emptiness-suchness, wherein the ten thousand things of nature and everyday life are revealed just as they are in their isness. Moreover, Huxley describes this lucid perception of things in the haecceity of their concrete particular suchness, thisness, or isness as the Zen experience of no-self, declaring: "This is how one ought to see, how things really are" (2009, 34–35).

Huxley goes on to explain his spiritual illumination triggered by psychedelic experience in terms of a depth psychology of the unconscious. In his analysis of the astonishing effects of mescaline on the human mind, Huxley describes how the psyche can be divided into various layers, including "consciousness," the "personal unconscious," the "collective unconscious" with its archetypes, and "the world of Visionary Experience" (2009, 84–85). By "the world of Visionary Experience," Huxley clarifies that he does not refer to illusory hallucinations but to the beatific vision of divine light, or what in *The Tibetan Book of the Dead* (Evans-Wentz, 1967) is termed the Clear Light of the Void. Moreover, by the ecstatic vision of clear light he refers both to the luminosity of the mind itself as well as the radiance of all effulgent things shining with the phosphorescent glow of an inner light. For Huxley, the illumination experience of awakening to dharmakaya emptiness as the clear light bliss of the void is "experiencing consciously something of that which, unconsciously, is always with us" (2009, 106). It must be further emphasized how for Huxley, the psychedelic experience of ultimate reality as clear light is to be described as superconsciousness. Huxley sums up his psychological understanding of mescaline-induced satori as follows: "The way to the superconscious is through the subconscious, and the way, or at least one of the ways, to the subconscious is through the chemistry of individual cells" (2009, 145). While he discusses various methods for bypassing the filtering mechanism of the cerebral reducing valve, including meditation, fasting, isolation, deep breathing, sensory deprivation, chanting, and hypnosis, Huxley views mescaline and other psychedelic drugs as the most direct and rapid means of access to the superconscious via the subconscious and from there to dharmakaya emptiness as clear light bliss of the void, whereupon the ten thousand things are disclosed just as they are in their isness. Thus like Suzuki, Huxley analyzes the beatific experience of illumination as opening to our deeper unconscious in superconsciousness. Yet at the level of practice, the difference is that for Huxley, the way to the superconscious is through the subconscious, and the most direct way to the subconscious is to radically alter brain chemistry through pharmacological science using psychedelic catalysts. For Suzuki, however, the shortcut path to satori as awakening to the cosmic Unconscious in superconsciousness is Zen koan meditation, especially focused concentration of the whole bodymind on the keyword MU!

Epilogue

D. T. Suzuki and Jean Gebser on Zen Satori as a Shift to the Integral Structure of Consciousness as Openness, Radiance, and Transparency

Suzuki's account of levels of the human psyche, including the cosmic Unconscious, collective unconscious, personal unconscious, semi-unconscious, and rational ego-consciousness, together with the integration of all these levels in Zen satori as superconsciousness, approximates the mutation of structures of consciousness articulated by the brilliant German-Swiss philosopher Jean Gebser (1905–1973). To begin with, Gebser was among the distinguished group of scholars regularly attending the Eranos Conferences in Switzerland, including C. G. Jung (archetypal psychology), Mircea Eliade (comparative religions), Gershom Scholem (Kabbalah), Henry Corbin (Islamic Sufism), Martin Heidegger (phenomenology), Suzuki (Zen), and other luminaries. In his masterwork *The Ever-Present Origin* (*Ursprung und Gegenwart*, 1949), Gebser uses Husserlian phenomenology to describe the constitutive "structures of consciousness" unfolding in the history of European civilization, including the archaic, magical, mythical, mental-rational, and newly emerging mutation toward the ego-free aperspectival/arational-integral structure (1985).[1] Transpersonal psychologist Ken Wilber, it should be noted, adopts Gebser's structures of consciousness to describe the emergent levels constituting the total "spectrum of consciousness" in his own integral philosophy.[2] According to Gebser's phenomenological account, mutation to the new ego-free integral structure of consciousness in European history is to be described as an awakening to the infinite openness of transparency, clarity, and diaphany. In Gebser's words: "We must, in other words, achieve the new integral structure without forfeiting the efficient forms of previous structures. . . . Transparency (diaphaneity) is the form of the manifestation (epiphany) of the spiritual" (1985, 299). Gebser further asserts that mutation to the nascent integral structure "opens space through the capacity of rendering it transparent, and thereby supersedes nihilistic 'emptiness,' re-attaining openness in an intensified [integral] consciousness structure." (1985, 353). He continues: "The openness that is transfigured into plentitude . . . does not lead to emptiness, to *nihil*, to [negative] nothingness or *nada*, but to transparency" (1985, 529). Moreover, this emergence of the new integral structure is "the mutation from an unconscious openness to a conscious openness, whose essence is . . . diaphaneity, that is, spiritual transparency" (1985, 436). He further clarifies that this awakening to the integral structure of openness and transparency "must not be equated with a relapse into unconsciousness" but is rather a leap to "superconsciousness" (1985, 42–43).

According to Gebser, an Eastern paradigm of this ego-free arational integral structure of consciousness is the Zen satori described by Suzuki: "In a conversation in Kitakamakura, Japan, in 1961, the aged Zen-master Daisetzu Teitaro Suzuki emphatically agreed with me that 'Satori' must in no way be confused with Indic 'Samadhi!' Satori is one possibility inherent in the arational (integral) consciousness structure for entering or participating in time freedom" (1985, 243, n. 84). Gebser sums up Suzuki's view of Zen satori as a "super-wakefulness" to what he describes as the leap or mutation to a new emergent structure, beyond the egoistic mental-rational structure, to the ego-free arational integral structure of consciousness as transparent wholeness: "Zen students seek to free themselves from it [the egoistic mental-rational structure] in order to attain, ultimately, a sudden leap or mutation to a satori, an elevated super-wakefulness of consciousness, evoked by one of the seemingly 'senseless' *koans* (a kind of paradoxical sentence). We have defined this consciousness structure of integrative effectiveness as the 'arational-integral'" (1985, 222–223). During his trip to Sarnath, India, where the historical Buddha delivered his first sermons after entering nirvana, Gebser himself had a consummatory experience of sudden enlightenment, described as a "super-wakefulness" to the clear light of radiant transparent openness. Gebser further describes his beatific experience of spiritual illumination as a "happening with crystal clarity in everyday life," which was simultaneously a "transfiguration and irradiation of the indescribable, unearthly, transparent 'Light' (Feuerstein, 1987, 173)."[3] As reported in *Structures of Consciousness: The Genius of Jean Gebser* by Georg Feuerstein, the eminent scholar of Indian yoga theory and practice: "Gebser discloses that he had enjoyed an experience that D. T. Suzuki later confirmed as an instance of *satori*" (1987, 173). Feuerstein adds: "For Gebser his moment of *satori* or 'enlightenment,' was a confirmation of the integral orientation of Zen Buddhism, which he had previously presumed, mainly on the strength of the works by Zen master D T. Suzuki" (1987, 174).

It should be remembered that Suzuki, like Gebser, distinguishes nihilism or nullifying emptiness from the emptiness-fullness of Zen satori and that one of his favorite synonyms for sunyata or emptiness in its positive designation is "transparency." Suzuki remarks: "The aim of Zen is . . . to return to the original state of purity and transparency" (ZJC, 359). Elsewhere, he says that in Zen satori one becomes "open, light and transparent" (AIZB, 47). Again, Suzuki described his own satori as a nondual experience of both himself and the natural world as "transparent" (SWS I, 209–210; FZ, 11). Similarly, in his phenomenological description of the ego-free integral structure of consciousness, Gebser says that "the world and we ourselves — the whole — become transparent" (1985, 263). Gebser's phenomenological description of mutation to the integral structure, like the philosophical psychology of Suzuki, thereby explains Zen satori as a leap from an unconscious openness to a fully conscious openness characterized by the diaphaneity or transparency of superconsciousness. Moreover, just as Gebser describes how the new integral-arational structure of consciousness as diaphaneity or transparency has become increasingly disclosed in twentieth-century European art and literature, Suzuki's Zen aestheticism likewise demonstrates how the transparent openness of absolute nothingness is manifested in traditional Japanese artforms developed under the aegis of Zen, such as haiku poetry, noh theater, and sumie ink painting.

Suzuki's Zen-Kegon understanding of satori as breakthrough to *mushin* or no-mind and *muga* or nonego as the cosmic Unconscious further approximates Gebser's mutation to the "aperspectival-integral structure" in that it designates a radical shift beyond the narrow uniperspectival vision of the rational-mental structure that sees things from only the single linear viewpoint determined by a fixed ego to an ego-free *multi*perspectival nonlinear vision of things as simultaneously viewed from multiple sides in the transparent openness of the dharmadhatu as the interconnected matrix of Indra's net. For according to Zen-Kegon Buddhism, in the transparent openness of the dharmadhatu as the resplendent Jeweled Net of Indra, every jewel in the dynamic interconnected network of relationships is like an illuminated mirror that simultaneously reflects and is also reflected by all the other jewels so as to be seen from every possible viewpoint thereby to multiply the beauty, splendor, and majesty of the universe ad infinitum.

From the standpoint of Gebser's phenomenology of structures of consciousness, Suzuki's account of Zen satori designates a leap to an elevated super-wakefulness that transcends and incorporates all previous structures, finally mutating from the egocentric perspectivism of the mental-rational structure to the ego-free aperspectival/arational-integral structure of consciousness, described in terms of its "openness," "radiance," and "transparency." Suzuki thus proclaims that while the ego and its imputed subject-object dualism make the Unconscious unconscious, nondual Zen satori makes the Unconscious fully conscious in superconsciousness, whereupon through Zen koan practices such as focusing the whole bodymind on the keyword "MU," one awakens to the diaphaneity, clarity, and luminosity of spacelike dharmakaya emptiness or absolute nothingness as the vast expanse of radiant transparent openness.

Abbreviations for the Works of D. T. Suzuki and Related Texts

AFM	*Aśvaghosha's Discourse on the Awakening of Faith in the Mahayana*
AIZB	*An Introduction to Zen Buddhism*
ARS	"A Reply [to Hu Shi] from D. T. Suzuki"
AZ	*The Awakening of Zen*
AZL	*A Zen Life: D. T. Suzuki Remembered*
BIL	*Buddha of Infinite Light*
DT	*Daisetsu tsurezuregusa*
EZB	*Essays on Zen Buddhism* (3 volumes)
FZ	*The Field of Zen*
FZAF	"Foreword" to *Zen in the Art of Flower Arrangement*
HRN	"How to Read Nishida"
IBN	"Is Buddhism Nihilistic?"
IZAA	"Introduction" to *Zen in the Art of Archery*
JS	*Japanese Spirituality*
LCP	"The Life of a Certain Person"
LS	*The Lankavatara Sutra*
LSE	*The Lankavatara Sutra: An Epitomized Version*
LZ	*Living by Zen*
M	無心と言うこと、[*Mushin to iu koto*]
MCB	*Mysticism: Christian and Buddhist*
MZB	*Manual of Zen Buddhism*
OIMB	*On Indian Mahayana Buddhism*
OMB	*Outlines of Mahayana Buddhism*
PM	"Preface" in *Mumonkan*
PPOH	"The Place of Peace in Our Hearts"
RD	"Religion and Drugs"
RHD	"Review of Heinrich Dumoulin: *A History of Zen Buddhism*"
RI	"Reason and Intuition"
SBN	*Swedenborg: Buddha of the North*
SDZ	鈴木大拙全集 [*Suzuki Daisetsu zenshū*]
SK	"Shinran and Kierkegaard"
SLS	*Studies in the Lankavatara Sutra*
SU	"Self the Unattainable"

SWS	*Selected Works of D. T. Suzuki* (4 volumes)
SZIP	*Sengai: The Zen of Ink and Paper*
SZ	*Studies in Zen*
TPZA	"Preface" to *Zen for Americans*
TZBM	*The Training of the Zen Buddhist Monk*
WI	"What Is the 'I'?"
WZ	*What is Zen?*
WZW	"The Way Zazen Works"
ZA	*Zen for Americans*
ZB	*Zen Buddhism: Selected Writings of D.T. Suzuki*
ZBIJC	*Zen Buddhism and Its Influence on Japanese Culture*
ZDNM	*The Zen Doctrine of No Mind*
ZJC	*Zen and Japanese Culture*
ZKMA	*The Zen Koan as a Means of Attaining Enlightenment*
ZNB	禅と日本文化 [*Zen and Japanese Culture*]
ZP	*Zen Buddhism and Psychoanalysis*
ZRHS	"Zen: A Reply to Hu Shih"
ZSB	"The Zen Sect of Buddhism"
ZTZ	禅のつれずれ [*Zen no tsurezure*]

Notes

Introduction

1. The best scholarly overview of Suzuki's life and thought in English is Richard M. Jaffe's introduction to his edited volume *Selected Works of D. T. Suzuki, Volume 1: Zen* (2015, xi-lvi).

2. Insightful critiques have been leveled against Suzuki's Zen by scholars, including Louis de La Valée Pousin (1908), Hu Shih (1953), Peter Dale (1986), David Dilworth (1978), Thomas Kasulis (1981), Robert Magliola (1986), Bernard Faure (1993), Robert Sharf (1994, 1995), Urs App (1995), the Critical Buddhism of Matsumoto Shirō and Hakamaya Noriyaki (Paul Swanson and Jamie Hubbard, 1997), Dale S. Wright (2000), Judith Snodgrass (2003), Brian Victoria (2006), David McMahan (2008), Yamada Shōji (2009), Christopher Ives and Ichikawa Hakugen (Ives, 2009), and others.

3. Sueki Fumihiko here refers to a conference "Reflections on D. T. Suzuki: Commemorating the Fiftieth Anniversary of His Death," December 5 to 6, 2016, held at Nichibunken (International Research Center for Japanese Studies) in Kyoto, Japan. Some of the papers delivered at this commemoration event were published in *The Eastern Buddhist: New Series*, Vol. 47, No. 2, 2016. For the proceedings of this conference, see *Beyond Zen* (2022) edited by Breen et al.

4. Recent studies on Suzuki's thought include Avram Alpert's *Global Origins of the Modern Self, from Montaigne to Suzuki* (2019), the final chapter of which provides a non-Eurocentric, creolized, deracialized, and decolonized reading of Suzuki's Zen notion of global selfhood, thereby including Suzuki within an expanded canon of world philosophy. Rossa O. Muireartaigh's *The Zen Buddhist Philosophy of D. T. Suzuki* (2022) has provided a much needed overview of Suzuki's philosophical writings that is extremely concise, yet rigorous and insightful. *Beyond Zen: D. T. Suzuki and the Modern Transformation of Buddhism* (2022) edited by Breen et al. contains a valuable collection of essays on various aspects of Suzuki's work.

5. While Richard M. Jaffe is the general editor of *The Selected Works of D. T. Suzuki*, each individual work has its own volume editor. *Volume I: Zen* (2015) is edited by Richard M. Jaffe; *Volume II: Pure Land* (2015) is edited by James C. Dobbins; *Volume III: Comparative Religion* (2016) is coedited by Jeff Wilson and Tomoe Moriya; and *Volume IV: Buddhist Studies* (2021) is edited by Mark L. Blum. In addition to the carefully selected writings of Suzuki, the volume editors have contributed outstanding introductory essays using the most updated research from contemporary Zen and Japanese Buddhist studies.

Chapter 1

1. Regarding this Dunhuang manuscript, Suzuki notes: "This discourse ascribed to Bodhidharma is not mentioned in any of the Zen histories we have at present and there is no way to decide its authenticity" (EZB III, 8–9, fn. 3).

2. See my review article, Jackson, *Buddhadāsa*.

3. Hisamatsu's view on the unconscious stands in agreement with the Kyoto School philosopher Nishitani Keiji. In a passage from Religion and Nothingness, Nishitani argues that religion is not based on the preconscious or subconscious (1982, 13; 宗教とは何か, 1961, 18). As said by Nishitani in this passage, religion cannot be explained by "the viewpoint of preconscious life and sympathy" (*izen no seimei ya kannō no ba*, 以前の生命や感應の場) (宗教とは何か, 1961, 18). For Nishitani, religion is not a return to the preconscious or subconscious but instead requires a breakthrough to the more encompassing Zen Buddhist standpoint of sunyata or emptiness, otherwise referred to as the field of absolute nothingness.

4. Nishihira explains that Izutsu's 1969 lecture at the Eranos conference in Switzerland was a response to Suzuki's Zen lecture on *mushin* or no-mind delivered at previous Eranos conferences in 1953 and 1954 ("Subjectivity of 'Mu-shin,'" 2015, 2).

5. As summed up by Barbara O'Brien in her concise history of Zen titled *The Circle of the Way*, modern historical scholarship demonstrates that this contest between Huineng and Shenxiu is most likely fictional, as are many of the stories and legends about the early Chan patriarchs, Bodhidharma, and even the Buddha himself (2019, 76). The debate between Huineng and Shenxiu is meant to show two competing notions of Buddha nature, or tathagatagarbha. Huineng's verse teaches that Buddha nature is already present and only needs to be realized through sudden awakening, whereas Shenxiu's verse teaches that Buddha nature exists within us only as a seed or potential that must be gradually cultivated through arduous practice.

6. In his early 1907 work *Outlines of Mahayana Buddhism*, Suzuki attempts to correct Western misunderstandings of Zen and Mahayana Buddhism as nihilistic and, at this point in his writings, associates nihilism with "absolute nothingness" or "absolute void." Suzuki maintains that sunyata or emptiness "must never be understood in the sense of annihilation or absolute nothingness, for nihilism is as much condemned by Buddhism as naïve realism" (OMB, 193). In his later work, however, Suzuki employs the distinction made by Nishida and the Kyoto School of modern Japanese philosophy, between nihilism as "relative nothingness" and true sunyata or emptiness as "absolute nothingness," comprehended as the plenary vacuum where emptiness is fullness and fullness is emptiness.

7. After World War II, Suzuki returned to the US as a celebrity at which time he began giving public lectures and teaching classes at Columbia University in New York City. The main topic of Suzuki's popular lectures and classes was Kegon (C. Huayan; Skt. Avataṃsaka) Buddhist philosophy (Larson, *Where the Heart Beats*, 170).

8. His 1960 essay "How to Read Nishida" in Nishida Kitarō's *A Study of Good*, Suzuki explains how toward the end of his life, Nishida took a new interest in Kegon (Huayan) philosophy and that they often discussed Kegon Buddhism together. Thus, Nishida would come to articulate his early Zen-colored notion of "pure experience," as well as its reformulation in his later Zen philosophy of "absolute nothingness," as the locus (*basho*) of unimpeded harmonic interpenetration between multiplicity and unity or objectivity and subjectivity (HRN, iii–vi).

9. This passage makes an interesting cross-cultural reference to Hegel, arguing that the Kegon Buddhist notion of *riji muge* or "interpenetration between particular and universal" is akin to the "concrete universals" of Hegel's dialectical philosophy. Suzuki thus says that the "doctrine of interpenetration . . . is a thought somewhat similar to the Hegelian philosophy of concrete universals" (SWS IV, 155).

10. Suzuki's discussion of "just enough" in the Zen *wabi*-style of tea (ZJC, 295) is a reference to the saying engraved on the stone water basin of Ryōanji and other Zen temples: "I know what 'just enough' means" (*ware tada taru wo shiru*, 吾唯足を知る).

11. Suzuki makes reference of this synaesthetic experience of interfusion between the multivariate sense modes in his recorded 1958 university lecture *Zen no tesugaku ni tsuite* (On Zen Philosophy). In this lecture Suzuki discusses how Zen satori is a nondual experience of undiscriminated totality where there is no division between conscious and unconscious, subject and object, or the various sense modes, so that one "sees with the ears," and "hears with the eyes" (D. T. Suzuki: CD Audio Resources, 2017; Disc 4/Track 4).

12. Suzuki's view of synaesthesia thus coincides with the medical research of Dr. Richard Cytowic, who concludes: "In synesthesia, a brain process that is normally unconscious becomes bared in consciousness" (*The Man Who Tasted Shapes*, 166). Dr. Cytowic further gives personal testimony of how Zen meditation cultivates the experience of synesthesia as interpenetration of multiplicity-into-unity.

13. Suzuki's translation of *The Awakening of Faith* renders *ālaya-vijñāna* as "all-conserving mind" (AFM, 43, 61, 75, 151). In Y. S. Hakeda's translation of this text, *ālaya-vijñāna* is rendered as the "storehouse consciousness" (1967). Hakeda's translation explicitly identifies the *ālaya-vijñāna* or storehouse consciousness with the subconscious mind, rendering it "the mind [subject to the influence] of karma [operating] in subconsciousness" (1967, 89; brackets in original text). For both Suzuki and Hakeda, the *ālaya-vijñāna* or storehouse consciousness is the subconscious mind functioning as the universal repository for all karmically inherited *vāsanās* or habit-energies in an ancient stream of accumulated memories flowing from the beginningless past.

14. See Albert Low's commentary on Hakuin's text *The Four Ways of Knowing of an Awakened Person* (2006), where he provides a detailed analysis of Hakuin's view of *ālaya-vijñāna* as the Great Mirror Knowing. As explained by Low, Hakuin clarifies that after the "turning around" (*parāvritti*), which occurs in the Zen awakening of kensho or satori, the *ālaya-vijñāna* is cleansed, purified, and transformed, whereupon one realizes the Great Perfect Mirror Wisdom as the boundless light of dharmakaya emptiness (2006, 29–30).

15. Although in his Zen writings Suzuki generally ignores, dismisses, or criticizes the Sōtō tradition due to sectarian preference for Rinzai Zen, authentic Sōtō Zen theory and practice as transmitted by Dōgen would later be brought to America in 1959 by the Zen monk Shunryu Suzuki Roshi (1904–1971), author of *Zen Mind Beginner's Mind* (1970), who founded the San Francisco Zen Center and Tessajara Mountain Retreat Center in California.

16. In *Zen Master Hakuin*, Philip Yampolsky explains: "The exact details of the koan system Hakuin used are not clearly known. . . . It emphasized the use of the *Mu* koan and later the Sound of the Single Hand for the initial awakening" (1971, 15). Thus, while initially Hakuin's Zen kōan practice system emphasized focusing on the keyword Mu, he later introduced his own kōan, "The Sound of One Hand" (*sekishu no onjō*, 隻手の音声).

17. In *Oretagama* Hakuin claims that he learned his "introspection" and "melted butter" techniques of *tanden soku* as methods of breathing down into the *tanden* or navel energy center at the lower abdomen from a reclusive Daoist yoga adept called Hakuyū living in the remote mountain caves of Japan (Yampolsky, *Zen Master Hakuin*, 30–32). The Daoist *neidan* or alchemical yoga of inner heat that Hakuin learned from the Daoist master Hakuyū has many similarities to the *tummo* or "inner fire" yoga of Tibetan Vajrayana Buddhism. See *The Bliss of Inner Fire* by Lama Yeshe (Boston: Wisdom Publications, 1998). As explained by Meido Moore in *Hidden Zen*, Hakuin taught meditative techniques of full deep breathing (*tanden no soku*) focused on the *tanden* (丹田) or navel as the energy center in the *hara* or lower abdomen, including both "introspection" (*naikan*, 内観) and the "soft butter method" (*nanso no hō*, 軟酥の法). Instructions for Hakuin's abdominal breathing exercises, and the soft butter or healing ointment technique, are also given by Julian Daizan Skinner in *Practical Zen*.

18. Elsewhere, Suzuki also makes reference to *The Practice of the Presence of God* by Brother Lawrence, a seventeenth-century Carmelite friar who taught one to abide in the holy presence of God by continuous conversation with Him in everyday life (ZB, 23).

19. The term "kenotic" here refers to the biblical tradition of *kenōsis* (Philippians, 2:5–11) or the self-emptying of God in Jesus Christ for universal salvation. In the writings of Nishida Kitarō and the Kyoto School of modern Japanese philosophy, comparisons between Christian *kenōsis* or "self-emptying" and Buddhist *śūnyatā* or "emptiness" are central themes for interfaith dialogue.

20. Suzuki further develops this comparison between the doctrine of parinamana or transference of merit in Mahayana Buddhism and vicarious sacrifice of Jesus on the Cross for the sins of all mankind in Christianity, in his essay "Development of Mahayana Buddhism" (SWS IV, 72–76).

Chapter 2

1. In the West, everyday aesthetics is exemplified by John Dewey's protest against the "compartmentalization" of art into museums, exhibitions, or galleries in separation

from the ordinary activities of daily life. Dewey's philosophy of art is therefore directed toward "recovering the continuity of esthetic experience with normal processes of living" (1980, 10). For Dewey, the arts should be understood as "celebrations . . . of the things of ordinary experience" (1980, 11). The Japanese tradition of "everyday aesthetics" has been admirably developed by Saito Yuriko (2007).

2. Viglielmo explains that in Nishida Kitarō's essay on aesthetics "An Explanation of Beauty" (Bi no setsumei, 美の説明, 1900), the Zen colored term *muga* (無我) or nonego is best translated as "ecstasy." See Viglielmo, "Nishida Kitarō.

Chapter 3

1. In *Zen and Psychoanalysis*, Suzuki refers to this film as "the Magnificent Seven," describing it as "a Japanese film play, recently introduced to American audiences" (ZP, 21). However, *The Magnificent Seven* (1960) was actually the title an Old West–style remake of Kurosawa Akira's 1954 film *The Seven Samurai*, which was released the same year as *Zen and Psychoanalysis* (1960) by Suzuki et al. However, in his discussion of this film, Suzuki is clearly speaking about the workings of unconscious intuition developed by the master swordsman as depicted in Kurosawa's Japanese film, *The Seven Samurai*, and not the fast draw gunslinger cowboys of its Western remake.

2. This famous scene from Akira's 1954 film *The Seven Samurai* was inspired by a tale about the master swordsman Tsukahara Bokuden (1489–1571), which Suzuki summarizes in his chapter on "Zen and the Samurai" from *Zen and Japanese Culture* (ZJC, 75–76).

3. Suzuki also wrote the introduction to *Zen in the Art of Flower Arrangement* by Gustie L. Herrigel, the wife of Eugen Herrigel (FZAF, xi), where he gives a similar Zen interpretation of *ikebana* (生花) or flower arrangement as a religio-aesthetic path to satori based on his psychology of a deeper unconscious mind (FZAF, xi).

4. Yamada Shōji exposes a serious duplicity, hypocrisy, and inconsistency in Suzuki's ethnocentric attitude, not only toward Herrigel but also toward all Westerners who have written on Zen. Suzuki gives a strong endorsement in his introduction to Herrigel's *Zen in the Art of Archery*: "In this wonderful little book, Mr. Herrigel, a German philosopher who, came to Japan and took up the practice of archery toward an understanding of Zen, gives an illuminating account of his own experience" (IZAA, x). Yamada, however, then points out how during a conversation with the Zen scholar Hisamatsu Shin'ichi in 1959, Suzuki divulges his true feelings: "Hisamatsu: What about Herrigel? Suzuki: Herrigel is trying to get to Zen, but he hasn't grasped Zen itself. Have you ever seen a book written by a Westerner that has?" (cited by Yamada, 2009, 208). Suzuki here expresses an arrogant, condescending, and dismissive attitude of sheer contempt toward all Western scholars and practitioners of Zen, while also exposing an aspect of his character that inclines toward Japanese exceptionalism, ethnic chauvinism, and ultranationalism.

5. In *Zen for Americans* (*Sermons of A Buddhist Abbot*, 1906/1974) written by Shaku Sōen as translated and modified by Suzuki, this same passage on Buddhist ethics from

Dhammapada is cited: "Commit no wrong, but good deeds do, And let thy heart be pure, All Buddha's teach this truth" (ZA, 69). Suzuki's Zen teacher Shaku Sōen clarifies the message of this verse is as follows: "Let a man do what is good and avoid what is bad and have his heart as pure as he can of all egotistic impulses and desires" (ZA, 70). Moreover, all deeds of goodness flow from "sympathy" (AZ, 74), "pure-heartedness" (AZ, 74), and "a heart of compassion" (AZ, 177). Here it is taught that Buddhist ethics is to do good and avoid evil and that to do good is to act selflessly from a pure heart of sympathy, kindness, and compassion. Nonetheless, in this same work, with the spirit of ultranationalism Shaku Sōen defends and praises Japan's actions in the Russo-Japanese war fought in 1904–1905 between the Russian and Japanese empires over their rival imperialist ambitions in Korea and Manchuria (TPZA, 201).

Chapter 4

1. In an illuminating essay Roy Starrs (2022) emphasizes how the Unconscious is the source of "inspiration" for haiku poetry in D. T. Suzuki's Zen interpretation of Japanese literature.

2. Although Suzuki, a representative of Rinzi Zen Buddhism, describes how Zen-inspired haiku poetry celebrates the ephemeral beauty of perishability, he does not thematize the Japanese aesthetic category of *mono no aware* or the sadness and beauty of evanescence. By contrast, *The Zen Poetry of Dōgen* (2005) by Steven Heine analyzes how the poetry of Dōgen (1200–1253), the founder of Sōtō Zen, expresses the primacy of temporal becoming with the doctrines of *uji* (有時) or "being-time" and *mujō busshō* (無常仏性) or "impermanence-buddha-nature" as well as its corresponding Japanese religio-aesthetic principle of *mono no aware* (物の哀れ) or the pathos of things.

3. In his work *Long Strange Journey: On Modern Zen, Zen Art, and Other Predicaments* (2011), Gregory Levine discusses the difficulty in establishing what is "Zen art," who has been influenced by Zen art, and what is the extent of the relation between Zen and art in traditional Japanese culture.

4. In *Zen and Oriental Art*, Hugo Munsterberg describes the influence of Suzuki's Zen, not only on the new wave artists in New York City on the East Coast but also on West Coast artists in San Francisco and Seattle (1965, 142).

5. Zaehner, *Zen, Drugs and Mysticism*, 125.

6. Margaret Salinger, the daughter of J. D. Salinger, confirms that her father was studying Zen before *The Catcher in the Rye*, that he developed a friendship with Suzuki, and that through Suzuki he became extremely knowledgeable about Zen (2001, 11).

7. Margaret Salinger, the daughter of J. D. Salinger, confirms that her father was studying Zen before The Catcher in the Rye, that he developed a friendship with Suzuki, and that through Suzuki he became extremely knowledgeable about Zen (2001, 11).

Chapter 5

1. James was a member of the Society for Psychical Research founded in 1882 by Frederic Myers.
2. The largest New Thought organization in the world today is *Seichō-no-Ie* (生長の家), founded by Taniguchi Masaharu. In his major work *Truth of Life* (Volume 8), Taniguchi Masaharu explains his New Thought view that the human mind is constituted by the conscious, subconscious, and superconscious minds (1962, 139–140).
3. See John Haller, *The History of New Thought*.

Chapter 6

1. Avram Alpert remarks on Suzuki's interest in Kant's philosophy and use of Kantian vocabulary, adding: "This was not only through his engagement with Paul Carus, but also in his own reading. Suzuki's library in Kamakura retains to this day some dozen volumes on or by Kant" (2019, 256; 375, fn. 46).

Chapter 7

1. For Suzuki's detailed linguistic analysis of Yakusan Igen's koan in terms of its threefold distinctions of *shiryō* or "to think," *fushiryō* or "not-thinking, and *hishiryō* or "the Unthinkable" [the Unconscious], see Suzuki (SWS I, 112).
2. James Heisig points out that the Kyoto School philosopher Nishitani Keiji was resistant to Jungian depth psychology and its Japanese development by Kawai Hayao: "As an indication of Nishitani's resistance to overtures from psychologists, see his discussions with the Jungians David Miller and Kawai Hayao, where Nishitani [1988] plays skeptic in a playful but decisive manner" (2001, 339).
3. Stretcher gives an edifying interpretation of Murakami's fiction in terms of the French psychoanalyst Jacques Lacan's "semiotic unconscious" or what Lacan terms the "unconscious Other," as the unconscious system of language that interacts with the conscious self (2002a, 84).

Chapter 8

1. My discussion of Rancière's political aesthetics is indebted to Tanke's book, *Jacques Rancière: An Introduction. Philosophy, Politics, Aesthetics* (2011). The discussion of Rancière's three "regimes" of art, and its relation to Foucault's three epistemic orders (*epistemes*) or conceptual grids, is likewise based on Tanke's book *Foucault's Philosophy of Art* (2009).

2. In contradiction to his claim that the Zen aestheticism of tea establishes a democratic spirit of nonhierarchical equality beyond class distinctions, Suzuki elsewhere states: "Zen is meant for the élite, for specially gifted minds and not for the masses. . . . Unless aristocracy in one form or another is admitted and to a certain extent encouraged, the artistic impulses are suppressed and no religious geniuses will be forthcoming" (TZBM, 114).

3. Aside from the topological structure of the unconscious as a Möbius band, there are also many other significant points of convergence between Lacanian psychoanalysis and Zen, including Lacan's notion of the empty subject, and the radical nature of his short therapy session. Lacan himself often notes the resemblance of his own psychotherapy to Zen (1988b, Book I, 1; 1975, 115; 2002, 98).

4. Nik Fox clarifies how in later works such as his biographical study of Flaubert titled *The Family Idiot*, Sartre reintroduces a Freudian notion of the unconscious. See Nik Fox, *The New Sartre*, 24.

5. Influenced by Suzuki, the modern Japanese philosopher Izutsu Toshihiko likewise argues that Qingyuan's koan of mountain/no mountains/real mountains is a threefold process of articulation/non-articulation/articulation-in-nonarticulation, wherein the third stage of *mushin* or no-mind is the satori awareness of the self and all things as being "ontologically transparent" (1977, 125–128), a stage he also identifies in the same text as consciousness of the not-conscious in supra-consciousness (1977, 15–17).

Chapter 9

1. Influenced by various Eastern and Western traditions, including Suzuki's Zen doctrine of the Unconscious and the Yogacara Buddhist theory of eight levels of consciousness, Wilber developed his own map of the psyche and theory of the unconscious. Wilber's transpersonal psychology based on his full spectrum model consciousness enumerates five basic types of the unconscious: the ground unconscious, the archaic unconscious, the submergent unconscious, the embedded unconscious, and the emergent unconscious (1996a, 97–108).

2. *Transpersonal Psychologies* (1975) edited by Charles Tart, examines both Zen Buddhism and the work of Gurdjieff as systems of "transpersonal psychology," including chapter 4 on "Zen Buddhism" by Claire Myer Owens and chapter 7 on "Gurdjieff" by Kathleen Riordan. Insofar as French psychotherapist Hubert Benoit synthesizes Suzuki's modern Zen psychology of the Unconscious with the work of Gurdjieff, I have included him in the section on Transpersonal Psychology.

3. Segal was an artist, a friend of Suzuki, a student of various Zen masters, as well as a disciple of Gurdjieff. The life, art, and philosophy of William Segal is showcased in a documentary by filmmaker Ken Burns, titled *Seeing, Searching, Being — William Segal* (2010), now available on YouTube, as well as in DVD format (Mystic Fire Videos, PBS). This documentary explores Segal's paintings and his practice of Gurdjieff's "self-remembering" technique, as well as his views on Zen and Zen art.

4. Gurdjieff's sacred dance movements and music influenced by the whirling dervishes of Sufi mysticism are showcased in the grand finale of *Meetings with Remarkable Men* (1979), a film biopic on the early life of Gurdjieff directed by Peter Brooks and now available on DVD/Blueray formats. Also, performances of Gurdjieff's sacred dances and music can by viewed on YouTube.

5. In *Hidden Minds: A History of the Unconscious*, F. Tallis recounts how the literary-artistic movement of Romanticism in the tradition of William Wordsworth and Samuel Coleridge explored the unconscious as "the font of inspiration and creativity" (2012, 6). Moreover, for Romantics such as Coleridge, "the opium poppy" was regarded as "Nature's passport to the unconscious" (2012, 7). However, as discussed by neurologist Dr. James Austin MD in *Zen and the Brain*, the human brain itself naturally manufactures its own opiates (1999, 212). From here, Austin points out the relation of opium to the Buddhist path of emancipation from suffering: "Consider three items. Opiates have relieved suffering for ages. Marx is passé, but his dictum lingers: religion is 'the opium of the people.' Finally, the Buddha's central message, as summed up in the key phrase, 'suffering do I teach, and the way out of suffering'" (Austin, 1999, 213).

Like Suzuki's essay "Religion and Drugs" (RD, 129; SWS III, 233), Austin thus notes the ironic connection between Buddhism and Marx's description of religion as an opiate. But Austin adds: "Are these items [Buddhism and opioids] separate? Or could this message — the relief of suffering — be connected with the opiate-like substances found recently in our own brains?" (Austin, 1999, 213).

6. In his 1962 book on psychedelic experience called *The Joyous Cosmology: Adventures in the Chemistry of Consciousness*, Alan Watts writes: "The Westerner must borrow such words as *samadhi* or *moksha* from the Hindus, or *satori* or *kensho* from the Japanese, to describe the experience of oneness with the universe" (2013, 107).

7. See "'Drugs and Buddhism' — A Symposium" in *The Eastern Buddhist* (New Series, vol. 4. no. 2, October 1971]. The symposium on Zen and psychedelics includes essays by Suzuki, Watts, Ray Jordan, Robert Aitken Roshi, Richard Leavitt, and Ueda Shizuteru. *The Eastern Buddhist* is a journal that began in 1921 under the editorship of Suzuki. After Suzuki's death in 1966, the journal was continued under the editorship of Nishitani Keiji (1900–1990), Abe Masao (1915–2006), and other scholars associated with the Kyoto School of modern Japanese philosophy.

Epilogue

1. In Gebser's phenomenological description of the *leap* or mutation to the newly emerging aperspectival-arational integral structure of consciousness in European history, the prefix "a-" does not signify a negation but rather "freedom from" as well as "freedom towards." Hence the *a*rational is neither irrational nor rationalistic, but "freedom from" narrow egocentric rationalism, as well as "freedom towards" the new integral structure of transparency. Likewise, for Gebser, *a*perspectival is neither unperspectival nor perspectival, but "freedom from" a single fixed egocentric perspective, thereby signifying

a transparent openness that is able to simultaneously view things from multiple perspectives. Gebser's mutation to the new arational-aperspectival structure of integral consciousness in European history designates a breakthrough to radiant transparent openness, which is neither egoistic nor egoless but *ego-free*, thereby designating "freedom-from" both the egocentrism of Descartes' *cogito* as well as the "egolessness" of previous structures.

2. Wilber adopts Gebser's structures of consciousness to articulate his own "full spectrum" model consciousness in a number of works, for instance, *Up from Eden* (1996b, 27–28).

3. For a scholarly account of Gebser's life and works, including his encounters with Suzuki and discussions of Zen satori as a leap to the ego-free aperspectival/arational integral structure of consciousness as "transparency," see Feuerstein's *Structures of Consciousness: The Genius of Jean Gebser.*

Bibliography

Selected Works by D. T. Suzuki

AFM (1900) 2007. *Aśvaghoṣa's Discourse on the Awakening of Faith in the Mahayana.* Translated by D. T. Suzuki. Open Court Press. Republished by Forgotten Books.

AIZB (1934) 1960. *An Introduction to Zen Buddhism.* With a forward by Carl Jung. Grove Press.

ARS 1961. "A Reply [to Hu Shih] from D. T. Suzuki." *Encounter* (October): 55–58.

AZ 1980. *The Awakening of Zen.* Edited by Christmas Humphreys. Prajna Press.

AZL 1995. *A Zen Life: D. T. Suzuki Remembered.* Edited by Abe Masao. Weatherhill.

BIL 1998. *Buddha of Infinite Light.* Shambhala Publications.

DT 1966. *Daisetsu tsurezuregusa.* Yomiuri Shinbunsha.

EZB I (1927) 1949. *Essays on Zen Buddhism.* First Series. Grove Press. First published by the Eastern Buddhist Society.

EZB II 1933. *Essays on Zen Buddhism.* Second Series. Luzak.

EZB III 1969. *Essays on Zen Buddhism.* Third Series. Luzak.

FZ (1969) 1970. *The Field of Zen.* Edited with a foreword by Christmas Humphreys. Harper and Row.

FZAF 2006. "Foreword" to *Zen and the Art of Flower Arrangement* by Gustie L. Herrigel. Penguin Press. First published in German, 1958; First published in English, 1987.

HRN 1960. "How to Read Nishida." In *A Study of Good* by Nishida Kitarō. Translated by Valdo H. Viglielmo. Ministry of Education.

IBN 1906. "Is Buddhism Nihilistic?" *Light of Dharma* 6: 3–7.

IZAA	(1953) 1961. "Introduction" to *Zen in the Art of Archery* by Eugen Herrigel. Translated by R. F. C. Hull. Vintage Books.
JS	(1972) 1988. *Japanese Spirituality*. Greenwood Press.
LCP	2007. "The Life of a Certain Person." *Eastern Buddhist: New Series* 38 (1–2): 3–7.
LS	(1932) 1973. *The Lankavatara Sutra*. Translated from the original Sanskrit by D. T. Suzuki. Routledge and Kegan Paul.
LSE	(1932) 2003. *The Lankavatara Sutra: An Epitomized Version*. Translated by D. T. Suzuki. Edited by Dwight Goddard. Monkfish Book Publishing. Originally published as *Self-Realization of Noble Wisdom: The Lankavatara Sutra*.
LZ	(1950) 1972. *Living by Zen*. Edited by Christmas Humphreys. Samuel Weiser.
M	(1939) 2012. 無心と言うこと *Mushin to iu koto* [*On the Unconscious*]. Daitō shuppansha.
MCB	(1957) 2002. *Mysticism: Christian and Buddhist*. Routledge.
MZB	(1935) 1994. *Manual of Zen Buddhism*. Grove Press.
OIMB	1968. *On Indian Mahayana Buddhism*. Edited by Edward Conze. Harper Torchbooks.
OMB	(1907) 2016. *Outlines of Mahayana Buddhism*. SophiaOmni Press.
PM	1966. "Preface" in *Mumonkan: The Zen Masterpiece*. Translated by R. H. Blythe. Hokuseido Press.
PPOH	(1894) 2022. "The Place of Peace in Our Hearts." In *The Zen Buddhist Philosophy of D. T. Suzuki: Strengths, Foibles, Intrigues, and Precision*. Translated by Rossa O Muirearthaigh. Bloomsbury Academic.
RD	1971. "Religion and Drugs." Edited by Nishitani Keiji. *Eastern Buddhist* 4 (2): 128–133.
RHD	1965. "Review of Heinrich Dumoulin: *A History of Zen Buddhism*." *Eastern Buddhist: New Series* 1 (1): 123–126.
RI	1967. "Reason and Intuition." In *The Japanese Mind*. Edited by Charles A. Moore. University of Hawaii Press.
SBN	1996. *Swedenborg: Buddha of the North*. Translated by Andrew Bernstein. Swedenborg Foundation.

SDZ	1968. 鈴木大拙全集 [*Suzuki Daisetsu zenshū*] [*Collected Works of Suzuki Daisetsu*]. Iwanami.
SK	1998. "Shinran and Kierkegaard." In *Popular Buddhism in Japan: Shin Buddhist Religion and Culture*. Edited by Esben Andreasen. University of Hawaii Press.
SLS	(1930) 1972. *Studies in the Lankavatara Sutra*. Routledge and Kegan Paul.
SU	(1970) 1982. "Self the Unattainable." In *The Buddha Eye: An Anthology of the Kyoto School*. Edited by Fredrick Frank. Crossroad. Originally published in *Eastern Buddhist* 3, (2): 1–8.
SWS I	2015. *Selected Works of D. T. Suzuki. Volume I: Zen*. Volume editor and general editor, Richard M. Jaffe. University of California Press.
SWS II	2015. *Selected Works of D. T. Suzuki. Volume II: Pure Land Buddhism*. General editor, Richard M. Jaffe. Volume editor, James C. Dobbins. University of California Press.
SWS III	2016. *Selected Works of D. T. Suzuki. Volume III: Comparative Religions*. General editor, Richard M. Jaffe. Volume editors, Jeff Wilson and Tomoe Moriya. University of California Press.
SWS IV	2021. *Selected Works of D. T. Suzuki. Volume IV: Buddhist Studies*. General editor, Richard M. Jaffe. Volume editor, Mark L. Blum. University of California Press.
SZ	1955. *Studies in Zen: A Delta Book*. Dell Publishing.
SZIP	(1971) 1999. *Sengai: The Zen of Ink and Paper*. Shambhala. Originally published as *Sengai: The Zen Master*.
TPZA	(1906) 1974. Translator's preface to *Zen for Americans*, by Soyen Shaku. Open Court Press. Originally published as *Sermons of a Buddhist Abbot*.
TZBM	(1934) 2007. *The Training of the Zen Buddhist Monk*. Cosimo. Originally published by the Eastern Buddhist Society.
WI	(1971) 1982. "What Is the 'I'?" In *The Buddha Eye: An Anthology of the Kyoto School*, edited by Fredrick Frank. Crossroad. Originally published in *Eastern Buddhist* 4 (1): 13–27.
WZ	1971. *What Is Zen?* Harper and Row.

WZW	(1914) 2020. "The Way Zazen Works." In *The Middle Way*, translated with an introduction by Wayne S. Yokoyama, Spring 2021.
ZA	1974. *Zen for Americans* by Soyen Shaku. Translated with a preface by D. T. Suzuki. Open Court.
ZB	2006. *Zen Buddhism: Selected Writings of D.T. Suzuki*. Edited by William Barrett. Doubleday.
ZBIJC	1938. *Zen Buddhism and Its Influence on Japanese Culture.* Eastern Buddhist Society.
ZDNM	(1949) 1969. *The Zen Doctrine of No Mind*. Edited by Christmas Humphreys. Rider.
ZJC	1979. *Zen and Japanese Culture*. Princeton University Press.
ZKMA	1994. *The Zen Koan as a Means of Attaining Enlightenment*. Charles E. Tuttle.
ZNB	2005. 禅と日本文化 [*Zen and Japanese Culture*]. Translated by Kitagawa Momo'o. Kodansha. Originally published in English as Ze*n Buddhism and Its Influence on Japanese Culture* by the Eastern Buddhist Society in 1938 and originally published in Japanese translation as *Zen to nihon bunka* by Iwanami Shoten in 1964.
ZP	1960. *Zen Buddhism and Psychoanalysis.* D. T. Suzuki, Erich Fromm, and Richard De Martino. Harper and Row.
ZRHS	1953. "Zen: A Reply to Hu Shih." *Philosophy East and West* 3 (1): 25–46.
ZSB	1906–1907. "The Zen Sect of Buddhism." *Journal of the Pali Text Society* 5: 8–43.
ZTZ	2017. 禅のつれずれ [*Zen no tsurezure*] [*Idle Thoughts on Zen*]. Kawade shobo shinsha.

Multimedia Resources for D. T. Suzuki

2006. *A Zen Life: D. T. Suzuki.* A documentary by Michael Goldberg. Japan Intercultural Foundation.

2017. 鈴木大拙講演集 禅―東洋的なるもの [Collected Lectures of Suzuki Daisetz]. Tokyo, Japan: Art Days. 4 Disc Box Set.

Bibliography of Other Texts

Abdul-Jabbar, Kareem. 2017. *Coach Wooden and Me*. Hachette Books.

Abe Masao. 1985. "True Person and Compassion — D. T. Suzuki's Appreciation of Lin-chi and Chao-chou." In *Zen and Western Thought*, edited by William R. LaFleur. University of Hawaii Press.

Abe Masao. 1991. "Kenotic God and Dynamic Sunyata." In *The Emptying God*, edited by John B. Cobb, Jr. and Christopher Ives. Orbis Books.

Abe Masao. 1995. *A Zen Life: D. T. Suzuki Remembered*. Edited by Abe Masao. Weatherhill.

Abe Masao. 1997. *Zen and Comparative Studies*. Edited by Steven Heine. University of Hawaii Press.

Alpert, Avram. 2019. *Global Origins of the Modern Self, from Montaigne to Suzuki*. State University of New York Press.

App, Urs. 1995. "Treatise on No-Mind: A Chan Text from Dunhuang." Translated with an introduction by Urs App. *Eastern Buddhist: New Series* 28 (1): 70–107.

Ashton, Dore. 1992. *Noguchi: East and West*. Knopf.

Assagioli, Roberto. 2007. *Transpersonal Development: The Dimension Beyond Psychosynthesis*. Inner Way Productions.

Assagioli, Roberto. (1973) 2010. *The Act of Will*. Synthesis Center Press.

Assagioli, Roberto. (1965) 2012. *Psychosynthesis*. Synthesis Center Press.

Asada Akira. 1983. *Kōzō to chikara*. Keisō Shobō.

Aśvagosa. 1967. *The Awakening of Faith*. Translated by Y. S. Hakeda. Columbia University Press.

Atkinson, William Walker. (1909) 2010. *Subconscious and the Superconscious Planes of Mind*. Cosimo Classics.

Austin, James. 1999. *Zen and the Brain*. MIT Press.

Austin, James. 2016. *Living Zen Remindfully: Retraining Subconscious Awareness*. MIT Press.

Azuma Hiroki. 2009. *Otaku: Japan's Data Base Animals*. Translated by Jonathan E. Abel and Shion Kono. University of Minnesota Press.

Badiner, Allan. (2002) 2015. *Zig Zag Zen: Buddhism and Psychedelics*. Edited by Allan Hunt Badiner and Alex Grey. Synergetic Press.

Bargh, John. 2017. *Before You Know It: The Unconscious Reasons We Do What We Do*. Touchstone.

Beardsley, Monroe. 1966. *Aesthetics from Classical Greece to the Present*. University of Alabama Press.

Benoit, Hubert. 1990. *Zen and the Psychology of Transformation: The Supreme Doctrine*. Foreword by Aldous Huxley. Inner Traditions.

Benoit, Hubert. 2004. *The Light of Zen in the West: Incorporating the Supreme Doctrine and the Realization of the Self*. Translated by Graham Rooth. Sussex Academic Press.

Bishop, John. 1976. *A Study of the Religious Dimensions in the Fiction of J. D. Salinger*. MA thesis, McMaster University.

Bowring, R. J. 1979. *Mori Ōgai and the Modernization of Japanese Culture*. Cambridge University Press.

Breen, Sueki, Sueki Fumihiko, and Yamada Shōji, eds. 2022. *Beyond Zen: D. T. Suzuki and the Modern Transformation of Buddhism*. University of Hawaii Press.

Bucke, Richard, M. (1901) 1991. *Cosmic Consciousness*. Arcana.

Buddhadāsa Bhikku. 1994. *Heartwood of the Bodhi Tree: The Buddha's Teaching on Voidness*. Wisdom Publications.

Cage, John. 1961. *Silence: Lectures and Writings by John Cage*. Wesleyan University Press.

Carus, Carl Gustav. 1970. *Psyche, On the Development of the Soul. Part One: The Unconscious*. Spring Publications.

Cunningham, Eric. 2007. *Hallucinating the End of History. Nishida, Zen and the Psychedelic Eschaton*. Academia Press.

Cytowic, Richard E. 1993. *The Man Who Tasted Shapes*. Putnam.

Cytowic, Richard E. (1989) 2002. *Synesthesia*. 2nd ed. MIT Press.

Dale, Peter N. 1986. *The Myth of Japanese Uniqueness*. St. Martin's Press.

Danto, Arthur, C. 1981. *Transfiguration of the Commonplace*. Harvard University Press.

Danto, Arthur, C. (1972) 1988. *Mysticism and Morality: Oriental Thought and Moral Philosophy*. Columbia University Press.

Danto, Arthur, C. 1997. *After the End of Art*. Princeton University Press.

Danto, Arthur, C. 1999. *Philosophizing Art*. University of California Press.

Danto, Arthur, C. 2002. "The World as Warehouse: Fluxus and Philosophy." In *What's Fluxus? What's Not? Why?* Gilbert and Lila Silverman Fluxus Collection Foundation.

Danto, Arthur, C. 2003. *The Abuse of Beauty: Aesthetics and the Concept of Art*. Open Court.

Danto, Arthur, C. 2004. "Upper West Side Buddhism." In *Buddha Mind in Contemporary Art.*, edited by Jacquelynn Baas and Mary Jane Jacob. University of California Press.

Danto, Arthur, C. 2019. "The Artworld." In *Aesthetics: The Classic Readings*, edited by David E. Cooper. Originally published in *Journal of Philosophy*, 61 (19), 1964.

Davis, Bret. 2022. *Zen Pathways: An Introduction to the Philosophy and Practice of Zen Buddhism*. Oxford University Press.

Dehaene, Stanislas. 2014. *Consciousness and the Brain*. Penguin Books.

Deleuze, Gilles. 1993. *The Fold: Leibniz and the Baroque*. Translated by Tom Conley. University of Minnesota Press.

Deleuze, Gilles, and Felix Guattari. 1987. *A Thousand Plateaus: Capitalism and Schizophrenia*. Translated by Brian Massumi. University of Minnesota Press.

Dewey, John. 1980. *Art as Experience*. Perigee Book.

Dilworth, David. 1978. "Suzuki Daisetz as Regional Ontologist: Critical Remarks on Reading Suzuki's 'Japanese Spirituality.'" *Philosophy East and West* 28 (1): 99–110.

Doi, Takeo. 1971. *Amae no kōzō*. Kobundo.

Doi, Takeo. 1973. *The Anatomy of Dependence*. Translated by J. Bester. Kodansha International.

Dumoulin, Heinrich. 1963. *A History of Zen Buddhism*. Random House.

Dumoulin, Heinrich. 1992. *Zen Buddhism in the 20th Century*. Translated by Joseph S. O'Leary. Weatherhill.

Ellenberger, Henri F. (1970) 1994. *The Discovery of the Unconscious: The History and Evolution of Dynamic Psychiatry*. Fontanna Press.

Evans, Dylan. 1996. *An Introductory Dictionary of Lacanian Psychoanalysis*. Routledge.

Evans-Wentz, W. Y., ed. 1967. *The Tibetan Book of the Dead*. Galaxy Publishers.

Faber, Roland. 2014. *The Divine Manifold*. Lexington Books.

Faure, Bernard. 1993. *Chan Insights and Oversights*. Princeton University Press.

Feuerstein, George. 1987. *Structures of Consciousness: The Genius of Jean Gebser*. Foreword by Gary Snyder. Integral Publishing.

Feuerstein, George. (1996) 2008. *Buddhism and the Art of Psychotherapy*. Texas A&M University Press.

Fink, Bruce. 1997. *A Clinical Introduction to Lacanian Psychoanalysis: Theory and Technique*. Harvard University Press.

Firman, John, and Ann Gila. 2002. *Psychosynthesis: A Psychology of the Spirit*. State University of New York Press.

Ford, James, and Melissa Blacker, eds. 2011. *The Book of MU: Essential Writings on Zen's Most Important Koan*. Wisdom Books.

Foucault, Michel. 2002. *The Order of Things: An Archaeology of the Human Sciences*. Routledge.

Fox, Nick. 2003. *The New Sartre*. Continuum.

Frank, Frederick, ed. 1982. *The Buddha Eye: An Anthology of the Kyoto School*. Crossroad.

Frankl, Victor, E. (1946) 1975. *The Unconscious God: Psychotherapy and Theology*. Simon and Schuster.

Freud, Sigmund. (1923) 1960a. *The Ego and the Id*. Translated by J. Riviere. W. W. Norton.

Freud, Sigmund. (1905) 1960b. *Jokes and Their Relation to the Unconscious*. W. W. Norton.

Freud, Sigmund. (1900) 1965. *The Interpretation of Dreams*. Translated and edited by James Strachey. Avon Books.

Freud, Sigmund. (1930) 2005. *Civilization and Its Discontents*. Norton.

Fujita Masakatsu. 2019. "The Postwar Development of the Kyoto School and Its Significance." In *Contemporary Japanese Philosophy: A Reader*, edited by John Krummel. Rowman and Littlefield.

Fukushima Keido. 2017. *Zen Bridge: The Zen Teachings of Keido Fukushima*. Edited by Grace Schireson and Peter Schireson. Wisdom Publications.

Fuller, Andrew. 2008. *Psychology and the Unconscious*. Rowman and Littlefield.

Fuller, Robert, C. 1986. *Americans and the Unconscious*. Oxford University Press.

Galliano, Lucian. 2019. *Japan Fluxus*. Lexington.

Gardner, Sebastian. 1999. "Schopenhauer, Will, and the Unconscious." In *the Cambridge Companion to Schopenhauer*, edited by Christopher Janaway. Cambridge University Press.

Gardner, Sebastian. 2010. "Eduard von Hartmann's Philosophy of the Unconscious." In *Thinking Through the Unconscious*, edited by A. Nicholls and M. Liebscher. Cambridge University Press.

Gebser, Jean. (1949) 1985. *The Ever-Present Origin*. Translated by Noel Barstad with Algis Mickunas. University of Ohio Press.

Griffin, David. 1989. *Archetypal Process: Self and Divine in Whitehead, Jung, and Hillman*. Edited by David Ray Griffin. Northwestern University Press.

Grof, Stanislav. (1975) 2009. *LSD: Doorway to the Numinous*. Park Street Press. Originally published by Viking Press as *Realms of the Human Unconscious*.

Grof, Stanislav. 2017. "Observations from 4,000 LSD Sessions." In *Psychedelic Medicine*, edited by Richard Louis Miller. Park Street Press.

Guattari, Felix. 2011. *The Machinic Unconscious: Essays in Schizoanalysis*. Translated by Taylor Adkins. Semiotext(e).

Guattari, Felix. 2016. *Lines of Flight*. Bloomsbury.

Hagiwara Takao. 2014. "Derrida and Zen." *Philosophy East and West* 64 (1): 123–150.

Hakuin. 1999. *Wild Ivy: The Spiritual Autobiography of Zen Master Hakuin*. Translated by Norman Waddell. Shambhala.

Haller, John. 2012. *The History of New Thought: From Mind Cure to Positive Thinking and the Prosperity Gospel*. Swedenborg Foundation Press.

Harada Sogaku. 2011. "Commentary on Joshu's Mu." In *Kawai The Book of Mu*, edited by James Ford and Melissa Myozen Blacker. Wisdom Publications.

Hartmann, Eduard von. (1869) 1931. *The Philosophy of the Unconscious*. Translated by William C. Coupland. Harcourt, Brace. New edition with three volumes published in one volume.

Hayao Kawai. 1995. *Dreams, Muths and Fairy Tales in Japan*. Daimon.

Hayao Kawai. 1996. *The Japanese Psyche: Major Motifs in the Fairy Tales of Japan*. Translated by Kawai Hayao. Spring Publications.

Hayao Kawai. (1996) 2008. *Buddhism and the Art of Psychotherapy*. Texas A&M University Press.

Hayao Kawai and Murakami Haruki. 1996. *Murakami Haruki, Kawai Hayao ni ai ni iku* [村上春樹、河合隼雄に会いに行く]. Iwanami.

Hayao Kawai and Murakami Haruki. 2016. *Haruki Murakami Goes to Meet Hayao Kawai*. Translated by C. Stephens. Daimon.

Heine, Steven. 2005. *The Zen Poetry of Dōgen*. Dharma Communications.

Heine, Steven. 2008. *Zen Skin, Zen Marrow: Will the Real Zen Buddhism Please Stand Up*. Oxford University Press.

Heine, Steven. 2009. *Bargainin' For Salvation: Bob Dylan, A Zen Master?* Continuum.

Heine, Steven. 2014a. *Like Cats and Dogs: Contesting the Mu Kōan in Zen Buddhism*. Oxford University Press.

Heine, Steven. 2014b. *Zen Koans*. University of Hawaii Press.

Heisig, James. 2001. *Philosophers of Nothingness*. University of Hawaii Press.

Heisig, James, Thomas Kasulis, and John Maraldo, eds. 2011. *Japanese Philosophy: A Sourcebook*. University of Hawaii Press.

Herrera, Hayden. 2015. *Listening to Stone: The Art and Life of Isamu Noguchi*. Straus and Giroux.

Herrigel, Eugen. (1953) 1961. *Zen in the Art of Archery*. Introduction by D. T. Suzuki. Translated by R. F. C. Hull. Vintage Books.

Herrigel, Eugen. (1960) 1974. *The Method of Zen*. Vintage Books. Originally published by Routledge and Kegan Paul.

Herrigel, Eugen. (1953) 1981. *Zen and the Art of Archery*. Introduction by D. T. Suzuki. Translated by R. F. C. Hull. Random House.

Herrigel, Gustie, L. (1958) 1999. *Zen in the Art of Flower Arrangement*. Foreword by D. T. Suzuki. Souvenir Press.

Hisamatsu Shin'ichi. 2011. "Oriental Nothingness." In *Japanese Philosophy: A Sourcebook*, edited by James Heisig, Thomas Kasulis, and John Maraldo. University of Hawaii Press.

Hofstadter, Albert, and Richard Kuhns. 1976. *Philosophies of Art and Beauty*. University of Chicago Press.

Hori, Victor. 2016. "Suzuki and the Invention of Tradition." *Eastern Buddhist: New Series* 47 (2): 41–81.

Hu Shih. 1953. "Ch'an (Zen) Buddhism in China. Its History and Method," *Philosophy East and West* 3 (1): 3–24.

Hubbard, Jamie, and Paul L. Swanson, eds. 1997. *Pruning the Bodhi Tree: The Storm Over Critical Buddhism*. University of Hawaii Press.

Huxley, Aldous. 1999. *Moksha: Aldous Huxley's Classic Writings on Psychedelics and the Visionary Experience*. Edited by M. Horowitz and C. Palmer. Park Street Press.

Huxley, Aldous. (1954) 2009. *The Doors of Perception*. Harper Perrrenial Modern Classics.

Hymns, Joe. 1979. *Zen in the Martial Arts*. Jeremy P. Tarcher/Putnam.

Ives, Christopher. 2009. *Imperial Way Zen*. University of Hawaii Press.

Izutsu, Toshihiku. 1977. *Toward a Philosophy of Zen Buddhism*. Prajna Press.

Izutsu, Toshihiko. 1981. *The Theory of Beauty in the Classical Aesthetics of Japan*. Edited by Toshihiku Izutsu and Toyo Izutsu. Martinus Nijhoff.

Izutsu, Toshihiku. 2019. "Consciousness and Essence." In *Contemporary Japanese Philosophy: A Reader*, edited by John Krummel. Rowman and Littlefield.

Jackson, Peter. 2003. *Buddhadāsa: Theravada Buddhism and Modernist Reform in Thailand*. Silkworm Books.

Jaffe, Richard M., ed. 2015. *The Selected Works of D. T. Suzuki*. Vol. I. University of California Press.

Jaffe, Richard M. 2015. *The Selected Works of D. T. Suzuki*. Vol. II. Edited by James C. Dobbins. University of California Press.

Jaffe, Richard M. 2016. *The Selected Works of D. T. Suzuki*. Vol. III. Edited by Jeff Wilson and Tomoe Moriya. University of California Press.

James, Henry Sr. 1869. *The Secret of Swedenborg*. Fields, Osgood.

James, William. (1906) 1996. *Essays in Radical Empiricism*. Nebraska University Press.

James, William. (1902) 1982. *The Varieties of Religious Experience*. Penguin Books.

Jaspers, Karl. (1953) 2021. *The Origin and Goal of History*. Translated by Michael Bullock. Routledge.

Jiang, Tao. 2006. *Contexts and Dialogue; Yogācāra Buddhism and Modern Psychology on the Subliminal Mind*. University of Hawaii Press.

Johnson, Frank A. 1993. *Dependency and Japanese Socialization: Psychoanalytic and Anthropological Investigations into Amae*. New York University Press.

Jung, Carl Gustav. 1971. *The Portable Jung*. Edited by Joseph Campbell. Penguin Books.

Jung, Carl Gustav. 1978. *Psychology and the East*. Princeton University Press.

Jung, Carl Gustav. (1961) 1989. *Memories, Dreams, Reflections*. Edited by Aniela Jaffe. Translated by Richard Winston and Clara Winston. Vintage Books/Random House.

Jung, C. G., and Shin'ichi Hisamatsu. 1968. "On the Unconscious, the Self and the Therapy." *Psychologia* 11: 25–32.

Jung, C. G., and Shin'ichi Hisamatsu. (1958) 1971. *Zen and the Fine Arts*. Translated by Gishin Tokiwa. Kodansha International.

Kandel, Eric R. 2012. *The Age of Insight: The Quest to Understand the Unconscious in Art, Mind, and Brain, From Vienna 1900 to the Present*. Random House.

Kasulis, Thomas. 1977. "Zen Buddhism, Freud, and Jung." *Eastern Buddhist: New Series* 10 (1): 68–91.

Kasulis, Thomas. 1981. *Zen Action/Zen Person*. University of Hawaii Press.

Kasulis, Thomas. 1998. "Abe Masao as the D. T. Suzuki's Philosophical Successor." In *Masao Abe: A Zen Life of Dialogue*. Edited by Donald W. Mitchell. Charles E. Tuttle.

Kasulis, Thomas. 2007. "Reading D. T. Suzuki Today." *Eastern Buddhist: New Series* 38 (1–2): 41–57.

Kasulis, Thomas. 2018. *Engaging Japanese Philosophy: A Short History*. University of Hawaii Press.

Kawai Toshio. 2011. *Murakami Haruki no "monogatari": Yume tekisuto to shite yomitoku* [*Murakami Haruki's "Narrative:" Interpretive Reading of the Dream Text*]. Shinchōsha.

Kerouac, Jack. (1958) 1976. *The Dharma Bums*. Penguin Books.

Koestler, Arthur. 1960. "A Stink of Zen: The Lotus and the Robot (II)." *Encounter* 85 (October): 13–32.

Koestler, Arthur. 1960. *The Lotus and the Robot*. Macmillan.

Koestler, Arthur. 1961. "Neither Lotus nor Robot." *Encounter* 16 (February): 58–59.

Koryu Osaka. 2011. "Working with Mu." In *The Book of Mu*, edited by James Ford and Melissa Myozen Blacker. Wisdom Publications.

Kōsaka Masaaki. 1967. "The Individual in Japanese Society." In *The Japanese Mind*, edited by Charles A. Moore. University of Hawaii Press.

Kramer, Robert. 2019. *The Birth of Relationship Therapy*. Psychosozial-Verlag.

Krummel, John. 2019. *Contemporary Japanese Philosophy: A Reader*. Edited by John W. M. Krummel. Rowman and Littlefield.

Kurokawa Kisho. 1988. *Rediscovering Japanese Space*. Weatherhill.

Lacan, Jacques. 1975. *Encore: The Seminar of Jacques Lacan, Book XX*. Translated by Bruce Fink. Norton.

Lacan, Jacques. 1988. *The Seminar of Jacques Lacan: Book I: Freud's Papers on Technique, 1953–54*. Edited by Jacques-Allain Miller. Norton.

Lacan, Jacques. 1998. *The Four Fundamental Concepts of Psychoanalysis. The Seminar of Jacques Lacan Book XI*. Translated by Alain Sheridan. W. W. Norton.

Lacan, Jacques. 2015. *Anxiety: The Seminar of Jacques Lacan Book X*. Translated by A. R. Price. Edited by Jacques-Alain Miller. Polity Press.

Lacan, Jacques. 2002. *Ecrits*. Translated by Bruce Fink. W. W. Norton.

Larson, Kay. 2013. *Where the Heart Beats: John Cage, Zen Buddhism, and the Inner Life of Artists*. Penguin Books.

Leclerc, Ivor. (1958) 1975 . *Whitehead's Metaphysics*. Indiana University Press.

Lee, Bruce. 1999. *Bruce Lee: Artist of Life*. Compiled and edited by John Little. Tuttle Publishers.

Levine, Gregory. 2017. *Long Strange Journey: On Modern Zen, Zen Art, and Other Predicaments*. University of Hawaii Press.

Levine, Steven Z. 2011. *Lacan Reframed: A Guide for the Arts Student*. I. B. Tauris.

Li Zehou. 2010. *The Chinese Aesthetic Tradition*. University of Hawaii Press.

Li Zehou. 2020. *A History of Classical Chinese Thought*. Translated by Andrew Lambert. Routledge.

Low, Albert. 2006. *Hakuin on Kensho: The Four Ways of Knowing*. Shambhala.

Magliola, Robert. 1986. *Derrida on the Mend*. West Purdue University Press.

Makise, Hidemoto. 2017. "Lacanian Psychoanalysis and Japanese Zen (Hakuin Zen): The Relation Between 'The Impossible Thing,' Drawings, and Topology." *Annual Review of Critical Psychology* 13: 1–15.

Maraldo, John, C. 2021. *The Saga of Zen History and the Power of Legend*. Chisokudo Publications.

Marra, Michele. 1999. *Modern Japanese Aesthetics: A Reader*. University of Hawaii Press.

Maslow, Abraham. 1964. *Religions, Values, and Peak-Experiences*. Ohio State University Press.

Maslow, Abraham. 1971. *The Farther Reaches of Human Nature*. Viking Press.

Maslow, Abraham, H. 1968. *Toward A Psychology of Being*. 2nd Ed. D. Van Nostrand.

McCort, Dennis. 2008. "Hyakujo's Geese, Amban's Doughnuts and Rilke's Carrousel: Sources East and West for Salinger's 'Catcher.'" In *J. D. Salinger's The Catcher in the Rye*. New Ed, edited with an introduction by Harold Bloom. Infobase Publishing. Reprinted from *Comparative Literature Studies* 1997 34 (3): 260–268.

McGrath, S. J. 2012. *The Dark Ground of Spirit: Schelling and the Unconscious*. Routledge.

McMahan, David. L. 2002. *Empty Visions: Metaphor and Visionary Imagery in Mahayana Buddhism*. Routledge Curzon.

McMahan, David. L. 2008. *The Making of Buddhist Modernism*. Oxford University Press.

Merton, Thomas. 1967. *Mystics and Zen Masters*. Farrar, Straus and Giroux.

Merton, Thomas. 1968. *Zen and the Birds of Appetite*. Abbey of Gethsemani/ New Directions

Mills, Jon. 2014. *Underworlds: Philosophies of the Unconscious from Psychoanalysis to Metaphysics*. Routledge.

Miyamoto Musashi. 2005. *The Book of Five Rings: A Classic Test on the Japanese Way of the Sword*. Translated by Thomas Cleary. Shambhala.

Mlodinow, Leonard. 2013. *Subliminal: How Your Unconscious Mind Rules Your Behavior*. Vintage Books/Random House.

Moore, Charles, A. 1967. "Suzuki: The Man and the Scholar." *Eastern Buddhist*: *New Series* 2 (August).

Moore, James. 1991. *Gurdjieff: The Anatomy of a Myth*. Element.

Moore, Meido. 2020. *Hidden Zen: Practices for Sudden Awakening and Embodied Realization*. Shambhala.

Moriya, Tomoe. 2007. "'A Note from A Rural Town in America': The Young Suzuki Daisetsu and the Significance of Religious Experience." *Eastern Buddhist*: *New Series* 38 (1–2): 58–68.

Morris, Ivan. 1969. *The World of the Shining Prince: Court Life in Ancient Japan*. Penguin Books.

Munsterberg, Hugo. 1965. *Zen and Oriental Art*. Charles E. Tuttle.

Murakami Haruki. 2003. *The Wind-Up Bird Chronicle*. Translated by Jay Rubin. Vintage.

Murphy, Joseph. 1964. *The Miracle of Mind Dynamics: Use Your Subconscious Mind to Obtain Complete Control Over Your Destiny*. Prentice Hall.

Murphy, Joseph. 1968. *The Cosmic Power Within You*. Tarcher Perigee.

Murphy, Joseph. (1963) 2008. *The Power of Your Subconscious Mind.* Prentice Hall Press.

Myers, Gerald E. 1986. *William James: His Life and Thought.* Yale University Press.

Nicholls, Angus, and Martin Liebscher. 2010. *Thinking the Unconscious: Nineteenth-Century German Thought.* Cambridge University Press.

Nietzsche, F. 1967. *The Will to Power.* Translated by Walter Kaufmann and R. J. Hollingdale. Random House.

Nietzsche, F. 1974. *The Gay Science.* Translated by Walter Kaufmann. Vintage Books/Random House.

Nishida, Kitarō. 1987. *Last Writings: Nothingness and the Religious Worldview.* University of Hawaii Press.

Nishihira, Tadashi. (2013) 2015. "Subjectivity of 'Mu-shin' (No-mind-ness): Zen Philosophy as Interpreted by Toshihiko Izutsu." *Journal of Integral Creative Studies* 1–9.

Nishihira, Tadashi. 2024. *The Philosophy of No-Mind.* Translated by Catherine Sevilla-Liu and Anton Sevilla-Liu. Bloomsbury.

Nishitani Keiji. 1961. 宗教とは何か [*What Is Religion?*]. Sōbunsha.

Nishitani Keiji. 1982. *Religion and Nothingness.* Translated by Jan Van Bragt. University of California Press.

Nishitani Keiji. 1988. "The Divine in the Contemporary World: A Conversation with (Discussion with Kawai Hayao and David Miller)." Translated by Mark Unno. *Kyoto Journal* (Fall), 16–22.

Nishitani Keiji. 1991. *Nishida Kitarō.* Translated by Yamamoto Seikaku and James Heisig. University of California Press.

Noguchi, Isamu. 1967. *Isamu Noguchi: A Sculptor's World.* Thames and Hudson.

Northrop, F. S. C. 1979. *The Meeting of East and West.* Macmillan.

O'Brien, Barbara. 2019. *The Circle of the Way: A Concise History of Zen from the Buddha to the Modern World.* Shambhala.

O Muireartaigh, Rossa. 2022. *The Zen Buddhist Philosophy of D. T. Suzuki: Strengths, Foibles, Intrigues, and Precision.* Bloomsbury.

Odin, Steve. 1982. *Process Metaphysics and Hua-Yen Buddhism.* State University of New York Press.

Odin, Steve. 1985. "A Whiteheadian Perspective on the Yugen Style of Art and Literature in Japanese Aesthetics." *Japanese Journal of Religious Studies* 12 (1): 63.

Odin, Steve. 1985. "A Phenomenological Investigation into the Aesthetics of Darkness and Shadows in Japanese Culture" *Journal of Buddhist Philosophy* Spring.

Odin, Steve. 1986. "Blossom Scents Take Up the Ringing: Synaesthesia in Japanese and Western Aesthetics." *Soundings: An Interdisciplinary Journal* 69 (3): 256–281.

Odin, Steve. 1987a. *"Nihon no geijutsu to bungaku no yūgen yoshiki ni tsuite, Whiteheado-tetsugaku no kanten kara no bunseki"* ["A Whiteheadian Perspective on the Yugen Style of Art and Literature in Japanese Aesthetics"]. Translated by Tanaka Yutaka. *Shisō* 762.

Odin, Steve. 1987b. "An Explanation of Beauty: Nishida Kitarō's *Bi no setsumei*," *Monumenta Nipponica* 42 (2): 211–217.

Odin, Steve. 1990. "Derrida and the Decentered Universe of Ch'an/Zen Buddhism." *Journal of Chinese Philosophy*, 17.

Odin, Steve. 1994. "The Epochal Theory of Time in Whitehead and Japanese Buddhism: An East-West Study of Whitehead, Dōgen, and Nishida." *Process Studies* V 23 (2): 119–133.

Odin, Steve. 1995. "Buddhist Śūnyatā and Western Philosophy." *Pacific World: New Series* 11: 280–303.

Odin, Steve. 1996. *The Social Self in Zen and American Pragmatism.* State University of New York Press.

Odin, Steve. 2001. *Artistic Detachment in Japan and the West: Psychic Distance in Comparative Aesthetics.* University of Hawaii Press.

Odin, Steve. 2001. "Peace and Compassion in Whitehead and the Lotus Sutra." *Journal of Chinese Philosophy* 28 (4): 371–384.

Odin, Steve. 2003. Review of *Buddhadāsa: Theravada Buddhism and Modern Reform in Thailand.* By Peter A. Jackson. Silkworm Books.

Odin, Steve. 2005. "God as Peace-Bestowing Buddha/Christ." In *Deep Religious Pluralism*, edited by David Ray Griffin. Westminster John Knox Press.

Odin, Steve. 2012. "Whitehead on the 'Rhythm of Education' and Kitarō Nishida's 'Pure Experience' as a Developing Whole." In *Education and the Kyoto School of Philosophy*, edited by Paul Standish and Naoko Saito. Springer.

Odin, Steve. 2016. *Tragic Beauty in Whitehead and Japanese Aesthetics*. Lexington Press.

Odin, Steve. 2018. "Beauty as Ecstasy in the Aesthetics of Schopenhauer and Nishida Kitarō." In *New Essays on Japanese Aesthetics*, edited by Mihn Nyugen. Lexington Books.

Ohnuki-Tierney, Emiko. 2002. *Kamikaze Cherry Blossoms and Nationalism: The Militarization of Aesthetics in Japanese History*. University of Chicago Press.

Pearlman, Ellen. 2012. *Nothing and Everything: The Influence of Buddhism on the American Avant-Garde 1942-1962*. Evolver Editions.

Perkins, Franklin. 2004. *Leibniz and China*. Cambridge University Press.

Pickover, Clifford. 2006. *The Möbius Strip: Dr. August Mobius's Marvelous Band in Mathematics, Games, Literature, Art, Technology, and Cosmology*. Thunder's Mouth Press.

Price, Lucien. 1954. *Dialogues of Alfred North Whitehead*. Mentor Books.

Rancière, Jacques. 2010. *The Aesthetic Unconscious*. Translated by Debra Keates and James Swenson. Polity Press.

Saito Yuriko. 2007. *Everyday Aesthetics*. Oxford University Press.

Sakamoto, Hiroshi. 1977. "D. T. Suzuki and Mysticism." *Eastern Buddhist: New Series* 10 (1): 54–67.

Sakamoto, Hiroshi. 1978. "D. T. Suzuki as a Philosopher." *Eastern Buddhist: New Series* 11 (2): 33–42.

Salinger, J. D. 1959. "Seymour: An Introduction." *New Yorker*, June 6.

Salinger, J. D. 1961. *Franny and Zooey*. Little, Brown.

Salinger, J. D. (1951) 1979. *The Catcher in the Rye*. Little, Brown.

Salinger, J. D. (1953) 1981. *Nine Stories*. Little, Brown.

Salinger, J. D. (1963) 1987. *Raise High the Roof Beam, Carpenters and Seymour: An Introduction*. Little, Brown.

Salinger, Margaret. 2001. *Dream Catcher: My Life with J. D. Salinger.* Washington Square.

Sartre, Jean-Paul. 1988. *The Transcendence of the Ego.* Translated by Forrest Williams and Robert Kirkpatrick. Farrar, Straus and Giroux.

Sartre, Jean-Paul. (1956) 1992. *Being and Nothingness.* Translated by Hazel E. Barnes. Washington Square.

Satō, Kemmyō. 2008. "D. T. Suzuki and the Question of War." Translated from the Japanese in collaboration with Thomas Kirchner. *Eastern Buddhist: New Series* 39 (1): 61–120.

Sawada, Janine. 2004. *Practical Pursuits: Religion, Politics, and Personal Cultivation in Nineteenth-Century Japan.* University of Hawaii Press.

Segal, William. 2003. *A Voice at the Borders of Silence: An Intimate View of the Gurdjieff Work, Zen Buddhism, and Art.* Overlook Press.

Serrano, Miguel, C. 1997. *Jung and Herman Hesse: A Record of Two Friendships.* Daimon.

Sharf, Robert. 1993. "The Zen of Japanese Nationalism." *History of Religions* 33 (1): 1–43.

Sharf, Robert. 1994. "Whose Zen? Zen Nationalism Revisited." In *Rude Awakenings: Zen, the Kyoto School, and the Question of Nationalism,* edited by James W. Heisig and John Maraldo. University of Hawaii Press.

Sharf, Robert. 1995. "The Zen of Japanese Nationalism." In *Curators of the Buddha: The Study of Buddhism Under Colonialism,* edited by Donald Lopez. University of Chicago Press.

Shusterman, Richard. 2008. *Body Consciousness: A Philosophy of Mindfulness and Somaesthetics.* Cambridge University Press.

Skinner, Julian Daizan. 2017. *Practical Zen.* Jessica Kingsley Publishers.

Slawenski, Kenneth. 2010. *J. D. Salinger: A Life.* Random House.

Snodgrass, Judith. 2003. *Presenting Japanese Buddhism to the West: Orientalism, Occidentalism, and the Columbian Exposition.* University of North Carolina

Soga Ryōjin. 1982. "Dharmākara Bodhisattva." In *The Buddha Eye: An Anthology of the Kyoto School,* edited by Frederick Franck. Crossroad.

Starrs, Roy. 2022. "D. T. Suzuki's Theory of Inspiration and the Challenges of Cross-Cultural Transmission." In *Beyond Zen: D. T. Suzuki and the Modern Transformation of Buddhism*, edited by John Breen, Sueki Fumihiko, and Yamada Shōji. University of Hawaii Press.

Strassman, Rick. 2001. *DMT: The Spirit Molecule*. Part Street.

Strassman, Rick. 2015. "DMT Dharma." In *Zig Zag Zen: Buddhism and Psychedelics*, edited by Allan Badiner. Synergetic.

Stretcher, Matthew. 2002a. *Dances with Sheep: The Quest for Identity in the Fiction of Murakami Haruki.* University of Michigan.

Stretcher, Matthew. 2002b. *Haruki Murakami's The Wind-up Bird Chronicle.* Continuum.

Stretcher, Matthew. 2014. *The Forbidden Worlds of Haruki Murakami.* University of Minnesota Press.

Sueki Fumihiko. 2016. "Reading D. T. Suzuki with a Focus on His Notion of 'Person.'" *Eastern Buddhist: New Series* 47 (2): 1–26.

Swanson, Paul. 1997. "Why They Say Zen Is Not Buddhism: Recent Japanese Critiques of Buddha-Nature." In *Pruning the Buddha Tree: The Storm Over Critical Buddhism*, edited by Paul L. Swanson and Jamie Hubbard. University of Hawaii Press.

Tagawa Shun'ei. 2009. *Living Yogacara: An Introduction to Consciousness-Only Buddhism*. Translated by Charles Muller. Wisdom Publications.

Takeuchi Yoshinori. 1982. "The Philosophy of Nishida." In *The Buddha Eye: An Anthology of the Kyoto School*, edited by Frederick Frank. Crossroad Publishing.

Takeuchi Yasuhiro. 2008. "The Zen Archery of Holden Caulfield." In *The Catcher in the Rye*. New Ed, edited with an introduction by Harold Bloom. Infobase.

Tallis, Frank. 2012. *Hidden Minds: A History of the Unconscious*. Helios Press.

Tamdgidi, Mohammad. 2009. *Gurdjieff and Hypnosis*. Palgrave Macmillan.

Taniguchi Masaharu. 1962. *Truth of Life: Book of Meditative Practices*. Vol. 8. Nippon Kyo-Bunsha.

Taniguchi Masaharu. 1975. *Truth of Life*: The Mystical Power Within: Truth of Life: The Mystical Power Within. Vol. 5. Seicho-No-Ie.

Taniguchi Masaharu. 2017. *Seicho-no-Ie: Truth of Life*. Seicho-No-Ie.

Tanke, Joseph. 2009. *Foucault's Philosophy of Art*. Continuum.

Tanke, Joseph. 2011. *Jacques Rancière: An Introduction. Philosophy, Politics, Aesthetics*. Continuum.

Tart, Charles. 1975. *Transpersonal Psychologies*. Edited by Charles Tart. Harper and Row.

Taylor, Douglas. 2011. *The Hidden Levels of the Mind: Swedenborg's Theory of Consciousness*. Swedenborg Foundation.

Thompson, Evan. 2017. *Waking, Dreaming, Being*. Columbia University Press.

Troward, Thomas. 1989. *The Edinburgh and Dore Lectures on Mental Science*. DeVorss & Company.

Ueda Shizuteru. 2007. "'Outwardly, Be Open: Inwardly, Be Deep': D. T. Suzuki's 'Eastern Outlook.'" Translated by Thomas Kirchner. *Eastern Buddhist: New Series* 38 (1–2): 8–40.

Victoria, Brian Daizen. 2006. *Zen at War*. 2nd Ed. Rowman and Littlefield.

Viglielmo, V. H. 1971. "Nishida Kitarō: The Early Years." In *Tradition and Modernization in Japanese Culture*, edited by Donald H. Shively. Princeton University Press.

Vivekananda. (1896) 1955. *Raja Yoga*. Ramakrishna-Vivekananda Center.

Waldron, William S. 2003. *The Buddhist Unconscious: The ālaya-vijñāna in the Context of Indian Buddhist Thought*. Routledge Curzon.

Waldron, William S. 2006. "On Selves and Selfless Discourse." In *Buddhism and Psychotherapy Across Cultures*, edited by Mark Unno. Wisdom.

Watts, Alan. 1972. *In My Own Way*. Pantheon.

Watts, Alan. (1957) 1989. *The Way of Zen*. Vintage Books.

Watts, Alan. 1996. "Beat Zen, Square Zen, and Zen." *Chicago Review* 42 (3–4): 49–56.

Watts, Alan. (1962) 2013. *The Joyous Cosmology: Adventures in the Chemistry of Consciousness*. Vintage.

Weinberger, Joel, and Valentina Stovicheva. 2020. *The Unconscious*. Guilford Press.

Whitehead, Alfred North. 1933. *Adventures of Ideas*. Free Press.

Whitehead, Alfred North. 1938. *Modes of Thought*. Free Press.

Whitehead, Alfred North. 1958. *The Concept of Nature*. Cambridge University Press.

Whitehead, Alfred North. 1978. *Process and Reality*. Corrected Ed. Edited by David Ray Griffin and Donald Sherburne. Free Press.

Wilber, Ken. 1983. *Eye to Eye: The Quest for a New Paradigm*. Anchor/Doubleday.

Wilber, Ken. 1993. *The Spectrum of Consciousness*. Quest Books.

Wilber, Ken. 1996a. *The Atman Project*. Quest Books.

Wilber, Ken. 1996b. *Up from Eden*. Quest Books.

Wright, Dale, S. 2000. *Philosophical Meditations on Zen Buddhism*. Cambridge University Press.

Wumen Huikai. 2011. "The Koan Mu: Text, Commentary, and Verse." In *The Book of Mu*, translated by Robert Aitken. Wisdom Publications.

Yamada Shōji. 2001. "The Myth of Zen in the Art of Archery." *Japanese Journal of Religious Studies* 28 (1–2): 1–30.

Yamada Shōji. 2009. *Shots in the Dark: Japan, Zen and the West*. University of Chicago Press.

Yamada Shōji. 2015. *Tokyobugiugi to Suzuki Daisetsu*. Jinbun Shoin.

Yamada Shōji. 2022. *Tokyo Boogie-woogie and D. T. Suzuki*. Translated by Earl Hartman. University of Michigan Press.

Yampolsky, Philip. 1971. *Zen Master Hakuin: Selected Writings*. Columbia University Press.

Yanagi Sōetsu. (1972) 1989. *The Unknown Craftsman: A Japanese Insight into Beauty*. Revised Ed. Foreword by Hamada Shōji. Adapted by Bernard Leach. Kodansha International.

Yanagi Sōetsu. 2017. *The Beauty of Everyday Things*. Penguin.

Yeshe, Thubten. 1998. *The Bliss of Inner Fire*. Edited by R. Courtin and A. Cameron. Wisdom Publications.

Yoshizawa, Katsuhiro. 2009. *The Religious Art of Zen Master Hakuin*. With Norman Waddell. Counterpoint.

Yuasa Yasuo. 1987. *The Body: Toward an Eastern Mind-Body Theory.* Translated by Nagatomo Shigenori and T. P. Kasulis. State University of New York Press.

Yuasa Yasuo. 1993. *The Body, Self-Cultivation, and Ki-Energy.* Translated by Shignori Nagatomo and Monte S. Hull. State University of New York Press.

Yuasa Yasuo. 2008. *Overcoming Modernity: Synchronicity and Image-Thinking.* Translated by Nagatomo Shigenori and John W. M. Drummel. With an introduction by Nagatomo Shigenori. State University of New York Press.

Yusa, Michiko. 2002. *Zen and Philosophy: An Intellectual Biography of Nishida Kitarō.* University of Hawaii Press.

Zaehner, R. C. 1972. *Zen, Drugs and Mysticism.* Pantheon Books.

INDICES

Subject Index

abgrund, 166
abodelessness (no-abiding) (*wuzhu* / *mujū* / 無住), 17
absolute spirit, 84
abstract expressionism, 133, 138, 141
aesthetic experience, 94, 97, 156, 159, 176, 177, 180-182, 190, 253, 255
aesthetic unconscious, 65, 129, 213-215
alaya-vijnana, 46-52, 83, 128, 166, 172, 181, 182, 269
amae, 189-190
American transcendentalism, 127, 157, 173, 175, 240
Amida Buddha, 52, 60, 80-83, 86
analytical psychology, 1, 5, 46, 63, 183, 186, 193, 195, 196, 198, 202, 204, 207, 253
anātman. See *muga*
anime, 114
aperspectival-integral consciousness, 261-263, 276
archery, 21, 87, 91, 93, 95, 100-105, 113, 118, 133
archetypal process, 160
archetypes, 1, 23, 46, 78, 196-202, 206, 210, 211, 229, 260
Aśvaghosha (Awakening of Faith), 48
atman, 84, 108, 151, 203, 204, 242, 259

avant-garde art, 4, 133-138, 141, 222-223, 252
Avataṃsaka, see Kegon Buddhism

bardo, 201-202
beat generation, 133-135
The Book of Five Rings, ix, 118
borromean knot, 216, 217
brahman, 108, 151, 204, 242
Buddha mind, 1, 18, 49, 174, 220, 221, 244
Buddha nature (*busshō*), 1, 4, 8, 16-18, 29, 35, 39, 40, 58, 72, 106, 108, 109, 146, 174, 188, 190, 242, 248, 249, 268, 270
bunjinga, 120
bunraku, 114
bushidō, 87, 95-97
busshō. See Buddha nature

The Catcher in the Rye, 135
Chan (禪), 7, 11, 13, 14, 17, 21, 22, 27, 28, 29, 37, 38, 48, 54-56, 59, 72, 104, 105, 140, 141, 149, 150, 161, 183, 200, 204, 224, 231, 268, 270
chikhai bardo, 201-202
chit wang (void mind), 21
chonyid bardo, 201-202
Christian mysticism, 84-86, 146, 150, 154, 166-167, 218, 240-242

Christianity, 52, 84-86, 146, 150, 154, 156, 166, 210, 255, 270
clear light, 39, 51, 54, 201, 202, 204, 260, 262
collective unconscious, 1, 5, 23, 44, 46, 51, 61-65, 78, 174, 186, 193, 195-200, 202, 204, 206, 207-211, 214, 229-231, 251, 253, 260, 261
comedy, 122, 123, 251
communism, 109, 257
compassion (*karuṇā* / *jihi* / 慈悲), 16, 41-43, 60, 71, 80, 88, 106, 107, 109, 110-113, 115, 126, 210, 239, 251, 272
Confucianism, 52, 54
cosmic consciousness, 17, 23, 24, 148, 152, 153, 157, 158, 189, 194, 241, 246, 250
Critical Buddhism, 108-109, 267

Dadaism, 135, 139
Dao, 1, 18, 28, 54, 55, 56, 95, 259
Daodejing, 16
Daoism, 1, 5, 16, 17, 52, 54, 138, 150, 161, 206, 237, 240
Daoist alchemy, 195
Dhammapada, 112, 272
Dharani, 81
The Dharma Bums, 134-135
dharmakaya, 1, 4, 5, 6, 18, 27, 31, 34, 36, 39, 50, 51, 54, 64, 65, 66, 74, 78, 84, 85, 89, 90, 92, 98, 151, 170, 186, 198, 201-203, 212, 214, 243, 244, 256, 259, 260, 263, 269
Diamond Sutra, 140
The Divine Comedy, 251
The Doors of Perception, 254, 257
Dunhuang manuscripts, 14, 22, 268

ecstasy, 92-94, 97, 117, 120, 152, 218, 238-240, 254, 271
ek-stasis, 93, 218
ego, 65, 66, 70, 93, 101, 103, 113, 171, 172, 173, 174, 180, 181, 185, 188, 189, 190, 196, 200, 207, 211, 215, 222, 227, 243, 252, 263
ego-consciousness, 5, 14, 25, 43, 48, 63, 67, 76, 78, 83, 95, 96, 100, 102, 104, 105, 126, 162, 174, 180, 196, 199, 200, 207, 210, 211, 225, 226, 243, 248, 249, 261
egolessness, 93, 276
emptiness, ix, 1, 4, 5, 6, 11, 16, 20, 21, 24, 27-35, 41, 43, 50, 51, 53, 54, 55, 57, 58, 60, 61, 64, 65, 66, 67, 70, 71, 72, 74, 78-81, 84, 85, 87, 89, 90, 91, 92, 93, 96, 97, 98, 99, 101, 109, 113-115, 118, 120-124, 126-129, 134, 135, 137, 141, 148, 149, 150, 151, 152, 159-162, 166, 167, 170, 195, 198, 199, 200-208, 210, 211, 212, 214, 215, 219, 221, 222, 223, 225, 232, 233, 237, 238, 241, 244, 253, 255, 256, 259, 260, 261, 262, 263, 268, 269, 270. See also *śūnyatā*
enlightenment, 1, 1-6, 8, 9, 13-17, 22, 26, 29, 30, 32, 39, 46, 48, 50, 52, 54, 55, 58, 61, 66, 67, 68, 71, 72, 75, 78, 80, 85, 86, 108, 113-115, 121-126, 133, 134, 140, 141, 149, 152, 158, 161, 170, 180, 181, 184, 189, 190, 191, 192, 194, 195, 201, 202, 211, 223, 232, 233, 238, 241, 245, 250, 254, 256, 257, 258, 262
epiphany, 117, 134, 138, 198, 261
everyday aesthetics, 87, 88, 127, 271
evolution, 56, 174, 175, 178, 234, 243, 258
existential psychoanalysis, 222
existentialism, 32, 133, 135, 145, 187, 194, 222, 223, 239, 240

faith, 80-82, 86, 156, 157
fascism, 7, 109, 114
flower arrangement, 21, 107, 133, 265, 271

Flower Garland Scripture. See *Avataṃsaka Sūtra*
Fluxus, 135, 136, 138, 141
The Fold, 169, 217
Frankfort School, 193
fringe structure (focus/fringe), 157, 158
Ganda tradition of Mahayana Buddhism, 38, 49, 50
Gateless Barrier, 56, 61, 69, 72, 205, 256
Gateless Gate. See *Gateless Barrier*
Gaṇḍavyūha Sūtra, 37, 38, 42, 49
*Gegenwart (*present*)*, 261
geidō (芸道), 117-142
geist, 47, 181, 182
Genji. See *The Tale of Genji*
German Idealism, 157, 173, 181
German Romanticism, 173, 175, 177
Godhead, 85, 86, 150, 167, 197, 259
golden flower, 197
gradual enlightenment, 15, 30
great mirror wisdom (*ādarsana jñāna*), 50, 51, 64, 78

haiku poetry, 21, 87, 91, 93, 95, 107, 118, 120, 128-135, 193, 198, 214, 223, 259, 263, 272
hallucination, 196, 197, 201, 208, 256-260
hara center, 72, 75-80, 97, 98, 270
HCC (historical and cultural criticism), 7, 8. See also Critical Buddhism
Heian period, 110
Hinduism, 138, 204, 237
holotropic breathwork, 254
hongaku (本覚), 8, 190
Huayan (華嚴) Buddhism. See Kegon
Humanism, 145, 238-245

I Ching. See *Yijing*
id (Freud), 103, 185, 186, 188, 189, 194, 208, 214, 253

idealism, 109, 154, 157, 171, 173, 175, 181, 182
ikebana flower arrangement, 271
iki (chic), 190
Indra's net, 1, 11, 27, 36, 37, 38, 39, 40, 41, 42, 43, 49, 54, 167, 170, 226, 231, 232, 233, 234, 235, 263
inner fire, 270
interdependent origination, 30, 36, 49, 113, 159, 170
interpenetration, 1, 11, 27, 36-44, 49, 54, 58, 73, 117, 161, 163, 167, 170, 171, 214, 234, 235, 268, 269
intuition, 42, 43, 49, 55, 60, 64, 65, 70, 78, 81, 89, 91, 95, 97, 100, 105, 111, 113, 115, 118, 123, 129, 130, 131, 149, 150, 151, 152, 156, 159, 160, 161, 162, 170, 174, 175, 176, 177, 178, 192, 200, 204
istigkeit (isness), 259
Izanagi and Izanami, 209

Japanese uniqueness. See *Nihonjinron*
Jungian psychology, 195, 206, 207, 211

Kabbalah, 261
Kamakura, 3, 114, 262
Kannon, 43
Kegon Buddhism (Huayan / 華嚴), 1, 11, 27, 36-44, 49, 58, 167, 170, 171, 245, 231-235, 263, 268
kenshō (見性), 4, 13, 29, 70
kōan (公案), 3, 4, 11, 34, 50, 55, 56, 57, 61, 66, 68-79, 80, 81, 82, 84, 89, 97, 122, 126, 134, 135, 140, 155, 161, 192, 193, 199, 200, 204, 205, 206, 207, 217, 219, 220, 223, 224, 225, 259, 260, 262, 263, 266, 269, 273, 274
Kojiki, 209
Kojirin (居士林), 3
kokoro (心), 28, 51, 96, 167, 190
Kwannon. See Kannon

Lacanian psychoanalysis, 174, 226, 274
Laṅkāvatāra Sutra, 44, 48, 49, 243

Mahayana Buddhism, 1, 3, 5, 6, 9, 11, 21, 25, 27, 28, 30, 31, 32, 36, 37, 38, 41, 44, 47, 48, 49, 54, 79, 81, 84, 88, 110, 113, 115, 120, 151, 152, 165, 172, 178, 181, 182, 192, 195, 201, 204, 243
Maitreya, 37, 42
manas, 46, 48, 53, 243, 244
mandala, 196, 197, 198, 201, 211
Mandukya Upanishad, 204
manga, 114, 121, 123
martial arts, 87, 91, 95, 96, 97, 104, 105, 118, 133
middle path. See middle way
middle way, 20, 31, 280
militarism, 7, 8, 105-115
mind-only Buddhism. See *Yogācāra*
mindfulness, 55, 75, 88, 249
modernity, 206, 226, 230
Moebius strip, 215-221, 274
moksha, 256, 259, 275
monads, 159, 167-170, 181
mono no aware, 114, 190, 272, 273
morality, 42, 108, 110-113, 115, 127, 138
morning glory, 131-132, 192
Mount Sumeru, 170
mu (無) [keyword in Jōshū's koan], 4, 28-32, 34, 66-78, 81, 84, 126, 205, 223, 269
muga (無我), 13, 25, 28, 31, 52, 92-94, 106, 114, 122, 129, 180, 181, 182, 203, 218, 238, 240, 241, 256, 263, 271. See also ecstasy
muishiki (無意識), 21, 52, 53, 128
Mushinron (無心論), 14, 22
mysticism, 25, 36, 47, 81, 84, 85, 86, 108, 133, 138, 150, 166, 180, 241, 265, 272, 278

nembutsu, 80-81
New Thought, 145, 154-157, 273
Nichts, 166, 167
nihilism, 20, 27, 31-34, 35, 55, 85, 90, 91, 92, 113, 114, 115, 135, 188, 193, 225, 262, 268
nihonjinron (日本人論), 7
nirmanakaya, 200-204
nirvana, 24, 32, 134, 140, 166, 250, 256, 259, 262
no-mind (無心 / *mushin*), 1, 6, 7, 9, 11, 13, 14, 15, 16, 17, 18, 20, 21, 22, 23, 24, 25, 26, 27, 28, 29, 30, 31, 33, 50-59, 61, 65, 67, 74, 79, 80, 82, 84, 85, 87, 88, 89, 92-114, 117, 118, 120, 121, 122, 126, 127, 162, 172, 178, 180, 183, 192, 193, 200, 204, 205, 207, 214, 218, 223, 224, 241, 244, 248, 253, 256, 263, 265, 268
no-thought (無念 / *munen*), 13, 15-18, 22, 23, 25, 28, 31, 65, 92, 93, 94, 97, 98, 122, 129
noh drama, 21, 87, 88, 91, 92, 93, 95, 107, 113, 117, 118, 133, 198, 214, 263
nonduality, 8, 71, 160
nothingness, 1, 4, 5, 6, 11, 20, 24, 26-36, 50-53, 58, 61, 64-67, 78, 80, 85-87, 90-96, 108, 113, 115, 117, 120-129, 132, 134, 137, 141, 151, 166-170, 186, 187, 190, 191, 195, 197, 198, 200-214, 220-226, 232, 238, 253, 255, 259, 261, 263, 268

Oedipal/Oedipus, 185, 187, 214, 222, 229
ordinary mind (*heijōshin*), 27, 55, 56, 61, 87, 95, 96, 180, 256
Oretagama, 75, 270
original enlightenment, 1, 4, 8, 108, 200. See also *hongaku*
Orpheus, 209

oval diagram of the mind (Assagioli), 250-253
oxherding pictures, 124, 126, 209, 210

parāvritti (turning around), 48, 50, 51, 269
peak experience, 238-244, 250
personality development, 187
personal unconscious, 174, 186, 193-198, 202, 204, 207, 208, 211, 229, 251, 253, 255, 260, 261
perspective, 36-44, 159, 160, 167-171, 276
Platform Sutra, 17, 243
A Pluralistic Universe, 157
pop art, 138, 139, 141
prajñāpāramitā, 1, 11, 28, 30, 31, 35, 36, 43, 53, 54
prajñā-samādhi, 15
prehensions, 159-161
process metaphysics, 5, 146, 159, 160, 233, 234
prosperity gospel, 155
psychedelic, 152, 228, 238, 240, 254-260, 275
psychoanalysis, 1, 4, 5, 24, 50, 63, 91, 103, 160, 183-212, 213, 215, 217, 218, 221, 222, 226, 227 228, 229, 238, 239, 240, 245, 247, 249, 251, 253, 255, 266, 271, 274
psychosynthesis, 249-253
pure experience, 7, 8, 73, 92, 94, 108, 147-152, 157, 161, 190, 210, 239, 256, 268
Pure Land, 1, 37, 52, 60, 79, 80, 81, 82, 83, 84, 86, 136

radical empiricism, 40, 146, 147, 148, 150, 151, 152, 153, 158, 159
Raja Yoga, 25, 249
relative nothingness, 27, 32, 34, 35, 115, 124, 210, 225, 268
Renaissance, 141, 179, 232

rhizomatic unconscious, 213, 226-235
rhizome, 213, 226-235
Rinzai Zen, 1, 3, 4, 11, 28, 30, 50, 56, 57, 66, 67, 68, 69, 72, 73, 74, 75, 76, 78, 79, 80, 81, 82, 97, 120, 121, 124, 126, 167, 192, 204, 205, 211, 216, 218
Romanticism, 165, 173, 174, 175, 176, 177, 178, 254

sabi, 87, 88, 91, 127, 129, 136, 190
sambhogakaya, 201, 202, 204
samurai, 7, 65, 95-128
satori (悟り), 1, 3, 4, 7, 9, 13, 22-27, 30, 31, 36, 37, 38, 40-44, 47, 48, 50, 51, 52, 54-58, 61-75, 77, 80, 81, 84, 85, 88, 89, 95, 96, 99, 109, 111, 113, 115, 123, 124, 126, 128, 129, 130, 132, 134, 135, 138, 147, 148, 149, 151, 152, 155, 156, 158, 159, 161, 162, 163, 166, 167, 170, 171, 173, 174, 177, 178, 180, 182, 183, 184, 188, 189, 190, 191, 192, 193, 194, 195, 199, 204, 205, 206, 207, 212, 213, 214, 223, 224, 225, 226, 232, 238, 239, 240, 241, 242, 247, 245, 247, 248, 249, 250, 254, 255, 257, 258, 260, 261, 262, 263, 269, 271, 274, 275, 276
schizoanalysis, 227-232
schizophrenia, 227
self-nature, 17-20, 29, 35, 64, 253
semiotic unconscious, 174, 213-218, 226, 274
Seven Samurai [film], 99, 271
shamanism, 237
Shaolin, 104
shibui, 190
shibumi, 91, 127, 129, 136
shikantaza (只管打坐) (just sitting), 66
Shin Buddhism (真宗), 1, 60, 79, 80, 81, 84, 86
Shingon Buddhism, 37

Shinto, 83, 154, 209
sidpa bardo, 201-202
soku-hi logic of paradox, 137, 220-221, 233
Somaesthetics, 87-89, 118
Sōtō Zen, 66, 79, 107, 109, 191, 192, 269, 273
Southern School [Chan Buddhism], 14, 22
spectrum of consciousness, 242-245, 261
Square Zen, 133-134
storehouse consciousness. See *alaya-vijnana*
subconscious, 4, 5, 24, 26, 37, 44, 46, 47, 48, 88, 89, 132, 146, 147, 152-158, 167, 181, 197, 208, 209, 225, 226, 245, 246, 247, 249, 256, 258, 260, 269
subliminal, 1, 4, 6, 11, 18, 39, 43, 44-48, 53, 54, 55, 63, 75, 80, 87, 95, 97, 100, 102, 123, 145, 146, 151, 152-158, 174, 182, 193, 204, 222, 232, 254, 255, 256
suchness, 1, 4, 20, 27, 29, 31, 33, 34, 35, 54, 57, 67, 71, 87, 90, 91, 92, 109, 113, 120, 126, 127, 134, 148, 149, 150, 151, 166, 187, 198, 202, 203, 206, 210, 223, 225, 241, 256, 259
sudden enlightenment (*tunwu / tongo* / 頓悟), 4, 15, 17, 29, 30, 58, 66, 67, 72, 80, 124, 158, 211, 250, 262
Sufism, 82, 237, 261
sumie ink painting, 87, 88, 117-120, 126, 198, 219, 263
Sung Dynasty, 58, 72
sunyata, 1, 5, 11, 27-31, 33, 34, 35, 36, 41, 43, 49, 58, 85, 89, 90, 98, 113, 121, 124, 141, 149, 150, 151, 152, 159, 160, 161, 170, 189, 195, 211, 221, 223, 256, 259, 262, 268
super-consciousness, 1, 4, 5, 11, 17, 24, 25, 26, 31, 36, 43, 56, 58, 59, 61, 63, 66, 72, 73, 76, 77, 124, 126, 147, 148, 151, 154-158, 161, 163, 168, 173, 174, 177, 180, 182, 184, 188, 191, 193, 195, 204, 205, 223, 226, 242, 243, 244, 248-253, 254, 260, 261, 262, 263, 273
Surrealism, 197
swordsmanship, 7, 21, 51, 65, 87, 88, 91, 93, 95-118
synaesthesia, 42, 43, 269
synchronicity, 206

Tale of Genji, 110
tanden, 76, 270
Tantra, 134, 197, 202
Tao. See Dao
tathagatagarbha, 1, 4, 18, 108, 188, 190, 191, 268, 270
tea ceremony, 87, 88, 91, 93, 95, 97, 107, 117, 118, 126-128, 133, 134, 198, 214, 215
Ten Oxherding Pictures, 124, 126, 209, 210
Theravada Buddhism, 21, 25, 45
Tibetan Book of the Dead, 201, 260
Tibetan Buddhism, 194, 197, 198, 201, 204
topology, 213-218
transcendence, 54, 108, 141, 210, 222, 238, 240, 241
transcendental ego, 171-173
transcendental Idealism, 171-173
transcendental unity of apperception, 171-173
Transcendentalism, 127, 157, 165, 173, 175, 195, 240
transparency, 9, 27, 35, 222-226, 261-263
Transpersonal Psychology, 6, 9, 145, 237-259, 274, 275
trikāya (three bodies), 5, 31, 203
Tummo "inner fire" Yoga, 270

Unbenwusste Geist, 182

The Unconscious God, 188, 284
Upanishads, 204
Ursprung, 171, 261

Vairocana Buddha, 162
Vedanta, 25, 204
Vedas, 204
visionary experience, 260
void mind. See chit wang
Vorstellungen, 167, 171

wabi, 42, 87, 88, 91, 97, 127, 128, 129, 136, 137, 141, 166, 167, 190, 215, 269
The Wind-Up Bird Chronicle, 208-209
wunian (無念). See no-thought
wuwei (無為 / non-action), 16, 56, 59, 89, 121, 197
wuxin (無心). See mushin
wuzhu (無住). See abodelessness

Yijing, 195
Yoga, 21, 25, 44, 46, 75, 80, 155, 197, 204, 242, 243, 249, 262, 270
Yogacara Buddhism (mind-only Buddhism), 11, 23, 27, 43-50, 53, 54, 64, 78, 83, 166, 172, 181, 242, 243, 244, 274
yogin, 206
yūgen, 90, 91, 117, 129, 182

zazen (座禅), 3, 4, 66, 73, 75, 76, 83, 88, 123, 147, 211

Name Index

Abe Masao, 28, 60, 62–63, 167, 207, 276–277
Adler, Alfred, 188
Aeschylus, 179
Alpert, Avram, 8, 9, 267, 273
Anaxagoras, 185
App, Urs, 22, 267
Asanga, 243
Asahara Saichi, 83
Ashton, Dore, 137
Assagioli, Roberto, 238, 242, 249-253
Aśvaghoṣa, 277
Atkinson, W. William, 155, 249
Aurobindo, Sri, 242
Austin, James, 183
Austin, John, 141
Awa Kenzō, 100, 101, 104, 105
Azuma Hiroki, 229–230

Badiner, Allan Hunt, 282

Baizhang Huaihai, 59
Bankei, 78–79, 90
Bashō, 129-130, 137, 193
Beauvoir, Simone de, 222
Beethoven, Ludwig van, 179
Benoit, Hubert, 194, 238, 242, 244-249, 275
Bergson, Henri, 6, 122-123, 151, 159, 206, 213, 258
Blake, William, 41
Blum, Mark, 83, 267
Boehme, Jacob, 6, 165-167, 178-180
Bodhidharma, 13, 14, 15, 20, 28, 38, 48, 84, 268, 270
Bucke, Richard M., 148, 194
Buddhadāsa Bikkhu, 21
Bukkō Kokushi. See Wuxue Zuyuan

Cage, John, 135-138, 252
Carus, C. G. (Carl Gustav), 178

Charcot, Jean-Martin, 213
Ch'ing Yuan. See Qingyuan Weixin
Chiyo, 131-132, 192-193
Cunningham, Eric, 255–256
Cytowic, Richard, 269

Dahui Zonggao, 72, 73
Dale, Peter, 267
Dante (Dante Alighieri), 251
Danto, Arthur C., 137–142
Davis, Bret, 24
Deleuze, Gilles, 6, 169, 213, 217–234
DeMartino, Richard, 193
Dharmapala, Anagarika, 25
Derrida, Jacques, 215, 220–221
Descartes, René, 168, 266
Dilworth, David, 267
Dōgen, 66, 79, 191, 192, 195, 269, 272, 273
Doi Takeo, 189–190
Donovan (Donovan Phillips Leitch), 140
Duchamp, Marcel, 139, 141
Dumoulin, Heinrich, 50, 183-184
Dushun, 37
Dylan, Bob, 133, 217

Eckhart, Meister, 85-86, 150, 197, 241, 252, 259
Eisai, 120
Ellenberger, Henri, 153, 165, 213
Escher, M. C., 217
Eurydice, 209

Faber, Roland, 234
Fa-tsang. See Fazang
Faure, Bernard, 8, 22, 114, 183, 267
Fazang, 38, 40
Feuerstein, Georg, 262, 276
Fichte, Johann Gottlieb, 174, 177-178
Foucault, Michel, 213
Frankl, Viktor, 169, 188
Franklin, Perkins, 169

Freud, Sigmund, 1, 5, 46, 63-64, 103, 122-123, 145, 147, 157, 174, 183–190, 193–198, 202, 204, 207, 208, 211, 213, 214, 215, 222, 227, 228, 229, 238, 239, 249, 251, 253, 254, 255, 274
Fromm, Erich, 23, 192, 193, 194
Fukushima Keido Roshi, 3, 21, 22
Fuller, Robert C., 145-146, 193, 240

Gardner, Sebastian, 176, 179
Gebser, Jean, 9, 261-263, 276
Ginsberg, Allen, 133
Griffin, David, R., 160
Grof, Stanislav, 6, 238, 242, 254, 255
Guattari, Félix, 6, 213, 226-234
Gurdjieff, Georgij I., 238, 242, 245-248, 275

Hagiwara Takao, 216, 220-221
Hakamaya Noriyaki, 108
Hakuin Ekaku, 3, 50, 66, 74, 75, 76, 78, 79, 89, 135, 205, 216, 218, 219, 220, 270
Harada Sogaku, 205
Hartmann, Eduard Von, 6, 47, 155, 165, 174, 178, 179, 180, 181, 182
Hegel, G. W. F., 165-166, 174, 177, 178, 179, 181, 268-269
Heidegger, Martin, 32, 33, 101
Heine, Steven, 7, 8, 72, 73, 101, 109, 133, 272
Heisig, James, 273
Herrera, Hayden, 137
Herrigel, Eugen, 100-105, 218, 277
Hisamatsu, Shin'ichi, 24, 207, 271
Hori, Victor, 149
Huineng, 15, 16, 17, 18, 20, 28, 29, 30, 35, 38, 57, 67, 84, 123, 124, 268, 270
Huxley, Aldous, 238, 240, 254, 257, 260

Ichikawa Hakugen, 106-109

Imakita Kōsen, 3, 69
Ives, Christopher, 106, 267
Izutsu Toshihiko, 26, 27, 268, 270

Jackson, Peter, 21
Jaffe, Richard M., 9, 28, 105, 134, 146, 148, 181, 267
James, William, 5, 25, 34, 47, 145, 146, 148, 156, 159, 175, 183, 195, 239, 249
Janet, Pierre, 213
Japhy Ryder. See Gary Snyder
Jōshū. See Zhaozhou Congshen
Jung, C. G., 1, 5, 6, 23, 44, 46, 51, 63-65, 78, 160, 165, 174, 183, 186, 191-211, 214, 229, 240, 251, 253, 255, 261, 273
Junshu. See Shenxiu Yuquan

Kakuan Shien, 124
Kamiyama Kenji, 230
Kandel, Eric, 185-186
Kant, Immanuel, 6, 94, 165, 171-173, 178, 181, 198, 273
Kawai Hayao, 206-212, 273
Kerouac, Jack, 133–135
Koestler, Arthur, 101, 106
Kondo Akihisa, 188-189
Koryu Osaka, 205
Kurokawa Kishō, 137, 233
Kurosawa Akira, 99-100, 271

Lacan, Jacques, 6, 174, 213-218, 221, 239, 294
Laozi, 16, 56
Larson, Kay, 135, 251, 268
Lawrence, Brother, 270
Lee, Bruce, 104, 105
Leibniz, Gottfried Wilhelm, 6, 155, 159, 160, 165, 167-169, 178-181
Levine, Gregory, 92, 272
Li Zehou, 16–17
Linji, Yixuan. See Rinzai

Magliola, Robert, 221
Maslow, Abraham, 238, 239, 240, 241
Matsumoto Shirō, 108, 267
May, Rollo, 187
McMahan, David, 22, 42, 173, 175, 193, 267
Mazu Daoyi, 18, 20, 59, 61
Merleau-Ponty, Maurice, 206, 217
Merton, Thomas, 84
Miller, David, 273
Mills, Jon, 6, 160, 166
Miyamoto Musashi, 118
Möbius, August Ferdinand, 216
Moriya Tomoe, 246
Morris, Ivan, 110
Muireartaigh, Rossa O., 267
Mumon Ekai, 72, 205
Munakata Shiko, 137
Murakami Haruki, 206–208
Murphy, Joseph, 156
Myers, Frederic, 153, 154, 155, 273
Myers, Gerald, 157

Nanquan Puyuan, 56, 59, 61
Nansen. See Nanquan Puyuan
Newton, Isaac, 167
Nicholls, Angus, 165
Nietzsche, Friedrich, 32, 165
Nishida Kitarō, 2, 3, 34, 37, 53, 92-94, 106-108, 148, 149, 181, 190, 198, 206, 221, 265, 268, 270
Nishihira Tadashi, 26, 112
Nishitani Keiji, 24, 32, 34, 206, 273, 276
Noguchi Isamu, 137
Northrop, F. S. C., 146, 150, 160, 161

Ohnuki-Tierney Emiko, 114
Okamura Mihoko, 254
Ono Yoko, 136
Osaka Koryu, 205

Pearlman, Ellen, 133
Perkins, Franklin, 169

Pickover, Clifford, 216–217
Platner, Ernst, 168
Pollock, Jackson, 138, 141, 197

Qingyuan Weixin, 140, 224

Ramacharaka. See William W. Atkinson
Ramakrishna, 25
Rancière, Jacques, 6, 213-215, 274
Rank, Otto, 187–189
Raphael, 141, 148
Rikyū. See Sen no Rikyū
Rinzai, 59-61, 121, 124

Saito Yuriko, 271
Sakamoto Hiroshi, 195
Salinger, J. D., 135, 272, 274
Samuel Coleridge, 255, 275
Sartre, Jean-Paul, 222–225, 274
Sawada, Janine, 3
Schelling, Friedrich Wilhelm Joseph, 6, 165-166, 173-179
Scholem, Gershom, 261
Schopenhauer, Arthur, 31, 76, 155, 181
Sen-no-Rikyu, 127
Shusterman, Richard, 88
Sengai Gibbon, 120–124
Sesshū Tōyō, 119
Sharf, Robert, 8, 148-149, 267
Shenhui, 20
Shenxiu Yuquan, 29–30, 268, 270
Shinran, 60, 79, 83
Shunryu Suzuki Roshi, 269
Snyder, Gary, 133–134
Sōen Shaku, 3, 25, 69, 75, 147, 272
Soga Ryōjin, 83
Sophocles, 214
Spinoza, Baruch, 149
Starrs, Roy, 272
Strassman, Rick, 254, 256
Stunkard, Albert, 254
Sueki Fumihiko, 8, 59-60, 267

Suzuki, Beatrice Lane, 3
Suzuki Shunryu (Shunryu Suzuki Roshi), 269
Swedenborg, Emmanuel, 265

Takano Shigeyoshi, 113–114
Takeuchi Yoshinori, 148
Taniguchi Masaharu, 154
Tanke, Joseph, 214, 274
Takuan Sōhō, 97, 98, 99, 107, 111, 112
Tao Yuanming, 52, 53
Thoreau, Henry David, 127
Troward, Thomas, 156
Tsung-mi. See Zongmi

Ueda Shizuteru, 8, 207, 210, 257, 275

Vasubandhu, 243
Victoria, Brian Daizen, 107, 109
Viglielmo, Valdo H., 94, 271
Vivekananda, Swami, 25, 155, 249

Waldron, William S., 44-45
Warhol, Andy, 138–141
Watts, Alan, 23, 61, 133, 257
Whitehead, Alfred North, 5, 146, 159, 160, 161, 162, 169, 234
Wilber, Ken, 8, 238, 242-245, 261, 274, 276
Wilson, Jeff, 246, 267
Wittgenstein, Ludwig, 141
Wordsworth, William, 174, 275
Wumen. See Mumon
Wuxue Zuyuan, 205

Xuan Zang, 46

Yabuki Keiki, 14, 22
Yakusan Igen, 192–193
Yamada Shōji, 3, 101-103, 267, 271
Yanagi Sōetsu, 73, 127, 136
Yeshe, Lama, 270
Yosa Buson, 120

Yoshizawa Katsuhiro, 216, 219, 220
Yuasa Yasuo, 206
Yüeh-shan Hung-tao. See Yakusan Igen
Yunmen Wenyan. See Unmon

Zaehner, R. C., 133, 272
Zhaozhou Congshen, 56, 59, 61, 69, 72
Zhuangzi, 16
Zongmi, 37